MARKET LEADER

ADVANCED BUSINESS ENGLISH TEACHER'S RESOURCE BOOK

Iwonna Dubicka   Margaret O'Keeffe

PEARSON
Longman

FINANCIAL
TIMES

Pearson Education Limited
Edinburgh Gate
Harlow
Essex CM20 2JE
England

First published 2006
Third impression 2007

Pack:
ISBN: 978-1-4058-4347-8

Book for pack:
ISBN: 978-0-582-85463-5

CD-ROM for pack:
ISBN: 978-1-4058-4266-2

Set in 9/12pt Metaplus

Printed in Spain by Mateu Cromo, S.A. Pinto

Edited by Catriona Watson-Brown
Designed by Oxford Designers & Illustrators
Project managed by Chris Hartley
Produced for Pearson Education by Phoenix Publishing Services

www.market-leader.net

Acknowledgements
We are grateful to the following for permission to reproduce copyright materials:

Financial Times Limited for extracts adapted from 'Why I refuse to hobnob for advantage at vanity fair' by Lucy Kellaway, published in the *Financial Times* 24th January 2005; 'It's a brave new world out there … so should you relocate' by Henry Tricks, published in the *Financial Times* 20th March 2004; 'Goodbye to old-fashioned ideology' by Della Bradshaw, published in the *Financial Times* 1st August 2005; 'Emphasis should be on more skills investment' by Gill Plimmer, published in the *FT Report, Professional Development 2004* 11th October 2004; 'An Italian job takes its toll on Austrian roads' by Adrian Michaels, published in the *Financial Times* 22nd April 2005; 'India and its energy needs: Demand is rising but lags rest of the world' by Kevin Morrison, published in the *Financial Times* 17th January 2005; 'Nuclear energy: Come-back kid or ugly duckling?' by Fiona Harvey, published in the *Financial Times* 14th October 2004; 'Offshoring: A loss of jobs or a gain in profits?' by Brian Groom, published in the *Financial Times Business Reports, Future of Work 2004* 27th September 2004; 'Business bows to growing pressures' by Alison Maitland, published in the *Financial Times* 29th November 2004; 'Why Deutsche resists national champion status' by Patrick Jenkins, published in the *Financial Times* 16th February 2005; 'Floodgates open to a new style' by Dan Roberts, from FT.com 10th March 2005; 'Advice is once more in demand' by Simon London, published in the *Financial Times* 28th April 2005; 'A tougher outlook for Britain's advisors' by Michael Skapinker, published in the *Financial Times* 28th April 2005; 'Plan to think strategically' by Morgen Witzel, from the *FT Summer School Series* 9th August 2004; 'Why so many mission statements are mission impossible' by Sathnam Sanghera, published in the *Financial Times* 22nd July 2005; 'Groceries by the vanload' by Jonathan Birchall, published in the *Financial Times* 20th April 2005; 'Technology that put a shine on a growing business' by Marcus Gibson, published in the *Financial Times* 16th March 2005; 'Assolan's babies battle for market share' by Jonathan Wheatley, published in the *Financial Times* 16th March 2005; and 'Advent of the IT marriage broker' by Maija Pesola, published in the *Financial Times* 5th August 2005.

Sarah Murray for extracts adapted from her articles 'Partnerships: Campaigners use peace as a weapon', from the *FT Report, International Public Sector* 5th May 2005; 'Older people: Age and experience', from *FT Business Reports, Business and Diversity* 10th May 2004; and 'Business models: Take a good look at the local issues', published in the *Financial Times* 24th June 2004.

David Bowen for an extract adapted from his article 'Websites need to have both hard tools and soft touches', published in the *Financial Times* 14th February 2005.

Jay Conger and Edward Lawler for an extract adapted from their article 'People skills still rule in the virtual company', from *FT Summer School 2005* 26th August 2005.

In some cases we have been unable to trace the owners of copyright material and we would appreciate any information that would enable us to do so.

Introduction

Market Leader Advanced is the latest addition to this five-level series. Like the other Course Books in the series, it reflects the fast-changing world of business with materials from authentic sources, such as the *Financial Times*. The Advanced Course Book contains 12 main units and four revision units and retains the dynamic and effective approach that has made this series so successful in Business English classes worldwide. The Course Book is accompanied by a Practice File, Test File and Teacher's Resource Book (with photocopiable activities and Text bank material).

1 Course aims

Market Leader is an extensive new Business English course designed to bring the real world of international business into the language-teaching classroom. It has been developed in association with the *Financial Times*, one of the world's leading sources of professional information, to ensure the maximum range and authenticity of business content.

The course is intended for use either by students preparing for a career in business or by those already working who want to improve their English communication skills. It is most suitable for use with students who are at an advanced language level.

Market Leader combines some of the most stimulating recent ideas from the world of business with a strongly task-based approach. Role-plays and case studies are regular features of each unit. Throughout the course, students are encouraged to use their own experience and opinions in order to maximise involvement and learning.

An essential requirement of Business English materials is that they cater for the wide range of needs which students have, including different areas of interest and specialisation, different skills needs and varying amounts of time available to study.

Market Leader offers teachers and course planners a unique range of flexible materials to help meet these needs. There are suggestions in this book on how to use the unit material extensively or intensively, and how the material in the Practice File integrates with the Course Book. There are optional extra components, including a Business Grammar, videos and a series of special subject books to develop vocabulary and reading skills. This book contains extensive photocopiable material in the Text bank and Resource bank.

2 The main course components

Course Book

This provides the main part of the teaching material, divided into 12 topic-based units. The topics have been chosen following research among teachers to establish which are the areas of widest possible interest to the majority of their students. The Course Book provides input in reading, speaking and listening, with guidance for writing tasks, too. Every unit contains vocabulary development activities and a rapid review of essential grammar. There is a regular focus on key business functions, and each unit ends with a motivating case study to allow students to practise language they have worked on during the unit. For more details on the Course Book units, see *Overview of a Course Book unit* below.

There are also four revision units in the Course Book that revise and consolidate the work in the main units.

Practice File

This gives extra practice in the areas of vocabulary, grammar, business skills and pronunciation. There is a special focus on collocations, text grammar and developing fluency in spoken English. The Practice File includes an audio CD to enable students to work on their own as appropriate.

Audio materials

All the listening activities from the Course Book (interviews with business practitioners) and the Practice File (pronunciation exercises) are available on cassettes and audio CDs, depending on users' preference.

Teacher's Resource Book

This book provides you with an overview of the whole course, together with detailed teaching notes, background briefings on business content, the Text bank (24 optional extra reading texts) and the Resource bank (photocopiable worksheets practising communication skills).

Test File

Five copiable tests are available to teachers and course planners to monitor students' progress through the course. There is an entry test plus four progress tests and an exit text which review the work done throughout the course.

3 Overview of a Course Book unit

A typical unit consists of the following sections.

Listening and discussion

Students have the opportunity to think about the unit topic and to exchange ideas and opinions with each other and with the teacher. There is a variety of stimulating activities, such as listening to short extracts, expressing personal preferences and answering questions. Throughout, students are encouraged to draw upon their life and business experience.

The authentic listening texts are based on interviews with business people and experts in their field. Students develop listening skills such as prediction, listening for specific information, ordering facts, note-taking and correcting summaries.

Essential vocabulary related to the listening topic is presented and practised in each of these sections, through a variety of creative and engaging exercises. Students learn new words, phrases and collocations, and are given tasks which help to activate the vocabulary they already know or have just learnt. There is further vocabulary practice in the Practice File.

There are a number of discussion activities throughout the book. Their purpose is to activate students' world knowledge, improve their fluency in English and provide them with opportunities to respond to the content of the recordings and texts.

Reading and language

Students read interesting and relevant authentic texts from the *Financial Times* and other business sources. They develop their reading skills through a variety of tasks, such as matching headings and text, ordering items, completing summaries and pairwork information exchange. They also practise useful business lexis from the texts.

The texts provide a context for the language work and discussion in this section. The language work develops students' awareness of common problem areas at advanced level. The focus is on accuracy and knowledge of key areas of grammar, text cohesion and idioms. In many units, more than one language area is presented, and there are extra practice exercises in the Grammar reference section at the end of the Course Book.

Business skills

This section helps students to develop their spoken and written communication skills in the key business areas, such as presentations, meetings, negotiations, telephoning, problem-solving, social English, business correspondence and report writing.

Each section contains a Useful language box, which provides students with the support and phrases they need to carry out the business tasks in the regular role play activities. The Writing file at the end of the Course Book also provides students with useful model texts and writing guidelines.

Case study

Each unit ends with a case study linked to the unit's business topic. The case studies are based on realistic business problems or situations and are designed to motivate and actively engage students. They use the language and communication skills which they have acquired while working through the unit. Typically, students will be involved in discussing business problems and recommending solutions through active group work.

All of the case studies have been developed and tested with students in class and are designed to be easy to present and use. No special knowledge or extra materials are required. For teaching tips on making the best use of the case studies, see *Case studies that work* below.

Each case study ends with a realistic writing task. These tasks reflect the real world of business correspondence and will also help those students preparing for Business English exams. Models of writing text types are given in the Writing file at the end of the Course Book.

4 Using the course

Accessibility for teachers

Less experienced teachers can sometimes find teaching Business English a daunting experience. They may be anxious about their lack of knowledge of the business world and of the topics covered in the course. *Market Leader* sets out to provide the maximum support for teachers. The Business brief section at the beginning of each unit in the Teacher's Resource Book gives an overview of the business topic, covering key terms (given in **bold**, and which can be checked in the *Longman Dictionary of Business English*) and suggesting a list of titles for further reading and information.

Authenticity of content

One of the principles of the course is that students should deal with as much authentic content as their language level allows. Authentic reading and listening texts are motivating for students and bring the real world of business into the classroom, increasing students' knowledge of business practice and concepts. Due to its international coverage, the *Financial Times* has been a rich source of text and business information for the course.

The case studies present realistic business situations and problems, and the communication activities based on them – group discussion, simulations and role-plays – serve to enhance the authenticity of the course.

Flexibility of use

Demands of Business English courses vary greatly, and the material accordingly needs to be flexible and adaptable. *Market Leader* has been designed to give teachers and course planners the maximum flexibility. The course can be used either extensively or intensively. At the beginning of each unit in the Teacher's Resource Book are suggestions for a fast route through the unit if time is short. This intensive route focuses mainly on speaking and listening skills. If you want to extend this concentration on particular skills, optional components are available in the course (see *Extending the course* below).

5 Case studies that work

The following teaching tips will help when using case studies.
1 Involve all the students at every stage of the class. Encourage everyone to participate.
2 Draw on the students' knowledge of business and the world.
3 Be very careful how you present the case study at the beginning. Make sure your instructions are clear and that the task is understood. (See individual units in the Teacher's Resource Book for detailed suggestions on introducing the case study.)
4 Ensure that all students have understood the case and the key vocabulary.
5 Encourage the students to use the language and business skills they have acquired in the rest of the unit. A short review of the key language will help.

6 Focus on communication and fluency during the case study activities. Language errors can be dealt with at the end. Make a record of important errors and give students feedback at the end in a sympathetic and constructive way.

7 If the activity is developing slowly or you have a group of students who are a little reticent, you could intervene by asking questions or making helpful suggestions.

8 Allow students to reach their own conclusions. Many students expect there to be a correct answer. You can give your own opinion, but should stress that there usually is no single 'right' answer.

9 Encourage creative and imaginative solutions to the problems expressed.

10 Encourage students to use people-management skills, such as working in teams, leading teams, delegating and interacting effectively with each other.

11 Allocate sufficient time for the major tasks such as negotiating. At the same time, do not allow activities to drag on too long. You want the students to have enough time to perform the task, and yet the lesson needs to have pace.

12 Students should identify the key issues of the case and discuss all the options before reaching a decision.

13 Encourage students to actively listen to each other. This is essential for both language practice and effective teamwork!

6 Extending the course

Some students' needs will require more input or practice in certain areas, either in terms of subject matter or skills, than is provided in the Course Book. In order to met these needs, *Market Leader* provides a wide range of optional extra materials and components to choose from.

Teacher's Resource Book

The Text bank provides two extra reading texts per unit, together with comprehension and vocabulary exercises.

The Resource bank provides copiable worksheet-based communication activities, linked to the skills introduced in the Course Book units.

Business Grammar

For students needing more work on their grammar, this book provides reference and practice in all the most important areas of Business English usage. It is organised into structural and functional sections.

Video

Four *Market Leader* videos are now available at intermediate and post-intermediate levels to provide students with authentic and engaging examples of Business English in use. Each video is accompanied by a set of photocopiable worksheets and a transcript.

Special subject series

Many students will need to learn the language of more specialist areas of Business English. To provide them with authentic and engaging material *Market Leader* includes a range of special subject books which focus on reading skills and vocabulary development.

The series includes *Banking and finance*, *Business law* and *International management*. Each book includes two tests and a glossary of specialised language.

Longman Dictionary of Business English

This is the most up-to-date source of reference in Business English today. Compiled from a wide range of text sources, it allows students and teachers rapid access to clear, straightforward definitions of the latest international business terminology.

Market Leader website

http://www.market-leader.net
This website offers teachers a wide range of extra resources to support and extend their use of the *Market Leader* series. Extra texts of topical interest are added regularly, together with worksheets to exploit them. Links to other relevant websites are posted here, and the website provides a forum for teachers to feedback comments and suggestion on the course to the authors and publishers.

The Test Master CD-ROM

The Teacher's Resource Book includes a Test Master CD-ROM which provides an invaluable testing resource to accompany the course.

- The tests are based strictly on the content of the corresponding level of *Market Leader*, providing a fair measure of students' progress.
- Keys and audio scripts are provided to make marking the tests as straightforward as possible.
- Most tests come in A and B versions. This makes it easier for teachers to invigilate the test by making it harder for students to copy from each other.
- The audio files for the listening tests are conveniently located on the same CD.

Types of test
The Test Master CD contains five types of test:
- Placement Tests
- Module Tests
- Progress Tests
- Mid-Course Test
- End of Course Test

Flexible
Teachers can print the tests out and use them as they are – or they can adapt them. Teachers can use Microsoft® Word to edit them as required to suit their teaching situation, their students or their syllabus.

Test Master CDs are available for *Market Leader* Advanced and all levels of *Market Leader* New Edition.

Contents

Resource bank

Being international

At a glance

	Classwork – Course Book	Further work
Lesson 1: **Listening and discussion** (pages 6–7) *Each lesson is about 60–75 minutes. This time does not include administration and time spent going through homework in any lessons.*	**Discussion: Public speaking** SS are encouraged to discuss public speaking, inspirational speakers, effective presentations and international audiences. **Listening: Experiences of giving presentations** Three business people talk about their experiences of giving presentations in intercultural settings and give tips for speaking to international audiences. **Vocabulary: Tips for giving presentations** SS look at some tips for giving presentations to international audiences and use related vocabulary in context. **Discussion: Types of presentation** SS talk about setting up rooms for different types of presentations, colour connotations, audience reactions and advice for giving presentations in their country.	**Practice File** Word power (pages 4–5)
Lesson 2: **Reading and language** (pages 8–9) *Each lesson is about 60–75 minutes.*	**Vocabulary: Slang, buzzwords and jargon** SS look at examples of slang, jargon and buzzwords. **Reading: *How not to sound like a fool*** SS read some advice on how to adapt your language and presentation style to ensure success when speaking to an international audience. **Language review: Business idioms** SS look at some business idioms.	**Text bank** (TRB pages 156–159) **Grammar reference and practice** (CB page 118) **Practice File** Text and grammar (pages 6–7)
Lesson 3: **Business skills** (pages 10–11) *Each lesson is about 75–90 minutes.*	**Networking** SS discuss tips for communicating with people they don't know or don't know very well; listen to some delegates meeting for the first time and networking at a conference; introduce themselves to another participant at an international conference. **Writing: Replying to a formal invitation** SS look at a formal e-mail and write a reply, accepting the invitation.	**Resource bank** (TRB page 218) **Writing file** (CB page 134) **Practice File** Skills and pronunciation (pages 8–9)
Lesson 4: **Case study** (pages 12–13) *Each lesson is about 75–90 minutes.*	**Working for Logistaid** A non-governmental organisation in Amsterdam is training some logistics managers to be relocated to Indonesia. SS look at the job advert, exchange some notes from the course on intercultural training and network during the break with other participants. SS also write a reply to a formal invitation to a dinner held at the Regional Governor's residence in Jakarta.	**Writing file** (CB page 134)

For a fast route through the unit, focusing mainly on speaking skills, just use the underlined sections.

For one-to-one situations, most parts of the unit lend themselves, with minimal adaptation, to use with individual students. Where this is not the case, alternative procedures are given.

Business brief

Presentations

Many people have a **fear of public speaking,** but a certain amount of **adrenalin and nerves** can help make a presentation more successful. Plenty of preparation time, knowing your topic, **rehearsing** and adapting your talk and **presentation style** according to the audience are also essential. Apart from the actual content of a presentation, speakers should also consider the following: **room set-up, seating arrangements, pace of delivery** and **tone of voice, gestures and body language, signs of approval or disapproval,** which may all vary according to culture and audience type.

Visual aids make a presentation easier to follow, but speakers should acquaint themselves with technical equipment beforehand to avoid any unnecessary embarrassment should things go wrong. **PowerPoint** is a useful and commonly used program for presentations, although some speakers still prefer to use an **overhead projector** with **transparencies** or **slides** as well as **handouts.**

Presentations, it is often said, need a beginning, a middle and an end. The **use of humour** or **appropriate anecdotes** to open a presentation can help to **engage the audience** or **get them on your side**, although humour differs widely in each culture and should be used sensitively or not at all. Another way to start off a presentation is with some brief, interesting or **surprising facts and figures**. At the start of any presentation, speakers should also introduce themselves briefly, if they have not already been formally introduced by someone else, before giving an overview of the talk. Likewise, after presenting the company, product or research findings, etc., the speaker needs to **summarise** or **conclude the main points** of the presentation before **signalling the end** and **inviting any further questions** from the public.

The **question-and-answer session,** or **Q&A,** after a presentation is sometimes considered the most challenging part of speaking in public, as not all questions can be anticipated. The presenter, however, should be prepared to a certain extent, if only to be able to refer the **member of the audience** to another authority or suggest further e-mail correspondence to follow up a particular issue.

Networking

Some managers say an important part of getting work done is **building relationships** and having an **extensive network** of **contacts**.

Networks are largely built through work contacts, for example, in meetings and conferences and by **doing favours for others**. Managers can participate in **company retreats** and **training programmes**, as well as **getting to know people** socially during coffee breaks, business lunches or on the golf course! However, the extent to which employees socialise outside working hours varies tremendously according to personal preference, company and national culture.

Exchanging business cards, listening actively, making eye contact, asking suitable questions and **finding common ground** are all practical ways of networking, although certain practices or behaviours will vary from country to country.

Presentations, networking and your students

In-work students will be able to talk about company presentations they have given or those they have attended. They could also compare presenting styles from different international settings or different areas, such as technical presentations vs. commercial ones. Pre-work students may have experience of attending lectures or talks given at school and university. They can also talk about the speakers/lecturers they know that are good at presenting. It may also be appropriate for both types of students to express concerns about giving presentations and share tips for speaking in public.

With networking, in-work students will be able to discuss occasions when they may network or socialise in English and the potential difficulties of starting conversations at business lunches, coffee breaks, etc. Pre-work students may talk about the advantages of making contacts in business in general.

Read on

Dale Carnegie: *The quick and easy way to effective public speaking*, Pocket, reissue edition 1990

Gert Hofstede: *Cultures and organisations: software of the mind – intercultural co-operation and its importance for survival*, McGraw Hill, 1996

Tom Leech: *How to prepare, stage and deliver winning presentations*, 3rd Edition, AMACOM, 2004.

Fons Trompenaars: *Managing people across cultures*, Capstone, 2004

Lesson notes

Warmer

◎ Write three or four of the following views on public speaking on the board or on a transparency. Ask SS which ones they agree/disagree with most and what they mean.

1 *Only the prepared speaker deserves to be confident.*
   (Dale Carnegie, American writer and lecturer, 1888–1955)

2 *Tell the audience what you're going to say, say it; then tell them what you've said.*
   (Dale Carnegie, as above)

3 *All the great speakers were bad speakers at first.*
   (Ralph Waldo Emerson, American essayist and poet, 1803–1882)

4 *Talk low, talk slow and don't say too much.*
   (John Wayne, American actor and director, 1907–1979)

5 *It is delivery that makes the orator's success.*
   (Johann Wolfgang Von Goethe, German poet, 1749–1832)

6 *Most speakers speak ten minutes too long.*
   (James Humes, American lawyer and presidential speech writer)

7 *There is nothing in the world like a persuasive speech to fuddle the mental apparatus.*
   (Mark Twain, American humorist and writer, 1835–1910)

◎ Alternatively, ask SS what they understand by the title of the unit, 'Being international'.

Overview

◎ Tell the SS that they will be looking at 'being international' in the context of intercultural communication, namely giving presentations to international audiences and networking at conferences or meetings.

◎ Go through the overview panel at the beginning of the unit, pointing out the sections that SS will be looking at.

Quotation

◎ Get SS to look at the quotation and ask them what they think it means. (The idea is that understanding the power of language helps us not only to communicate but to understand each other more fully. SS may also be invited to comment on the power and usefulness of understanding English and other languages and the importance of communication in the business world.)

Discussion: Public speaking

SS are encouraged to discuss public speaking, inspirational speakers, effective presentations and international audiences.

Ⓐ

◎ Discuss question 1 with the whole class. Get SS to discuss the remaining questions in pairs or small groups and then go through the answers with the whole class.

Suggested answers

1 You can give your own examples of giving presentations or 'speaking in public' as a teacher or trainer. Encourage SS to talk about their general fears or concerns of speaking in public, in their own language and/or in English.

2 SS may suggest any of the following techniques used by effective speakers: good preparation and knowledge of the topic; an ability to explain complex things clearly; projection or good use of voice and style of delivery without reading slides, notes or handouts word for word; unusual or attention-grabbing opening to the presentation; ability to establish rapport and engage the audience with a warm personality or use of questions; use of humour; smart appearance; regular eye contact with the audience and absence of irritating gestures. SS's discussion may highlight some cultural differences in perceptions of what makes an inspirational speaker.

3 Answers could include any of the following: an interesting topic; expert knowledge of the subject matter; an engaging speaker; good preparation and organisation with appropriate introduction, middle and conclusion; presentations that are succinct and to the point; use of visual aids; appropriate room set-up; a stimulating question-and-answer session at the end of the presentation; effective use of technical equipment and technology such as video, PowerPoint, figures and graphs and so on. SS's discussion may highlight some cultural differences in perceptions of what makes a good presentation.

4 SS may pre-empt some of the speakers from the listening and suggest any of the following: cultural sensitivity to local customs or traditions; careful use of language; avoiding idioms, slang and colloquialisms; adjusting pace and tone of delivery so that all the audience understands; (non-)use of suitable jokes or anecdotes; seating arrangements; different ways of showing approval or reacting to the speaker, e.g. clapping, nodding your head or knocking on the table and so on.

Listening: Experiences of giving presentations

Three business people talk about their experiences of giving presentations in intercultural settings and give tips for speaking to international audiences.

Ⓑ 1.1

◎ Play the recording once and ask SS to choose the best summaries individually. Replay a second time if necessary.

◎ As a follow-up, you could ask the SS to guess the nationality of the different speakers (1 American, 2 Belgian/French, 3 British).

1 c	2 d	3 b

(C) 🎧 1.1

- Explain that the first speaker is called Michael, the second Arianne and the third Steve.
- Play the recording a second time, pausing if necessary to allow SS to take notes. You could also pause after the answer to the first question to elicit the answer from the class as an example. Replay a third time, referring SS to the audio scripts on page 162 if necessary.
- After listening, SS compare notes in pairs and discuss the answers with the whole class. As with all cultural issues, discuss the differences in international audiences with sensitivity.

Suggested answers
1 He was using a lot of language (slang) that people didn't understand.
2 Casual, fun and personal. People might not find it funny because they don't understand him or his sense of humour.
3 Review it to remove/reduce the jargon and colloquial language and ask a colleague to check it for him.
4 She found out that VIP guests and people in senior posts sit in the front row of the audience.
5 She normally uses a semi-circular, theatre style.
6 She put some nicer chairs at the front for important members of the audience and arranged for them to be escorted to their seats.
7 By closing their eyes and nodding their heads up and down slightly.
8 By knocking on the table instead of applauding.

Vocabulary: Tips for giving presentations

SS look at some tips for giving presentations to international audiences and use related vocabulary in context.

(D)

- Do the exercise as a quick-fire whole-class activity, then discuss the tips with the whole class.

1 visual aids 2 script 3 handout 4 pace 5 delivery
6 rephrase 7 gestures 8 greet
Row is not used.

Discussion: Types of presentation

SS discuss the practical aspects of a presentation.

(E)

- Get SS to discuss their answers in pairs or threes. Go round the room, helping where necessary with vocabulary.

- Bring the class together and encourage SS particularly to talk about advice for giving a presentation in their country and how it might differ from other cultures.

Vocabulary: Slang, buzzwords and jargon

(A)

- Go through the three dictionary definitions as a whole class. You could explain that the terms *colloquialism*, *idiom* and *cliché* are also sometimes used to refer to slang or buzzwords. Drill pronunciation of these terms if necessary, highlighting word stress on the board. Elicit the first answer.
- Get SS to look at the cartoon. Ask them what buzzword is used? (*proactive leadership*)
- Ask SS to do the exercise individually, then compare their answers in pairs.
- Go through the answers with the whole class. Ask SS to provide examples in English of jargon used in their particular school, university or business sector that other people would not understand. Ask them to give other examples of contemporary buzzwords currently used in their organisation, such as *cutting edge*, *synergy*, *blended learning*, etc. Ask SS how they feel about using this kind of language.

1 a	2 b	3 b	4 a	5 b	6 b

Reading: *How not to sound like a fool*

SS read some advice on how to adapt your language and presentation style to ensure success when speaking to an international audience.

(B)

- As a lead-in to the article on *How not to sound like a fool*, ask SS whether they have ever been in a situation where they felt embarrassed about their English. If SS are not very forthcoming, give an example of when you felt embarrassed about speaking in public in a foreign language. Explain that native speakers may also suffer from feeling embarrassed when speaking in their own language in public. Alternatively, ask SS whether they think it's a good idea to use idiomatic or colloquial language when giving international presentations. Don't reject any ideas at this stage.
- Ask SS to read the questions and explain that the idea is to scan the article quickly for this information. They should ignore any words or phrases they don't know at this stage and focus on the task. In order to make this a quicker reading exercise, set a time limit. As a guideline, read through the text quickly, do the task and time yourself. Then allow SS about twice the time you needed to read and do the task – probably about four or five minutes.
- Before SS read, ask them to predict the advice given in the article about using colloquial language, idioms, clichés, slang or buzzwords.
- Ask SS for their reactions to the article before checking the answers. Did they predict correctly?
- Go through the answers with the whole class.

Suggested answers
1 It's very colloquial, and the writer uses it to illustrate the point that many people in an international audience wouldn't understand it.
2 Suggested rewording: *We really appreciate the opportunity to talk to you, our colleagues from Japan. We have some new ideas we want to discuss with you which we think you will be very impressed by.*
3 The way you give your presentation.
4 Simplifying the language for a non-native English speaker (paragraph 6) and suggesting a colleague reduce his talk (paragraph 9).
5 The Department of Commerce, embassies, local business people with relevant experience, publications, organisations specialising in international meetings, managers of international hotel chains.
6 Make sure you understand the question and be patient if it takes a while for the audience to comprehend your message.
7 Yawning, closing your eyes, nodding or shaking your head, frowning, smiling, waving, staring.

◎ Ask SS follow-up questions about giving and attending presentations in English. How do they (or would they) rehearse their presentation? How much time do they think is necessary to prepare a presentation? (Some experts recommend up to ten hours for a 20-minute formal presentation.) Do they prefer native speakers to simplify their English in presentations or use more idiomatic language that is more advanced or 'authentic'? What kind of presentations, speakers or accents do they find the most difficult to follow?

Language review: Business idioms

SS look at some common business idioms.

Ⓒ

◎ Get SS to read the article again, explaining that the paragraphs are numbered. If a SS asks a question, throw it open to the whole class to find out if someone can provide an explanation before answering it yourself.

◎ If you are short of time, divide the class into pairs and ask SS A to find items 1–4 (paragraphs 1–4), and SS B, items 5–8 (paragraphs 4–11). SS then exchange answers.

◎ Go through the answers with the whole class.

1 The stakes can be high (and the pitfalls many)
2 (a) risky business   3 set the stage for   4 full-blown
5 head down the wrong track   6 Tap into
7 information overload   8 can't figure (you) out

◎ If SS are interested in finding out more, give them the details of the titles in the Read on section (page 9) and Tom Leech's website, www.winning-presentations.com

◎ You may also tell SS they will be looking at presentation introductions and presenting company information later (Unit 7), as well as summarising and dealing with questions (Unit 10). If SS are particularly interested in giving their own presentations in class during the course, you may wish to deal with these sections at an earlier stage.

◎ If SS are keen to practise giving presentations, tell them that at an appropriate stage in the course they will need to prepare a four- or five-minute presentation, or the start of a presentation, on a topic of their choice. For SS with little or no experience of giving presentations, suggest they use themselves as the topic. Other possible presentation ideas are: explaining the company or organisation where they work or study, their product or service, or a special interest. Encourage SS to vary the seating arrangements, use visual aids (PowerPoint/transparencies and/or handouts) and experiment with different ways of starting a presentation, such as with surprising facts or figures, a joke or an anecdote. Record their presentations on video, making notes on five or six language points. Give feedback after the presentations, praising good examples of presentation language used, reviewing short sections of the recorded video. SS who listen should take notes and write down any relevant questions for the speaker. Ask SS to evaluate their own presentations and say how they would improve them.

◎ Make sure SS are given sufficient time and notice to prepare their talks before speaking in public. SS who do not know each other very well may be reluctant to speak in public early in the course and/or reluctant to give feedback on each others presentations.

 Grammar reference: Business idioms page 118

◎ There is a further opportunity to practise business idioms in the Grammar reference section.

1 b   2 a   3 b   4 b   5 a   6 b   7 b   8 a

◎ Explain this is an exercise on transformations with vocabulary related to presentations and that SS can only use a maximum of five words for each gap. Go through the example with the whole class. Ask SS for the answer to item 2, then get them to do the rest of the exercise individually. SS compare in pairs, then go through the answers with the whole class.

1 (*example*)
2 give (us) a simple explanation
3 made (the) arrangements for
4 provided a summary of
5 someone who/that specialises in
6 to bring the seminar to
7 open to (mis)interpretation
8 make any assumptions

Networking

SS discuss tips for communicating with people they don't know, or don't know very well; listen to some delegates meeting for the first time and networking at a conference; introduce themselves to another participant at an international conference.

◎ You may like to use this quote on communication as a warmer:

'Good communication is as stimulating as black coffee and just as hard to sleep after.'

Anne Morrow Lindbergh, writer and aviation pioneer (1906–2001)

(A)

◎ As a lead-in to the section, ask SS:

What do you understand by the term 'networking'?
When do you network? Where? Who with?
In what situations have you/do you network in English?
Do you enjoy networking? Why (not)? How is it useful?

◎ Get SS to look at the tips individually.

◎ Go through reactions with the whole class.

(B)

◎ Ask SS if they would use questions like How much do you earn? or Do you come here often? Why (not)?

◎ Ask SS to look through the questions individually first and add some of their own.

◎ Get SS to compare their answers in pairs or threes. This way, if SS only think of a few of their own questions, they can add those of other SS to their list.

◎ Go through the additional questions quickly with the whole class. SS's answers will vary, depending on their culture.

Suggested questions for networking

What do you like most about (living in … /your job /this event)?
What's your opinion on (this restaurant/event/place)?
What do you recommend I do/see (in your town/country/region)?
All are examples of neutral and open questions.

What's the weather like in your country/city/region at the moment?
What do you think of the new boss?
What's the political situation in your country/city/region at the moment?
The first one is an acceptable question for the British, but possibly a non-starter in other cultures.
The above questions may be acceptable in some cultures, but not in others.

Unsuitable questions for networking

How much do you earn?
May be appropriate in India and other Asian countries, but not Anglo-American and European countries.
Do you come here often?
Considered to be a cliché in English-speaking countries; also a yes–no question.

Other possible questions

Where are you from? How long have you lived there?
How long have you been working for … /working as … / living here /coming to this event?
Could you recommend a nice restaurant (near here)?
How was your journey/trip to the office/event/this city?

(C) 🎧 1.2

◎ Refer SS to the list. Play the recording once and get them to mark their answers individually. Replay a second time if necessary.

◎ Go through the answers with the whole class.

		Melanie	Konrad
1	Ask for confirmation	✔	
2	Greet someone	✔	✔
3	Compliment someone	✔	
4	Accept a compliment		✔
5	Agree with someone		✔
6	Express interest	✔	✔
7	Refer to a previous conversation		
8	Exchange business cards	✔	✔
9	Refer to future contact	✔	✔
10	Introduce someone to a useful contact		

◎ After listening, invite SS to comment on James's intervention and why Melanie and Konrad had to stop their conversation.

◎ Refer SS to the audio script on page 162. Play the recording a second time if necessary while SS read the dialogue, underlining or noting the expressions used for the functions in the list. Point out that these expressions are important and worth learning by heart for situations that require networking or social English.

(D)

◎ Ask SS what kind of difficulties they experience when socialising in English in a professional context, such as an international conference. Ask them to brainstorm other situations when they might give someone their business card, for example at a business lunch, meeting, training course or with the passenger sitting next to them on a flight.

◎ Explain that they are going to do a role-play as delegates at an international conference. They will practise starting a conversation and trying to find common ground with the other delegate, using some of the tips in Exercise A and the questions in the Useful language box on page 10.

◎ Go through the expressions in the Useful language box on page 11 with the whole class. Ask SS to highlight or underline expressions they find particularly useful. Drill pronunciation of expressions, highlighting sentence stress and intonation on the board, if necessary.

Lesson notes

- Divide SS into pairs. SS A and SS B look at their corresponding information on pages 142 and 149. Ask SS to take notes of any questions they might ask their partner before they start the role-play. For SS who know each other well, ask SS A to invent their name, company, job position and personal interests. If SS do not know each other very well, tell SS A to be themselves.

- Monitor and circulate round the class as SS do the role-plays. Make a note of SS who carry out the task successfully, any useful language used and five or six language points for correction, including intonation and pronunciation.

- Ask SS what they found most difficult when networking in English. Give feedback to the whole class, praising those SS who found common ground, remembered to exchange business cards and set up a future meeting successfully.

- Ask one or two of the pairs to act out part of their conversations again, bearing in mind the previous feedback.

- Go through feedback with the whole class, praising appropriate language for networking and use of open vs. closed questions. Write up any points that need further work on the board.

Writing: Replying to a formal invitation

SS look at a formal e-mail and write a reply, accepting the invitation.

 E

- As a lead-in to this writing section, ask SS what kind of formal correspondence (letters or e-mails) they generally receive or write. Ask SS in work what kind of formal correspondence they receive in English, if any. Ask prework SS what recent writing tasks they have done in English. Note: Do not spend too much time on discussing less formal situations, as Unit 2 deals with writing effective e-mails.

- Get SS to read the e-mail and underline examples of any formal or polite language used, e.g. *We are writing to; subsequently arose; We would be honoured; extremely grateful; at your earliest convenience; should you require.*

- Ask SS if they think the people in the e-mail know each other or not. (They probably do, as the expressions *Dear Mr Grau* and *Warmest regards* are used.)

- Explain that although this is an e-mail, it is a formal invitation from a Chamber of Commerce. It is similar in style and language to a formal letter, with the exception perhaps of the ending. Ask SS how the correspondence might end if it was a letter, not an e-mail. (A letter would probably end in *Yours sincerely*, but this is not used in e-mails.)

- SS have to write a reply accepting the invitation to speak at the conference, including questions concerning conference details and promising to send a proposal for the talk. It should be formal – or at least semi-formal – in style.

- Circulate, monitor and help SS while they write. Make a note of any useful expressions used on the board.

 Writing file page 134

- If peer correction is appropriate in your setting, SS may compare their replies in pairs after completing the task. Is it the right length? What formal phrases did they both use? What could be improved?

- Go through feedback with the whole class, praising good examples of formal language and style and pointing out five or six areas that need further work.

- If necessary, photocopy the following sample answer, or write it up on the board. You may choose to elicit a similar model from SS, writing it up on the board sentence by sentence, or gap-fill parts of the letter.

Sample answer

Dear Mr McCarthy / Andrew McCarthy,

Thank you for inviting me to speak at the conference to be hosted by the Chamber of Commerce in Edinburgh next month. I would be delighted to give a plenary talk on the subject of 'Merging companies: merging cultures' and will send you my speaker proposal form shortly.

In the meantime, could you please let me know how long the talk needs to be so that I can plan it accordingly? I would also be grateful if you could confirm the conference venue.

I look forward to receiving your reply / meeting you at the conference,

Best regards,

Jaume Grau

Branch Director

Savings Bank of Girona, Edinburgh

- Alternatively, divide the class into pairs. SS A accept and SS B decline the invitation. SS then read each other's e-mails and compare.

- Early finishers may write a short reply declining the invitation politely or rewriting the invitation in a less formal style. These writing tasks could also be set for homework.

Case study: Working for Logistaid

In this case study, a non-governmental organisation (NGO) in Amsterdam is training some logistics managers to be relocated to Indonesia. SS look at the job advert, exchange some notes from the course on intercultural training and network during the break with other participants. SS also write a reply to a formal invitation to a dinner held at the Regional Governor's residence in Jakarta.

If this is the first case study you have done with the class, be sure to prepare it carefully beforehand. Read the information in the introduction of this Teacher's Resource Book (pages 4–5).

In class, pay particular attention to clearly breaking down the case study into the different tasks and making sure that SS understand and follow the structure of what you are doing.

There is no audio used in this case study. It focuses mainly on speaking skills, although a writing task is also included.

Background

- Get SS to focus on the photo of the lorry. As a lead-in to the case study, ask SS the following questions:
  What do you understand by the term 'NGO'?
  What are some of the NGOs you are familiar with in your country?
  Would you be interested in working for an NGO? Why (not)?
- Read the background information aloud (or ask a S to read it). Explain that Logistaid is a fictitious organisation. Deal with any other questions SS may have.
- Write the headings from the left-hand column of the following table on the board and elicit information from SS to complete the right-hand column.

Organisation	Logistaid
Purpose of organisation	An NGO that provides emergency assistance in more than 80 countries
Based in	Amsterdam
Training required	Intercultural training of logisticians/logistics managers for relocation to Indonesia
Training company	Centre for Intercultural Communication
Purpose of training	Help managers to adapt to the new environment and improve interaction in social and workplace settings

Task 1

- Ask SS what they think a logistics manager does, then refer them to the job advert and ask them to check their answers. Get SS's initial reaction to the job position and ask them if they would be interested in applying for it.
- Go through the answers with the whole class.

Suggested answers
Skills and experience required: leaderships skills, good command of English and another language, willing to travel and work in a challenging intercultural context, experience in logistics desirable but not essential, relevant experience in logistics, e.g. purchasing, transport and distribution, maintenance as well as training and administration and general liaising/co-ordinating.
Possible candidates for the position may include any of the following: candidates with a willingness to travel and learn about other cultures, suitable voluntary work experience and a strong background in working for similar organisations, young managers with no family commitments; another possible profile could be an older person who has been made redundant and is looking for new challenges.

- Time permitting, you may ask pre-work SS to write a formal letter of application for the job position, or set this as homework at the end of the class.

Task 2

- Refer SS to the brochure from the Centre of Intercultural Communication on their International Relocation Programmes. Ask SS:
  Why do you think intercultural training would be important for managers being relocated to Indonesia?
  What do you think this kind of training consists of?
  If appropriate for SS in work, ask them if they have ever done any intercultural training in their company or organisation. If appropriate, ask SS if they have ever been to Indonesia or South-East Asia and what they thought of it. For SS who have not been to the area, ask them to focus on the general idea of relocation and going to work in a foreign country, rather than Indonesia specifically. Note: it is not necessary for SS to have knowledge about Indonesia in order to complete the tasks in this case study.
- Get SS to look at the International Relocation Programmes and ask them:
  What is 'culture shock'?
  What do you think will be the most difficult aspect of being relocated to a country like Indonesia?
- Divide SS into pairs. Explain that in this role-play, they are trainee logisticians for Logistaid in Amsterdam on their lunch break and that they each have some notes missing and need to swap information. Deal with any questions the SS may have before they begin the task.
- Circulate and monitor, checking SS are carrying out the task correctly. Make a note of any useful language used and points for correction for later feedback.
- After SS have exchanged information, go through the points quickly with the whole class. Ask SS how they feel at this stage as trainees before relocation, for example nervous, excited, anxious, etc.

Task 3

- Divide SS into threes and tell them they will be getting to know some of the other participants from the course and that they have to find some common ground during this networking task.
- Refer SS to their role-play information in the Activity file. Explain that they all have different work experience and have worked in different countries, but they keep their own nationality during the role-play.
- Emphasise the importance of team-building and building relationships with people from the course, as they will feel very isolated once they have been relocated to Indonesia and may want to keep in contact with the other participants. Tell SS they may be working together with the other course participants in the future, but this has not yet been confirmed before they begin the task.

Lesson notes

- Circulate and monitor, checking SS are completing the task correctly. Make a note of key language being used and points for correction. Deal with any basic errors after the role-play if necessary. Deal with other points, such as intonation in questions, during feedback when SS have completed the case study.
- Alternatively, the role-play cards in Task 3 can be omitted if SS do not know each other very well; they can then carry out the task as themselves, so that the task becomes an authentic one.

Writing

- Tell SS that three months have now passed since they were relocated. Ask them to imagine how they think the experience has gone, for example adapting to cultural differences, difficulties at work, missing family and friends.
- Get SS to focus on the photo on page 13. Ask them what they think it is. Tell SS they have received a dinner invitation from the Regional Governor of Jakarta, and it is important they attend as a public-relations exercise. Explain they have recently found out that one of their colleagues, whom they met on the training course in Amsterdam, will also be joining them soon, and they would prefer to attend the dinner with a colleague. Explain that although they are working 'in the field' as representatives of Logistaid, they would occasionally be expected to attend this kind of formal event.
- Ask SS to read the letter and deal with any questions they may have.
- SS write a short, formal reply of no more than 100 words, accepting the invitation and mentioning the name of their colleague, taking care to word their request politely. Tell SS it is best to address a person of authority using his/her official title. Refer SS to the expressions used in the Business skills section for writing formal correspondence. This task may be set as homework or an out-of-class activity.

 Writing file page 134

- Circulate and monitor, checking SS are completing the task correctly.
- For early finishers, or as an extra activity, divide SS into pairs or groups of three. Tell them they are now at the dinner in Jakarta. Two of the SS are representatives from Logistaid and one is the Regional Governor of Jakarta. Give more confident SS the role of the governor. Explain they have to talk for five minutes before dinner and find some common ground. Alternatively, with SS that don't know each other very well, ask SS to give a short presentation on their company and/or their job.

Feedback

- When SS have finished the writing task, bring the whole class to order.
- Praise the strong language points and work on five or six points that need improvement, especially in relation to language used for networking, finding common ground, open and closed questions and intonation in questions.
- Ask one or two groups to say what happened in their groups and what they discovered about the other participants.
- Ask one or two SS to read out their reply to the invitation or, if appropriate, ask pairs of SS to read each other's and comment on any differences in language used. Alternatively, and if short of time, collect the writing task and go through writing errors at the beginning of the next class.

---

1 to 1

- Go through the information in the Course Book with your student. Explain any difficulties. In Tasks 2 and 3, you and your student are participants on the training course for logisticians. In Task 3, choose only two of the role-play cards, A and B. Don't dominate the conversation in this task, but say enough to keep it going and allow your student to ask and answer questions.
- At the same time, monitor the language that your student is using. Note down any good examples of language and points that need correction or improvement. Come back to these later, after the student has completed Task 3.
- Praise any good examples of language used and go over any errors, including pronunciation. Then repeat Task 3, swapping roles, or taking roles A or B and C. Record the second role-play if possible. If the student is reluctant to do the writing task, explain it is very short or do the additional role-play at the dinner as recommended for early finishers. Go through feedback with the student after the final task.

Training

	Classwork – Course Book	Further work
Lesson 1: **Listening and discussion** (pages 14–15) *Each lesson is about 60–75 minutes. This time does not include administration and time spent going through homework in any lessons.*	**Discussion: Training** SS discuss their experiences of training courses, different learning styles and what they know about coaching and mentoring. **Listening: Interview with a training consultant** A training consultant talks about the purpose of some of the training activities she does and the aims of coaching and mentoring programmes. **Vocabulary: Company training** SS learn some key training words and expressions and use them in context. **Discussion: Types of training** SS discuss training courses, their views on mentoring and coaching and their future training plans.	**Practice File** Word power (pages 10–11)
Lesson 2: **Reading and language** (pages 16–17) *Each lesson is about 60–75 minutes.*	**Discussion: Online learning** SS discuss their views on e-learning, other learning styles and online MBAs. **Reading: *Time to break out from campus*** SS read an article about Universitas 21 Global, an online university offering an MBA programme. **Language review: Multiword verbs** SS look at multiword verbs related to education and training.	**Text bank** (TRB pages 160–163) **Grammar reference and practice** (CB page 119) **Practice File** Text and grammar (pages 12–13)
Lesson 3: **Business skills** (pages 18–19) *Each lesson is about 75–90 minutes.*	**Telephone strategies: clarifying and confirming** SS listen to two telephone conversations where people need to clarify and confirm information. **Writing: E-mails** SS look at tips for writing e-mails, analyse some sample e-mails and practise writing e-mails in more and less formal styles.	**Resource bank** (TRB page 219) **Writing file** (CB page 135) **Practice File** Skills and pronunciation (pages 14–15)
Lesson 4: **Case study** (pages 20–21) *Each lesson is about 75–90 minutes.*	**Training at SmileCo** A leading confectionery company, based in the UK, has recently bought out a rival company. There is now a need to retrain all the sales force to update their skills and instil a sense of team spirit. The management team also want to roll out a new market information-gathering system.	**Writing file** (CB page 135)

For a fast route through the unit, focusing mainly on speaking skills, just use the underlined sections.

For one-to-one situations, most parts of the unit lend themselves, with minimal adaptation, to use with individual students. Where this is not the case, alternative procedures are given.

Business brief

Most companies recognise the benefits of training employees. It can give a company a **competitive edge** by increasing profits, productivity, creativity, staff motivation and customer satisfaction. The key lies in developing an **effective training strategy** for a business which identifies the **skills and knowledge** the company needs to achieve its aims, the skills and knowledge employees already have and, from that, the **skills gaps** to be filled. Organisations and managers are sometimes reluctant to spend money and time on training because of the short-term costs, the lack of a tangible **return on investment** and the possibility that staff might leave for better jobs or competitors might **poach** their highly trained employees. Furthermore, even when a company has a training **evaluation process**, it is often difficult to assess the benefits of certain types of **soft-skills** training such as **effective communication**, **leadership skills**, **team building** and **conflict management**.

Training can be done for many reasons and take many forms. As part of a **performance appraisal scheme**, a manager may identify areas where an employee is underperforming and recommend training. The company may have a career or **professional development** programme for its staff and managers. There may also be a specific requirement for all staff to learn a new scheme and to develop certain **computer literacy skills** as well as **technical** and **behavioural competences**.

Although most emphasis is placed on **formal training**, people often learn most about their jobs through informal **on-the-job training**, such as reading **self-study books** and instructional manuals, talking to their managers, dealing with clients and chatting with peers by the coffee machine or over lunch. The importance of this **informal training** is often overlooked in the belief that training is something that only takes place in a classroom.

Formal training takes a pre-determined form with **specific learning objectives**. It could be in the form of university or college courses, workshops, seminars, conferences, presentations or demos. It can be provided by an **in-house** expert, but increasingly businesses are turning to specialised **external consultants** and training providers. The programmes they offer may be **tailor-made** for the business or bought **off the shelf**. Courses may be **intensive** or **extensive** and be held **onsite** or **offsite**. Many companies also use the **cascade training model** to maximise the benefits from training.

As information and computer technology has developed, it has become possible to offer **distance learning courses** to business via the Internet. Some of the advantages of this model are that employees can have more flexibility and control over their training programme, and it is generally more economical for companies. However, not all courses are suited to the **e-learning** format, and it's also important to bear in mind the preferences and **learning styles** of employees. It seems likely that **blended learning**, combining **face-to-face classes** with **online materials**, may become a popular model for business training in the future.

Nowadays **mentoring** and **coaching** are popular forms of informal, personal development in business, particularly for senior executives. The two are very similar, but in general, coaching lasts for a set period of time. The word **mentor** comes from Greek mythology, meaning 'a trusted friend, counsellor or teacher'. **Mentoring programmes** tend to be long term and they allow new, inexperienced managers to be paired with a more experienced person, who is not their direct boss. The mentor offers 'a friendly ear' and advice as the newcomer progresses in her/his career.

In the past, many companies could offer an employee a **job for life**. In today's rapidly changing world, individuals, as well as companies, are aware of the need for **continuous** and **self-directed learning** throughout one's lifetime. More and more people are now taking more responsibility for planning their own **career paths**.

Training and your students

In-work students will be able to talk about the training strategy of their company and other companies they may know or have worked for. Pre-work students will have experience of training from school and university. They can also talk about the companies they know that have a good reputation for training programmes. All students will have general world experience of learning all-purpose life skills, such as time management.

Read on

P. Nick Blanchard, James W. Thacker and Andrew Stull: *Effective training – systems, strategies and practices,* Prentice Hall, 2003

Marcia L. Conner: *Learn more now – 10 simple steps to learning better, smarter, and faster,* Wiley, 2004

David Kay and Roger Hinds: *A practical guide to mentoring,* How To Books, 2004

Henry Mintzberg: *Managers not MBAs: a hard look at the soft practice of managing and management development,* Berrett-Koehler, 2005

Suzanne Skiffington and Perry Zeus: *The complete guide to coaching at work,* McGraw-Hill Education, 2000

Lesson notes

Warmer

◎ Ask SS to brainstorm all the learning situations they've been in as a child and adult. Set a three-minute time limit for this activity. To make sure SS understand what they have to do, elicit or give them an example, e.g. learning to tie your shoelaces, swim, ride a bicycle, cook, drive a car, etc. Write SS's ideas up on the board. Then ask SS to work in groups of three or four to discuss what they remember about any of these learning experiences, who taught them, how they felt and how they were taught.

Overview

◎ Tell SS they will be looking at different types of training and professional development.

◎ Go through the overview panel at the beginning of the unit, pointing out the sections that SS will be looking at.

Quotation

◎ Ask SS what the quote means and what they think of it.

◎ Ask SS if they have they ever had a mediocre/good/ superior/great teacher. SS may not feel comfortable being negative, so leave out the question about the mediocre teacher if you think it is inappropriate. Who were these teachers and what made them mediocre/good/superior/ great?

Discussion: Training

SS discuss their experiences of training courses, different learning styles and what they know about coaching and mentoring.

Ⓐ

◎ SS work in pairs to discuss the four questions. Set a three-minute time limit for this. Then get feedback as a whole class. Help SS with the names of different types of training courses in English. SS will probably say that the learning styles they prefer may depend on what they are learning – elicit some examples. It isn't necessary to spend much time contrasting face-to-face with online learning, as this subject comes up in the second lesson. For question 3, ask SS if they can prioritise the qualities they have listed. Add a few more qualities if SS haven't mentioned them, e.g. have a good sense of humour, and ask SS for their views. SS will have some ideas already about mentoring and coaching; if not, give them the section in the Business brief (see page 19) as a short introduction. It is not necessary to spend too long on this, as it forms part of the listening section.

Listening and discussion: Interview with a training consultant

SS listen to Rosa Soler, a training and development consultant based in Barcelona, Spain, who works with multinationals, local companies and universities. In the first part of the interview, she talks about her company and describes some of the training activities she does. In the second part of the interview, she talks about the differences between coaching and mentoring programmes.

Ⓑ 2.1

◎ Get SS to focus on the photo of Rosa, then to work in pairs and look through the sentences. Explain any difficult vocabulary and ask SS to try to predict the missing information.

◎ Play the first part of the interview.

◎ Get SS to check answers in pairs, then play the recording again, stopping in sections to allow SS time to write if necessary. Replay any difficult sections a third time if necessary.

◎ SS check their answers in small groups. Circulate and deal with any queries they have. If you can see that all SS have the correct answers, you may decide not to go through all the answers in open class, simply confirm for the class that everyone has the correct answers and deal with the problem questions. This saves class time.

---

1 analysing/assessing/evaluating/observing; training (programmes)
2 bridge-building; leadership; interpersonal
3 management skills; prioritise; cope under pressure
4 coaching; mentoring

Ⓒ 2.2

◎ Get SS to read the statements and predict if the answers are true or false.

◎ Play the second part so they can check their predictions. Ask SS if they need to listen again and play the second part again if required.

1	True	*Basically, when you coach people, you improve on their skills so that they can do a better job ... These skills may include many business management skills, such as negotiating, time management, preparing meetings and presentations or organisation.*
2	False	*But coaching isn't only for managers. Anyone in a company might do this sort of programme.*
3	True	*... they are long-term career programmes which are specially designed for a select few in multinationals.*
4	False	*The mentoring programme is in fact only part of a bigger picture because the participant, or mentee, may probably be attending other training and personal development programmes. Or he or she might be studying for an MBA*
5	True	*... but the mentor cannot be the mentee's direct manager or boss. Usually, the mentor is someone who is high up in the company, who has a lot of experience and know-how ... It has to be someone who can be objective if the mentee has a problem at work or comes for advice.*
6	True	*They invest a lot of time and energy; it's very difficult to find the right person.*

◉ You may want to refer SS to the audio script on page 163. It's often very useful for SS to listen and read the audio script. You may want to just listen to one part of the interview again, depending on the time available and SS's needs. Then ask SS to pick out a language area, such as ten words relating to training or some multiword verbs (e.g. *end up being managers*, *come up with solutions*). However, don't spend too long going over the audio script in detail.

Vocabulary: Company training

SS learn some key training words and expressions and use them in context.

Ⓓ–Ⓔ

◉ Explain the tasks and get SS to work in pairs on them.

◉ Go round the room and help where necessary. Correct any misspelling of words.

◉ With the whole class go through the answers. Drill pronunciation of difficult words (e.g. *coach*, *evaluation*, *mentoring*, *consultant*, *appraisal*, *participant*) and highlight word stress on the board. Note: *mentoree* is also sometimes used, instead of *mentee*.

D **2** coaching; coach **3** evaluation **4** mentor; mentoring **5** consulting/consultancy; consultant **6** assess; assessor **7** appraise; appraisal **8** instruct; instructor **9** participate; participant

E **1** training **2** assessment **3** training/coaching **4** instruction(s) **5** participants **6** mentor **7** assess/evaluate **8** appraisal

Discussion: Types of training

SS discuss training courses, their views on mentoring and coaching and their future training plans.

◉ Get SS to discuss the four questions in pairs.

◉ With the whole class, ask SS to report back on their views and future training plans.

Discussion: Online learning

SS discuss their views on e-learning, other learning styles and online MBAs.

◉ This section returns to the concepts of face-to-face and online or e-learning introduced in the first lesson. It introduces the idea of blended learning, which combines the two. Before discussing the questions, you might want to ask if any SS are already studying for an MA or an MBA or are planning to do so in the future. (This follows up from the discussion in the last class.) If they are, ask them more questions about the course(s): method of instruction, why they chose that course, how long it is, what the course requirements are, what are the advantages of having an MA/MBA, etc. It may not be appropriate to ask about course fees.

◉ Refer SS to the three questions and deal with any problem words. Then ask the SS to work in groups of three or four to discuss the questions. As feedback, ask each group in turn to give you an advantage of doing an MBA online, and write each new suggestion on the board so that the groups can compare their ideas and they are prepared for Exercise B.

◉ If you think your SS will appreciate the humour, you could tell them this joke and then, on a more serious note, ask them what they see themselves doing in five years' time.

Manager: What do you see yourself doing in five years' time?
Employee: I don't know. The TV guide only goes up to the end of the week.

Reading: *Time to break out from campus*

SS read an article about Universitas 21 Global, an online university offering an MBA programme.

(B)

◎ Once you have the list of advantages on the board, refer SS to the article and ask them to find the advantages of online MBAs mentioned in the text. Explain that the idea is to scan the article quickly for this specific information. Tell the SS that they should ignore any words or phrases they don't know at this stage and focus on the task. In order to make this a quicker reading exercise, set a time limit. As a guideline, read through the text quickly, do the task and time yourself. Then allow your SS about twice the time you needed to read and do the task. SS will probably need about four or five minutes.

◎ Ask SS, in pairs, to compare their list of advantages and also to compare it with their list on the board. What points had they made that were not in the text and vice versa. Discuss the answers with the whole class.

◎ Ask them for their initial reactions to the points made in the article. Do they agree or disagree with the advantages mentioned? Are there any disadvantages they can think of now after reading the article?

---

1 The MBA director at the Brisbane Graduate School of Business says *E-learning is engaging, authentic* (paragraph 2) – although this is debatable, it may be more motivating for certain students, and the use of new technologies makes it appear more up-to-date than traditional classroom methods.

2 More accessible / less elitist than other MBAs: *It also aims to break away from the elitist model of higher education by making tertiary education accessible to more people.* (paragraph 3)
'An online course is more democratic, everybody has a voice, where you don't have just your typical Anglo-Saxon who is loud and talks more,' says Mr Williams. (paragraph 4) This again is debatable, although it's possible that students who may sit quietly in a class will contribute more readily to an online discussion.

3 It's cheaper than other MBAs: *Universitas 21 Global says that it is offering an alternative route for students in Asia, who cannot afford to pay for higher education or travel to the US, UK or Australia. To make its online MBA programme affordable, the institute charges varying tuition fees, depending on where the students come from.* (paragraph 5)

4 Older working students can save time: ... *flexibility of both time and curriculum, offers a huge incentive for working professionals.* (paragraph 7)

(C)

◎ Get SS to read through the summary of the article first to check vocabulary. If someone asks a vocabulary question, throw it open to the whole class to find out if someone else can provide an explanation. If not, explain where necessary.

◎ SS read the text again and complete the summary individually. Circulate and check answers, clarify any doubts and confirm correct answers.

◎ SS compare answers in pairs. If they need extra help, put the missing words on the board with a few distractors and get SS to choose answers from there.

◎ If necessary, check answers with the whole class. If not, then confirm that SS have completed the summary correctly.

◎ Discuss SS's reactions to the information again as a whole class and ask a few more general discussion and comprehension questions:
Why do you think Universitas 21 Global MBA is popular in India? (Education is highly-valued and a leveller in a society with a caste system.)
Why is it difficult for the university to break into the Chinese market? (The government is still deciding whether to give approval and also the course only costs 25% of a face-to-face MBA course in China, so there may be resistant from Chinese universities.)
What is the typical profile of a student studying at a 'bricks and mortar' university? How is the student profile at Universitas 21 Global different and why? (University SS are usually young and single. This online university's SS are married, working professionals – presumably because they haven't got the time during the day to attend face-to-face classes, preferring to study at home at nights and weekends.)
Do you think Universitas 21 Global's pricing policy is workable?
What would Universitas 21 Global have to do to become a recognised brand in your country?
How do people pay for their education in your country?
What is being done/can be done to help people who can't afford to pay for higher education in your country?

◎ Alternatively, if you are short of time, or SS don't want to read the whole article again in order to complete the summary, then write the jumbled answers on the board along with a few distractors and get SS to complete the summary using the words you have given them.

---

1 online/international 2 universities 3 (tuition) fees
4 abroad 5 education/fees 6 market
7 recognised/accepted 8 mature/senior

(D)

◎ Explain that the paragraphs in the article are numbered and show SS where the numbering is.

◎ Do the first item together as a whole class. Then ask SS to work in pairs to find the other words and expressions. They may find they can do some of these items without referring back to the text, but they should look at the paragraph to check their answers.

◎ Circulate and confirm answers or indicate in which sentence a word or expression occurs where SS are having difficulties. Get early finishers to compare their answers with another pair.

- If necessary, check answers with the whole class. If not, then confirm that SS have completed the summary correctly. If you'd like to offer further practice, ask SS, individually, to write true example sentences about themselves using some of these words, e.g. *post, degree*. Also, drill the pronunciation of any new words that SS might like to have as part of their active vocabulary.

> **1** tertiary institutes   **2** (associate) professor   **3** tap into
> **4** degree conferred   **5** critical mass   **6** bricks-and-mortar universities

Language review: Multiword verbs

SS look at multiword verbs related to education and training.

Ⓔ

- As a lead-in to this language review section, refer SS to paragraph 3 of the article and ask them to find examples of two multiword verbs (*tap into* and *break away from*). The meaning of *tap into* was already explored in Exercise D. Now ask SS to try to work out the meaning of *break away from* in the context given.
- Put SS in pairs to do the same with the sentences in Exercise E. Note that sentence 2 is *break away from*. Point out that there is more than one multiword verb in sentence 6. Circulate and help where necessary.
- Go through SS's ideas with the whole class, asking each pair to give their explanations of the meanings and find out if the rest of the class agrees.
- Alternatively, you can use these synonyms to confirm SS answers or give them to SS to match with the multiword verbs after they have identified them in the sentences.
  1   stop doing something, such as a course, before you have completely finished
  2   leave / escape from
  3   divide into separate parts to analyse it
  4   pay for someone to study a course
  5   investigate
  6^1 fail to do something by the time that was expected
  6^2 do something that needs to be done, but which you did not have time to do before.

> **1**   *will **drop out*** = will leave before the course finishes
> **2**   ***broke away from*** = stopped doing or gave up (something mainstream)
> **3**   ***breaking** it **down*** = making it clear / summarising
> **4**   ***putting** its employees **through*** = making its employees study or do
> **5**   *have been **looking into*** = researching or investigating
> **6**   *fell **behind with*** = couldn't complete
>   *'s **catching up with*** = studying hard for / making the same progress as others

- As further practice, tell SS to work in pairs to write six sentences of their own using these multiword verbs.
- Alternatively, ask SS to work in pairs. They write gap-fill sentences for three of the multiword verbs from the exercise and pass them to another pair to complete. Do an example on the board to make it clear what they have to do, e.g. *I'll have to study this weekend to ... ... my MBA coursework.*

 Grammar reference: Multiword verbs page 119

- Refer SS to the Grammar reference for further information and another practice exercise.

> **1** breaking away from   **2** fallen behind with   **3** catch up
> **4** look into   **5** dropped out   **6** put her through   **7** coping with   **8** followed up

Ⓕ

- SS to do the gap-fill exercise in pairs. Circulate and help as necessary.
- Go through the answers with the whole class.
- Discuss SS's views on the article.

> **1** hype (it) up   **2** bring in   **3** set up   **4** get to   **5** think ahead   **6** put on

Telephone strategies: clarifying and confirming

SS listen to two telephone conversations where people need to clarify and confirm information.

> **What is staff induction?**
> A planned induction programme for new staff is a very important part of the employment process. It's an opportunity to make new employees familiar with the operating procedures of the company. They should also understand the company's business objectives, and what it is trying to achieve. A typical programme might include a tour of the company facilities, dealing with paperwork such as contracts and the staff handbook, a presentation about the company (e.g. the history of the organisation and a description of the company organigram), some information about the job, hours of work, dress code and personal development within the company.

Ⓐ 🎧 2.3, 2.4

- Ask SS if they know what 'staff induction' involves. You and they may have some anecdotes of your/their own experience of staff inductions.

Lesson notes

Lesson notes

- If SS don't know what a staff induction programme is, tell them the information on page 23. SS can listen and then, in pairs, reconstruct verbally what they heard. Repeat the information so SS can get more details if necessary.
- Discuss the reasons why companies have induction programmes and whether they are worthwhile. If there is time and interest, get SS to design an induction programme for their own company or institution, if one is not already on offer.
- SS listen to the first phone conversation and say who the speakers are (e.g. a manager, a new member of staff, a receptionist, someone from the human resources department) and what the purpose of the phone call is.
- Check answers in pairs, then confirm the information as a whole class. SS can give any details they heard.
- Repeat this procedure with the second phone call.
- With the whole class, ask SS which call sounded more formal and why.

---

1   In the first conversation, the main purpose of Leoni Taylor's call to Mel Van Der Horst in Human Resources is to find out where she has to go to attend the induction course. In the second conversation, the receptionist, Pierre, calls Mel to advise her that the meeting room has been double-booked and that she has to move her induction session to another room.

2   The first conversation between Mel Van Der Horst and Leoni Taylor is more formal than Mel's conversation with the receptionist, Pierre. That's because Mel and Pierre are clearly work colleagues who know each other quite well. Mel and Leoni have apparently never met, so they are more polite and formal with each other.

Ⓑ ⌒ 2.3

- Check the vocabulary with SS, particular items a–c, and explain functions like 'echoing/rephrasing' if necessary.
- SS do the exercise in pairs before listening to the first conversation again to check their answers.
- Drill the pronunciation of the phrases that use questioning intonation.
- Refer SS to the Useful language box, where there is a summary of the expressions used. Ask them if they can think of any more expressions that they use for these purposes. Try to sensitise the SS to English sentence stress, linking and intonation. Don't get them to repeat all the expressions, just one or two from each section that might be difficult in terms of pronunciation (e.g. *Would you mind ...?* or *Could I ask you to ...?*).
- Refer SS to the audio script on page 163 and ask them to practise the dialogue in pairs, using the correct intonation when checking and confirming information.

---

1 b   2 c   3 b   4 a   5 b

Ⓒ ⌒ 2.4

- Ask SS to look at the room booking form and put the grid on the board. Explain that they have to listen to the second conversation again and correct the form, adding any extra information. Play the recording. Allow SS time to compare ideas in pairs. Then complete the grid on the board, asking the SS for the correct details.
- Ask SS to listen to the second conversation and get them to find examples of checking and confirming. Where did the speakers use a) echoing/rephrasing, b) question intonation or c) direct questions? If necessary, SS can also read the second audio script to check their answers.

Room	a.m.		p.m.	
B2	9–11	Chairman's meeting	11–	Staff induction (for rest of day)
B3	9–12	Staff induction	2–4	Sales team meeting
C1			2–5	Interviewing

- For follow-up practice, go to the Resource bank on page 219.

Writing: e-mails

SS look at tips for writing e-mails, analyse some sample e-mails and practise writing more and less formal e-mails.

Ⓓ

- Ask SS to work in groups of three or four. Start with a discussion of SS's use of e-mail. Who do they write to? How often do they use e-mail? Does their writing style vary according to the recipient of the e-mail (how and why)? Do they ever have to write in English? How often do they write e-mails in English and who to?
- Circulate, monitor and assist with the discussions. Make a note of any useful vocabulary SS use relating to the topic of e-mail, and three or four common errors for correction with the whole group. Write these on the board, in two separate sections, while SS are completing the task. Earlier finishers can be referred to the board to see if they know all the words and if they can correct the errors.
- Go through the language points for praise and correction on the board with the whole class.
- As a round-up of the discussion, ask SS who writes the most e-mails in English in each group and find out more details about this.
- Ask SS to work in the same groups of three or four. Brainstorm five tips for writing effective e-mails. Tell all SS to write down the tips as they will need to refer to these later. Set a five-minute time limit for this. Circulate and monitor what SS are writing.
- Regroup SS, so that they now have a partner from a different group. Get them, in pairs, to compare ideas.

◎ Ask SS to read the tips and see if their ideas were mentioned. Go through any difficult words and phrases (e.g. subject line, headline, inverted pyramid, headings, recipient, proofread, on the receiving end) with the whole class.

◎ In pairs, ask SS to decide if the e-mails follow the tips. What things are good about each e-mail? What could be better?

---

1 It hasn't been proofread: there are two spelling mistakes (*jjust, seesion*) and a punctuation error (*Everyone*). It does not have a strong subject line. On the plus side, the sentences are short and clear.

2 This e-mail is generally better. There are no proofreading errors, and it leaves a better impression on the reader. The only problems are that all the information is in one long paragraph which could be split up. Also, essential information like the time and date of session 1 is missing.

(E)

◎ In pairs, SS look at the e-mails again. As follow-up, ask for some more examples of formal or informal openers and closers in e-mails. SS may mention some of the informal SMS abbreviations, which are also creeping into e-mails these days, e.g. *CU 2moro* and *TTFN*.

Suggested answers
E-mail 2 is more formal.
More formal
　Dear ...
　It is my understanding that ...
　I suggest that ...
　Please confirm that ...
　Best wishes
Less formal
　Hello
　Just a reminder that ...
　See you there
　Thanks
　All the best
Other openers: *Hi, Good morning, Good afternoon, Good evening*
Other closing remarks: *With best regards, Speak to you soon, Bye for now.*

(F)

◎ Ask SS to work in pairs to write an e-mail together. Refer back to the telephone conversations in Exercise A. Ask them to predict who might send an e-mail to whom after these phone calls, e.g. from conversation 1, the HR manager might write to all new recruits confirming details about the induction day. Or, from conversation 2, the receptionist might write to the HR manager to confirm the new room arrangements for the induction day. Ask SS to choose one of the possible scenarios and write an e-mail.

◎ Set out a template for an e-mail message on the board, similar to the ones on the page.

◎ Refer SS to the model e-mail in the Writing file (CB page 135). Go through the features of a typical e-mail with them.

◎ Circulate, monitor and help SS. Make a note of any useful expressions SS use and put these on the board.

◎ To help SS be more aware of the impact their e-mails have on the reader, put each pair of SS with another pair. They exchange and read each others' e-mails. If they spot any words and expressions they don't know, they can ask their colleagues who wrote the e-mail about the meaning. If peer correction is appropriate in your setting, SS could also be asked to proofread each others' writing task and point out any spelling mistake or grammatical error they spot. Be on hand to help with this, if necessary, but leave most of the feedback and discussion to SS.

◎ If necessary, change the pairs around and repeat the process.

◎ Go through any common errors and the useful vocabulary and phrases on the board to round off the activity.

◎ If they would like or need further e-mail writing practice, SS can do Exercise F in class or as homework. Repeat the procedures above.

Case study: Training at SmileCo

A leading confectionery company, based in the UK, has recently bought out a rival company. There is now a need to retrain all the sales force to update their skills and instil a sense of team spirit. The management team also want to roll out a new market information-gathering system.

Background

◎ Get SS to study the background information in the Course Book.

◎ Write the headings on the left-hand side of the table and elicit information from SS to complete the right-hand side.

Company	SmileCo
Based in	UK
Industry	confectionery / fast-moving consumer goods (FMCG)
Recent acquisition	Reedley
Combined sales team	over 200
What's needed from the sales team	up-to-date / timely market information on the company and rival products, including merchandising, promotions, number and type of customers and rival sales-force activity
Why this information is important	So that it can be analysed for planning purposes.

Lesson notes

Listening ⏱ 2.5

- Get SS to read the listening task. Ask them to try and predict what might be wrong with the present information-gathering system. SS may be able to predict from reading the background that the information is not being received on time or that new staff from the acquired company haven't had adequate training with the system, or that the system itself is antiquated. Don't reject any ideas at this stage or give the answers away.

- SS listen and compare ideas in pairs. If necessary, listen again. Go through points with the whole class.

- Discuss their initial reactions to the problem. What do they think takes priority in terms of training and why? (There is no right answer to this question. SS may or may not reach a consensus.)

---

1 Problems with the sales team's current information gathering system are:
  - lack of information and out-of-date information;
  - staff can't afford to spend time in the office completing what they see as a complicated database, so it just gets left;
  - internal training for the regional managers was inadequate and they weren't equipped to train their staff;
  - sales team from Reedley have only had very ad-hoc informal training with the system.

2 Solutions discussed:
  Use iPAQ, a sort of palm pilot which the sales team could use to record details directly in the shops. The information is then be uploaded immediately via modem for analysis.

3 Training needs initially identify:
  - Training for the new iPAQ system implementation. Need to ensure that the regional managers buy in. Kamal suggests that they need to train staff up as quickly as possible and that a consultancy firm should do it.
  - Updating sales skills, e.g. customer awareness training to help sales staff become more 'pro-active' in their approach to selling.
  - The merged teams aren't integrating well. It could become a problem for staff motivation and morale. Team building is needed.

Task 1

- Divide SS into two groups. Refer each group to a different role card: Student A turns to page 143 and Student B turns to page 150. Ask them to read and deal with any questions they have.

- Pair the SS up with someone from the other group to do the role-play. Since the role-play is in the form of a phone call, it is useful for SS not to sit facing each other.

- Circulate and monitor the language they use during the role-play. Make a note of any key language used and any common errors for correction.

- After the discussion, draw attention to some key language that SS used correctly and give praise. Also work on five or six points for correction, e.g. pronunciation, vocabulary, structural errors.

Task 2

- Revise some of the expressions SS used in the Business skills section for clarifying and confirming information.

- SS work in pairs again and take the same roles as in the previous role-play. Student A turns to page 143 and Student B turns to page 150. Ask them to read and check their role cards before starting the task.

- Circulate and monitor, checking that SS are completing the task correctly.

---

1 to 1

- If this is a one-to-one class, you take the role of Geraldine Parker in Task 1. Since the role-play is in the form of a phone call, it is useful not to sit facing each other. This avoids visual clues and also allows you to take notes without distracting the student from the task.

- Monitor the language that you both use. After the discussion, draw attention to some key language that your student used correctly and give praise. Also work on five or six points for correction, e.g. pronunciation, vocabulary, structural errors.

- If there is time and interest, do the role-play again, this time swapping roles.

- Repeat the procedure for Task 2.

- It's also well worth recording activities such as role-plays, summaries and presentations with a one-to-one class for intensive correction work from time to time.

Reading

- Ask SS to read the text about the training course run by Everly Consultants. Go over any new words, e.g. *sets out to, make the most of, sales pitch, paid off*.

- Ask them to discuss whether they think they would like to do this type of training and explain why (not). Ask them to consider if this type of training would be good for the SmileCo sales team. (There is no correct answer to this question, but given the conversation SS have heard about outdated skills and the need for team building, this course might seem useful.)

Task 3

- Put SS in groups of three or four to discuss the questions. One student should be appointed secretary to make a note of the decision reached and feed back to the class. Another should chair the discussion and make sure everyone participates and that a consensus is reached. Set a 10–15-minute time limit for this task. If most groups still haven't finished the discussion after this time limit, allow them to run on a few more minutes. Remind any group that finishes early that the secretary will be asked to present their decisions to the whole class, and that they should help her/him to prepare for this.

◎ Call the class to order. Ask the secretary from each group to give a two-minute presentation.

◎ SS listen to each presentation and say which of their programmes coincided and differed and justify their programme in the light of any differences.

◎ Alternatively, if the class size is more than ten or 12, ask all SS in each group to make a note of the decisions reached. Then regroup SS so that one person from each of the original groups reports to the newly formed group. This ensures SS get more speaking time and speeds up the feedback process. They may then want to continue the discussion until they reach a new decision.

◎ To round off the activity, summarise some of the presentations, stating whether there had been any consensus between the groups on the training priorities, intensive/extensive courses, etc. and highlighting the best ideas in how all staff could benefit from the training a few people receive and how to build team spirit within the sales team.

Writing

◎ Brainstorm the information that should go in the e-mail and put these points on the board. All this information has come up in the role-plays in Tasks 1 and 2.

◎ Ask SS to look at the writing tips in the Business skills section again and the model e-mail in the Writing file (CB page 135).

◎ Get SS to write the final e-mail either as a class activity in pairs or for homework. This could probably be quite a long e-mail if SS include the background information as to who needs training and why the training is necessary. Alternatively, this could be made into a report-writing task.

 Writing file page 135

Lesson notes

Partnerships

At a glance

	Classwork – Course Book	Further work
Lesson 1: **Listening and discussion** (pages 22–23) *Each lesson is about 60–75 minutes. This time does not include administration and time spent going through homework in any lessons.*	**Discussion: Private provision of public services** SS discuss examples of private-sector involvement in public services. **Listening: PPPs in the UK** SS listen to a radio programme where experts debate the pros and cons of PPPs in the UK. **Vocabulary: PPPs** SS look at words relating to public private partnerships. **Discussion: Views on PPPs** SS discuss their views on PPPs.	**Practice File** Word power (pages 16–17)
Lesson 2: **Reading and language** (pages 24–25) *Each lesson is about 60–75 minutes.*	**Reading: *Infrastructure: Experience of the 1990s has put people off*** SS read about the successes and failures of PPP projects in developing economies. **Language review: Verb and dependent preposition; passive forms and causative *have*** SS work on two language areas: verb + preposition collocations and the passive verb form.	**Text bank** (TRB pages 164–167) **Grammar reference and practice** (CB pages 120–121) **Practice File** Text and grammar (pages 18–19)
Lesson 3: **Business skills** (pages 26–27) *Each lesson is about 75–90 minutes.*	**Negotiating: being vague and being precise** SS look at expressions for negotiating, listen to a conversation where they are used and apply them in a role-play. **Report writing: Layout and structure** SS talk about when they need to write reports, complete report-writing tips and write a short report.	**Resource bank** (TRB pages 220–221) **Writing file** (CB pages 138–139) **Practice File** Skills and pronunciation (pages 20–21)
Lesson 4: **Case study** (pages 28–29) *Each lesson is about 75–90 minutes.*	**Konopnicka Airport takes off** SS get information about the expansion project for an airport in Poland. They then participate in a role-play involving the negotiation of a PPP agreement.	**Writing file** (CB pages 138–139)

For a fast route through the unit, focusing mainly on speaking skills, just use the underlined sections.

For one-to-one situations, most parts of the unit lend themselves, with minimal adaptation, to use with individual students. Where this is not the case, alternative procedures are given.

Business brief

Common types of partnership

The *Longman Business English Dictionary* defines a partnership as a relationship between two people, organisations or countries that work together. In business terms, it is usually an association of two or more people who **go into partnership** by **pooling resources** and **sharing ownership**, responsibility, control, profits, losses and **liabilities** of the business. Each person contributes something to the business, such as ideas, expertise, money or property. The partners define their management rights and personal liability in a legal contract. A **silent partner** is a person who invests in a company or partnership and shares in the profits or losses, but does not take part in management of the business.

Another type of partnership is a **strategic alliance** between two or more companies to achieve a set of **specific goals** while remaining independent businesses. Strategic alliances come in many forms, including **joint ventures** and investments, and the development of common processes (e.g. supply chain) to increase the performance of both companies.

A third form of partnership is a **co-operative relationship** between people or groups who agree to share responsibility for achieving some specific goal. For instance, a charity might collaborate with a local government department in order to co-ordinate services. In this case, there may not be any **shared equity** or formal legal contract.

Public private partnerships

A **public private partnership** (PPP) is an agreement between the public and private sector on the provision of **public infrastructure projects**. In a PPP, or P3, scheme elements of a service previously run solely by the public sector are now provided through a partnership between a government agency and one or more private-sector companies. Unlike full **privatisation,** when the service is expected to operate like a private business, the government continues to participate in a PPP in some way and may maintain ownership of the assets.

When public and **private sector** try to work together, there is often a clash of cultures. However, there is a lot to be gained for both partners from working together. The **public sector** benefits from the **expertise** and resources of private business. The private sector offers better-quality services and responds more quickly to public demand. Then there are commercial benefits to the private sector of working on large, lucrative public contracts. A private company can also enhance its image and try to influence public policy-making.

This private-sector involvement is not without its controversy: Why should governments turn to the private sector when they have traditionally provided these services themselves? Aren't private companies less **accountable** than governments to the public? Will private companies take short cuts in order to increase profits? Will the need for public private partnerships increase?

Private-sector provision in developing economies

In many developing countries, the business sector has virtually taken over the delivery of public services because these governments do not have the resources to undertake large infrastructure projects. Poor countries may be required to **liberalise** their industrial, service or agricultural sectors through **trade negotiations** at the World Trade Organisation. Critics of this approach argue that there must be government controls to ensure that business delivers fair services to people.

Partnerships and your students

Your in-work students will be able to talk about the strategic alliances and business partnerships formed by their companies. They may even work for a business that has public-sector clients. Both pre-work and in-work students will certainly have views on public versus private provision of services – get them to talk about their experiences. They may also have views on the privatisation of state monopolies and the quality of public versus private services in their country.

Read on

Helen Sullivan and Chris Skelcher: *Working across boundaries,* Palgrave Macmillan, 2002

Alan Taylor et al.: *Partnership made painless,* Russell House Publishing, 2003

Lesson notes

Warmer

◎ Ask SS to brainstorm famous 'partnerships' for a few minutes this can include comedy double acts*, singing or acting duos and business partnerships. Give them a few examples you think they'll be familiar with (see answers below) to get them started. Alternatively, if SS enjoy trivia games, give them some of the first names of partnerships from the list below and ask them to give you the second name. SS then tell you what type of partnerships the pairs are.

*A 'double act', also known as a comedy duo, is used to describe the comic tradition of a pair of performers. One of the most famous double acts ever was Laurel and Hardy.

◎ Laurel and Hardy (early film comedy duo)
◎ Batman and Robin, 'The Dynamic Duo' (cartoon and film action heroes)
◎ Simon and Garfunkel (singing duo)
◎ Thelma and Louise (film characters)
◎ Starsky and Hutch (1970s TV detective show)
◎ Cagney and Lacey (1980s TV detective show)
◎ Romeo and Juliet (tragic lovers in Shakespeare's play)
◎ Lilo and Stitch (Disney cartoon characters: an orphaned Hawaiian girl and her extraterrestrial 'dog')
◎ Tom and Jerry (cartoon cat and mouse)
◎ Fred Astair and Ginger Rogers (dancing and acting duo)
◎ Paul McCartney and John Lennon (singer–songwriter team for the Beatles)
◎ Fortnum and Mason (luxury goods department store in Piccadilly, London)
◎ Marks & Spencer (British department store)
◎ Ben and Jerry (US ice-cream company founded in the 1970s in the US by childhood friends Ben Cohen and Jerry Greenfield, who had done a correspondence course in ice-cream making)
◎ Procter & Gamble (world's no.1 maker of household cleaning, beauty, health and baby-care products. William Procter and James Gamble formed their partnership in the 19th century in the US. One a soap maker, the other a candle maker, they had married two sisters and were encouraged to go into business together by their father-in-law.)
◎ Johnson and Johnson (leading US producer of healthcare products, ranging from toiletries to pharmaceuticals and medical diagnostic equipment. In 1876, Robert Wood Johnson developed a new type of ready-to-use surgical dressing, set up shop and formed a partnership with his brothers, James Wood and Edward Mead Johnson.)
◎ Tate & Lyle (founded in England in the late 19th century, the leading sugar and ingredients company grew from the separate sugar-cane refining businesses of Henry Tate and Abram Lyle)

Overview

◎ Tell SS they will be looking at the subject of private-sector involvement in public-sector services.
◎ Go through the overview panel at the beginning of the unit, pointing out the sections that SS will be looking at.

Quotation

◎ Ask SS if they've heard of John D. Rockefeller, who made his fortune in the 19th century with oil refineries and became so rich that he bought out most of his competitors and controlled almost 90% of the oil refined in the US. This near-monopoly position became the subject of much controversy and led to the US antitrust laws. The Rockefellers are still one of the richest families in the world today.
◎ Ask SS to read the quote and check the meaning of any words. Deal with any questions they may have, e.g. *found* in this context meaning 'start/begin with, based on'.
◎ Then ask SS what they think the quote means and if they agree with it. Discuss the pros and cons of setting up a business with a friend or family member.
◎ Ask SS if they can guess which famous businessman once said, 'Our success has really been based on partnerships from the very beginning' (Bill Gates, founder of Microsoft Corporation). Then ask them if you know which partnerships he was referring to. (He was referring to partnerships with industry and governments.) It's interesting to note that the richest man in the world recognised the importance of partnerships to his business.

Discussion: Private provision of public services

SS discuss examples of private-sector involvement in public services.

◎ Ask SS to look at the list of services. In small groups, they discuss what percentage of each service is provided by the government in their country and if there is also private-sector provision. They may mention any services that were formerly state-owned but which are now being or have been privatised. They can also discuss their views on the quality of public versus private services.
◎ As a round-up, ask SS if they know if the situation is similar or different in neighbouring countries or countries they may know through business contacts.

Listening: PPPs in the UK

SS listen to a radio programme where experts debate the pros and cons of PPPs in the UK.

(B) 3.1

◎ As a possible lead-in to the listening, explain that in the post-war era of the 1950s, there was a major expansion of public-sector provision of health, education and housing services in the UK, and many industries were 'nationalised' (i.e. brought under public ownership), including the railways and coal mining. The Thatcher government of the 1980s reversed this trend. The public housing stock has largely been sold off to tenants; public utilities, nationalised industries and transport services have all been reprivatised; and there is increasing private-sector involvement in health and education services. However, the vast majority of people still use these two public services.

◎ Before listening to the first part of the radio discussion, ask SS to look through the notes, check vocabulary and try to predict the missing information.

◎ SS listen and complete the notes. Then they compare their ideas in pairs.

◎ Play the recording a second time so SS can check their notes and get more information.

◎ Elicit the answers and put them on the board.

◎ Ask SS how this compares to their country:
What services have been outsourced?
Is the private sector financing public infrastructure projects?
Does that seem like a viable model at the moment? Why (not)?

---

1 outsourcing services   **2** cleaning   **3** catering   **4** public-sector buildings   **5** capital-intensive   **6** increasing public spending   **7** schools, hospitals, prisons, roads
8 a decade / ten years

(C) 3.2

◎ Before SS listen to the second part of the radio programme, ask them to look at the notepad, which shows the first point in favour of PFIs.

◎ In groups of three or four, SS quickly brainstorm one argument in favour and one possible criticism of PFIs.

◎ Put SS's ideas on the board in two columns, as per the Course Book.

◎ Ask SS to listen and see if any of their ideas were mentioned. They should also make a note of any other points mentioned.

◎ SS compare their notes in groups.

◎ Ask them how many points they heard. There are four points in favour and three criticisms.

◎ SS listen again to check their answers and pick up more details.

◎ Go through the answers with the whole class, putting key information on the board.

◎ Ask SS for their reactions to the debate. Which of the speakers seemed pro- and which seemed anti-PFI?

◎ Ask SS if they would like to listen again while reading the audio script.

◎ As follow-up to this, ask SS to identify five words or expressions in the text that relate to private provision of services, e.g. *outsourcing*, *competitive tendering*. Help them with any words they don't understand. This stage will also be useful for Exercise D.

Arguments in favour of PFI	Criticisms of PFI projects
1 The government can commission public services it couldn't otherwise afford.	**1** PFI projects designed to generate as much profit as possible for private consortiums.
2 New money is poured into public services.	**2** Buildings might/would be cheaper to build and manage if they were traditionally funded.
3 As the private sector is more efficient than the public sector, they can run public services more cheaply than the state could.	**3** Cheap-looking buildings being built. When the buildings become run-down and dated in a few years' time, the government will still be paying for them. The real cost won't be known for another 30 years or so.
4 Time and cost overrun is significantly reduced when the private sector manages a project.	

Vocabulary: PPPs

SS look at words related to public private partnerships.

(D)

◎ Give SS the instructions for this exercise and ask them to work in pairs. The first answer is given as an example.

◎ Go through the answers with the whole class.

◎ Focus on the pronunciation features such as word stress, vowel sounds and diphthongs that SS might have difficulty with.

---

1 Privatisation   **2** competitive; tendering   **3** running; maintenance; outsourced   **4** spending; privatised; ownership

---

Discussion: Views on PPPs

SS discuss their views on PPPs.

(E)

◎ Go through the four questions. Ask SS if they can give you a definition of *accountability*. (Individuals and organisations are responsible for their actions and may be obliged to explain them to others.)

◎ Get SS to discuss the points in pairs. Go round the room and help where necessary. Make a note of any common errors for correction, any useful new vocabulary and any points that are raised that would be good to discuss with the whole class.

◎ Write errors and new words on two separate parts of the board. Do the correction work with the whole class and go through the new words.

◎ With the whole class, SS report back on their opinions. Raise any interesting points that you heard SS mention in their pairwork discussion if they don't do so themselves, e.g. *Clara made an interesting point about ... Clara, would you like to tell us what you said?* This shows that you have been listening to the discussions, ensures that the discussion isn't dominated by the same SS every time and encourages participation from people don't normally speak in whole-group discussions. Obviously, only use this technique if, in your judgement, SS can cope with this.

Reading: *Infrastructure: Experience of the 1990s has put people off*

SS read about the successes and failures of PPP projects in developing economies.

(A)

◎ Put SS in pairs to discuss the two questions.

◎ Refer SS to the title of the article. Ask them what *to put someone off* means (make someone dislike or not want to do something), and who could be put off by PPP schemes and why.

◎ Ask SS to read the first two paragraphs quickly and say what the title refers to.

◎ Go through the answers with the whole class.

> Suggested answers
> lack of investment; projects in countries with high risk, e.g. political or economic instability; inefficient government/departments; corruption between private companies and government officials; lack of legal or regulatory structures; no public involvement in the project

(B)

◎ Ask SS to read the two parts of the sentence summaries and help them with any difficult words.

◎ SS attempt to match the two parts before reading the text and compare their ideas in pairs.

◎ SS read the full text to check their answers and put the items in the order in which they appear. At this stage, tell them not to focus on words they don't understand (some vocabulary items come up in the next exercise).

◎ If you want to exploit the vocabulary from the text further, a good exercise is to tell SS you will only explain five words or expressions from the text today. SS look at the text individually and choose their five words/expressions. Then they agree on five words in pairs and so on in a pyramid discussion, until the whole class comes up with the final five words/expressions. What usually happens in this process is that SS help each other with the meaning of words, can usually guess words from context and they make decisions about which words are essential to an understanding of the text. All these are good learner-training techniques.

> **1** f **2** e **3** c **4** d **5** b **6** a
> Text order is: 1f, 2e, 5b, 3c, 4d, 6a

Language review: Verb and dependent preposition; passive forms and causative *have*

SS work on two language areas: verb + preposition collocations and the passive verb form.

(C)

◎ Ask SS to work in pairs to do the vocabulary exercise. In the first instance, they should refer to the text to help them guess the meaning from the context. Circulate and help as necessary.

◎ Go through the answers with the whole class.

> **1** b **2** a **3** a **4** a

 Grammar reference: Dependent prepositions page 120

◎ For extra language practice related to the article, you can refer SS to the Grammar reference and practice on page 120 of the Course Book.

◎ Go through the answers with the whole groups.

◎ Ask SS in pairs to write an example sentence for any items they had difficulty with. Draw their attention to the fact that all of the verbs, except *prefer*, always require a direct object.

> to: advise, forbid, persuade, prefer, supply
> on: advise, build
> with: build, provide, supply

(D)

◎ Read the example from the text with the whole class and ask SS to identify the passive form: passive infinitive.

◎ If necessary, quickly revise how the passive is formed and when it is used.

- Ask SS to read all the sentences and deal with any difficult words, e.g. *top down*, *think tank*, *under the table*.
- SS work in pairs to complete the sentences. Circulate and help as necessary.
- Go through the answers with the whole class.

> **1** needs to be made **2** will be set up / is going to be set up **3** (will) have to be persuaded / have been persuaded **4** should not be built **5** has been forbidden **6** was / had been signed; was forced

 Grammar reference: Passive page 121

- For extra practice, see the exercise in the Grammar reference (CB page 121). If done in class, SS work in pairs to group the verbs.

> **1** The private sector has recently been involved by several US states in international marketing campaigns.
> **2** How much private money should be put into public projects, when there is an existing government budget?
> **3** The problem has been partly solved by the state of Alabama by giving the private sector an almost free hand.
> **4** But critics say it is hard for the private sector to know how far it should be involved when government funding exists.
> **5** Vice-president of the Economic Development Partnership of Alabama says his department was privately funded by 70 businesses last year.
> **6** Another model is provided by the public-private Indiana Economic Development Corporation.
> **7** The IEDC president says companies have been encouraged to locate to Indiana, and export promotion is now handled by the state.
> **8** Twice as many deals have already been closed by the state of Indiana compared with the same period last year.

E

- Put the example sentence (sentence 1) on the board. Ask SS to identify the structure (causative *have/get*) and elicit how it is formed. Elicit a sentence in the negative and question form as well.
- Ask SS to read all the sentences and deal with any difficult words and expressions, e.g. *joint venture*, *bring business in line*.
- SS work in pairs to rewrite the sentences. Circulate and help as necessary.
- Go through the answers with the whole class.

> **2** The TV company is still trying to get/have the joint venture approved by the government.
> **3** The Polish minister hopes to get/have a highway built in two years.
> **4** Many still believe the only way to get/have business brought in line is through the establishment of global rules, such as are being discussed in Geneva.
> **5** PPPs are types of contracts whereby the public sector gets/has some kind of service built or managed by the private sector.
> **6** PPPs have often failed because governments haven't got / don't have the public involved in the projects.

 Grammar reference: Passive page 121

Negotiating: being vague and being precise

SS look at expressions for negotiating, listen to a conversation where they are used and apply them in a role-play.

A

- Brainstorm the type of negotiations we have to do in our everyday life, e.g. what to watch on the TV, doing household chores, what to have for dinner, as well as more formal negotiations at work or college, e.g. the deadline for a project.
- Ask SS if they have seen the film *Jerry Maguire* and what they thought of it. Tell them that the film was based on the life of Leigh Steinberg, who wrote the book *Leigh Steinberg has a game plan*, based on his negotiation techniques.
- Ask SS to read the six tips for successful negotiation and help with any difficult words (e.g. *party*, *set the stage*, *give up*).
- SS discuss the questions in pairs.
- Ask SS if they think Steinberg's techniques would work in their country and ask them to explain why (not). Go through any other tips SS have with the whole class.

B

- SS work in pairs to match the functions and expressions.
- Drill the pronunciation, highlighting the features of sentence stress and intonation.
- Refer SS to the cartoon. Ask SS what they think the man is saying? Why? Do SS think he is being vague or precise here?

> **1** c **2** b **3** e **4** f **5** a **6** d **7** h **8** g

C **3.3**

- Tell SS they will hear part of a negotiation. Ask them to listen and decide what is being negotiated and what the outcome is.
- SS listen and then compare their ideas in pairs.

◎ If necessary, play the recording again so SS can confirm answers and listen for more details.

◎ Go through the answers with the whole class.

Topic: Pricing and special delivery terms (for olive oil)
Outcome: Giovanni will look into the possibility of a 5% discount.

(D) 🎧 3·3

◎ SS listen again and complete the chart.

◎ Refer them to the audio script on page 164 to check their answers and find any more expressions that were used.

◎ SS in pairs take the roles of Kathy and Giovanni and repeat the dialogue, paying particular attention to pronunciation. Circulate and help with any pronunciation problems.

◎ SS swap roles and repeat the dialogue.

Speaker	Vague	Precise	Asking for precise information	Expressions used *Suggested examples*
Kathy			✓	Couldn't you offer us a 5% discount?
			✓	Could you include the special delivery conditions at no additional cost?
Giovanni	✓			We can offer you exceptional delivery terms. (*doesn't specify*)
		✓		I'll speak to my manager and see what I can do.
	✓			I can't promise anything, but it'll be somewhere in the region of 5%.

(E)

◎ Ask SS to work in pairs. Tell Student A to turn to page 143 and Student B to turn to page 150. SS read the instructions. Deal with any problem words.

◎ Tell SS to refer to the negotiating expressions in Exercise B.

◎ Remind them that there are two separate situations to role-play.

◎ Give SS time to read and check their role cards. SS take a minute or two to think about what they are going to say. Ask them to try to incorporate as many of the useful expressions as possible. In general, the longer SS take to prepare a role-play, the longer their utterances will be and the better the level of accuracy.

◎ Circulate while SS are doing the role-play and help them when necessary. Make a note of any points for correction and points for praise, focusing particularly on how SS use the negotiating language.

◎ Call the class to order and go through the correction work, praising examples of good use of the language.

◎ Refer SS to the questions at the end of the exercise which ask them to review their performance. Ask SS about the outcome of their negotiations. Did they get what they wanted in both role-plays? What would they do differently another time? Get feedback from each pair, or if time is limited, get feedback from a one or two pairs of SS only.

Report writing: Layout and structure

SS talk about when they need to write reports, complete report-writing tips and write a short report.

(F)

◎ Do a brief needs assessment with the whole class on report writing. Ask SS how often they have to write reports in English, what type of reports they write, who they write reports for, how long they reports are expected to be. Ask them how they organise their reports, i.e. what sections they include (e.g. introduction, executive summary, conclusion, index, bibliography).

◎ Refer SS to the sections in Exercise F. SS work in pairs to put the sections into a logical order and say if there are any other sections they would add (e.g. index, bibliography).

◎ Go through answers with the whole class, discussing any differences of opinion.

Formal reports usually keep to the following order, although there are variations depending on the type of report.
◎ executive summary
◎ introduction
◎ findings
◎ conclusion
◎ recommendations

Other sections in a longer technical report may include contents page, graphics, bibliography, appendices, etc.

(G)

◎ Ask SS how they go about writing a report.

◎ Tell the whole class to check the words in the box. Help with any difficulties.

◎ SS work individually to complete the tips and then compare their ideas in pairs. Circulate and help as necessary.

◎ Go through the answers with the whole class.

◎ In pairs, SS discuss which of these techniques they already use, which they think it would be a good idea to use, and which they would never do and why.

---

1 plan   **2** register   **3** errors   **4** layout   **5** headings
6 Re-edit   **7** draft

(H)

◎ Tell SS to read the sentences and then read the report on page 159.

◎ Tell SS to put the sentences in the correct part of the report. Note that there is one extra sentence. Circulate and check that the SS are completing the report correctly, pointing out if the answers are not correct to give SS an opportunity to try again.

◎ SS compare their answers in pairs.

◎ Go through the answers with the whole class.

◎ Ask SS for their views on and reactions to the content of the report.

1 D **2** G **3** I **4** E **5** H **6** F **7** B **8** A	

◎ With the whole class, brainstorm what information they would put in a report about each of the role-play situations in Exercise E.

◎ SS work individually to choose one role-play to write about and produce a short first draft of their report.

◎ SS, in the same pairs as they were for the role-play, read each other's reports and make suggestions for changes or correct any factual mistakes.

◎ Refer SS to the model report on pages 138–139 of the Writing file.

Writing file pages 138–139

Case study: Konopnicka Airport takes off

SS get information about the expansion project for a major airport in Poland. They then participate in a role-play involving the negotiation of a PPP agreement.

Background

◎ With the whole class, look at the title of the case study and ask SS what the word *takes off* means in this context (i.e. to become successful). Then contrast this with the literal meaning of when a plane takes off. Explain that this use of double meaning is known as a 'pun'.

◎ Put the following table on the board and write the headings on the left. Tell SS to read the two sections on page 28 with the background information and complete the chart. Do the first item together as an example.

◎ Elicit the answers from SS and complete the right-hand side of the table.

Name of the airport	Konopnicka Airport
Location	Poland
Operated by	Polish Airports Agency (PAA)
Passenger numbers	5.5 million last year
Number of passenger terminals	1
Maximum passenger capacity	12 million a year
Expected growth in next four years	9.4 million
Scope of building project	A second runway, a new passenger terminal, a cargo terminal, a catering base
Reason for the expansion	To make it an international hub airport to relieve air congestion in western Europe.

Listening 🎧 3.4

◎ Get SS to read the listening instructions and the partially completed notes from the meeting, on the right-hand side of the page.

◎ Ask them to try and predict some of the missing details. SS may be able to predict some items from personal experience working on PPPs. Don't reject any ideas at this stage or give the answers away.

◎ SS listen and complete the notes.

◎ Ask SS to compare answers in pairs. If necessary, listen again. Go through answers with the whole class.

◎ SS may also like to listen and read the audio script on page 164.

◎ Ask SS for their initial reactions to the experience of and advice from the UK visitors.

1	making sure that ownership of the assets remains with the state.
2	agreeing that the PAA continues to operate airport services.
3	lower interest rates over a longer timescale, but tend to want more guarantees
4	Private investment firms: looking for a much higher rate of return in exchange for funding riskier ventures.
5	part public, part private finance
6	out to competitive tender
7	propose the method of finance.
8	building contractor is responsible for delays in the schedule.

Reading

◎ Ask SS to read the Laumann text. Ask them what type of text it is (a press release).

◎ Ask SS to read the press release again and answer these three questions:
  1 *What did the PAA do to get a contractor?*
  2 *Which private companies will be involved in the expansion project and what are their roles?*
  3 *Do you think Laumann is a suitable choice? Why (not)?*

1 Put the project out to competitive tender, as suggested in the meeting.

2 Laumann – building contractors; Weber-Merkel Bank – providing the finance

3 Laumann would appear to be a good choice, as they are a large company with a lot of experience of international projects.

Task

◎ Tell SS that they are going to negotiate the agreement between the Polish government and its private partners on the airport project.

◎ Refer SS to the language of negotiation on page 26.

◎ Elicit from SS what type of issues they think might be discussed in the negotiations. Then, put these heading on the board:
Financing
Operations and management
Repayment terms of the loan
Building schedule
Risk allocation

◎ Split SS into two groups. Group A turns to page 144 and Group B turns to page 151 and they both read the information. Help with any vocabulary items SS don't understand.

◎ Regroup SS into A + B pairs. Alternatively, SS can do this role-play in groups of four or five. SS appoint a note-taker in each group to write down the decisions made. Or they both take notes of the decisions made, if they work in pairs.

◎ When SS are ready, get them to start their meeting. Circulate and monitor the language being used. Note down any points for praise and any common errors during this stage. Allow SS plenty of time for the task as there are a lot of issues to cover.

Feedback

◎ Bring the class together again and praise five or six good language points that you heard and elicit the corrections to six or seven errors that you spotted.

◎ Ask the note-taker or a representative from each group/pair to report back on what agreement was reached on each of the five points above. SS in the other groups listen and identify any differences in the agreements they negotiated. They then report back on their agreements.

◎ SS decide which was the best negotiated agreement. There's no right answer to this, and opinions may vary.

1 to 1

◎ If this is a one-to-one class, you can take one of the roles in the negotiation task.

◎ Monitor the language that you both use. After the discussion, draw attention to some key language that your student used correctly and give praise. Also work on five or six points for correction, e.g. pronunciation, vocabulary, structural errors.

◎ If there is time and interest, do the role-play again, this time swapping roles.

◎ It's also well worth recording activities such as role-plays, summaries and presentations with a one-to-one class for intensive correction work from time to time.

Writing

◎ Refer SS to the executive summary section of the model report on page 138.

◎ Ask SS to use their notes from the meeting to write a 200–300-word executive summary, addressed to the Directors of the Polish Airports Agency and the Ministry of Infrastructure. The summary must include the five points discussed during negotiations. SS could do this for homework or in the same pairs or groups in class.

◎ If the executive summary is written in class, circulate and help SS with their written work and pointing out errors for correction.

 Writing file page 138

Revision

This unit revises and reinforces some of the key language points from Units 1–3, and links with those units are clearly shown. This revision unit, like Revision units B, C and D, concentrates on reading and writing activities. Some of the exercise types are similar to those in the Reading and Writing section of the Business English Certificate examination (Higher level) organised by the University of Cambridge ESOL Examinations (Cambridge ESOL).

For more speaking practice, see the Resource bank section of this book beginning on page 211. The exercises in this unit can be done in class, individually or collaboratively, or for homework.

1 Being international

Vocabulary: business idioms

◎ This exercise gives SS further practice of the business idioms from pages 8 and 118.

> **1** ran out of / 've run out of **2** got back on track **3** going over **4** sticks to the point
> **5** get; input **6** kicks off **7** kick around **8** keep track of

Business skills: networking

◎ SS are given further practice in using language related to networking from the Business skills sections on pages 10–11.

> **1** h **2** d **3** e **4** a **5** g **6** b **7** c **8** f

Presentations

◎ This exercise gives SS practice in the theory of public speaking, following work on presentations skills on pages 8–9.

> **1** e Only the prepared speaker deserves to be confident. (Dale Carnegie)
> **2** a All the great speakers were bad speakers at first. (Ralph Waldo Emerson)
> **3** f Once you get people laughing, they're listening and you can tell them almost anything. (Herbert Gardner)
> **4** d It is delivery that makes the orator's success. (Johann Wolfgang Von Goethe)
> **5** c Most speakers speak ten minutes too long. (James Humes)
> **6** b There is nothing in the world like a persuasive speech to fuddle the mental apparatus. (Mark Twain)

Writing: formal correspondence

◎ SS write a formal letter confirming attendance at a conference and write about some intercultural issues as further practice to the Business skills on page 11.

Sample answer

Dear Hendrickje De Vries,

With reference to your letter of September 15, I am writing to confirm my attendance at the conference on Intercultural Relationships in Business, to be held at the International Business School in Amsterdam. The title of my talk is 'Business Culture for the British Manager'. As requested, here is an outline of the main points.

Research has shown that understanding local systems is essential when communicating in an international context and that communication can break down for a variety of reasons.

1 Managers may find it difficult to adapt to the challenges of living and working in a different culture. I will give examples of British managers who have been relocated to emerging markets such as Brazil, Russia and China.

2 Not only language difficulties but also misunderstandings about attitudes to hierarchy and loss of face can cause problems. I will suggest that British business people need to use an 'international English' when doing business in an international setting. I also recommend that managers take care to respect the hierarchy in other countries and that the use of the British sense of humour does not always travel well.

3 Relationship-building is especially important for many non-Western cultures. I will highlight the importance of building trust and entertaining foreign visitors with regard to networking and establishing business contacts.

Please do not hesitate to contact me should you require further information.

I look forward to meeting you at the conference.

Best regards
Emile Laszlo

(246 words)

2 Training

Reading

◎ This exercise gives SS further practice in using the vocabulary associated with training and professional development (pages 14–15).

> **1** business schools   **2** three-year programmes   **3** the school   **4** training for executives
> **5** will be offered   **6** coaching   **7** developing partnerships   **8** develop

Business skills: telephoning

◎ This exercise gives SS further practice in confirming, clarifying or correcting information on the phone (page 18).

> **1** b (clarifying/confirming)   **2** f (clarifying/confirming)   **3** e (clarifying/confirming)
> **4** c (clarifying/confirming)   **5** d (correcting)   **6** a (correcting)

Writing: e-mails 1

◎ SS correct an e-mail to an HR manager, practising e-mail writing (page 19). If SS have not done this type of exercise before, draw their attention to the rubric and the fact that there isn't an error on every line.

> **1** a   **2** of   **3** do   **4** others / ✓   **5** ✓ / managers   **6** it   **7** for   **8** ✓   **9** themselves
> **10** ✓   **11** ✓

Writing: e-mails 2

◎ SS practise writing styles by rewriting the e-mail in the previous exercise in a more formal style (page 19).

Sample answer

Dear Angus Eliot

I have been informed by my line manager, Joanne Westwood, that there will be a staff training and development day in the near future. I would be grateful if you could send details about this, including course information and dates. Could you also please confirm whether course participants need to pay for this kind of training themselves?

On a personal level, I would be interested in doing a training course in Six Sigma, whereas other managers in my department have expressed an interest in coaching-style programmes.

Finally, it would be greatly appreciated by all staff members if a feedback form were to be given to participants at the end of each course. I think you will agree that this kind of feedback is very useful for analysing staff training needs and planning future courses.

I look forward to your reply.

Best regards
Carla Johnson
(147 words)

Vocabulary: word-building

◎ This exercise gives SS further practice in word-building associated with training and professional development (pages 14–15).

1 Mentoring   2 lecturer   3 assessing   4 appraisal   5 instruction   6 consultant
7 demotivated   8 trainees

3 Partnerships

Vocabulary: word partnerships

◎ This exercise gives SS further practice in word partnerships associated with public private partnerships, following the listening and vocabulary sections on pages 22–23.

1 h   2 a   3 b   4 g   5 f   6 c   7 d   8 e
1 private sector; delivery of services   2 lack of money; poor planning   3 reputation for; change their ways   4 far from perfect; make life better

Grammar: dependent prepositions

◎ This exercise gives SS further practice in dependent prepositions (page 120).

1 invest   2 (have) declined   3 applying/hoping   4 encouraged   5 expects
6 hopes / is hoping   7 try / are trying   8 needs   9 depend

Negotiating: being vague or precise

◎ This exercise gives SS further practice in being vague or precise in negotiating by reading a short dialogue between a government official and a manager of a construction company (pages 26–27).

1 I'm afraid it's looking unlikely (V)   2 But you signed a contract (P)   3 the project suffered serious delays when (P)   4 your company would be responsible for any delays (P)
5 that will involve taking on extra labour (P)   6 look at the refinancing of this project (P)
7 whatever it takes (V)   8 otherwise we have no alternative but (P)   9 see what can be done (V)   10 look into the possibilities very carefully (V)

Writing: report layout and structure

◎ This exercise give SS further writing practice in report layout and structure following pages 27 and 159. SS write a progress report as the manager for the construction project mentioned in the previous exercise.

Sample answer

Progress Report

Construction of government offices

Executive summary

Roberts & Walters Construction <u>was contracted</u> to build new government offices as part of a public private initiative. Following serious delays in construction work due to the findings of archaeological remains during excavation, the project is unlikely to be completed until early next year. Roberts & Walters therefore recommend a series of emergency measures to ensure the work is completed by December.

Introduction

In accordance with the present contractual agreement, all risk is assumed by Roberts & Walters. Failure to meet the expected completion date will result in severe penalty fines. It is therefore a matter of urgency that risk allocation is immediately reviewed. As the existing government offices are due to be vacated by the end of December, the new offices will need to be completed by the end of this year.

Findings

The discovery of Roman archaeological remains during excavation has caused serious setbacks in the project schedule. As these delays were due to circumstances beyond our control, we recommend risk allocation is reviewed and that both parties assume 50% of the risk. In addition, Roberts & Walters <u>will have</u> the current work schedule <u>revised</u> and employ additional labour, although this will affect project costs.

Recommendations

We strongly recommend the following measures to ensure construction is completed by December of this year:

1 An urgent meeting <u>needs to be held</u> by both parties to discuss the refinancing of the project.
2 Roberts & Walters <u>will need to have</u> the refinancing of the project <u>approved</u> by the end of this month in order to meet the new proposed completion date.
3 Regarding any extra labour costs incurred on the project, our recommendation is that both parties share these additional costs.

Conclusion

Roberts & Walters will ensure the new completion date is met, provided that risk allocation in the contractual agreement is revised to allow for the extenuating circumstances. Furthermore, we recommend that any resulting additional labour costs are shared by both parties.

(331 words)

UNIT 4 Energy

At a glance

	Classwork – Course Book	Further work
Lesson 1: **Listening and discussion** (pages 34–35) *Each lesson is about 60–75 minutes. This time does not include administration and time spent going through homework in any lessons.*	<u>**Discussion: Sources of energy and energy saving**</u> SS discuss sources of energy and ways of saving energy. **Listening: The future of natural gas** SS listen to an energy expert talking about developments in the gas industry. <u>**Discussion: Trends in the energy sector**</u> SS discuss implications of rising energy costs and mergers of energy companies. **Vocabulary: Energy and the environment** SS learn key words used in talking about energy and sustainable business.	**Practice File** Word power (pages 22–23)
Lesson 2: **Reading and language** (pages 36–37) *Each lesson is about 60–75 minutes.*	**Reading: *A dream of a hydrogen economy*** SS read about moves to develop hydrogen as the energy source of the future. **Language review: Discourse devices** SS look at the use of written and spoken discourse devices.	**Text bank** (TRB pages 168–171) **Grammar reference and practice** (CB page 122) **Practice File** Text and grammar (pages 24–25)
Lesson 3: **Business skills** (pages 38–39) *Each lesson is about 75–90 minutes.*	**Problem-solving** SS listen to two problems being discussed, look at the language of problem-solving and role-play a problem-solving scenario. **Writing: Proposal writing** SS look at the structure of proposals and use linking expressions for writing proposals in context.	**Resource bank** (TRB page 222) **Writing file** (CB pages 138–139) **Practice File** Skills and pronunciation (pages 26–27)
Lesson 4: **Case study** (pages 40–41) *Each lesson is about 75–90 minutes.*	<u>**Energy saving at Supersun**</u> SS look at the problems of energy cost at a supermarket chain and make proposals for savings.	**Writing file** (CB pages 138–139)

For a fast route through the unit, focusing mainly on speaking skills, just use the underlined sections.

For one-to-one situations, most parts of the unit lend themselves, with minimal adaptation, to use with individual students. Where this is not the case, alternative procedures are given.

Business brief

There has been an enormous increase in the demand for energy since the mid-20th century as a result of **industrial development** and population growth. According to The Energy and Resources Institute (TERI), the world's population has more than tripled in the last 150 years, while per capita use of **industrial energy** has increased about 20-fold. About 15% of the world's population living in the wealthy **industrialised nations** consume over half the energy used in the world. The number of cars and other motor vehicles has more than doubled since 1970. It is now widely acknowledged by industry experts that the **energy market** is already operating at close to full capacity as a result of **surging economic growth** in China and India. Volatile energy costs are also pushing up the prices of **petrol** and products.

Until recently, the main **primary sources** of energy in developed countries have been **oil** and **coal**. There are many environmental problems associated with **fossil fuels**, primarily the emission of **carbon dioxide** (CO_2) and other **greenhouse gas emissions** which are contributing to the destruction of the **ozone layer** and **global warming**. Adding to that, fossil fuels are **non-renewable** energy sources. Oil and coal supplies are soon expected to be exhausted, although there are no reliable figures on how soon supplies will run out. Nowadays, the demand for natural gas – the cleanest fossil fuel – is increasing, and it now plays a key role in the energy policies of many industrialised countries, because it is an **environmentally friendly** alternative. Most of the new **power stations** developed around the world are gas-fired. In the UK, for example, the displacement of coal by gas in power generation helped the country more than meet its emissions reduction commitment as part of the **Kyoto Agreement**.

While previously **gas reserves** were often too far away to bring to markets, **liquefied natural gas** (LNG) and gas-to-liquids technologies have virtually eliminated mobility as a problem. According to the International Energy Administration (IEA), natural gas accounts for 22% of the world energy supply, and its share is growing significantly. Demand for LNG is rising so fast that by 2020 to 2025, it may overtake oil as the world's **primary fuel**.

Nuclear energy can also produce power on a large scale without burning fossil fuel. Some countries, such as France, depend heavily on nuclear power, as it is a locally produced source of energy that crucially doesn't depend on imports from other countries, although most **green lobbyists** are opposed to nuclear power because of the potential risks.

The overall efficiency of energy production remains extremely low: on average, more than 90% of energy consumed is lost or wasted in the process of conversion from **raw materials** such as coal to the final energy service, such as electricity. The main problem isn't that we use energy, but how we produce and consume energy resources. **Conserving energy** has become the need of the day, be it in the transport, household or industrial sectors.

Alternative energy sources have become important and relevant in today's world, with many companies, such as Ford Motors and British Telecom, now looking at ways to generate their own energy using technologies based on **renewable energy sources**. Wind, wave and solar power can be replaced rapidly by a natural process and can never be exhausted. At present, though, these renewable energy sources account for no more than about 4% of the world's total electricity consumption, according to a recent report in the *Financial Times*, with most of this coming from **hydro-electric power**, a well-established form of renewable energy.

Fuel cells have also attracted attention recently as a potentially clean source of energy, harnessing hydrogen, the most abundant element in the universe. **Hydrogen fuel cells** produce electricity, with water as the main by-product, making them an attractive way of reducing air pollution and greenhouse gas emissions. It could become an alternative to fossil fuels in cars and in a wide range of household and industrial applications. However, making hydrogen fuel economically is not at all simple.

Energy and your students

Both pre-work and in-work students should be able to talk about energy sources and energy costs as consumers and be aware of the environmental issues and the dwindling supply of fossil fuels. They may also have views on the merger of energy companies, nuclear power and their governments' energy policies.

Read on

Godfrey Boyle (editor): *Renewable energy,* Oxford University Press, 2004

Jeremy Rifkin: *The hydrogen economy,* Polity Press, 2002

Paul Roberts: *The end of oil,* Bloomsbury, 2005

Vijay V. Vaitheeswaran: *Power to the people,* James Bennett Pty Ltd, 2005

Lesson notes

Warmer

◉ Give SS this list of modern devices and ask them to prioritise them in terms of how essential they are to their lives: the plane, the car, the mobile phone, the computer, the fridge, the television, the lift (elevator), the light bulb, the microwave oven, the washing machine.

◉ Get SS to tell you what the sources of energy are for all these devices (electricity and petrol, both essential for providing heat, light and power for human activities). Point out that these secondary energy sources are actually dependent on primary sources and elicit from SS what these are (coal, oil, natural gas, nuclear power and alternatives such as wind, solar, wave energy and hydrogen). Tell the SS that electricity has been generated for the purpose of powering human technologies for at least 120 years. Ask them if they know what the first power plants were run on (wood) and what we mainly rely on today (petroleum, natural gas, coal, hydroelectricity, nuclear power and a small amount from hydrogen, solar energy, tidal harnesses, and wind generators).

◉ Get SS to brainstorm other devices they think they would find it difficult to live without. Tell SS to discuss the relative importance of these items.

Overview

◉ Tell SS they will be looking at developments in the energy industry.

◉ Go through the overview panel at the beginning of the unit, pointing out the sections that SS will be looking at.

Quotation

◉ Ask SS to define what a proverb is and why they think we have them in every culture. According to the *Longman Dictionary of Contemporary English*, a proverb is 'a short well-known statement that gives advice or expresses something that is generally true'. It's worth noting that they exist in every culture because they are essentially words of wisdom to help guide our lives. Proverbs can also give us some insight in the values of a culture.

◉ Tell SS to read the quote and ask them what they think it means. Note that many proverbs have been borrowed and adapted from Chinese culture. The English equivalent of this proverb is 'There is no smoke without fire'. It means if people are saying bad things about someone or something, there is probably a good reason for it.

◉ Ask SS if a similar proverb exists in their language.

◉ Ask SS how they think this quotation can be related to the topic of the unit. In the context of energy, you could argue that it means all of our human activities need an energy source to drive them.

Discussion: Sources of energy and energy saving

SS discuss sources of energy and ways of saving energy.

(A)

◉ SS work in small groups of three or four to discuss the two questions. Set a five-minute time limit for this. Circulate and help SS by providing any vocabulary they need.

◉ Call the class together. Drill the word stress of any vocabulary relating to energy which SS might have had difficulties with, e.g. *nuclear, environment, electricity, fossil fuels, coal, oil, petrol,* etc. This will help SS to recognise some of these words when they hear them later in the recording.

◉ Get SS's feedback on their ideas as a whole class.

Suggested answers
1 Sources of energy that are generally considered to be environmentally friendly:
   ◉ Wind power, although some say that wind turbines ruin the natural landscape
   ◉ Solar energy
   ◉ Nuclear energy produces power on a large scale without burning fossil fuel and therefore does not contribute to effects of global warming; it is becoming popular again in countries like France, but is still considered to be a more controversial source of energy.
   ◉ Photovoltaic power (electricity caused by electromagnetic radiation) is one of the newer energies and is becoming more popular in countries like Germany.
   ◉ Hydrogen, e.g. hydrogen-fuelled cars (see Reading and language review)
   ◉ Natural gas, arguably, as it's cleaner than other fossil fuels such as oil or coal (see Listening)
2 a) Turning off lights and electronic equipment when not necessary or when not being used; having showers instead of baths (to save on heating and water); opening and closing fridge/freezer doors quickly; installing double-glazed windows; using low-energy light bulbs, etc.
   b) Turning off lights and electronic equipment when not necessary or when not being used; using low-energy light bulbs, avoiding air-conditioning systems if possible; turning down office heating systems to avoid people opening windows because it's too hot; having a heating/air-conditioning system that can be regulated in individual offices and not just through a centralised system; etc. (see also Case study)
   Also, although not strictly at home or in the workplace, students may mention transport, e.g. saving energy by walking or cycling to work/place of study; car-sharing as opposed to individuals driving to work; reducing the number of cars per household / company parking spaces; etc.

Listening: The future of natural gas

SS listen to an energy expert talking about developments in the gas industry.

(B) 🎧 **4.1**

◎ Get SS to work in pairs, look through the five questions and try to predict the correct option. Explain any difficult vocabulary.

◎ Play the recording once and ask SS to check their answers in pairs.

◎ Replay if necessary, although SS should be able to do this first listening task after hearing the recording once. This time, stop after each question to allow SS time to decide on an answer.

◎ Go through the answers with the whole class.

> **1** a   **2** b   **3** a   **4** b   **5** a

◎ As a follow-up, you could ask the SS how popular natural gas is as a source of energy in their country and if they have natural gas in their homes, and if so, for what appliances.

(C) 🎧 **4.1**

◎ Get SS to read through the summary and tell them there are eight errors. Deal with any vocabulary questions they have.

◎ Replay the recording.

◎ After listening, SS compare notes in pairs.

◎ Go through the answers with the whole class. One way to do this is to ask SS, in turn, to read out a section of the summary with the correct information. The other SS listen and say if they agree.

> Natural gas is far ~~less~~ **more** environmentally friendly than other fossil fuels like oil and coal, but it is also being replaced by newer sources of energy, as it will probably run out in ~~50~~ **150** years' time.
>
> The gas sector is ~~unlikely~~ **likely** to continue doing well for some time to come, and the opening up of markets, together with deregulation, has created more competition in the industry.
>
> Changes in how the sector is regulated mean that gas suppliers can now ~~sell~~ **buy** from anywhere. New regulations have also forced some companies to ~~bundle~~ **unbundle** their activities, dividing their companies into separate areas of business.
>
> Apart from competition, other factors that have affected the sector include a ~~fall~~ **rise** in the use of natural gas, as well as attracting a wider customer base. This has led to mergers between gas and ~~oil~~ **electricity** companies, as seen in Germany, and the creation of energy giants.
>
> Other concerns in the gas sector include security of supply and diversification: the ~~Middle East~~ **EU** relies heavily on certain countries and regions for its gas supply, so countries like Spain now import gas from a variety of countries.

◎ As a final stage in the listening, you may want to refer SS to the audio script on page 165. SS often like to listen and read at the same time. After listening, ask SS to focus on a language area, e.g. get them to find ten words relating to energy. Don't spend too long going over all the vocabulary items in the audio script in detail.

Discussion: Trends in the energy sector

SS discuss implications of rising energy costs and mergers of energy companies.

(D)

◎ Get SS to look at the four questions. SS discuss their answers in small groups of three or four. Circulate and monitor, helping where necessary with vocabulary. Make a note of any problems SS may still be having with the lexis associated with energy and five or six points for correction. Also, listen for any good points that SS make which can be brought up later when you round off the discussion with the whole class.

Vocabulary: Energy and the environment

SS learn key words used in talking about energy and sustainable business.

(E)

◎ Get SS to look at the vocabulary items in the box. Explain any difficult words (*watchdog* might need explaining – it's an organisation whose job is to protect the rights of consumers and to make sure that companies do not do anything illegal or harmful).

◎ Get SS to complete the articles in pairs. Circulate and monitor, helping where necessary by telling SS if they have the right answers or not.

◎ Go through the answers as a quick-fire whole-class activity.

> **1** energy consumption   **2** greenhouse gas emissions   **3** energy watchdog   **4** renewable energy   **5** energy efficiency   **6** wind power   **7** fossil fuel   **8** global warming

◎ As further speaking practice, you might like to ask SS for their reactions to the articles, e.g. What are the implications for the global energy market of the growth of demand in India and China? How would they feel about their government raising taxes in an effort to protect the environment? Would they mind having a nuclear power station near their home or place of work/study?

Reading: *A dream of a hydrogen economy*

SS read about moves to develop hydrogen as the energy source of the future.

- Get SS to look at the photo of the car and ask them if they'd like to have a car like that. Why (not)? Ask them how much petrol a car like that would need. (On average, a small car uses 6–8 litres per 100 kilometres, a large luxury car uses 12–15 litres and the average four-wheel drive uses 20–25 litres.)

- Get SS to read the extract *How 'green' is your car?* Deal with any vocabulary questions, e.g. *sport* in this context is a verb and means 'to wear or have visibly displayed'. Ask SS what the title means (*green* means 'environmentally friendly'). NB New petrol cars currently emit 100–170 grams of carbon dioxide a kilometre, but the average four-wheel drive emits more than 185 grams.

- Get SS to look at the four questions. Deal with any problem words, e.g. *petrol-guzzling* which means 'using a large amount of petrol in a wasteful way'.

- Ask SS to discuss the questions in pairs. Go round the room and help where necessary.

- Get the class together and go through their suggested answers. Ask SS why we will need alternatives to petrol-driven cars. (Because oil supplies are expected to run out in 50–60 years' time. This fact was mentioned by the gas expert in the recording in the previous spread.)

Suggested answers

1   Heavy marketing, people feel safer in them, status symbol.

4   Electric cars, solar-powered cars, hydrogen (see article), people using public transport more, or walking and cycling instead.

B

- As a lead-in to the article *A dream of a hydrogen economy*, ask SS whether they can predict why switching to hydrogen from fossil fuels could present challenges. Don't reject any ideas at this stage.

- Tell SS that they are looking for four challenges mentioned in the text. Explain that the idea is to scan read the whole article quickly for this information. Tell SS to underline the key phrases when they find them. They should ignore any words or phrases they don't know at this stage and focus on the task. In order to make this a quicker reading exercise, set a time limit. As a guideline, read through the text quickly, do the task and time yourself. Then allow your SS about twice the time you needed to do the task. SS will probably need about four or five minutes.

- Tell SS to check their answers in pairs. Then bring the class together and go through the answers with the whole class, asking SS to tell you the paragraphs and extracts where the challenges are mentioned.

- Ask SS about the tone of the article, i.e. the general attitude or feeling of the text. Ask SS if the writer seems confident that the hydrogen economy is a possibility in the near future, or if he seems more sceptical about it. After a first quick reading, SS should be able to tell that the article has a sceptical tone, as the writer has mentioned so many problems associated with a hydrogen economy.

- Get SS to work in pairs and ask them for more evidence from the text to suggest that the tone of the article is rather sceptical. Alternatively, if the task appears to be too challenging for your SS, refer them to one or two of the phrases yourself.

Four main challenges:

- finding ways to produce hydrogen: *Top of the list of difficulties is finding a simple and economical way to produce hydrogen.* (paragraph 3)

- finding ways to store it: *... storing enough of it on board a car has them utterly confused. Because hydrogen is the lightest element, far less of it can fit into a given volume than other fuels.* (paragraph 5)

- converting it to electricity by the use of fuel cells: *(... the fuel cells that convert hydrogen to electricity. Fuel cells have been used to power spacecraft, but their high cost and other drawbacks have kept them out of everyday applications such as cars.* (paragraph 6)

- infrastructure required to supply it to consumers: *Hydrogen fuel-cell cars also face an obstacle from outside: the infrastructure they need to refuel.* (paragraph 7)

Another issue mentioned is the safety concerns: *Various technical challenges – such as making them rugged enough to withstand the shocks of driving and ensuring the safety of cars loaded with flammable hydrogen gas* (paragraph 6)

The tone of the article seems somewhat sceptical about the viability of switching to a hydrogen economy. This is shown by the number of problems mentioned in the article and comments such as: *... have **sunk** billions of government dollars into hydrogen initiatives* (paragraph 1), *The only problem is that the bet on the hydrogen economy is **at best a long shot*** (paragraph 2), *Years of research in all these areas, however, **have yet to yield decisive progress*** (paragraph 4), *If producing hydrogen cheaply has researchers **scratching their heads**, storing enough of it on board a car has them **utterly confused*** (paragraph 5), *... the **litany of concerns** over making the transition to a hydrogen economy* (paragraph 9).

(C)

- Get SS to read the vocabulary items and see if they can predict the answers before reading the text again. It is worth pointing out that both definitions for items 1 and 8 are possible, but only one is correct in the context. Tell SS to read the relevant sections of the text, and check the meaning of the words and phrases in context.

- Get SS to compare their answers in pairs. If they do not agree, tell them to refer back to the text to help them decide.

- Call the class together and go through the answers with the whole class.

1 b	2 a	3 b	4 b	5 a	6 a	7 a	8 a	9 b	10 a

- As further practice, ask SS to write example sentences using three of the words or phrases.

(D)

- This exercise relates back to the topic of 'environmentally friendly' energy, first raised in the previous lesson, and explores the topic further. Put these three phrases – 1 environmentally friendly, 2 alternative energy, 3 renewable energy – on the board. Ask SS what the expressions mean to them. (1 does not harm the environment; 2 energy derived from sources that do not use up natural resources or harm the environment; 3 an energy resource that is replaced rapidly by a natural process, such as power generated from the sun or from the wind.)

- Get SS to work in small groups of three or four to discuss the three questions. Set a five-minute time limit for this. Circulate and help SS by providing any vocabulary they need. Alternatively, this could be an Internet research project. First, brainstorm the sources of alternative energy as a whole class (see answers to 1 below). Then split the SS into groups. Give each group an alternative energy to research its advantages, disadvantages and technological drawbacks. If this is done in class time, set each group a time limit of one hour to research the topic. Or set the task for homework and allow SS time in class to compare and put together a presentation of their findings. Ask each group of SS to give a five-minute presentation of their findings. SS listen to each presentation and decide at the end which alternative energies seem most/less viable and why.

- Call the class together. Deal with one source of alternative energy at a time. Get one student from each group to feedback on their ideas as a whole class. Ask SS to decide what they think seem the most/less viable sources of energy and why.

Suggested answers
1 Solar, wind, wave, tidal, hydroelectric, geothermal, biomass/bio fuel (e.g. straw, algae, cow dung, wood)
2 Experts think it is still unclear whether any of the alternative/renewable energies could be a viable global alternative to fossil energy. Hydrogen, solar energy and bio-fuels are the most debated options as part of the EU's energy strategy.
- Solar energy is not very effective on cloudy days, in winter, at night or in areas without much sunlight. The problem is how to store significant amounts of electricity when the sun is not available to produce it.
- Wind energy is similar to solar energy in that it is not dependable. Also, wind turbines are expensive, windy areas are often in isolated locations a long way from the power grid system, and some say that wind turbines ruin the natural landscape. Salt water would quickly damage wind turbines placed at sea.
- Many sorts of installations have been tried to obtain energy from waves, but without much success. Waves are not a dependable source of energy. As for tidal power, there are currently very few sites, it is considered ecologically damaging and not a significant power source.
- Hydroelectric dams destroy the local natural environment, wildlife and communities are displaced.
- Geothermal power is limited to certain locations.
- Using biomass such as wood can lead to deforestation. Ethanol (grain alcohol) produced from biomass (e.g. crops such as sugarcane) is a cleaner fuel than petrol as it produces less carbon monoxide. However, it produces just as much nitrogen oxide. In addition, ethanol production contributes to air pollution. Another drawback is that organic material, while low in cost, tends to be bulky, making it uneconomic to transport over long distances to power stations.

Language review: Discourse devices

SS look at the use of written and spoken discourse devices.

 Grammar reference: Discourse devices page 122

- If SS would like to do some language work following on from the text, refer them to page 122 of the Grammar reference on linking expressions. Get SS to read the information in the table on the left and look at the example sentences. Ask them to find three examples of linking expressions used in the article on page 37, e.g. *But 15 per cent of the energy in natural gas is lost as waste heat during the re-forming process* (paragraph 3), *Years of research in all these areas, **however**, have yet to yield decisive progress* (paragraph 4), ***Because** hydrogen is the lightest element, far less of it can fit into a given volume than other fuels* (paragraph 5), ***Yet**, if that is the case, many*

energy experts argue, governments should be spending far more money to lower the technical and economic barriers to all types of alternative energy (paragraph 10).

◉ Get SS to work in pairs to complete the sentences on page 122. Do the first one with the whole class so that SS know what is expected. Circulate and help where necessary.

◉ Call the SS together and go through the answers with the whole class.

---

1   to buy smaller cars unless
2   since (the) oil (supply) is
3   in spite of (their) reservations / in spite of having reservations
4   so they can / so as to
5   cheap because it costs
6   on water (supplies) because of

Problem-solving

SS listen to two problems being discussed, look at the language of problem-solving and role-play a problem-solving scenario.

Ⓐ 🎧 4.2

◉ You may like to use this quote on problems as a lead-in to the section. Read it aloud, dictate it to the class or write it on the board. Get SS to say what it means, if they agree with it and ask them who they think said it.
We can't solve problems by using the same kind of thinking we used when we created them. (Albert Einstein)

◉ Ask SS to look at the right-hand photo. Get SS in pairs to discuss what they can see in it and decide where they think it was taken. Set a two-minute time limit for the discussion. Circulate and help with any vocabulary where necessary.

◉ Call the class together and ask if they guessed the city. (Rotterdam)

◉ Refer SS to the left-hand photo and ask them what they see. (Air-conditioning / air-con units)

◉ Tell SS they will listen to two separate dialogues. SS listen and identify what the two problems are, and who they think is speaking in each dialogue.

◉ SS compare their ideas in pairs. Only if necessary, play the recording again to allow SS an opportunity to confirm their ideas. Go through the answers with the whole class.

---

1   In the first conversation, the speakers are talking about the high level of staff turnover in one of the company offices. It is probably a regional manager and a manager from the Human Resources Department.
2   In the second conversation, the speakers are discussing the shortage of air-conditioning units for sale. They are probably the owners or managers of an electrical goods shop.

Ⓑ 🎧 4.2

◉ Tell SS that they will listen to the dialogues again. Ask them to read the extracts in pairs and try to predict the missing words. Deal with any vocabulary questions, e.g. *staff turnover* means 'the rate at which people leave an organisation and are replaced by others'; *branches* are individual banks, shops, offices, etc. that are part of a large organisation; *sold out of* means 'have no more left in a shop'.

◉ SS listen to the dialogues again and complete the phrases. SS compare their answers in pairs. Play the recording again if required.

◉ Go through the answers with the whole class.

---

1 notice   2 could be   3 As I understand it   4 to jump to any conclusions   5 would be a good idea to   6 looks like   7 should reconsider   8 only problem I can see   9 let's sleep on it

---

Ⓒ

◉ SS work in pairs to identify the function of each of the phrases. Tell SS to write the number of the phrase next to the items (a–d). Do the first one together as an example. Circulate and help where necessary.

◉ Go through the answers with the whole class as a quick-fire activity.

◉ As follow-up, drill the pronunciation of some of the expressions from the two conversations.

---

a) 1, 6, 8   b) 2, 3   c) 5, 7   d) 4, 9

Ⓓ

◉ SS work in pairs again to match the two parts of the phrases.

◉ As follow-up, draw SS's attention to the verb patterns with *suggest*, *consider* and useful expressions like *If (someone) were …*, *provided*, *might as well*.

◉ Drill the pronunciation of some of the expressions from the two conversations.

---

1 g   2 d   3 f   4 a   5 b   6 c   7 h   8 e

Ⓔ 🎧 4.2

◉ Explain that SS are going to role-play two situations based on the conversations in Exercise A. If necessary, play the conversations again to remind SS of the problems or elicit the problems from SS.

◉ Tell SS to incorporate some of the problem-solving language from Exercises B and D in their discussions.

- Divide SS into pairs. SS A and SS B look at the first situation on their corresponding role cards on pages 144 and 150. Allow SS time to read them and prepare what they are going to say. Tell SS they have a minute to do this. This preparation time is vital, as second-language acquisition research has shown that it improves the accuracy and length of SS's utterances. Deal with any vocabulary questions.

- Circulate and monitor the class as SS act out the role-plays. Make a note of SS who are carrying out the task successfully, any useful language used and five or six language points for correction, including intonation and pronunciation.

- Call the class together. Give feedback to the whole class, praising SS who used the expressions correctly. Put the items for correction on the board and elicit the correct versions from SS. Drill any pronunciation items again, where necessary.

- Refer SS to the second situation. Repeat the procedures above, reminding SS to pay particular attention to avoiding the same errors. Circulate and monitor SS performance. Again, make a note of SS who carry out the task successfully, any useful language used and five or six language points for correction, including intonation and pronunciation.

- Call the whole class together and praise their efforts. Go through the corrections together as before. Finally, ask each pair of SS for feedback on the tasks; were they able to come up with any proposals or solutions to the problems? If time is limited, just ask one or two groups for their feedback.

- For follow-up practice, go to the Resource bank in this book.

Proposal writing

SS look at the structure of proposals and use linking expressions for writing proposals in context.

- Tell SS that you are going to look at writing proposals. If you have in-work SS, ask if they ever have to write proposals and what they think the purpose of a proposal is (to persuade the reader to do or accept something, e.g. fund a project, buy your product, etc.). Ask them what they expect to find in a proposal and how it might be organised. SS may have different experiences or no experience of proposal writing. You could copy and distribute the following information if SS will find it useful or go through these points by giving SS an oral presentation.

Proposals are both **informative and persuasive** writing because they attempt to educate and to convince the reader to do something. Therefore, it necessary to **get your audience's interest** in the project before you present them with timescales and costs. It's always important to **highlight the benefits** the reader will receive, as well as the cost of the solution.

There are many ways to set out a proposal, and the tips and guidelines here are by no means definitive. You can use a **memo** for internal proposals and the **business-letter format** for proposals written from one external organisation to another. One simple framework is as follows:

- The **introduction** presents and summarises the problem and your proposed solution(s). It includes a summary of the benefits the reader will receive from the solution and the total cost.
- The **body** of the proposal provides a detailed explanation of the solution, including a breakdown of the method, tasks, equipment and personnel that will be required. It can also present a detailed breakdown of the timescale and costs.
- The **conclusion** emphasises the benefits that the reader will receive from your solution to the problem and should encourage and persuade the reader to take your proposed course of action.

Some proposal writers provide an **executive summary** written in non-technical language for those outside your specific area of expertise. Alternatively, you might include a **glossary of terms** that explains technical language used in the body of the proposal and/or attach **appendices** that explain technical information in language that is easy to understand. In addition, if your proposal is going to people in the organisation or clients who don't know you, include your **qualifications** for the project.

- Get SS to look at the Useful language box and identify the more formal linkers that might be used in reports and the less formal words that might be more common in spoken English.

- SS compare their ideas in pairs.

- Go through the answers with the whole class.

Suggestions for less formal, more frequently spoken expressions are:

Adding extra information
too, also, as well as

Contrasting information
but

Introducing the result of previous information
so

Giving the reason for something
because, that's why

Expressing a sequence of events
then, after that, finally

(G)

- Tell SS they are going to write a proposal. Refer them to the writing-style tips at the bottom of the page. Deal with any vocabulary questions, e.g. 'gender-neutral' language means using words that do not assume people are always male – writers should use *he or she* rather than just *he*.

- Ask SS some questions about the tips, e.g. Why is it particularly important to write with the reader in mind when doing proposals? (Because you want your reader to do/accept what you propose); For which audiences do/would they use a semi-formal writing style and when do/would they write in a more formal style?

- Now tell SS to imagine that they are managers in a company that is about to relocate. Ask SS to suggest reasons why a company might relocate. Ask SS to suggest some reasons why employees might be happy or unhappy about such a move. SS may have personal experience of office moves which they can tell you about.

- Get SS to read the instructions and the notes to incorporate into their introduction. Deal with any vocabulary questions, e.g. *outskirts*.

- SS work in pairs to write their introductions. Circulate and help SS with the task, pointing out any errors as they are writing, but allowing SS the opportunity to make the corrections themselves.

- SS exchange proposals with another pair and read each others' versions. If culturally appropriate, you could ask SS to proofread each other's work and point out any errors.

- Copy the model answer below and distribute it to SS for them to compare with their versions. Ask them to underline the linking expressions and any expressions they find useful.

Model report

Transport service for relocated staff

Introduction

Given the high cost of office space in the city centre, the company has decided to relocate to a new business park on the outskirts of the city in January next year. This move will provide more spacious facilities, allow for expansion and have the added advantage that the offices and warehouse will be finally integrated on one site.

Despite these benefits, a major concern of the administration staff due to be relocated is the lack of public-transport links to the business park. I have investigated existing transport facilities and, as the business park is a new development, the local transport companies do not, as yet, have any plans to reroute any services or create any new services for the foreseeable future.

As a solution to this problem, I propose that the company provide a morning, lunchtime and evening mini-bus service from Kings Square, a location in the city that provides easy access for onward journeys via bus, underground and train networks. At an estimated annual cost of 53,000 euros, this solution is both cost-effective and efficient and will ensure staff morale is not adversely affected by the company relocation.

Case study: Energy saving at Supersun

SS look at the problems of energy cost at a supermarket chain and make proposals for savings.

Background

- Get SS to focus on the photo of the supermarket freezers. As a lead-in to the case study, ask SS where they usually shop for food and if they buy much frozen food. Ask them if they think the demand for frozen food is likely to increase or decrease in the future and to give reasons for their answers.

- Get SS to study the background information in the Course Book. If you think it's useful, read it aloud or ask a student to read it aloud. Deal with any vocabulary questions they may have, e.g. *the bottom line* means 'the figure showing the company's total profit or loss', *shelf stock* means 'all the items that the store sells'.

- Write the following headings on the left-hand column of the table and elicit information from SS to complete the right-hand column.

Company/organisation	Supersun
Based in	California
No. of stores	30
Current threats and weaknesses	• tight profit margins • strong competition • increasing energy bills • government's 'clean air' legislation
Main operating costs	• shelf stock • energy bills
Strengths and opportunities	• creative marketing strategies to retain and increase customers • reduce energy costs by improving efficiency

Reading

- Put these numbers on the board: 2, 50, 10, 9, 10, 400.

- Get SS in pairs to read the CERG newsletter extract and say what the numbers refer to.

- Go through the answers with the whole class as a quick-fire activity. Deal with any vocabulary problems, e.g. *earnings per share* means 'a company's profits for a period of time divided by the number of shares'.

Profit margins are below **2**% in supermarkets.

Energy costs are as high as $**50** or more per square metre.

It's estimated that a **10**% reduction in annual costs increases profit margins by **9**%, increases share earnings by nearly **10**% and is equivalent to a $**400** increase in sales per square metre.

◎ Ask SS if they think energy saving is a good idea for supermarkets based on what they've read. (It would certainly seem so from the increase in profit margins claimed by the CERG newsletter.)

◎ Ask SS why they think supermarkets have such high energy costs. What do they think are the main sources of energy consumption in supermarkets? Don't spend too long on this discussion, as the sources of energy consumption are outlined in the pie chart on the next page.

◎ Refer SS to the pie chart on page 41. Deal with any vocabulary problems. Ask SS as a whole class to brainstorm ways supermarkets could reduce costs in these areas. You and SS may be able to talk from personal experience of walking into a store that was too hot/cold, or which had the doors open in winter and the heating on, etc.

Listening 🎧 4.3

◎ Get SS to look at the agenda for the store managers' monthly meeting and read the listening task.

◎ Play the first part of the recording and ask SS which agenda items the group are discussing. (They start with item 2, but go into items 3 and 4 as well during the course of the discussion.)

◎ Play the whole recording and ask SS to make a list of the tasks the new Energy Project Team will have to work on.

◎ SS listen. In pairs, they compare ideas. If necessary, replay the recording. Go through points with the whole class.

Suggested action points for Energy Project Team
◎ Collect and analyse data on energy costs.
◎ Think of ways to make energy saving a priority for everyone in the company.
◎ Come up with ideas for reducing CO_2 emissions by 10% in the next seven years.
◎ Make proposals for energy savings and possible investment in new equipment/technologies.

◎ As a follow-up, ask SS what energy-saving and waste-reducing measures people came up with in the meeting; were they the same ideas as SS had mentioned earlier in their brainstorming session? Play the recording again to get more details and check SS's answers.

◎ SS compare their answers in pairs. Then go through the answers with the whole class.

◎ Turn air-con down.
◎ Turn off lighting inside and outside the supermarkets.
◎ Use skylights.
◎ Buy/use more energy-efficient refrigeration units.
◎ Buy energy from renewable sources.
◎ Sell less frozen food and cut number of fridges.
◎ Cut transportation costs through buying more produce locally.

Task 1

◎ Tell SS they are now part of the newly formed Energy Project Team. One of their duties is to collect information about ways to save energy and report back to the group.

◎ Divide the class into two groups. Refer one group to the Student A role card on page 145 (Energy Efficient Lighting in Shops) and the other group to the Student B role card on page 151 (Refrigeration). Tell them to read the information and try to memorise it, retelling it in their own words. Deal with any vocabulary questions. They can look at the card quickly if they need to. Allow them time to practise this in their group.

◎ Regroup SS in A+B pairs. Tell them to report their information to their partner. They can look at the role cards if they need to check something, but should try to retell the information in their own words as much as possible. SS listen to each other and take brief notes. Circulate and monitor SS's performance and what they are writing. Note down strong points, any useful language used and five or six language points for correction, including vocabulary and pronunciation features.

◎ Call the class together. Praise SS's performance. Go through the points for correction, eliciting the answers from SS wherever possible. Ask SS which techniques they read and hear about would save the company most money and which would be the cheapest to implement, e.g. checking fridge door temperature settings, using low-energy light bulbs.

Reading

◎ Get SS to read the news extract at the top of page 41. Deal with any vocabulary problems, e.g. *hike* means 'a large increase in prices'. Ask SS what impact these price rises will have on Supersun. (It will increase operating costs and reduce the profit margin. Supersun may decide to increase product prices as a result, but this could cost it customers. Alternatively, they could look at energy-saving measures to counteract the price rise.)

Task 2

◎ Tell SS to read Task 2 and to look at the CO_2 emissions chart on the right. Deal with any questions they have.

◎ Refer SS back to the problem-solving language used in Exercises B and D on page 38. Drill a few of these expressions again.

◎ Divide SS into small groups. Tell them to discuss the points and to come up with some solutions and proposals. One person from each group should lead the discussion, and a note-taker should write down their solutions and proposals.

◎ One way to encourage SS to use certain expressions is to give each of them a card with three expressions on. SS have to try to get all three of their expressions into the conversation.

- Circulate and monitor, checking SS are carrying out the task correctly. Make a note of any good language being used and common errors for correction, including pronunciation.
- Alternatively, another way to deal with errors is to write them down on pieces of paper and pass them to SS to look at and try to self-correct.

Feedback

- Bring the class together. Praise some of the strong language points that you heard, and work on five or six points that need improvement, especially in relation to language used for problem-solving. Get SS to model the correct forms.
- To round off the activity, ask the note-taker from each group to report back on their proposals. Highlight some of SS's best ideas.
- If there is time and interest, ask SS if they think energy saving is an issue in industry and companies in general. They may be able to give you examples of initiatives they know of, such as new office buildings that make the most of natural light and which have been equipped with energy-saving devices, such as solar panels.

Writing

- SS look at the rubric for the Writing task.
- Get SS to brainstorm the information that should go in this proposal and put these points on the board. All this information has come up in the listening and in Tasks 1 and 2.
- Ask SS to look back at the tips for proposal writing (CB page 39) and in the lesson notes (TRB page 49). Revise the structure and purpose of a proposal. Get SS to look at the Useful language box on page 39 again as well.
- Get SS to write their drafts in pairs or individually.
- Circulate and monitor, checking SS are completing the task correctly.
- If time is limited, SS can write just a 200-word introduction as a class activity and do the full report for homework.
- For early finishers, or as an extra activity, tell SS to proofread each others' proposals.
- Put all the proposals on the wall and ask SS to circulate and read the other proposals and decide what other points were mentioned that they would have liked to include in their proposals.

 Writing tips (CB page 39) and guidelines (TRB page 49)

---

1 to 1

- Go through the information in the Course Book with your student. Explain any difficulties. In Task 1, get the student to prepare one of the roles and you take the other. At the same time, monitor the language that your student is using. Note down any good examples of language and points for error correction or improvement. Come back to these later. Praise any good examples of language used and go over any errors, including pronunciation.
- Do Task 2 together. Don't dominate the conversation in this task, but say enough to keep it going and allow your student to ask and answer questions. You could record the discussion on cassette or video, if the student agrees, and use it for intensive correction work afterwards.

Lesson notes

Employment trends

At a glance

	Classwork – Course Book	Further work
Lesson 1: **Listening and discussion** (pages 42–43) *Each lesson is about 60–75 minutes. This time does not include administration and time spent going through homework in any lessons.*	**Listening 1: Work patterns** SS listen to short extracts and decide what type of employment the speaker is talking about. **Listening 2: Trends in employment** SS listen to an interview with a business studies lecturer, who talks about recent research into employment trends in the UK. **Vocabulary: Employment** SS look at words related to employment. **Discussion: Employment trends 1** SS talk about employment trends.	**Practice File** Word power (pages 28–29)
Lesson 2: **Reading and language** (pages 44–45) *Each lesson is about 60–75 minutes.*	**Discussion: Job satisfaction** SS discuss the factors that affect job satisfaction. **Reading: *India: Call centres ring the changes*** SS read about staff attrition rates at call centres in India. **Language review: Cohesive devices and using inversions for emphasis** SS look two language areas arising from the text: cohesive devices and using inversions for emphasis. **Discussion: Employment trends 2** SS talk about jobs of the future, unpopular jobs and how companies can retain staff.	**Text bank** (TRB pages 172–175) **Grammar reference and practice** (CB pages 123–124) **Practice File** Text and grammar (pages 30–31)
Lesson 3: **Business skills** (pages 46–47) *Each lesson is about 75–90 minutes.*	**Resolving conflict** SS discuss their views on conflict in the workplace; listen to a conversation where a conflict is being discussed; do a role-play and listen to an expert talking about misunderstandings that arise in e-mail communication. **Writing: e-mails** SS write a reply to an abrupt e-mail.	**Resource bank** (TRB page 223) **Writing file** (CB page 135) **Practice File** Skills and pronunciation (pages 32–33)
Lesson 4: **Case study** (pages 48–49) *Each lesson is about 75–90 minutes.*	**Delaney: call-centre absenteeism** SS read about the problems of absenteeism in a Dublin call centre, role-play an interview about absenteeism with a member of staff, prioritise the issues and discuss how to resolve the problems.	**Writing file** (CB pages 138–139)

For a fast route through the unit, focusing mainly on speaking skills, just use the underlined sections.

For one-to-one situations, most parts of the unit lend themselves, with minimal adaptation, to use with individual students. Where this is not the case, alternative procedures are given.

Business brief

The way we work is undergoing constant change as the world moves from the **industrial age** to the **information age**. In many industrialised countries, this transition has generally led to a loosening of relationships between **employers** and **employees** and far greater **flexibility** in terms of employment contracts and **working hours,** with more people working on **fixed-term contracts** and greater levels of **self-employment**.

Information and communication technologies, such as the Internet and broadband connections, are having a major impact on the way we work and will continue to do so in the future. Many jobs and **careers** will become 'extinct', and new ones will replace them. Other jobs will be transformed by technology out of all recognition in today's world. Experts predict that most of today's children will be doing jobs in the future that do not even exist yet.

The trend of moving manufacturing operations to countries with **low labour costs** has existed for many decades. This drive towards **increased productivity** and **lower production costs**, combined with technological advances, has more recently allowed companies to **outsource** and **offshore** other parts of their operations to these countries and regions. Companies are now able to distribute their work around the globe and operate 24 hours a day, seven days a week.

According to the FT's *Future of Work* Report, Asia is the top destination, with 37 per cent of **outsourcing projects**. But western Europe also benefited, with 29 per cent – the favoured locations being the UK, Ireland, Spain and Portugal – and eastern Europe with 22 per cent. India has become one of the major suppliers of **call centres** for the Britain and the United States because of the huge number of English-speaking graduates. However, it is not only the **low-skilled** jobs that are being transferred to Asia. Increasingly, multinationals are recruiting **highly skilled** engineering and programming staff in Asian countries and transferring their **research and development** operations to these countries as well.

Free marketeers argue that European countries, like France and Germany, suffer from excessive **labour market regulation**, such as **minimum wage legislation** and EU directives controlling working hours. In many eastern European countries, large-scale **unemployment** and the **informal economy** are still major problems, and ones that the expanded EU will have to find ways to deal with. Many predict there will be greater **mobility** of the workforce as people move from east to west to find work. Western Europe, Japan and the United Sates are all **ageing societies**. As the **active workforce** continues to fall in proportion to the total population, many have expressed concerns about the impact that this will have on these societies.

India and China are now playing an increasing role in the world economy. According to Kim Clark, dean of Harvard Business School, 'We simply have not comprehended yet the full impact of 2.5 billion people coming into the world economy who were not part of it before.' There is no doubt of the benefits and opportunities for those developing economies that have invested in technology in terms of increased **employment opportunities** and economic development. Secondly, **higher incomes** in these developing economies not only benefit the domestic economy, but also the global economy, as these are huge potential markets for goods and services.

Employment trends and your students

Your in-work students will be able to talk about how their jobs and careers have changed as technology has developed. They may also have experienced a change in direction in their careers, have retrained or envisage the need to do so in the future. Pre-work students will be able to talk about the jobs of members of their family and the type of job they expect they'll be doing in the future. Both pre-work and in-work students will certainly have views on employment trends in their country/region and in the wider world.

Read on

Rebecca Corfield: *Successful interview skills: How to present yourself with confidence,* Kogan Page, 2006

Matthew J. DeLuca: *201 answers to the toughest job interview questions*, Schaum, 1996

Spencer Johnson: *Who moved my cheese?* Putnam Adult, 1998

Richard Nelson Bolles: *What color is your parachute? A practical guide for job-hunters and career changers,* Ten Speed Press, 2005

Lesson notes

Warmer

◎ Get SS to look at the opening picture. Tell them to work in pairs for two minutes and talk about what they can see in the picture and how they think it relates to the unit title. Call the class together and ask them what they think the connection is between the unit title and the picture. (He seems to be working from home, or at least an isolated location, thanks to modern technology (note that there is a satellite dish on the roof). This photo shows one way that employment is changing in the 'information age'. The unit deals with different aspects of this change.)

◎ Put some of these jobs on the board and ask if SS know what they are: butler, cobbler, servant, tailor, shoeshine, farmer. Ask SS if these jobs exist today in their country and in what form. Ask SS if they can give you any more examples of jobs which are virtually 'extinct' today.

◎ Get SS to think about some jobs that exist now that didn't exist a hundred years ago. Put some of these jobs on the board: printer, nurse, reporter, secretary, bank clerk, doctor, engineer, miner, airline check-in staff, travel agent, supermarket cashier. Get SS to say how they think technology will affect these jobs in the future. Will they become extinct or how will they be transformed? This activity can be done in small groups if you prefer.

◎ This could lead into a discussion of outsourcing and insourcing. Don't spend too long on this, because SS will get an opportunity to discuss the issues in more detail in the reading section.

Information box

It is estimated that medical knowledge is doubling every eight years, and that half of what students learn in their first year at university about science and technology is obsolete or revised by their final year.

Some futurists predict that the type of jobs that will 'survive' are those that involve face-to-face contact with clients or that don't involve routines that can be automated, or jobs that require high levels of teamwork and flexibility. Examples are retail salesperson, health-care provider, lawyer.

Overview

◎ Tell SS they will be looking at some issues related to employment trends around the world.

◎ Go through the overview panel at the beginning of the unit, pointing out the sections that SS will be looking at.

Quotation

◎ Put some of the following abbreviations and acronyms on the board – or add some others, as appropriate for your SS – and ask SS what they represent. Do this as a quick-fire activity with the whole class.
BA (Bachelor of Arts) degree: first university degree in subjects relating to the broad definition of arts, usually lasting three years in the UK
BSc (Bachelor of Science) degree: see BA
BEC Business English Certificate (UCLES)
CAE Certificate in Advanced English (UCLES)
MD Doctor of Medicine: degree in medicine usually studied after a first degree. Medical training takes between six and seven years in total in the UK.
PhD Doctor of Philosophy: a degree of a high level that involves advanced research. Studying for a PhD can take anything from three years to a lifetime.

◎ Ask SS these questions:
What qualifications do you think are important to get a good job nowadays?
Has this changed in the last 50 years?
Do people need more qualifications nowadays?
What is the average length of a degree course and vocational training in your country for doctors, lawyers, architects and other professionals?
Has this changed in recent decades?
NB In some European countries, such as the UK, the average degree course is three years in length, but it can be four or even five years in countries like Spain.

◎ Get SS to give you some of the acronyms and abbreviations for courses and exams they can study for in secondary school, university and in further and higher education. What are the minimum requirements to get into university? Do people put letters after their names (e.g. BA, MSc)? In what circumstances?

◎ Get SS to look at the quotation and ask them what they think it means. Deal with any questions SS have about the vocabulary, e.g. *fellow* is an old-fashioned way to say 'man'. Alternatively, ask SS to look at their dictionaries to find definitions for the word *fellow* and any related words and report back to the rest of the class.

◎ Then get SS to read the quotation and explain what it means. Ask them if it is the case in their country or region that highly qualified people can't get work in their profession.

◎ As follow-up, SS might want to look at the use of abbreviations and acronyms in business, e.g. CEO, VIP, VP. Depending on the area of business, there may be a lot of standard international abbreviations, e.g. importation and exportation, or banking and finance. Put some of these common business abbreviations and acronyms on the board and elicit the meaning from SS in a quick-fire activity. Ask SS if they can add a few more. NB Some companies are best known by their initials as well, e.g. GM, IBM, BMW, CK, DHL, BA, FT.

Listening 1: Work patterns

SS listen to short monologues and decide what work pattern the speaker is talking about.

(A) 🎧 5.1

◎ Get SS to read through the eight work patterns. Deal with any questions they have, e.g. *casual labour* (also *informal employment*) is any work that is done without a legal contract, social security and income-tax payments.

◎ Play all six extracts without stopping. SS work in pairs to compare their answers. Monitor to see if SS are getting most of the answers.

◎ Play each extract again. Tell SS to listen for words and expressions which helped them decide their answers. This time, pause after each speaker and elicit the answer from the whole class. Ask SS to tell you what words or phrases they heard which helped them.

> **1** a **2** h **3** e **4** b **5** c **6** d

◎ If time allows and SS are interested, refer them to the audio script on pages 165–166. Get SS to listen again and read. Ask SS to identify any other words and expressions that relate to work patterns and gave clues to the answer.

◎ As further practice, refer SS to the two extra work patterns they didn't hear described (*shift work* and *fixed-term/temporary contract*) and get them to write a short monologue which describes some aspect of one of these forms of work. In pairs, SS then read their short extract to each other and decide which work pattern is being described.

◎ To round up, ask SS questions about some of these work patterns:
Is seasonal work common and in which sectors (e.g. agriculture, hotel and tourism)?
In which jobs is it common to work shifts (e.g. hospital staff)?
Do people migrate to or from their country/region to work? Where to/from?
Are fixed-term contracts common?

Listening 2: Trends in employment

SS listen to an interview with Sean McGuinness, a business studies lecturer and governor at Hammersmith and West London College in London. In the first part of the interview, he talks about recent research into work patterns in the UK. In the second part, he describes how new technologies have changed the way we work.

(B) 🎧 5.2

◎ Get SS, in pairs, to look through the questions and try to predict which statements are true and which are false. Explain any difficult vocabulary.

◎ Play the first part of the interview.

◎ Get SS to check answers in pairs. Go through all the answers in open class after SS have listened only once. SS should have understood enough with one listening to do this true/false task. Tell them they will be listening to the recording again, though.

> **1** False **2** True **3** True **4** False

◎ Put the following items on the board. Tell SS to listen to the interview again and identify what the items refer to.
ESRC, 80, 90, 5, 7, 6 and 2, 7 and 4, portfolio workers

◎ Play the recording again all the way through.

◎ SS check their answers in small groups. Circulate and deal with any queries SS have.

◎ If you can see that all SS have had difficulties with a particular item, play that section of the recording again.

◎ Go through all the answers in open class.

> ESRC = the Economic and Social Research Council
> 80 = percentage of people in permanent employment ten years ago
> 90 = percentage of people in permanent employment today
> 5 = percentage of employees with temporary contracts nowadays
> 7 = percentage of people in self-employment
> 6, 2 = the average length of time (years, months) people stayed in their jobs ten years ago
> 7, 4 = the average length of time (years, months) people stay in their jobs now
> portfolio workers = a flexible and mobile workforce that goes from job to job

◎ As a follow-up, you could ask SS if any information they heard in the interview surprised them.

(C) 🎧 5.3

◎ Ask SS to look at the picture on the left of the exercise and ask if they know what this object is and what it's used for. (An hour glass, an old-fashioned device filled with sand, used for telling the time.) Tell SS that *hour glass* will be mentioned in the recording in another context.

◎ SS, working in pairs, to look through the items a–e. Deal with any questions they have (e.g. *enlargement,* from the root word *large*, meaning 'to increase in size or amount'; commonly used to refer to photocopies, images or photographs).

◎ Play the full recording through a first time.

◎ SS compare answers in pairs. Go through the answers with the whole class. It should be possible for advanced SS to do this first task having heard the recording only once.

> Correct order: c, b, e, a, d

Lesson notes

(D) 🎧 5.3

- Tell SS to listen again and make notes about each of the five points.
- Play the recording, this time pausing briefly after each item to allow SS time to finish writing their notes.
- SS go through their notes in small groups. Circulate and monitor, dealing with any questions SS have and checking if there was any important information that SS did not pick up on.
- Go through the answers with the whole class.
- If necessary, based on your assessment of SS's feedback, play any difficult parts of the recording a third time, to allow SS an opportunity to hear the information again.

Suggested answers

Proportion of people using the Internet and e-mail at work

- Over 80% of higher professional and senior managers use the Internet and e-mail at work.
- Only 29% of administrative staff and 14–15% of skilled, semi-skilled and unskilled manual staff use the Internet and e-mail in their jobs.

Development of job enlargement

- People are taking on additional skills and roles and sharing out middle-management roles.
- Higher professional jobs have risen by 3% to 37% in the last ten years, but the middle-ranking jobs have been squeezed out.

Description of the 'hour-glass' economy

- The theory suggests that there will be large numbers of highly skilled and unskilled workers and very few people in the middle-ranking occupations.

Occupations that are experiencing growth

- Traditional and low-paid occupations: sales assistants, call-centre operators, security guards, care workers and generally service-sector jobs are growing.
- The fastest growing occupation in the UK is hairdressing – up by over 300% from ten years ago.

Recommendations for government employment policy

- Need for minimum wage legislation and controls over working hours.

- Ask SS to describe what is meant by the 'hour-glass economy'. (There will be more higher professionals and unskilled workers and fewer middle-ranking jobs. Therefore, the implication from this is that employment in the UK will resemble an hour-glass shape – wide at the top and bottom, but narrow in the middle. The speaker thinks this will make social mobility difficult.)
- For further practice, you may want to refer SS to the audio script on page 166. It's often useful for SS to listen and read the script, but it's also valid for SS just to read without listening again. Ask SS to pick out a language area, such as ten words and expressions relating to the lexical set of employment. Don't spend time going over all the words in the audio script in detail; focus SS on a particular language item and just deal with questions relating to that language. This task will also help SS prepare for the next exercise.

Vocabulary: Employment

SS look at words related to employment.

(E)

- Refer SS to the items in the box, but do not explain any expressions at this stage. Encourage them to use the context of the sentences to help with the meaning.
- SS work in pairs to complete the sentences. Circulate and monitor. Tell SS if their answers are right or wrong so that they can try again if necessary.
- Call the class together and go through the answers. Drill the word stress and pronunciation features of some of the more difficult vocabulary items.

---

1 service sector   **2** employment tenure   **3** mobile workforce   **4** job stability   **5** middle-management   **6** bargaining power   **7** skilled manual   **8** minimum-wage

---

Discussion: Employment trends 1

SS talk about employment trends.

(F)

- Get SS to read the questions and deal with any questions (e.g. *overtime* means working extra hours; some companies pay for this, but most don't; *foreseeable* means 'fairly soon').
- Get SS to discuss their answers in small groups of three or four. Circulate and monitor, helping where necessary. Note down five or six common errors for correction related to the theme of employment and any new words that have come up which might be useful for the whole class. Write these on the board for later. You could also make a note of any interesting/controversial points raised during these discussions to refer back to in the final feedback stage.
- Bring the class together and go through the corrections, eliciting the correct forms from SS. Ask them to explain the new words on the board. Drill pronunciation where necessary.
- As a final feedback stage, ask a person from one group for a brief summary of their discussion and whether they agreed or not. Ask one person from each group to feedback if time and interest allows. SS may want to continue the debate as a whole class if there are a lot of differences of opinion. Encourage this and act as a leader/moderator.

An argument in favour of employment legislation is that it protects employees with less bargaining power from long working hours and very low wages. An argument against legislation is that employers want greater flexibility and freedom and may employ fewer people as a consequence of legislation.

Discussion: Job satisfaction

SS discuss the factors that affect job satisfaction.

- Before the task, ask SS what factors they think affect job satisfaction. Do this as a quick-fire activity with the whole class.
- Go through the list of factors. Deal with any questions (e.g. *perks* are something in addition to money that you get for doing your job; other examples are luncheon vouchers and free medical insurance).
- Drill the pronunciation of these factors, highlighting word stress on the board.
- SS do the exercise individually and then compare their ideas in small groups of between three and five. Remind SS to think about some other factors they think are important. Allow five minutes for this activity.
- Call the whole class together and find out if there was any consensus about the items that were marked with a 1 (very important). Ask SS to provide examples of other factors they consider to be important (e.g. long holidays, close to home).

Reading: *India: Call centres ring the changes*

SS read about staff attrition rates at call centres in India.

- As a lead-in to the article *India: Call centres ring the changes*, ask SS to explain what a call centre is and which businesses generally use them. (A place equipped to take a large number of phone calls, generally dealing with customer bookings and queries. Banks, insurance companies, computer firms, transport, utilities and telephone companies are just some examples of businesses that use them.) Do this as a quick-fire activity.
- Ask SS which countries now outsource/offshore a lot of call-centre work and where it is outsourced to. (Examples are France to Morocco, Spain to Morocco and Latin America, the USA and Britain to India, Germany to neighbouring central and eastern European countries. There is a lot of outsourcing within a region too, e.g. England to Scotland and Ireland. Basically, thanks to modern technology, this work is generally outsourced to countries with lower labour costs.)
- Ask SS what they think are the main benefits and problems of managing a call centre in India. Do this as a quick-fire activity and don't reject any ideas at this stage. Put SS's ideas in two lists on the board.
- Get SS to read the first two paragraphs of the article and to underline the benefits and problems they find. Allow only a couple of minutes for this. Call the whole class together. Ask SS to refer back to their lists on the board. Which points were made? Were there any other benefits/problems they hadn't anticipated?

Possible benefits

- Growth in the sector: *the sector has almost quadrupled ... in the past three years to more than 350,000 employees and looks set to continue expanding at 50 per cent a year.*
- Other possible answers not mentioned in the first two paragraphs: low labour costs, English-speaking workforce (paragraph 3), cheap office space, etc.

Problems

- Main problem is the 'revolving-door' work culture, i.e. high staff turnover / high attrition rates: *Attrition rates, particularly in the larger hubs of Bangalore, Delhi and Mumbai, have jumped to more than 50 per cent a year in the past 18 months.* This leads to problems with staff loyalty, hierarchy, patience and discipline.
- Added stress for HR mangers who are recruiting and training staff: *these young call-centre workers think nothing of taking a job, doing four weeks of training and leaving without anything else in the bag.*
- Other possible answers: low staff motivation/morale, lack of job security, lack of continuity in the workplace, etc.

C

- Get SS to read the questions and multiple-choice options. Deal with any questions.
- Explain that the idea is to read the whole article in close detail. Tell SS they should ignore any words or phrases they don't know at this stage and focus on the task.
- Monitor SS to see how long the task is taking. Allow enough time for most of the SS to finish the task.
- Early finishers can compare their answers in pairs/small groups. Get SS to identify where they found the information in the article. This allows slower readers time to finish the task.
- Go through the answers with the whole class. If necessary, SS say where they found the answers in the article to help their colleagues who may not have answered correctly.
- Ask SS for their initial reactions to the points made in the article. Were they surprised to discover that staff retention was now such a problem in Indian call centres? Why (not)? (SS may say it's not surprising, as there is more demand than supply, so people can change jobs easily. Also, they may know that staff attrition rates are generally high in call centres anywhere in the world.)

1 b *its revolving-door work culture is also undermining virtues such as loyalty, hierarchy, patience and discipline* (paragraph 1)

2 c *'Until very recently, India had a culture where you took a job for life and never dreamed of leaving it unless you had a firm counter-offer' ... 'But these young call-centre workers think nothing of taking a job, doing four weeks of training and leaving without anything else in the bag'... 'There is a circuit where new companies come in and poach employees at higher salaries'* (paragraphs 2 and 3)

3 b *One solution has been for companies to choose more isolated locations* (paragraph 4). Note that SS may be tempted to choose option c), which is not correct because the text states in paragraph 5: *'You can only really attract people with such gimmicks,' says Mr Chawla. 'Retaining them is a different matter.'*

4 c *Another solution – still in its infancy – is to hire part-time older employees, including housewives, and to allow them to telecommute from home* (paragraph 7)

5 a *there is little to suggest the problem of an inherently footloose workforce will pose a mortal threat to India's continued expansion. 'Call-centre attrition is a universal problem,' says Mr Bhatnagar. 'It has got worse in India, but not nearly to the extent you would see in the West'* (paragraph 10)

◉ As a final stage to the reading, you might want to exploit some of the vocabulary items SS didn't understand in the text. A good exercise is to tell SS you will only explain five words/expressions from the text today. SS look at the text individually and choose their five words/expressions. Then they agree on five words in pairs and so on in a pyramid discussion, until the whole class comes up in with the final five words/expressions. What usually happens in this process is that SS help each other with the meaning of words, can usually guess words from context and they make decisions about which words are essential to an understanding of the text. All these are good learner-training techniques.

Language review: Cohesive devices and using inversions for emphasis

SS look two language areas arising from the text: cohesive devices and using inversions for emphasis.

 Grammar reference: Cohesive devices page 123

◉ As a lead-in to cohesive devices, refer SS to *such anxieties* (paragraph 1 of the article) and ask them whether this phrase is referring backwards or forwards in the text and what it's referring to (see answer key).

◉ Get SS to turn to page 123. Talk through the example and ask SS to do the exercise individually. Alternatively, write items 1–8 and the paragraph numbers on the board so SS don't have to keep turning from the Grammar reference at the back of the book to the article on page 45. Circulate and monitor SS, confirm their answers and help where necessary.

◉ SS compare in pairs. Then go through the answers with the whole class.

1 The anxieties of more demanding consumers (*a brash new generation of profligate consumers*) and a high turnover of staff (*revolving-door work culture*) that is undermining virtues such as loyalty, hierarchy, patience and discipline. (Anaphoric reference: referring back to something in the text)

2 *Attrition rates, particularly in the larger hubs* (cities) *of Bangalore, Delhi and Mumbai, have jumped to more than 50 per cent a year ...* (Anaphoric reference: referring back to something in the text)

3 *In spite of India's ... supply of English-speaking graduates ... the industry's rate of expansion has meant that demand has often outstripped supply.* (Anaphoric reference: referring back to something in the text)

4 Omits *companies.* (Anaphoric reference: referring back to something in the text)

5 Substitutes *people/employees.* (Anaphoric reference: referring back to something in the text)

6 Although some companies are trying to attract young workers with *gimmicks* (salsa classes, multi-cuisine canteens, on-site recreational facilities, such as football tables and cafés), the more serious solution is dealing with employee trauma. (Cataphoric reference: referring forwards to something that is coming in the text)

7 Omits *employees.* (Anaphoric reference: referring back to something in the text)

8 Omits *as these two core problems existing* (i.e. that few people like to work at night and the work is repetitive). (Anaphoric reference: referring back to something in the text)

 Grammar reference: Using inversion for emphasis page 124

◉ As a lead-in to inversions, ask SS to close their books. Dictate this sentence and get SS to compare what they've written in pairs.
They say that the booming sector has helped spawn a brash new generation of profligate consumers, and its revolving-door work culture is also undermining virtues such as loyalty, hierarchy, patience and discipline.

◉ Get SS to open their books again on page 45 and find a sentence with a similar meaning (*Not only has the booming sector helped spawn a brash new generation of profligate consumers, they say, but its revolving-door work culture is also undermining virtues such as loyalty, hierarchy, patience and discipline* (paragraph 1)).

◎ Ask SS why the writer uses the construction *Not only ... but also* and what happens to the verb *has helped* in this construction. (To emphasise a point. The auxiliary verb goes before the subject and the main verb goes after it.)

◎ Get SS to turn to page 124 and read the information about the four types of inversion. Point out that where there is no auxiliary verb, we use the auxiliary *do* in inversion structures, e.g. *Not only **did** she study at the university, but she also teaches there now.* If the verb in the first phrase is *to be,* it is moved before the subject, e.g. *Not only **is she** a qualified engineer, she is also an accomplished musician.*

◎ Do the first sentence transformation with the whole class. SS work on the other questions individually. Circulate and monitor, confirm SS answers and help where necessary.

◎ SS compare in pairs. Then go through the answers with the whole class.

---

1 Not only is call-centre work repetitive, (but) it's also stressful.
2 Not only did the company increase salaries, (but) it also created recreational facilities for staff.
3 Only when he had worked in IT for two years did Paul realise he wasn't cut out for the job.
4 Never had I found a job so rewarding until I started working for myself.
5 Hardly had he started interviewing candidates for the new job vacancies when three more people handed in their notice.
6 On no account will she (ever) accept a cut in salary.

Discussion: Employment trends 2

SS talk about jobs of the future, unpopular jobs and how companies can retain staff.

◎ Get SS to read the three questions. Deal with any queries.

◎ SS work in small groups to discuss the questions. Circulate and monitor their discussions. Help with any questions. Make a note of five or six points for correction, any new vocabulary items and points for praise. Put the items for correction and new vocabulary on the board. Early finishers can be asked to work on these.

◎ Call the class together and elicit the corrections and the meaning of new vocabulary from SS. Praise any good use of language you heard.

◎ Get feedback from SS on their discussions. If time is limited, just get feedback from one or two groups.

Resolving conflict

SS discuss their views on conflict in the workplace, listen to a conversation where a conflict is being discussed, do a role-play and listen to an expert talking about misunderstandings that arise in e-mail communication.

(A)

◎ The issue of conflict may be very culturally sensitive. Some cultures don't like to have any public display of disagreement or conflict, for instance Thais. Other cultures seem to be more comfortable expressing themselves forcefully, e.g. Spanish and Americans. As a lead-in to this section, ask SS when was the last time they had a disagreement with someone in the family, at work or a stranger in the street. Ask them what the conflict was about and how they resolved the issue. Alternatively, you can give a simple example yourself, e.g. when someone jumped in front of you in a queue in a supermarket and what you did or said.

◎ Get SS to look at the photo at the top of page 46. Ask SS to imagine how the two speakers are feeling and what the conversation is about.

◎ Get SS in pairs to write a short dialogue for the photo. Circulate and help where necessary.

◎ Get SS to act out their dialogues for the whole class. If time is limited, just ask one or two pairs to do this.

◎ Put SS into small groups to discuss their views on the statements. There are no correct answers, this is a consciousness-raising exercise to make SS aware of their own feeling about conflict and maybe think about their culture's attitude to conflict.

◎ Call the class together and ask them if other types of workplace conflict can arise, e.g. between departments, between boss and staff.

(B)

◎ Get SS to look at the checklist. Deal with any questions, e.g. *give in*.

◎ SS work individually to complete the chart, answering the question 'Which do you most often use?'.

◎ Put SS into pairs to compare their charts and answer the other two questions.

◎ Call the class together and go through the last two questions with the whole class, asking SS which conflict resolution techniques get the best results and other techniques that they have used or seen used.

(C)

◎ Get SS to read the extract. Deal with any questions. Tell them they have to memorise the essential information.

◎ SS close their books and work in pairs to tell a summary of what they've read. They can look back very quickly if there is something they've forgotten, but usually between both SS they can remember and relate the essence of what they've read in their own words.

◎ Ask the whole class if they think they are good listeners. Most of us like to think we are. Ask them to give you examples of how they show other people they are listening.

Some suggestions for ways to show you're listening: nodding, smiling, eye contact, asking more questions.

Lesson notes

(D) 🎧 5.4

- Tell SS that they are going to listen to a conversation between two work colleagues. Tell them to listen out for what the conversation is about and what techniques Terry uses to show he is listening to Yolanda.
- Play the recording once and get SS to write their answers individually, then compare in pairs.
- Ask what the conflict is about. (Terry's phone calls disturb Yolanda when she's working.)
- Play the recording a second time so that SS can identify all the techniques Terry uses.
- Go through the answers with the whole class.

> 1 Terry paraphrases what Yolanda's said to check his understanding: *Let me see if I follow you. You're saying that you can't work because I disturb you when I'm using the phone.*
>
> 2 Then he asks her to continue rather than interrupting her or defending himself: *No, please go on.*
>
> 3 Next he shows he understands her point of view before explaining his position: *I appreciate how you feel, Yolanda. The thing is, it's important for me to talk to clients and engage in some friendly small talk. It really helps to get sales.*

- Refer SS to the Useful language box on page 47. Ask SS to listen again and tick the phrases Terry uses. (See answers above.)
- Get SS to work in pairs. Refer SS to the audio script on page 166. Deal with any questions. Get SS to read the dialogue aloud, paying attention to their intonation. Monitor SS's performance and make a note of any problems SS are having with the features of connected speech.
- Call the class together and drill any phrases SS had difficulties reproducing at a natural speed and rhythm, e.g. *driving me up the wall, when I'm using the phone, most of the time*, etc.
- SS swap roles and repeat the dialogue, trying to reproduce it at as natural a speed and rhythm as possible.
- Finally, call the class together and ask SS how they would resolve the situation. Don't reject any ideas at this stage. Ask SS at the end to decide what they thought was the best solution mentioned.
- For further practice, SS, in the same pairs, might like to finish the conversation between Terry and Yolanda. Get SS to incorporate at least one more phrase from the Useful language box. Circulate and help as necessary.
- Call the whole class together and ask one or two pairs to read out the resolution of the conflict between Terry and Yolanda.

(E)

- Explain that SS are going to do a role-play and should try to use some of the expressions in the Useful language box.

- Go through the expressions in the Useful language box with the whole class. Drill pronunciation of some of the phrases SS might have difficulty with.
- Divide SS into two groups. Group A and Group B look at their corresponding information on pages 145 and 152. Deal with any questions, although SS will probably be able to help each other in their groups. SS read and prepare what they are going to say.
- Put SS into A+B pairs. SS role-play the situation. Monitor and circulate as SS act out the role-plays. Make a note of SS who carry out the task successfully, any target language used and five or six language points for correction, including pronunciation.
- Go through feedback with the whole class, praising appropriate language used for active listening, paraphrasing and checking understanding. Write up any points that need further work on the board and elicit the corrections from SS.
- Ask SS if they were able to resolve the conflict between Orsolya and Bohdan and how.
- For follow-up practice, go to the Resource bank at the back of this book.

(F) 🎧 5.5

- As a lead-in to this section, ask SS what kind of e-mails they generally write and receive, how many e-mails they deal with in the course of a day, if they ever react badly to the e-mails people write to them and what sort of problems they sometimes have.
- Get SS to look at the emoticons and ask SS if they know what some of them mean.

> Some common emoticons
> | | |
> |---|---|
> | :-) | I'm smiling |
> | :-(| I'm sad/upset |
> | :-[| I'm cross |
> | :-D | I'm laughing |
> | :-o | I'm shocked/embarrassed |
> | ;-) | I'm joking/winking |
> | :-p | I'm sticking my tongue out |
> | :-l | I'm confused |
> | —>: -@ | I'm angry |
> | :'-(| I'm shedding a tear |
> | :-? | I'm doubtful |

- Ask SS if they ever use emoticons and what their views on them are. (People might argue that it's a lazy or immature way to write e-mails.)
- Go through the three questions as a quick-fire activity with the class. Don't reject any ideas at this stage.
- Get SS to look at the photo of Rob Giardina on the left and tell them they are going to listen to his views on these questions. Split the class into three groups. Tell each group to listen for the answers to just one of the question and to take notes while they listen.

- SS compare their notes in their groups and add any extra information their colleagues heard which they didn't. Circulate and monitor, dealing with any questions or doubts.
- Play the recording again, this time pausing briefly after each question to allow SS time to complete their notes. Again, each group compares their answers.
- Put the SS into groups of three, with one person from each of the previous groups. Tell them to exchange the answers to the three questions.
- Go through the answers with the whole class.
- Discuss SS's views on what they heard. Have they ever experienced misunderstandings of the type mentioned in the interview? In-work SS who work with multinational teams might be able to talk abut the different communication styles of their different cultures.

1
- No visual information and feedback that you have in a face-to-face conversation, e.g. smiles or nods, being able to say 'I don't understand.' This makes it easy to get nasty and 'flaming' can occur, i.e. people sending angry and insulting e-mails.
- Your context is different from their context, for example you write a quick e-mail because you're in a rush, and it can be interpreted as brusque and direct.
- Some people don't express themselves well in writing.

2
- When you read an e-mail, don't always believe your first impression – think about other possible interpretations.
- When you write e-mails, think about how the other person could maybe misinterpret what you're writing and then make it clear that you don't mean that. Emoticons sometimes seem silly, but they can help express the tone you want.
- When in doubt, ask open, neutral questions.

3
- E-mail can help resolve conflict by removing the visual information, and this is particularly useful for multicultural teams because you can avoid misunderstandings that can be caused by different communication styles and differences in things like body space or eye contact. If a conflict exists, people can't see you're angry and you have more control over what you communicate.
- Secondly, you have the time to make your e-mails more rational and less emotional if you choose.
- Finally, you can't interrupt and you can't be interrupted.

Writing: e-mails

SS write a reply to an abrupt e-mail.

- Get SS to look at the e-mail from Yolanda's manager. Explain that it has been a very busy period at work for the whole department. Ask them how Yolanda might feel about receiving that e-mail and other possible interpretations for the e-mail. (Yolanda might feel offended/stressed out by the brusque nature of the e-mail and its brevity. However, her manager could have written it in a rush and had not intended to cause offence.)
- Set out a template for an e-mail on the board, much like the one on the page.
- Refer SS to the model e-mail on page 135 of the Writing file and briefly go through the features.
- Get SS to work in pairs to write a reply from Yolanda to her manager. Circulate, monitor and help SS to formulate their ideas whilst they write. Point out any mistakes and allow SS an opportunity to make corrections. Make a note of five or six common errors and any useful expressions used. Put these on the board for later feedback.
- Earlier finishers can be referred to the board to see if they know all the new words/expressions and if they can correct the errors.
- After completing the task, if peer correction is appropriate in your setting, SS may compare their replies with another pair. Is it the right length? What phrases did they both use? What could be improved? If they spot any words and expressions they don't know, they can ask their colleagues who wrote it about the meaning. This task helps SS be more aware of the impact their writing has on the reader.
- Go through feedback with the whole class, praising good examples of language and style and ask SS to correct the errors on the board.
- Alternatively, if time is limited, this writing task could also be set for homework.

Sample e-mail

To:	Lynne Atkins
From:	Yolanda Fowler
Subject:	Monthly sales

I'm so sorry, Lynne, but, as you know, it's been an extremely busy period at work, and I'll need more time to finish the sales report. I can have it ready by the end of the week. Hope that's all right.

Regards
Yolanda

 Writing file page 135

Case study: Delaney: call-centre absenteeism

SS read about the problems of absenteeism and low morale in a Dublin call centre, role-play an interview about absenteeism with a member of staff, prioritise the issues and discuss how to resolve the problems.

Background

◎ Get SS to focus on the case-study title, the photo of Dublin and the call-centre staff. As a lead-in, ask SS what *absenteeism* means (regular absence from work or school without a good reason) and why they think staff at a call centre might be absent from work regularly. Don't spend too long on this discussion, as most of the issues come up in the case study.

◎ Get SS to study the background information. Read it aloud, or ask SS to read it aloud. Deal with any questions they may have.

◎ Write the headings from the left-hand column of the following table and elicit information from SS to complete the right-hand column.

Company	Delaney
Based in	Dublin, Ireland
Client	Major car-hire company, which has outsourced its European operation to Delaney
Number of staff	240 full-time and part-time
Staff profile	Mostly young women in their mid- to late 20s. Many of them are fluent in Spanish, French and German.
Average employment tenure	three years
Problems associated with staff turnover	• high costs of recruitment, selection and training • newer staff have lower productivity levels • the competitiveness of the call centre

Report

◎ Put the following sentence stems on the board, then get SS to read the report and complete the sentences.
1 HR spent … monitoring absenteeism.
2 The annual sick absence is …
3 Typical reasons for sick absence are …
4 Some consequences are …
5 Most seriously, this could lead to …
6 The company must …

◎ SS complete the sentences individually and then compare their ideas in pairs.

◎ Go through the possible answers with the whole class.

1 HR spent **a year / 12 months** monitoring absenteeism.
2 The annual sick absence is **(on average) seven days per agent**.
3 Typical reasons for sick absence are **headaches, migraines, colds, flu, back problems and stress.**
4 Some consequences are **delays in answering calls, extra work and stress, cost of replacements, uncertainty for future planning.**
5 Most seriously, this could lead to **client and customer dissatisfaction with the level of service.**
6 The company must **find ways to deal with and reduce absenteeism**.

Task 1

◎ Divide SS into two groups. Refer each group to a different role card: Group A turns to page 146, and Group B turns to page 152. Ask them to read the role cards and deal with any questions they have, after they have discussed their ideas as a group. It's a good idea in the first instance to allow time for peer teaching. Tell Group A to think about possible reasons why Tricia is off sick so often and what you, as her manager, could say to her in the interview. Tell Group B to discuss and plan what Tricia could say in this delicate interview with her manager. Giving SS time to prepare for the role-play helps to increase the length of their utterances and the level of accuracy.

Possible reasons for absence
◎ Personal problems she doesn't want the company to know about
◎ Pretending to be ill to take a day off work when she feels like it
◎ Lack of motivation, low morale, low pay
◎ Pressure of workload, lack of control over workload
◎ Feeling bored, undervalued, or overqualified for the job

◎ Refer SS to the Useful language box on page 47. Go through and drill the pronunciation of some of the phrases for active listening, paraphrasing and checking understanding. Remind SS to try to incorporate at least two or three of these in their role-play.

◎ Pair SS up with someone from the other group to do the role-play. Circulate and monitor the language that they use. Make a note of any target language used and five or six common errors for later correction.

◎ After the discussion, draw attention to some key language SS used correctly and give praise. Also work on the points for correction, put these on the board and elicit the correct form, pronunciation, word, etc. from SS.

◎ Ask SS for feedback on how their discussions went, if they were able to avoid a conflict and resolve the problem, and if so how? Ask the SS who played Tricia if they felt their manager had been supportive or not.

The consultant's report

◎ Get SS to read the report and underline the main problems and sources of conflict. Deal with any questions.

> Suggested answers
> Boredom, stress, unfriendly environment, pressure of workload and performance targets, call-monitoring

Task 2

◎ Get SS to read Task 2. Deal with any questions.

◎ Divide the SS into small groups of five or six. Tell them they will be the management team from Delaney during this task. Get them to allocate role among themselves (e.g. the Operations Manager, the Human Resources Manager, the Chief Financial Officer, one or two Team Managers). NB The Operations Manager is the senior member of staff that all the others report to. They could also have a representative from the consultants, APP. One student should lead the discussion and one should be note-taker.

◎ Circulate and monitor, checking SS are carrying out the task correctly. Make a note of any useful language being used and five or six common errors for correction, including pronunciation, for later feedback.

Feedback

◎ When most groups have finished the task, bring the whole class together. Praise the strong points that you heard and work on five or six points that need correction, getting SS to provide the correct forms.

◎ Ask the note-taker from one or two groups to report back on how they prioritised the tasks and any solutions they came up with. There is no right answer to this question. SS may or may not reach a consensus.

◎ To round off the activity, highlight and summarise some of SS's best ideas.

◎ As further practice, SS could be asked to write up action minutes from their management meeting (see Writing file page 136).

Writing

◎ Get SS to study the writing task and deal with any questions.

◎ Brainstorm the information that should go in the e-mail and put these points on the board. Alternatively, this could be made into a report-writing task.

◎ Get SS to look at the model e-mail on page 135 of the Writing file again (or report writing on pages 138–139).

◎ Get SS to write their first draft in pairs or individually. Circulate and monitor, helping where necessary, making corrections and checking SS are completing the task correctly.

◎ Get SS to write the final e-mail either as a class activity or for homework. This could probably be quite a long e-mail.

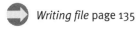 *Writing file page 135*

---

1 to 1

◎ Go through the information in the Course Book with your student. Explain any difficulties. In Task 1, you and your student are a team manager and a call-centre agent. Allow the student time to prepare her/his role. During the role-play, monitor the language that your student is using. Note down any good examples of language and points for error correction or improvement. Come back to these later. Praise any good examples of language used and go over any errors, including pronunciation.

◎ Do Task 2 together. Don't dominate the conversation in this task, but say enough to keep it going and allow your student to suggest ways to resolve these issues. You could record the discussion on cassette or video, if the student agrees and use it for intensive correction work afterwards.

UNIT 6 Business ethics

At a glance

	Classwork – Course Book	Further work
Lesson 1: **Listening and discussion** (pages 50–51) *Each lesson is about 60–75 minutes. This time does not include administration and time spent going through homework in any lessons.*	**Discussion: Ethical issues** SS discuss the affects of competitive labour and production costs and companies that have suffered bad press as a result of unethical business practices. **Listening: Corporate social responsibility** SS listen to Miguel Morán, international dean of a business school in Barcelona, talk about business ethics and corporate social responsibility. **Vocabulary: CSR terms** SS look at language for giving opinions in the context of CSR.	**Practice File** Word power (pages 34–35)
Lesson 2: **Reading and language** (pages 52–53) *Each lesson is about 60–75 minutes.*	**Reading: *Corporate responsibility without the waffle*** SS read about the types of CSR reports that companies are producing. **Discussion: Who is responsible?** SS discuss the ethics of advertising junk food to children and social responsibility in general for companies. **Language review: Multiword verbs** SS look at multiword verbs in the context of CSR reports.	**Text bank** (TRB pages 176–179) **Grammar reference and practice** (CB page 125) **Practice File** Text and grammar (pages 36–37)
Lesson 3: **Business skills** (pages 54–55) *Each lesson is about 75–90 minutes.*	**Ethical problem-solving** SS discuss three situations involving ethical problem-solving at work and listen to three people giving their opinions on some ethical problems. **Managing meetings** SS look at tips for effective meetings, listen to an extract of a meeting and discuss an agenda on managing meetings. **Writing: Action minutes** SS write up action points as discussed in the meeting on managing effective meetings.	**Resource bank** (TRB page 224) **Writing file** (CB page 136) **Practice File** Skills and pronunciation (pages 38–39)
Lesson 4: **Case study** (pages 56–57) *Each lesson is about 75–90 minutes.*	**Stitch Wear clothing** Stitch Wear is a US-based company manufacturing casual wear and sports clothing, with factories in developing countries. It faces allegations of using child labour in its factories in Pakistan. SS listen to a corporate responsibility consultant giving advice on improving the company's commitment to CSR. SS then discuss ways of improving the company's image regarding corporate responsibility in a management meeting. SS write up action points for the meeting.	**Writing file** (CB page 136)

For a fast route through the unit, focusing mainly on speaking skills, just use the underlined sections.

For one-to-one situations, most parts of the unit lend themselves, with minimal adaptation, to use with individual students. Where this is not the case, alternative procedures are given.

Business brief

Corporate social responsibility, or **CSR**, is fundamentally about the obligations of a company to society and the ways in which it can affect society and the environment. CSR has recently become a fashionable item on the **corporate agenda**. Even tobacco companies now make reference to CSR in corporate literature.

However, as **demands and expectations** of governments and society have become greater, many think that businesses need to show a **stronger commitment** to issues such as social responsibility, **sustainability** and **transparency**.

The fashion business particularly faces significant challenges. In the 1990s, Nike hit the headlines with **allegations** that some of its products were made in **sweatshop conditions** and by **child labour**. In 2005, Nike published the names and locations of more than 700 suppliers that manufacture its goods in an attempt to highlight the sportswear group's **ethical working practice** in developing countries. Companies are now seriously considering the **commercial viability** of **ethical fashion**.

The tendency to **switch production frequently,** to achieve the cheapest prices, means that relationships between brand owners and their producers in developing countries are often short term. Nevertheless, many believe the time is right for companies to market their **ethical stance** and that brands can **leverage their position** internationally by being ethical. A brand's value nowadays may not just be about profit and loss, but also **accountability** – being able to demonstrate clearly where and how a product is made.

Brand owners also risk being criticised for exploiting the concept of being ethical for **commercial gain**. Some would argue that the product comes first and ethics will always be secondary to the **consumers' self-interest**. Nevertheless, evidence suggests that consumers, especially younger ones, do care about where and how the clothes they buy are made.

Companies need to be specific and transparent about every aspect of their business. Transparency has always been an important aspect of corporate responsibility, and a growing number of companies are struggling with the challenge of reporting on **social, environmental and economic issues**, encouraged by governments and **regulatory authorities.** The Netherlands, Denmark and Norway have required environmental disclosures for several years.

A growing number of companies are voluntarily producing **CSR** or **sustainability reports** about non-financial issues and impacts that could significantly affect the business. But there are many multinationals which say nothing about issues such as **carbon-dioxide emissions, suppliers' labour conditions** or **community relations**.

The nature and standard of CSR reports varies widely. Sustainability experts say that companies should integrate **financial and non-financial reporting** and that many reports are too vague to provide useful information, but that is beginning to change.

Certain companies, such as Andersen, Enron and Worldcom, have suffered from allegations of unethical **corporate governance** or **financial irregularities** at management level, demonstrating that business ethics play a role on both the macro and micro level.

Business ethics and your students

In-work students will be able to talk about the sustainability of their company's products or services, labour conditions, ethical manufacturing and purchasing, the effect of their company's products/services on society and the environment, the company's financial and non-financial reports and contribution, or lack of contribution, to CSR.

Pre-work students may have experience of labour conditions and environmental impacts when working for companies on work placements or as part-time or temporary employees. Pre-work SS may also be more aware than in-work SS regarding issues such as (un)ethical fashion labels.

All students will have general world experience of buying (non-)ethical brands as consumers and may discuss the importance of corporate social responsibility when creating a positive or negative corporate image. They can also talk about whether companies should demonstrate greater responsibility and accountability to stakeholders such as employees, the local community and developing countries.

Read on

Robert E. Frederick: *A companion to business ethics*, Blackwell Publishing, 2002

Tom Hoskins: *The ICSA corporate social responsibility handbook*, ICSA Publishing, 2005

Sarbanes-Oxley: *A corporate director's compliance guide*, John Wiley & Sons Inc, 2005

Lesson notes

Warmer

◎ Ask SS to brainstorm a list of adjectives to describe attributes of an ethical business leader or manager. Write on the board: *An ethical business leader or manager should be …* (honest, trustworthy, open, fair, transparent, etc.). Then ask SS to brainstorm nouns related to ethics. Write on the board: *An ethical business should establish a corporate culture based on …* (e.g. honesty, trust, integrity, good conduct, values, openness, fair-mindedness, courage, transparency, etc.). Write SS's ideas up on the board.

◎ Alternatively, ask SS what they understand by the title of the unit, 'Business ethics'.

Overview

◎ Tell SS that they will be discussing business ethics and corporate social responsibility.

◎ Go through the overview panel at the beginning of the unit, pointing out the sections that SS will be looking at.

Quotation

• Get SS to look at the quotation and ask them what they think it means. (The idea is that a business should contribute to society and/or the local community in some way apart from just making a profit; for example, by improving labour conditions of its workers, reducing carbon-dioxide emissions and damage to the environment, setting up education or health programmes for employees, especially in developing countries and so on.)

Discussion: Ethical issues

SS discuss the affects of competitive labour and production costs and companies that have suffered bad press as a result of unethical business practices.

◎ SS work in pairs to discuss the two questions. Set a time limit (three to five minutes) for this. Then get SS's feedback as a whole class. Help SS with expressing their opinions and vocabulary related to ethics and business practice in English.

◎ For the first question, SS will probably say that competitive labour and production costs can affect a company's employees because companies in the retail industry particularly often switch suppliers and outsource production, depending on local labour costs. Workers may lose their jobs to countries where labour is cheaper and suffer from low wages, poor working conditions or job insecurity as a result.

◎ In the second question, SS may refer to recent scandals in the news and allegations of ethical misconduct and the question of corporate governance. Do not spend too much time on these questions, as unethical practices, such as child labour, are discussed in the Listening section.

Listening: Corporate Social Responsibility

SS listen to Miguel Morán, international dean of a business school in Barcelona, talk about business ethics. In the first part of the interview, he defines corporate citizenship and corporate social responsibility and talks about competitive labour costs. In the second part of the interview, he talks about child labour and some of the challenges companies face regarding ethical business practice.

Ⓑ 🎧 6.1

◎ Get SS to work individually, looking through the two summaries. Explain any difficult vocabulary (e.g. *pay lip service to*) and ask for SS's initial reaction to the questions raised in the summaries.

◎ Explain briefly that SS are going to listen to an international dean of a business school.

◎ Play the first part of the interview once and give SS time to look at the summaries again.

◎ Replay if necessary, stopping in sections to allow SS time to take notes.

◎ SS check answers in pairs. Circulate and deal with any queries SS have.

◎ Go through the mistakes in summary 1 quickly with the whole class, playing the recording a third time if necessary.

> Summary 2 is correct. Summary 1 has four mistakes:
>
> Miguel Morán says that corporate responsibility or citizenship is largely to do with the action taken by companies in relation to the local environment **and community/society** and is a kind of compensation paid back to society. **The interviewer** says many companies only pay lip service to these issues. However, if a company is involved in unethical practices, it will be found out by its **stakeholders** in the long run. He adds it's also difficult for multinationals to ensure workers in developing countries have decent wages due to local labour **costs**. Finally, he says it is up to governments to ensure that companies respect not only labour laws but also the human dignity of their employees.

Ⓒ

◎ Ask SS to *individually* read and mark the statements with the symbols.

◎ Deal with any difficult vocabulary.

◎ Ask SS to compare their answers in pairs or groups of three. Set a time limit (seven to ten minutes) for this discussion question.

◎ Bring the class to order and go through their reaction to the statements, discussing those questions that caused most disagreement.

(D) 6.2

◎ Ask SS to listen to the second part of the interview and compare their answers with those of the interviewee.

◎ Play the recording a second time, if necessary.

◎ After listening, SS compare their answers in pairs.

◎ Go through the answers with the whole class. Do not refer SS to the audio script at this stage, as SS listen to the recording again in Exercise E.

---

1 F *Nestlé, the well-known Swiss food company, produces a lot of its products in Asian countries where 11- and 12-year-olds are legally allowed to work.*

2 NS MM only gives the example of Nestlé that gets children to work part-time then pays for their education the rest of the time; he doesn't state this as a general rule.

3 NS MM states these children need money for their families who are living in poverty, not that banning child labour will cause extreme poverty.

4 NS This is implied by the interviewer's second question, but not stated by MM.

5 F *it's not just the fault of Western companies that child labour exists; it's also the fault of the state and the government ... I think it's a mix.*

6 F *There are an awful lot of well-known companies that have a reputation for being ethical but are producing unethically. And I'm talking about a lot of major companies ...*

◎ As a follow-up, ask SS if their opinions changed after listening to Miguel Morán or after discussing their answers with the other SS.

(E) 6.2

◎ Explain to SS that they are going to listen to the second part of the interview again. If time is short, do not replay the recording, but just refer SS to the audio scripts on page 167.

◎ SS check their answers in pairs, referring to the audio script if necessary. Don't spend too long going over the script in detail, only the expressions in items 1–8.

◎ Go through the answers with the whole class, writing the missing words in each sentence on the board. If you can see that all SS have the correct answers, you may decide not to go through all the answers in open class, simply confirm for the class that everyone has the correct answers and deal with the problem questions. This saves class time.

---

1 They hire these children part-time

2 need money for their families

3 not just the fault of

4 demanding lower and lower prices

5 starting to think about whether

6 trying to repair the damage

7 have a reputation for being

8 the difference in production costs

Vocabulary: CSR terms

SS look at language for giving opinions in the context of CSR.

(F)

◎ Explain that SS will be looking at expressions from the interview for giving opinions.

◎ Get SS to do the exercise individually. Circulate and monitor, helping where necessary with vocabulary.

◎ SS discuss their answers in pairs.

◎ Bring the class together and go through the answers.

◎ As an additional activity and time permitting, get SS to write their own opinions on CSR and child labour using the expressions in Exercise F, as well as other similar expressions (e.g. *I must say ..., it all comes down to ...*).

---

1 If I had to 2 Let's be 3 face it; two sides of the same coin 4 pay lip service to 5 the time has come for; the bottom line

---

◎ For follow-up practice, go to the Resource bank on page 224.

Reading: *Corporate responsibility without the waffle*

SS read about the types of CSR reports that companies are producing.

(A)

◎ Get SS to discuss the questions in Exercise A in small groups.

◎ Go through answers as a whole-class activity. SS may point out the quote by Milton Friedman was mentioned in the interview with Miguel Morán in the previous listening section. SS may suggest the following for other stakeholders: NGOs/pressure/special interest groups, women, ethnic minorities, local/national governments, end-users.

(B)

◎ As a lead-in to the article *Corporate responsibility without the waffle*, ask SS to comment on the accompanying photo: What does it show? Where is the factory? What do you think about employees' working conditions in these kinds of textile factories?

◎ Explain that the idea is to scan the first part of the article on page 52 quickly to find the meaning of *waffle* and the writer's opinion. Tell SS they should ignore any words or phrases they don't know at this stage and focus on the task of finding this information. In order to make this a quicker reading exercise, set a time limit. SS will probably need about three or four minutes for the first part of the article.

◎ Get SS to read the first part of the article, then ask for their initial reactions to the points made before checking their answers to the questions.

◎ Go through the answers with the whole class.

Lesson notes

- The writer is clearly quite sceptical about the forewords of corporate responsibility reports and critical of the lack of meaningful content.
- *Waffle* (colloquial) means 'talking or writing using a lot of words without saying anything important'. SS may be able to paraphrase this based on their reading of the text.

- Ask SS follow-up questions about whether they have read their company's CSR report and what they think of it. Alternatively, ask SS to list some of the vocabulary from the article that is used as waffle, e.g. *passion, commitment, engagement, trust, governance, credibility,* etc. You may like to point out that some of these words have become CSR 'buzzwords'.

Ⓒ

- Get SS to read the article again, explaining the paragraphs are numbered. If SS ask questions, throw them open to the whole class to see if someone can provide an explanation. If not, explain where necessary.
- Alternatively, if time is short, or SS don't want to read the first part of the article again, write the jumbled answers on the board along with a few distractors and get SS to complete the exercise using the words you have given them.
- Ask SS to do the exercise individually, then compare their answers in pairs.
- Monitor and circulate as SS do the task, indicating in which sentence a word or expression occurs where SS are having difficulties.
- Go through the answers with the whole class.
- Drill pronunciation of these words and expressions, if necessary, highlighting word stress on the board, e.g. ′stakeholders, ′tackling, com′mitment, ′foreword.

---

1 being a turn-off **2** stakeholders **3** tackling **4** lawsuits **5** cut off from **6** work out **7** fuzzy **8** commitment **9** foreword **10** tracks

---

Ⓓ

- Write these two headings on the board: *Points for CEOs to address; Examples of good company practice.*
- Get SS to read the second part of the article on page 53 and do the exercise individually.
- Monitor and circulate as SS do the task. Deal with any questions they may have.
- Get early finishers to compare their answers with another pair.
- Go through the answers with the whole class. Ask each student or pair to give their example and find out if the rest of the class agrees.

Points for CEOs to address	Examples of good company practice
1 Specific challenges/ risks and proposals for dealing with them	Arun Sarin, CEO Vodafone, talks about how the company will tackle human rights abuses in the company's supply chain.
2 Transparency	Bob Eckert, CEO Mattel, mentions audits by an external organisation of the company's CSR record and that the company publishes the result of this study on the website.
3 Governance	Bob Eckert says the company has a special committee to deal with this. Novo Nordisk improved the risk-management system last year, gets board members to do self-evaluations and has introduced a share-based incentive scheme.
4 Credibility	Paul Pressler, CEO Gap, mentions the poor reputation the company has in terms of working conditions and how they are going to improve conditions.

- As a follow-up, ask SS in work to provide some of their own company's examples of the four points mentioned. Ask pre-work SS to give other examples of the four points mentioned, thinking of a company they know or that has been in the press recently.

Discussion: Who is responsible?

SS discuss the ethics of advertising junk food to children and social responsibility in general for companies.

Ⓔ

- Ask SS to discuss the questions in pairs or groups of three.
- Give SS a time limit, e.g. five to seven minutes.
- As a follow-up to the first question, ask SS: *To what extent do you think other types of industries (tobacco, mobile, pharmaceutical, etc.) should take responsibility for people's health problems?*
- SS may suggest the following answers for the second question:
  – CEOs of food companies could mention the risks associated with added sugar, salt and fat in their products and talk about their company's commitment to healthier food and limiting advertising to children.
  – A computer and mobile phone company CEO could talk about the environmental impact of their obsolete products and show a commitment to recycling hardware or its safe disposal.
  – A CEO of a major clothing firm could demonstrate concern about the labour conditions in the supply chain, undertake to ensure decent conditions and label their clothes accordingly.

Language review: Multiword verbs

SS look at multiword verbs in the context of CSR reports.

 F

◎ As a lead-in to this language review section, refer SS to Exercise C again. Ask SS to give examples of multiword verbs, or words that derive from multiword verbs, in the first part of the article (*being a turn-off* in paragraph 1; *cut off from* in paragraph 4; *work out* in paragraph 4).

◎ Go through the exercise as a quick-fire activity with the whole class.

> 1 h   2 d   3 c   4 a   5 f   6 e   7 b   8 g

 Grammar reference: Multiword verbs page 125

◎ For revision or further practice, you may want to refer SS to the Grammar reference on multiword verbs from Unit 2 (page 119) again, if necessary.

> 1   **1** set out   **2** held to account   **3** phase out   **4** shy away from   **5** follow suit
> 2   **1** c   **2** a   **3** a   **4** b   **5** c   **6** a   **7** b   **8** a

Ethical problem-solving

SS discuss three situations involving ethical problem-solving at work and listen to three people giving their opinion on some ethical problems

 A

◎ As a lead-in to this section, ask SS what they understand by the following quote on ethics and personal behaviour.
It is important to remain focused on changing individual behaviour. After all, it is individuals who make unethical decisions, not faceless, corporate bodies.
(John Plender and Avinash Persaud, writers)

◎ Alternatively, if there is a good class atmosphere, you may want to describe a moral dilemma of your own that happened in the workplace and then ask SS the following questions:
What kind of ethical problems have you faced at work? What happened?
Do you think you took the right decision? Why (not)?
If you were facing an ethical dilemma at work, who would you ask for advice? Why?

◎ Get SS to look at the three situations. If time is short, ask SS to read all three situations, but only discuss one of them. (They will need to read all three situations in order to do the following listening exercises.)

◎ Go through initial reactions with the whole class. Were any of the dilemmas similar to ones previously discussed?

Ⓑ 🎧 **6.3**

◎ Explain to SS they are going to listen to three people talking about the situations in Exercise A.

◎ Play the recording once and ask SS for their initial reactions.

Ⓒ 🎧 **6.3**

◎ Play the recording a second time, pausing, if necessary, to give SS time to mark their answers individually.

◎ Get early finishers to compare their answers in pairs.

◎ Go through the extracts from the speakers with the whole class. Point out the frequent use of the contraction *I'd / I wouldn't ...* when hypothesising, giving advice or problem-solving.

◎ Go through pronunciation with the whole class and drill some of the expressions, if necessary, paying attention to words that are stressed for emphasis and to highlight the hypothetical meaning (e.g. *if it **were** the case ...*).

> 1   The first step would be to
> 2   In that case, I'd
> 3   In this situation, I wouldn't
> 4   Having said; it were the case; on the grounds that
> 5   could argue that
> 6   I'd have no problem

◎ Refer SS to the audio script on page 167. Play the recording a third time, if necessary, whilst SS read the monologues, underlining or noting the pronunciation of expressions from the Useful language box on page 54. Ask SS if they can think of any more expressions for these purposes.

◎ Try to sensitise the SS to English sentence stress, linking and intonation. Don't get SS to repeat all the expressions, just one or two from each section that might be difficult in terms of pronunciation (e.g. *There are a lot of issues at play here*).

Managing meetings

SS look at tips for effective meetings, listen to an extract of a meeting and discuss an agenda on managing meetings.

Ⓓ 🎧 **6.4**

◎ Ask SS to look at the tips for effective meetings and writing up action points. Point out that the tips use the mnemonic 'PARTAKE'.

◎ Tell SS they are going to listen to a group of people having a problem-solving meeting, discussing procedures for employing staff. Tell them to focus on what the agenda was, and whether the meeting was managed effectively or not.

◎ Play the recording once. Ask SS to compare their answers in pairs.

◎ Go through feedback with the whole class. Play the recording a second time, asking the SS to note down all the things that go wrong in the meeting. Refer to the audio script on page 167 if necessary. It is not necessary to spend too much time on this, as the listening is a humorous look at how *not* to manage meetings. Make sure SS are given plenty of time to discuss the next task and role-play the meeting.

Agenda or purpose of meeting: to discuss guidelines / company policy for taking on staff / the recruitment and selection process. Is it transparent? (The purpose of the meeting is stated clearly.)

The meeting, however, is not managed well generally, as Alan is not an especially effective chairperson: he says he doesn't have much time and has to finish by 10.15. Alan's also quite aggressive and even sarcastic to the participants, although he asks for people's opinions and asks Alison to get to the point.

The meeting is also ineffective or unsuccessful because the participants are disorganised, e.g.

1 The HR manager (Francine) is not present at the start.
2 Minutes from a previous meeting are not mentioned.
3 Alison has notes from Francine, but didn't distribute them beforehand.
4 Ian is not listening / hasn't read the agenda.
5 Alison goes off at a tangent.
6 The meeting is interrupted with Francine's late arrival.

SS may argue, however, that these kinds of problems are realistic.

(E)

◎ Refer SS to the language for problem-solving in the box on page 54. Go through the expressions and drill some of them for pronunciation and intonation if necessary.

◎ Ask SS to discuss the questions about the kind of meetings they have. SS in work may want to spend more time on this task. With pre-work SS, you may want to skip the exercise and move on directly to the meeting role-play (Exercise F).

(F)

◎ Explain to SS that they are going to simulate or role-play a company meeting, using the suggested tips. Tell them the meeting is about how to manage internal meetings more effectively.

◎ Divide SS into small groups of about four or five. Appoint a stronger student in each group to chair or lead the meeting. Ask SS to look at the meeting agenda page 160 and deal with any questions they have.

◎ Get SS to take notes before they start the meeting. Giving SS time to prepare for the role-play helps to increase the length of their utterances and the level of accuracy.

◎ Monitor and circulate round the class while SS role-play the meeting, helping the chairperson, if necessary, but not taking control of the meeting. Make a note of whether SS are following the tips and using language for problem-solving, as well as five or six language points for correction.

◎ Go through feedback with the whole class, asking the person who chaired or led the meeting to summarise any decisions made. If appropriate, ask SS if they thought the meeting was managed effectively. Praise those SS who followed the advice for effective meetings and any appropriate language used. Write up any points that need further work on the board.

◎ For follow-up practice, go to the Resource bank on page 224.

Writing: Action minutes

SS write up action points as discussed in the meeting on managing effective meetings.

(G)

◎ As a lead-in to this writing section, ask SS in work what kind of action points or minutes they generally receive or write. Ask pre-work SS what they would expect to read in action points of a company meeting.

◎ Tell SS they are going to write up a summary of the meeting they have just had in pairs.

◎ SS write a summary in the form of action points for what was decided in the previous meeting. Make it clear to the SS that they do not need to write detailed minutes.

◎ Circulate, monitor and help SS whilst they write. Make a note of any useful expressions used on the board, together with five or six common errors.

◎ Early finishers can be referred to the board to see if they can correct the errors.

 Writing file page 136

◎ After completing the task, SS may compare their action minutes with another pair. Were all the main points mentioned? Is it clear who is responsible for each point? Are there deadlines or suggested dates for the actions? What could be improved?

◎ To help SS be more aware of the impact their writing has on the reader, put each pair of SS with another pair from the same group. They exchange and read each others' action points. SS compare their summaries and ask their colleagues about any differences.

◎ If peer correction is appropriate in your setting, SS could also be asked to proofread each others' writing task and point out any spelling mistakes or grammatical errors they spot. Be on hand to help with this, but leave most of the feedback and discussion to SS.

◎ Go through feedback with the whole class, praising good examples of language used and pointing out five or six areas that need further work.

◎ Go through any common errors and the useful phrases on the board to round off the activity.

◎ This writing task could also be set for homework.

Case study: Stitch Wear clothing

Stitch Wear is a US-based company manufacturing casual wear and sports clothing, with factories in developing countries. It faces allegations of using child labour in its factories in Pakistan. SS listen to a corporate responsibility consultant giving advice on improving the company's commitment to CSR. SS then discuss ways of improving the company's image regarding corporate responsibility in a management meeting. SS write up action points for the meeting.

◎ In class, pay particular attention to clearly breaking down the case study into the different tasks and making sure that SS understand and follow the structure of what you are doing.

◎ The audio in this case study could be omitted if necessary, although you will have to give some prompts and ideas from the audio script for improving Stitch Wear's commitment to CSR and improving its public image.

Background

◎ Ask SS to focus on the photo of the clothing factory. As a lead-in to the case study, ask SS where they think the photo was taken and to predict what kind of problems the company might be facing.

◎ Ask SS to read the background information.

◎ Write the following headings from the left-hand column of the table and elicit information from SS to complete the right-hand column.

Company/organisation	Stitch Wear
Purpose	Clothing company that manufactures and sells casual wear and sports clothing
Based in	US
Retail outlets in	US and Europe
Factories in	Pakistan and Indonesia
Problems	Allegations by the press and the WLA of using child labour and poor working conditions in factories in Pakistan. Boycott campaign of Stitch Wear clothes, led by the WLA.
Tasks	Rethink CSR policy / Devise a new CSR strategy: corporate sponsorship of community projects, boost company sales, remain competitive, present more positive ethical image to the public.
Department responsible	PR

The media

◎ Refer SS to the newspaper article on page 56. Get SS's initial reaction to the news story.

◎ Ask SS to read the article and look at the graphs above it showing sales figures for the two companies and answer the questions:
How will the scandal affect Stitch Wear?
How do sales figures for the two companies compare?

◎ Go through the answers with the whole class.

◎ Deal with any questions the SS may have regarding difficult vocabulary. Note on the company name – Stitch Wear – and the newspaper headline: one of the Longman dictionary entries for the multiword verb *stitch up* is 'to deceive people for financial gain' (British English). Another informal definition of *stitch up* is to 'frame someone'; to make someone seen guilty of a crime by providing false information. The name Stitch Wear could therefore have negative repercussions in the UK.

◎ Customers, especially younger people, may boycott Stitch Wear's clothes as a result of the allegations and the WLA's campaign.
◎ Sales for Stitch Wear have fallen from 5.1bn dollars to 4.9bn dollars, while sales for its main competitor have risen from 4.9bn dollars to 5.1bn dollars in the last quarter. Stitch Wear is therefore losing a significant amount of its market share to the competition.

Listening 🎧 6.5

◎ Get SS to read the listening task. Ask them to try and predict what advice the consultant may give. SS may be able to predict from reading the background information that Stitch Wear needs to rethink its CSR policy and devise a new CSR strategy including corporate sponsorship of community projects, boost company sales, remain competitive and present a more positive ethical image to the public. Ask SS what kind of projects the company could sponsor that would appeal to younger customers. Don't reject any ideas at this stage or give the answers away.

◎ Play the recording once, pausing after sections if necessary, to allow SS time to take notes. You may choose to pause and elicit the consultant's second suggestion and the response from the Head of PR.

◎ SS compare their notes in pairs.

◎ If necessary, play the recording a second time, referring to the audio script on page 167. Go through the suggestions with the whole class, writing them up on the board. This information will help SS in the next stage of the case study.

◎ Discuss SS's initial reactions to the suggestions made and whether they think the ideas are appropriate or not. There is no right answer to this question. SS may or may not reach a consensus, but do not spend too much time on this at this stage, as they will be discussing these and further suggestions in the meeting.

Suggestions for CSR improvement	Response
1 Consultant: be careful with language in the CSR report; has to sound real and sincere.	Head of PR agrees
2 Consultant: Stitch Wear also needs to stay competitive. Any action plan / CSR programme needs to be financially feasible, e.g. adjust profit margins and review pricing.	Head of PR confused/ sceptical; asks for examples in the industry
3 Consultant gives example of company in Pakistan that set up educational programmes and healthcare for ex-child labourers.	Head of PR says it's expensive.
4 Head of PR: competitor runs a 're-use a shoe' program.	Consultant thinks it's a good idea.
5 Consultant: recommends a partnership with the Ethical Trading Initiative to screen suppliers.	Head of PR sounds interested.

Task

◎ Refer SS to the CSR meeting agenda and task on page 57. Deal with any questions they may have regarding vocabulary (e.g. *sustainable supply chain*, *supplier screening policy*).

◎ Divide the SS into groups of three or four. Explain to SS that the meeting has been called by the Head of PR, following his conversation with the ethics consultant. In this role-play, they are managers from different departments at Stitch Wear. Get SS to look at their respective role-play information on pages 146, 152, 156 and 158. Stronger or more confident SS could take the role of Student A, Head of PR, as this person needs to lead the meeting. Deal with any questions SS may have before they begin the task.

◎ With groups of three, make sure someone is Student A, but eliminate one of the other roles, according to SS's interests.

◎ Get SS to take notes before they begin on how these issues will affect their own department. They can also add any other ideas they may have on how to improve the company's commitment to CSR and its public image.

◎ Tell SS to take notes during the meeting, as they will need to write up action points later.

◎ SS hold the meeting. Circulate and monitor, checking SS are carrying out the task correctly. Make a note of any useful language being used for problem-solving and five or six common errors for correction, including pronunciation, for later feedback. Write these up on the board.

◎ Early finishers may correct the errors on the board.

Feedback

◎ When SS have finished the task, bring the whole class to order.

◎ Ask each group to summarise the outcome of each meeting briefly for the whole class. Ask one or two groups to say what happened in their groups, whether the meeting was managed effectively and whether the outcome was successful or not. You may like to ask the whole class to choose the best proposal. Alternatively, SS may like to present their proposals formally to the rest of the class. The other SS act as company shareholders and/or board of directors and vote on the best solution.

◎ Praise the strong language points and work on five or six points that need improvement, especially in relation to language used for managing meetings, problem-solving and discussing business ethics.

Writing

◎ Get SS to focus on the writing task on page 57 and deal with any questions they may have. Stress that their final proposals will need to be financially viable, as well as attractive to the public and media.

◎ Ask SS, in pairs or groups of four, to check the information that should go in the action points, referring to their meeting notes. All this information has come up in the listening and meeting role-play.

◎ Go through one group's first action point and put these points on the board as an example.

◎ Get SS to write in pairs or individually.

 Writing file page 136

◎ Circulate and monitor, checking SS are completing the task correctly.

◎ Get SS to write the final draft of the action points, either as a class activity in pairs or for homework. Alternatively, this could be made into a report-writing task following their presentation to the board of directors.

◎ For early finishers, or as an extra activity, tell SS that there have been rumours of financial irregularities involving management at Stitch Wear. The PR department has to issue an internal e-mail to all staff, allaying their concerns about the recent allegations in the press surrounding the company's unethical employment practices and what the company plans to do, as discussed in the recent management meeting.

1 to 1

- Go through the information in the Course Book with your student. Explain any difficulties. In the task, your student is Student A (Head of PR) and you are Student B (Head of Production). Don't dominate the conversation in this task, but say enough to keep it going and allow your student to ask and answer questions.
- At the same time, monitor the language that your student is using. Note down any good examples of language and points for error correction or improvement. Come back to these later.
- Praise any good examples of language used and go over any errors, including pronunciation. Then repeat the task, as Students C and D respectively. Record the meetings on video or cassette, if possible.

This unit revises and reinforces some of the key language points from Units 4–6, and links with those units are clearly shown. This revision unit, like Revision units A, C and D, concentrates on reading and writing activities. Some of the exercise types are similar to those in the Reading and Writing section of the Business English Certificate examination (Higher level) organised by the University of Cambridge ESOL Examinations (Cambridge ESOL).

For more speaking practice, see the Resource bank section of this book beginning on page 211. The exercises in this unit can be done in class, individually or collaboratively, or for homework.

4 Energy

Linking ideas

◎ These exercises give SS further practice of linking expressions on pages 39 and 122.

> **A** 1 The homes are designed to use solar panels **as well as** electricity for heating.
> 2 He talks about protecting the environment, **yet** his car's a real petrol guzzler.
> 3 The hydrogen economy is still a dream, **despite** the years spent on scientific research.
> 4 I always take the bus to work **as** you can never find a parking space.
> 5 There was a power cut **due to** a sudden surge in demand.
> 6 The world's oil supplies will soon run out, **so** we'll have to find other fuels.
> **B** as well as → in addition to
> yet → even though
> despite → in spite of
> as → because/since
> due to → because of / as a result of
> so → therefore
> **C a)** as well as, in addition to   **b)** yet, even though, despite, in spite of   **c)** due to, because of, as a result of, so, therefore   **d)** as, because, since

Vocabulary

◎ SS are given further practice in using language related to energy from the Listening and Reading sections on pages 34–37.

> **1** fossil fuels   **2** Wind power; renewable energy   **3** greenhouse gases   **4** four-wheel drive   **5** Global warming; carbon-dioxide emissions   **6** energy consumption   **7** environmentally friendly   **8** energy-efficient

◎ This exercise gives SS word-building practice following the case study on pages 40–41.

> **1** reduction   **2** investment   **3** legislation   **4** improvement   **5** performance   **6** competitive

Writing

◎ SS write a proposal for energy efficiency as further practice to the Business skills on page 39.

Sample answer

Report
Proposals for energy efficiency

Introduction

I have been asked by the management team to make proposals for energy savings in the company as part of our drive to reduce energy costs. Some of these proposals can be implemented immediately without incurring major costs. Others require some capital investment. A detailed breakdown of energy bills over the last five years and an estimate of the implementation costs and projected savings are provided in the appendices to this report.

Executive summary
Lighting

Using low-energy florescent lighting would produce a saving of 25–30%. Although these are more expensive to buy, they last up to twice as long as normal florescent lights, so we will soon recoup the cost. I also propose the installation of time switches in staff lavatories.

Heating

The heating system is old and inefficient and does not distribute heat equally in all areas of the building. Some staff open the windows in winter to cool down, while staff in other parts of the buildings are using extra electric heaters to keep warm. I recommend we replace the current system as soon as possible. Estimated savings would allow us to recoup our investment within six to seven years.

Air-conditioning

Our costs in this area have risen dramatically and are now on a par with our heating bills. Lack of maintenance means that the units are not working efficiently. These should be checked by a qualified technician once a year.

Staff awareness

In addition, information about energy efficiency should be posted on noticeboards to encourage staff to save energy.

(259 words)

(B)

◎ SS write an introduction to a report as further practice of the Business skills on page 39.

Sample answer

Overcapacity at Mitos 3 Gym

Introduction

Mitos has a chain of five gyms in the city. Mitos 3 opened six years ago, with a 25-metre indoor pool, a sun deck, a 200-square-metre weight and machine training area, five rooms for programmed exercise classes, in addition to a bar and a beauty saloon.

Membership of Mitos 3 is at record levels. There are now over 4,000 members, the vast majority young adults in their 20s and 30s. The peak periods are between 1 and 3 p.m. and in the early evening between 6 and 8 p.m.

Because of the number of active members, the gym is running at full capacity during peak lunchtime and evening periods. This has generated some problems and complaints from members. Specifically, people have to wait to use the training machines, and classes are sometimes full. There are also queues for the showers, and the boiler can't generate enough hot water to cope with demand.

As a solution to this problem, I propose we offer a cheaper-rate membership at off-peak times. I also recommend putting notices in the shower area asking members to be more conscious of water conservation.

(192 words)

5 Employment trends

Vocabulary

◎ This exercise gives SS further practice in using the vocabulary associated with employment (page 42).

> **1** Part-time   **2** Seasonal work   **3** Shift work   **4** Fixed-term/Temporary contract
> **5** Teleworking   **6** Unemployed   **7** Migrant worker   **8** Self-employment

Cohesive devices

◎ This exercise gives SS further practice in cohesive devices (page 123).

> **1** This   **2** them   **3** in this respect   **4** its   **5** its   **6** this knowledge   **7** their

Inversion for emphasis

◎ SS correct an e-mail from a dissatisfied customer, practising inversions after the case study on pages 48–49. If SS have not done this type of exercise before, draw their attention to the rubric and point out that all six errors relate to inverted forms.

> I'm writing to complain about the service I received when I phoned to reserve a car today. I can't believe how rude the operator was. Not **only did** she rush me through the reservation, but she also finished the call when I was in the middle of a question. No sooner **had I** given her my details than she ended the call without confirming the price. I had to phone back and **only after** my third call **was I** able to speak to the same operator. I'm going to tell all my family and friends about this experience and tell them **that on** no account **should they** reserve a car with your company.

Writing e-mails

◎ SS practise writing e-mails by replying to the customer's complaint in the previous exercise.

> **Sample answer**
>
> Dear Mrs Moore
>
> Thank you for informing us about your experience and please accept my apologies. We appreciate feedback from our clients and we take customer service very seriously. All our call agents are trained to deal with customer enquiries politely. We also operate a monitoring scheme to check that calls are handled correctly. We do our best to ensure that all our operators confirm the booking details and enquire if the customer has any further questions before ending the call. I am sorry that this did not happen when you made your reservation and I would like to offer you a 5% discount on your booking. I hope this is to your satisfaction.
>
> Best regards
> Anita Hodden
> (118 words)

Communication skills

◎ This exercise gives SS further practice in the useful language for active listening, paraphrasing and checking understanding on page 47.

> **1** f   **2** c   **3** b   **4** a   **5** e   **6** d

6 Business ethics

Reading

◎ SS correct a short article on business ethics by identifying the extra word that appears on some but not all of the lines. If SS have not done this type of exercise before, draw their attention to the rubric and the fact that some of the lines are correct.

> **1** ✓ **2** out **3** for **4** the **5** at **6** ✓ **7** that **8** there **9** ✓ **10** you **11** not **12** ✓

Vocabulary

◎ This exercise gives SS further practice of words related to corporate social responsibility after the case study on pages 56–57.

> **1** passionate **2** commitment **3** trust **4** persuasive **5** scepticism **6** risky
> **7** environmental **8** threat **9** development **10** successful **11** progressive **12** inspiration

Reading

◎ This exercise gives SS further practice of multiword verbs from page 53.

> **1** set up **2** hold us to account **3** shy away from **4** set out **5** falls into **6** phase out
> **7** carried out **8** follow suit

Writing

◎ This exercise gives SS further e-mail writing practice after the case study on pages 56–57. SS write a reply to one of Stitch Wear's customers who is concerned about the company's use of child labour.

> **Sample answer**
>
> Dear Ms Powell
>
> Thank you very much for your e-mail. I can assure you that Stitch Wear is taking this issue very seriously. We now screen all our suppliers to ensure that children under 14 are not employed anywhere in the world in the production of our goods.
>
> We are also planning to introduce health and educational facilities for children who once worked in our Asian factories. Stitch Wear is deeply committed to child welfare, and we sponsor several fund-raising events for children's charities in this country, including the annual Happy Child Fun Run. Please click on this link to our website to find out more about Stitch Wear's commitment to responsible business www.stitchwear.com.
>
> With best regards
> Harriet Pratt
> (119 words)

UNIT 7 Finance and banking

At a glance

	Classwork – Course Book	Further work
Lesson 1: **Listening and discussion** (pages 62–63) *Each lesson is about 60–75 minutes. This time does not include administration and time spent going through homework in any lessons.*	**Discussion: Banking 1** SS are encouraged to discuss banks, Internet banking and how personal and international banking have changed. **Vocabulary: Banking terms** SS look at some banking terms and use related vocabulary in context. **Listening: Changes in international banking** SS listen to Joan Rosàs, from La Caixa savings bank in Barcelona, talk about current trends and changes in banks and banking services. **Discussion: Banking 2** SS talk about how trends in banking are affecting business and the future of banking.	**Practice File** Word power (pages 40–41)
Lesson 2: **Reading and language** (pages 64–65) *Each lesson is about 60–75 minutes.*	**Discussion: Financial difficulties** SS discuss factors that can cause a company financial problems. **Reading: *Marconi repays £669m of debt, US Airways vows to rise again*** SS read two short texts on company debt and recovery in relation to Marconi and US Airways. **Vocabulary: Debt and recovery** SS look at vocabulary related to company debt and recovery in context. **Discussion: Profitable sectors** SS discuss which companies/sectors are doing well/badly.	**Text bank** (TRB pages 180–183) **Grammar reference and practice** (CB page 126) **Practice File** Text and grammar (pages 42–43)
Lesson 3: **Business skills** (pages 66–67) *Each lesson is about 75–90 minutes.*	**Giving presentations** SS listen to someone introducing a presentation and practise the language of introducing a presentation. **Describing financial performance** SS listen to a presentation and describe financial performance using the language of trends. **Writing: Introduction to a presentation** SS write the introduction of a presentation on a company's financial performance.	**Resource bank** (TRB pages 225–226) **Grammar reference and practice** (CB page 126) **Practice File** Skills and pronunciation (pages 44–45)
Lesson 4: **Case study** (pages 68–69) *Each lesson is about 75–90 minutes.*	**Cost-cutting at Erstaunliche Autos** SS listen to some radio business news concerning the financial crisis at Erstaunliche Autos (EA), a German car manufacturer; act as financial consultants; and devise a cost-cutting programme, which they present to management at EA.	**Grammar reference and practice** (CB page 126)

For a fast route through the unit, focusing mainly on speaking skills, just use the underlined sections.

For one-to-one situations, most parts of the unit lend themselves, with minimal adaptation, to use with individual students. Where this is not the case, alternative procedures are given.

Business brief

Finance is the part of economics concerned with providing **funds** to individuals, businesses and governments. Finance allows these entities to use **credit** instead of **cash** to purchase goods and **invest in** projects. For example, an individual can **borrow** money from a bank to buy a home. A company can **raise money** through **investors** to build a new factory. Governments can **issue bonds** to raise money for projects. There are many other aspects of finance, such as **corporate finance** and **public finance.**

Institutions such as **stock exchanges** provide a market for existing **securities**, which include **stocks** and **bonds**. Banks and other **financial institutions** provide credit.

Banking is the business of providing **financial services** to consumers and businesses. Some of basic banking services are **checking accounts** (**current accounts** in the UK) and **savings accounts** and **deposit accounts** that can be used to save money for future use. Other services include **loans, credit cards** and basic **cash management** services such as **foreign currency exchange**.

Banking institutions include **commercial banks, savings and loan associations** (SLAs) and **savings banks**. The major differences between these types of banks lie in how they are owned and how they manage their **assets and liabilities**. Bank assets are typically cash, loans, securities (bonds, but not stocks) and property in which the bank has invested. Liabilities are mainly the **deposits** received from the bank's customers, which are still owned by, and can be withdrawn by, the **depositors**.

Other financial institutions that are not banks but nevertheless provide banking services include: **finance companies, investment companies, investment banks, insurance companies, pension funds, security brokers and dealers, mortgage companies** and **real-estate investment trusts**.

Business recovery

All business activity **carries risk,** and any company can fail. **Cashflow** is not the same thing as **profitability,** and a common cause of failure is **rapid growth,** causing costs to **rise steeply ahead of income**.

The causes of failure are complex. Once-stable markets **go into decline,** reducing **income** and cashflow. Operational problems create large, **unforeseen costs** that **eat up profits**. Investors begin to **lose confidence,** the **share price** falls, **credit ratings** are reduced and it becomes more difficult to borrow. Profitable parts of the company may be **sold off** to **raise cash**; this works in the short term, but **long-term revenue** declines.

Sometimes the senior management team is changed, also known as **corporate restructuring,** in the hope that new managers will make a difference. However, studies of US companies that change their top management in response to crises show that only about one-third make **a full recovery**.

As a last resort, declarations of **insolvency** or **bankruptcy** can create a breathing space, and compel lenders and investors to **come to terms with** problems and bear some of the **losses**. Not every **insolvent company** is **written off**; many recover and return to **successful trading**. In other cases, insolvency exposes deeper problems. Then the only choice is **liquidation,** with **assets sold at auction** and **staff made redundant**.

Finance and banking and your students

In-work students will be able to talk about aspects of company finance, describing company performance, and will possibly have some knowledge of international banking transactions such as letters of credit used for import/export. Pre-work students may have experience of reading about company performance.

All students will have some experience of personal banking and banking services, possibly including online banking, and may also be able to discuss growth and recovery regarding companies that are in the news.

Read on

Michael Brett: *How to read the financial pages,* Random House, 2003

Ron Chernow: *The house of Morgan: an American banking dynasty and the rise of modern finance,* Grove Press, 2001

Longman Business English Dictionary, Pearson Education, 2000

Lesson notes

Warmer

◎ Ask SS to brainstorm the names of some high-street banks and say what sort of banks they are, e.g. commercial, savings banks or building societies, and whether they are regional, national or 'global' banks. Write SS's ideas up on the board, but do not spend too long on this, as it leads into the first discussion question in Exercise A. Ask SS to name some well-known international banks if they haven't already done so, e.g. J.P. Morgan, Deutsche Bank, etc., and whether they prefer to bank with lesser-known regional banks or a global bank.

Overview

◎ Tell SS that they will be looking at finance and banking in this unit.

◎ Go through the overview panel at the beginning of the unit, pointing out the sections that SS will be looking at.

Quotation

◎ Get SS to look at the quotation and ask them what they think it means. (The idea is that money is obviously essential and is an example of Woody Allen's irony.)

Discussion: Banking 1

SS are encouraged to discuss banks, Internet banking and how personal and international banking have changed.

 A

◎ SS work in pairs to discuss the questions. Set a three-minute time limit for this. Then get SS's feedback as a whole class. Help SS with banking terminology in English. With this kind of specific vocabulary, it is a good idea to read the Business brief (page 81) before starting the unit and have a good dictionary, such as the *Longman Business English Dictionary,* to hand during class.

---

1 SS may say that they think certain banks are successful because they charge a lot for their services, or have a good reputation for customer service, or have developed online banking and more sophisticated banking services in order to attract more clients. Many Spanish banks offer 'points' to customers, depending on the number of banking transactions carried out on debit or credit cards. Customers can thereby accumulate and exchange points in return for various gifts. Ask SS if their banks offer similar promotions.

2 SS will probably say Internet banking is easier and quicker than going to their high-street bank, although SS may also have reservations about carrying out online transactions for security reasons. It is not necessary to spend too long on this point, as the future of banking forms part of the discussion after the listening section.

3 SS may say that banking transactions are faster or more efficient than five or ten years ago, with the development of Internet banking and new technologies. SS's answers will vary here, depending on their experience of company finance and/or payments of export/import. It is not necessary to spend too much time on this question with pre-work SS.

Vocabulary: Banking terms

SS look at some banking terms and use related vocabulary in context.

 B

◎ Refer SS to the words in the box. The vocabulary is taught here before the listening, as SS may have varied experience of banking terminology.

◎ With pre-work SS particularly, you may prefer to pre-teach some of these items, and/or have a good business dictionary, such as the *Longman Business English Dictionary*, to hand. One way of pre-teaching vocabulary items is to write the words and their definitions on the board. SS then match the items. Alternatively, give SS one of the words and get them to look it up in the dictionary. SS then explain their word to the rest of the class in their own words. As a follow-up activity, ask SS if they have ever invested in bonds or company shares. Why (not)?

ATM: Automated Teller Machine or cash point (BE)

bond: a document which can be bought and sold and which is produced by a government or organisation, promising that it will pay back money it has borrowed, usually with interest

equity (or equities): the capital that a company has from shares rather than from loans; trading equities means trading in companies' shares on the stock market, rather than trading on other markets

letter of credit: used to guarantee payment and delivery of goods, whereby the importer's bank guarantees payment to the exporter's bank once it receives the related shipping documents

securities: a financial investment such as a bond or share, or the related certificate to show who owns it

share: one of the parts into which the ownership of a company is divided

◎ SS do the exercise in pairs, then compare answers.

◎ Go through the answers with the whole class. Deal with any further vocabulary questions SS may have.

1 ATM   2 letters of credit   3 corporate restructuring
4 bonds   5 trading   6 capital

◎ Tell SS they will also be dealing with vocabulary for finance and growth in the following reading section.

Listening: Changes in international banking

SS listen to Joan Rosàs, from La Caixa savings bank based in Barcelona, talk about current trends in banks and banking services. In the first part of the interview, he talks about recent changes and trends in international banking. In the second part, he talks about the future developments in international banking.

Ⓒ 🎧 7.1

◎ Get SS to focus on the short explanatory text on La Caixa. You may also like to tell SS that La Caixa's success in Catalonia, Spain, is partly due to its extensive branch network, with ATMs on every high street, despite current trends towards online banking. If SS are interested, refer them to the bank's website: www.lacaixa.es

◎ Get SS to work in pairs, look through the questions and try to predict whether the information is true or false. Explain any difficult vocabulary.

◎ Play the first part of the interview and elicit the answer to the first question.

◎ Play the rest of the recording once, stopping in sections to allow SS time to mark their answers.

◎ Get SS to check answers in pairs.

◎ Go through the answers with the whole class, playing any difficult sections a third time if necessary, or referring SS to the audio script on page 168 if necessary.

1   True
2   False (J. Rosàs mentions new technologies, not new regulations.)
3   False (He refers to electronic letters of credit, not e-mails.)
4   True
5   True
6   False (He says they are examples of sophisticated/non-traditional/investment banking.)

◎ If SS are interested in recognising accents, you may like to explain that Joan Rosàs is Catalan, but travels a great deal in his job and spent ten years working in New York, and therefore has a mixture of a Catalan and American accent.

Ⓓ 🎧 7.2

• Refer SS to the cartoon. Ask SS what the woman is doing and what it says on the screen. (She's checking her bank balance on the TV with a remote control, and the account is overdrawn.) Ask SS if they can already do their banking transactions in this way, or if they think this will be the future of banking for individual customers.

◎ Ask SS to read through the notes under the three headings and see if they can predict any of the answers. Note: it is not important for them to complete all the gaps, as the focus is on familiarising them with the vocabulary.

◎ Play the second part of the recording, pausing where necessary to give SS time to write their answers

◎ After listening, SS compare their answers in pairs; circulate and deal with any queries SS have.

◎ If necessary, play the recording a second time and refer SS to the audio script on page 168. However, don't spend too long going over the script in detail, as SS will need time to discuss the questions in Exercise E.

◎ Go through the answers with the whole class. Ask SS if they know what WAP stands for (Wireless Application Protocol, which is a protocol that turns mobile telephones into small Internet browsers).

1 global   2 (large) regional   3 Smaller   4 do well
5 strategic market segments   6 bundled   7 savings
8 credit cards   9 insurance and consumer   10 bricks
11 retail branch   12 Internet   13 Clicks and clicks
14 cell phones   15 Digital TV   16 TV remote control

Discussion: Banking 2

SS talk about how trends in banking are affecting business and the future of banking.

Ⓔ

◎ Get SS to discuss their answers in pairs or threes. Circulate and monitor, helping where necessary with vocabulary.

Lesson notes

◎ Bring the class together and encourage SS particularly to talk about new banking products and services, the way new technologies are changing the world of banking and how companies carry out payment transactions (e.g. *international cheque truncation*). Some SS may want to discuss recent bank mergers in the news and the feasibility of cross-border mergers. Other SS may want to talk more about security issues with Internet banking. You may like to point out to SS you will be dealing with online business in Unit 10.

◎ During the discussion, monitor and circulate. Make a note of any good examples of vocabulary and five or six language points for correction, including pronunciation.

◎ Go through feedback with the whole of the class, praising appropriate language for finance and banking. Write up any further points on the board.

◎ SS with a specialist interest in finance may want to compare British and American terms for finance and banking services – see table below. It is worth pointing out, however, that some American financial terms are also used in the UK and maybe more widely used internationally.

◎ Write up both columns without the headings and ask students to guess which column is British English and which is American English, and then elicit what the terms mean. Alternatively, mix up the words in the column of American English, then ask students to match the terms to the British equivalent. Ask SS if they are more familiar with the British or American terminology in their country or business.

British English	American English
cheque	check
current account	checking account
share	stock
shareholder	stockholder
stock	inventory
building society (or savings bank)	Savings and Loans Association (SLA)
merchant bank	investment bank
unit trust	mutual fund or Mutual Savings Banks (MSB)
creditors	accounts payable
debtors	accounts receivable

◎ If SS are interested in further finance and banking vocabulary, you can also refer them to the following website: www.investorguide.com

Discussion: Financial difficulties

SS discuss factors that can cause a company financial problems and read a short article on the topic.

◎ As a lead-in to the exercise, you may like to use this quote and ask SS what they understand by it:
Money is to a business what food is to a living organism. Businesses that run out of money effectively starve to death.
(Morgan Witzel, writer)

◎ Explain to SS that the idea is that 'just as the nutrition requirements of organisms change as they grow and age, so a business's money needs change as it matures. Private borrowing may be enough when the business is in its "infant" stage, but more sophisticated types of funding may be needed as the business grows' (from *An essential commodity* by Morgan Witzel for the FT, 4 August 2004)

◎ Alternatively, refer SS to the photo of the closing-down sale. Elicit from SS why the shop might be closing down, e.g. the owner is retiring, a larger shop has taken away its business, there's no demand for the goods it sells, etc.

◎ Refer SS to the questions, asking them to think of some factors, first of all individually, then compare their answers in groups of three or four.

◎ Go through the answers with the whole class.

> **1** Most of the items listed, with the possible exception of executive salaries, can cause a company financial problems and lead to financial crisis. Other potential external or internal factors are:
> - ◎ slow company response to change in the industry or major societal/environmental/technological issues, e.g. the advent of the PC, mobile phones or the Internet;
> - ◎ dramatic changes in corporate structure;
> - ◎ weak Financial Director;
> - ◎ over diversification;
> - ◎ corruption and scandal;
> - ◎ autocratic Chairman/CEO and passive board members;
> - ◎ high administration costs (this could include executive salaries).
>
> According to John Argenti, UK business consultant and designer of the A-score, 'It's not change that causes corporate failure, it's management mistakes. And those depend on the original defects in a company.' He divides corporate break-down into three phases:
> **Defects:** sees the emergence of crucial gaps and imbalances in a company's management, and consequently its internal and external monitoring systems.
> **Mistakes:** when these defects lead to inappropriate business decisions.
> **Symptoms:** the company starts to show the symptoms of failure, from staff turnover to cashflow crisis.
> (Adapted from http://news.ft.com/)

◎ Get SS to read the short newspaper extract on business recovery.

◎ SS compare their answers in pairs.

◎ Go through the answers with the whole class.

2 For turnaround: it stops the shareholders from losing their investment and saves jobs.
Against turnaround: it prevents consolidation in a highly competitive sector.

Reading: *Marconi repays £669m of debt, US Airways vows to rise again*

SS read two short texts on company debt and recovery in relation to Marconi and US Airways.

◉ As a lead-in to the articles, ask SS what they know about the two companies, e.g. Marconi is a maker of telecom equipment; US Airways used to be one of the big US airlines. Both companies experienced financial crisis. SS may know that Marconi almost went bankrupt, but don't spend too long on this, as the SS will answer some of these points in the following reading task.

◉ Divide the class into pairs: SS A read the text on Marconi and SS B read the article on US Airways. Tell SS they are going to verbally summarise what they read and the answers for the three questions for their partner. Explain that the idea is to scan the articles quickly for this information. Tell SS they should ignore any words or phrases they don't know at this stage and focus on the questions. In order to make this a quicker reading exercise, set a time limit.

◉ Get SS to read the articles. With less confident SS or larger groups, you may decide to divide the class into groups A and B: Group A reads the Marconi article together in pairs and Group B reads the US airways text. SS then summarise their answers for another pair.

◉ SS summarise their answers to the questions and what they have read for their partner. Circulate and monitor, helping SS with vocabulary if necessary.

◉ Ask SS for their initial reactions to the points made in the article before checking the answers.

◉ Go through the answers with the whole class.

1 **Marconi's** crisis was brought about by the decision to focus on telecommunications and to sell the profitable defence division. The company also bought a lot of other companies, but there was a collapse in demand in the hi-tech and telecoms sector.
US Airways' problems appear to have been caused by high fuel costs and competition from low-budget airlines. Although it isn't mentioned in the article, the aviation industry was also badly hit by the 9/11 terrorist attack (11 September 2001).

2 **Marconi** has restructured the company, sold many businesses, sacked thousands of staff and given control of the company to bondholders. In exchange, the debt has been written off, and the original shareholders have lost almost all of their investment.
US Airways is declaring bankruptcy to conserve cash and avoid paying creditors. The company has also been trying to get staff to agree to 'savings' (presumably salary cuts, staff reductions and increased productivity) and wants legal permission to suspend pension payments and cancel the pension fund for some staff.

3 **Marconi** seems to be surviving the crisis – the company has been able to sell some businesses and pay off some debts earlier than expected, and profits and share values are improving.
US Airways seems almost certain to go bankrupt unless the government intervenes or they are bought out by another company.

◉ Alternatively, if time is short, or with one-to-one SS, SS read one of the articles and exchange information about the second article with you.

◉ After reading, ask SS follow-up questions:
What has happened to the two companies since the articles were written?
Do you know other companies that are experiencing similar financial difficulties?
How are these companies dealing with decline and turnaround?
Do they seem likely to go bankrupt? Why (not?)

Note: There is no language review for this section – see Business skills.

Vocabulary: Debt and recovery

SS look at vocabulary related to company debt and recovery in context.

◉ Get all SS to read both articles again, pointing out that the paragraphs are numbered. If SS ask questions, throw them open to the whole class to see if someone can provide an explanation. If not, explain where necessary.

◉ Alternatively, if short of time, ask SS to read only one of the articles, or ask SS A to do questions 1–7 (Marconi) and SS B, questions 8–14 (US Airways). SS then exchange answers.

◎ Get SS to do the exercise individually.

◎ Circulate and confirm answers or indicate in which sentence a word or expression occurs where SS are having difficulties. Get early finishers to compare their answers with a partner.

◎ Go through the answers with the whole class, asking SS to give their explanations of the meanings and find out if the rest of the class agrees.

1 b	2 a	3 a	4 b	5 a	6 b	7 b	8 a	9 b	10 b
11 a	12 a	13 b	14 a				

◎ If SS are interested in finding out more, give them the reading list in the Read on section (page 81) and the website: www.investorguide.com

Discussion: Profitable sectors

SS discuss which companies/sectors are doing well/badly.

◎ SS discuss the questions in pairs or small groups.

◎ Circulate and monitor during the discussion, making a note of any useful language used.

◎ Go through the answers with the whole class. SS will give their own answers for question 1. In question 2, SS may say that in Europe, the science R&D and banking sectors are doing very well, but the traditional manufacturing sectors, such as car plants, are struggling due to high labour costs and overseas competition. The airline industry appears to be in crisis globally. The hi-tech and telecoms sector is recovering from the downturn of the late 1990s.

Giving presentations

SS listen to someone introducing a presentation and practise the language of introducing a presentation.

Ⓐ 🎧 7.3

◎ As a lead-in to this section, ask SS some of the following questions about introducing presentations:
When was the last time you gave a presentation? Where? Who to?
How did you introduce or start the presentation?
Did you write and rehearse it beforehand or did you improvise?
How could you improve the introduction?

◎ Alternatively:
When was the last time you saw someone give a presentation? Where? Who to?
How did they introduce or start the presentation?
Do you think they improvised it, or was it written and rehearsed?

◎ Point out that if they are going to give a presentation in English, it's a good idea to write at least their introduction and conclusion and rehearse it beforehand. It is not necessary to memorise the introduction word for word, but it's important to be able to read it without looking too much at your notes.

◎ Play the recording once, pausing if necessary to give SS time to write their answers.

◎ SS compare in pairs.

◎ Play the recording a second time if necessary.

◎ Go through the answers with the whole class.

1 to talk to you	**2** start by reporting	**3** we'll look at
4 I'm sure you'll	**5** ask any questions	

The speaker uses expressions like *the bright future ahead* and *growing from strength to strength* to get the audience's interest in what's she's going to talk about. She also addresses them directly when she says *I'm sure you'll agree*.

◎ Drill pronunciation of some of the expressions used, highlighting word stress on the board. It's often a good idea for SS to read the audio script aloud to each other to practise the pronunciation and intonation of the key words and phrases.

◎ Refer SS to the presentation tips. Deal with any questions and ask SS to add any further tips they may have for giving presentations.

Describing financial performance

SS listen to a presentation and describe financial performance using the language of trends.

Ⓑ 🎧 7.4

◎ As a lead-in to this section, ask SS some of the following questions about giving or attending financial presentations:
How often do you give financial presentations?
When was the last time you saw a presentation on company performance?
What do you think are some of the difficulties of giving these kinds of presentations?
What kind of visual aids do/would you like to use in this kind of presentation (e.g. PowerPoint, graphs from financial reports, etc.)?

◎ Ask SS to read the short explanatory text on CME.

◎ Refer SS to the graph and the description of CME's performance and projections. Make sure SS are given enough time to do this before playing the recording.

◎ Play the recording once, pausing where necessary to give SS time to write their answers.

◎ Get SS to compare their answers in pairs.

◎ Go through the answers with the whole class.

> **1** outperform **2** medium term **3** gradually recover
> **4** over double

◎ Refer SS to the audio script on page 168 and deal with any questions they may have regarding language for describing trends.

◎ Try to sensitise the SS to English sentence stress, linking and intonation. Don't get SS to repeat all the expressions, just one or two from each section that might be difficult in terms of pronunciation, drilling pronunciation and intonation of any difficult items and highlighting word stress on the board where necessary, e.g. **What** we've got **here**; **What** you can **see**; by **year seven** will be over **double**. SS may find it useful to read the audio script and listen to the recording a third time, at the same time as highlighting stressed words.

◎ For further practice of the language of trends, refer SS to the Grammar reference on page 126 in the Course Book.

 Grammar reference: Language of trends page 126

> **1** **1** a **2** b **3** c **4** b
> **2** **1** gradually declined **2** falling from **3** rapid upturn
>   **4** soar to **5** slight drop **6** stabilised at **7** recovered

ⓒ 🎧 7.5

◎ Refer SS to Exercise C and the bar chart on page 160.

◎ Play the recording once and get SS to correct the five errors in the chart individually, pausing at relevant sections when necessary to give SS time to write their answers and check the graph.

◎ SS compare answers in pairs, playing the recording a second time if necessary.

◎ Go through the answers with the whole class, referring SS to the audio script on page 168 if necessary.

> **Errors in chart**
> **1** In Year 1, revenue more than doubled between Q3 and Q4 to $40m, not $50m.
> **2** In Year 2, revenue rose to $40m in Q2 (not $42m).
> **3** In Year 3, growth in Q2 and Q4 was $48m and $62m, not vice versa.
> **4** In Year 3, Q4 should match Q4 of Year 4, not Q1.
> **5** In Year 4, Q3 revenue dipped slightly to $46m, not $55m.

ⓓ

◎ As a lead-in to the exercise, write the following five verbs for describing trends on the board and elicit from the SS whether they are used to describe rising or falling figures: *sink* (fall), *leap* (rise), *plummet* (fall), *surge* (rise) and *slip* (fall). Ask SS which of these verbs expresses only slight movement (*slip*) and explain the others express a significant rise or fall.

◎ Divide SS into pairs and ask them to look at the Language of trends box on page 126.

◎ Monitor and circulate as SS do the activity, helping them, where necessary, to identify the expressions in the financial press and add them to the appropriate section in the Grammar reference.

◎ SS compare their answers with another pair.

◎ Ask SS to add to the table any more expressions that they use for these purposes.

◎ Go through the answers with the whole class.

> Suggested answers
> **1** *The firm sank deep into the red* ... (add to end of the table)
> **2** ... *has seen profits leap* (add to *Profits have rocketed* section of the table. Point out the construction of this sentence is different from the others and that *Profits have leapt* is also possible.)
> **3** ... *shares plummeted* (add to end of the table)
> **4** *Shares* ... *have slipped* (add to *Profits have decreased* section of the table)
> **5** *Shares* ... *dropped sharply* (add *sharply* to the list of adverbs in the *Profits have* section of the table.
> **6** ... *numbers climbed from* ... *to* ... (add to *Profits have doubled* section of the table)
> **7** ... *surged* (add to *Profits have recovered* section of the table)
>   ... *almost tripling* (add to *Profits have doubled* section of the table)
>   ... *in the last quarter.* (add to first section of the table)
> **8** ... *soar* (add to *Profits have recovered* section)
>   ... *four-fold* (add to the list of adverbs)

◎ Try to sensitise the SS to English sentence stress, linking and intonation. Don't get SS to repeat all the expressions, just one or two from each section that might be difficult in terms of pronunciation (e.g. *plummeted*, *tripling*, *four-fold*).

◎ You may also tell the SS they will be looking at presentations again later in the CB (Unit 10 looks at summarising a presentation and dealing with Q&A). If SS are particularly interested in giving presentations, you may wish to deal with this section at an earlier stage.

◎ For follow-up practice, go to the Resource bank on page 225.

Writing: introduction to a presentation

SS write the introduction of presentation on their company's financial performance.

ⓔ

◎ Get SS to read the Useful language box.

◎ Elicit the first few sentences of the presentation from the SS, or refer them to the presentation given by Diana Holden on page 66.

◎ SS write their introduction to the presentation on CME's financial performance in pairs.

◎ Alternatively, if SS do not generally give these kinds of presentations, ask them to write the introduction for a presentation they have already given or will possibly give in the future, e.g. on their company or department or line of work.

◎ Circulate, monitor and help SS whilst they write. Make a note of any useful expressions used and five or six points for correction on the board.

◎ Early finishers can be referred to the board to see if they can correct the errors.

◎ After completing the task and, if peer correction is appropriate in your setting, SS may compare their introductions in pairs. Are the sentences too long? What expressions did they both use? What could be improved? Tell SS not to bother too much with spelling mistakes, as this introduction is meant to be spoken. If they spot any words and expressions they don't know, they can ask their colleagues who wrote it about the meaning. This task helps SS be more aware of the impact their presentation has on the audience.

◎ Go through feedback with the whole class, writing up any common errors and useful vocabulary and phrases on the board.

◎ Ask SS to memorise as much of the introduction as they can. SS then give their short presentation to the rest of the class. This activity may also be recorded on video or cassette, as SS will find it a more challenging and realistic task if they are recorded, rather than just 'talking' to their peers.

◎ Go through feedback with the whole class, praising good examples of language and style, including pronunciation and pointing out five or six areas that need further work. If presentations have been recorded in larger classes, do not replay the whole presentation each time, as you may not have time. Just replay sections and make sure you praise SS as much as commenting on their errors. It may not be appropriate to comment on SS's body language and delivery, depending on SS's culture and the teaching setting, as in the case of SS who may be rather shy, or, indeed, professional SS who are in work and well practised at giving presentations in their own language.

◎ Alternatively, or if time is short, this writing task could also be set for homework.

Case study: Cost-cutting at Erstaunliche Autos

SS listen to some radio business news concerning the financial crisis at Erstaunliche Autos (EA), a German car manufacturer; act as financial consultants; and devise a cost-cutting programme which they present to management at EA.

◎ In class, pay particular attention to clearly breaking down the case study into the different tasks and making sure that SS understand and follow the structure of what you are doing.

Background

◎ Get SS to focus on the photo of the new model of a car and the accompanying headline. As a lead-in to the case study, ask SS the following questions:
Where do you think the car was produced?
Would you buy a Chinese car? Why (not)?
Which countries are famous for their car industry? (the US, Germany and Japan)

◎ Elicit some well-known car companies from these countries and ask SS to tell you which ones are doing well or badly, and why. Elicit from SS the implications of the headline and the information 'reading between the lines'. (There's been some restructuring: there's a new chief. Earnings need to be boosted: Erstaunliche Autos are probably doing badly.)

◎ Get SS to study the background information. Tell SS the case study is based on a fictitious German car company.

◎ Write the following headings from the left-hand column of the table and elicit information from SS to complete the right-hand column. Deal with any further questions SS may have.

Company	Erstaunliche Autos (EA)
Industry	Car manufacturer
Based in	Frankfurt, Germany
Size	Medium-sized
Employment conditions for workers	(Very) good: enjoy a four-day week and good salaries
Problems EA is facing	Production costs are high (40% more than similar companies); serious competition from China.
Possible solutions	The new company chairman wants a cost-cutting programme with job losses; help with the refinancing package from financial consultants, Tompkins and Kosters.

Task 1

◎ Refer SS to the graph on three Chinese car manufacturers over the last three years. Get SS's initial reaction to the graph, then ask them to write down a sentence for each of the companies, describing the graph in more detail.

◎ If SS write their answers, circulate and monitor whilst they write, helping them with language for describing company performance, if necessary.

◎ Go through the answers with the whole class and write up their answers on the board.

Graph on Chinese car manufacturers

1 Sales for Car Company 1 (*purple line*) increased dramatically in the first quarter of Year 1 and reached 12% by the middle of Year 2, following a joint venture with a US company. Since then, figures have fluctuated significantly, dropping to just under 8% in Year 3.

2 Sales for Car Company 2 (*orange line*) fluctuated throughout Year 2, then rose dramatically at the start of Year 3 with the introduction of a new Mini model and now remain at just over 6%.

3 Sales for Car Company 3 (*red line*) also fluctuated throughout Year 2 and increased to over 4% in the early months of Year 3. Sales have been rising steadily and are now at 5%.

Conclusion: the graph shows that despite major fluctuations and a sharp rise in sales for Car Company 1 in Year 2, sales figures have converged in Year 3, and the companies now have a market share of between 5–8%. Competition is tough, although Car Company 1 is still ahead.

◎ As a follow-up to the activity, tell SS the following three facts about the Chinese car industry. Alternatively, write up the sentences on the board and elicit the bold figures. Point out that EA is concerned about competition from the Chinese car manufacturers in the global market, if SS do not comment on this themselves.

The Chinese car industry

Less than **1%** of the Chinese population had a car in 2005. China is the world's **third** biggest car market.

Capacity for car production in China is close to six million cars a year, while domestic demand was around **three million** in 2005.

Listening 🎧 7.6

◎ Get SS to read the listening task. Ask them to try and predict what plans have been leaked to the press. SS may be able to predict some of the answers from reading the background. They may also guess that the company may have plans to relocate, possibly to China or elsewhere, if production and labour costs in Germany are very high. Don't reject any ideas at this stage or give the answers away.

◎ SS listen to the recording. After listening, they compare ideas in pairs. If necessary, play the recording a second time, pausing after relevant sections.

◎ Go through the answers with the whole class.

Information about EA that has been leaked to the press

1 Chairman of EA wants to increase productivity and boost profits by €4 billion over the next three years. This will involve cost cuts of up to €7 billion.

2 Inside sources claim EA chief, Bernd Wulf, is looking into closing the Belgian car plant.

3 There's a possibility of EA opening a factory in India.

◎ Discuss SS's initial reactions to the problem and ask these questions:
Do you think it might be better to open a factory in China in the light of previous information? Why (not)?
What do you think is going to happen at EA and why?
SS may say the Chinese market is more difficult to get into than other markets; that German car workers need to be more productive. There is no right answer to these questions. SS may or may not reach a consensus.

Task 2

◎ Get SS to focus on the photo on page 69. Ask SS what it represents (a robot-operated assembly line). Ask SS:
What do you think will be the future of car assembly workers in the world?
What's the current situation of the car industry in your country?
SS will probably say that job losses are to be expected as robots take over car production, as they have done already in France and other countries.

◎ Refer SS to the first part of Task 2. (Note this task is in two stages.)

◎ Divide SS into groups of three. Explain to SS they are financial consultants at Tompkins and Kosters and have to decide on the best proposals for a cost-cutting package which they will later present to management at EA. Get SS to look at their role-play information on pages 146, 153 and 157. Deal with any questions the SS may have before they begin the task.

◎ SS exchange information and decide on the best proposals in groups. The information includes: proposed figures and areas where cuts can be made (see pie chart for Student A); annual productivity rates in Germany and Belgium for EA compared to other car manufacturers in China and India (see bar chart for Student B); average hourly rates for assembly-line workers in three countries (see bar chart for Student C).

◎ Circulate and monitor, checking SS are carrying out the task correctly. Note that any proposals should be supported by the facts and figures they have. Make a note of any key language being used and five or six points for correction, including pronunciation, for later feedback.

◎ Bring the class together. Go through the main points quickly with the whole class, making a note of their ideas on the board.

◎ Refer SS to the second part of Task 2. Tell them they will need to present these cost-cutting measures to management using these figures and graphs.

Lesson notes

- Give SS five or ten minutes to prepare their presentations. If SS are working in groups of three, ask them to divide the presentation into three parts (introduction, main proposals and conclusion). Note that this presentation time is important if SS are to carry out the task correctly and confidently.

- SS present their proposals to the rest of the class. Make a note of any key language being used and five or six points for correction, including pronunciation, for later feedback.

- Alternatively, or if time is short, ask SS to prepare only the introduction of their presentation with the main proposals included.

Feedback

- When SS have finished the task, bring the whole class to order.

- Ask one or two groups to say what happened in their groups and, if appropriate in your setting, ask SS to comment on the best proposals and give reasons for their choice.

- Praise the strong language points and work on five or six points that need improvement, especially in relation to language used for finance and describing company performance.

- To round off the activity, highlight some of SS's best ideas and praise those students that gave successful presentations.

Writing

- Refer SS to the writing task and deal with any questions they may have.

- Get SS to look at the rubric. Brainstorm the information that should go in the summary and put these points on the board. All this information has come up in Listening, Tasks 1 and 2 and their presentations.

- Ask SS to look at the Useful language box on page 67 again and the Grammar reference on page 126, if necessary.

 *Grammar reference: Language of trends* page 126

- Circulate and monitor, checking SS are completing the task correctly.

- Get SS to write the final summary of their proposals either as a class activity in groups of three or individually. Alternatively, this writing task could be set for homework.

- For early finishers, and if appropriate in your setting, ask SS to read and compare each others' summaries. SS could comment whether graphic information and figures were described correctly and appropriately in the summary.

---

1 to 1

- Go through the information in the Course Book with your student. Explain any difficulties. In Task 1, you and your student are financial consultants. Don't dominate the conversation in this task, but say enough to keep it going and allow your student to describe the graph showing Chinese car makers. In Task 2, you and your student are financial consultants SS A and B. Praise any good examples of language used and go over any errors, including pronunciation. Then repeat this task, alternating roles, e.g. SS B and C. Alternatively, your student may look at information for SS A and you look at both bar charts and proposals for SS B and C.

- During these tasks, monitor the language that your student is using. Note down any good examples of language and points for error correction or improvement. Come back to these later.

- Record Task 2 on video or cassette, if possible.

Consultants

At a glance

	Classwork – Course Book	Further work
Lesson 1: **Listening and discussion** (pages 70–71) *Each lesson is about 60–75 minutes. This time does not include administration and time spent going through homework in any lessons.*	**Discussion: Consultants** SS discuss the benefits of taking on external consultants and appropriate steps for recruiting a consultant. **Listening: Radio interview on recruiting consultants** SS listen to business advisor Michelle Geraghty talking about the different stages of recruiting consultants and managing consultancies during an assignment or project. **Vocabulary: Managing consultancies** SS look at managing consultancy projects and use related vocabulary in context. **Discussion: Disadvantages of consultancies** SS talk about some of the disadvantages of hiring consultants.	**Practice File** Word power (pages 46–47)
Lesson 2: **Reading and language** (pages 72–73) *Each lesson is about 60–75 minutes.*	**Discussion: Using consultants** SS discuss the use of consultancy firms and business sectors that spend the most money on consultants. **Reading: *Could it be you when they need an expert?*** SS read an article on the benefits and drawbacks of becoming a consultant and the consultancy industry in general. **Language review: Negation using prefixes/Conditionals** SS look at negation using prefixes (in the context of the reading) and conditionals (as an optional activity in the Grammar reference).	**Text bank** (TRB pages 184–187) **Grammar reference and practice** (CB pages 128–129) **Practice File** Text and grammar (pages 48–49)
Lesson 3: **Business skills** (pages 74–75) *Each lesson is about 75–90 minutes.*	**Negotiating sales** SS listen to a sales manager giving a training session on sales negotiations, look at some negotiating tips for making concessions and do a role-play to negotiate a car deal for their company. **Writing: Terms and conditions** SS write up the terms and conditions agreed in a previous sales negotiation.	**Resource bank** (TRB page 227) **Writing file** (CB page 137) **Practice File** Skills and pronunciation (pages 50–51)
Lesson 4: **Case study** (pages 76–77) *Each lesson is about 75–90 minutes.*	**Mobi-net: it's their call** SS study proposals from two consultancy firms for Mobi-net, a mobile service provider based in Austria that needs to keep its lead in the competitive mobile-phone market. SS negotiate with both consultancies and write a summary of the terms agreed with the preferred consultancy.	**Writing file** (CB page 137)

For a fast route through the unit, focusing mainly on speaking skills, just use the underlined sections.

For one-to-one situations, most parts of the unit lend themselves, with minimal adaptation, to use with individual students. Where this is not the case, alternative procedures are given.

Business brief

A consultant is an **independent contractor** that provides **specialised services** or **skills** to a client for a **fee**. As **experts in their fields**, consultants can help with analysing and **solving problems, completing projects** and **specific tasks**. They can also help a company to **focus on results**, based on the **client's objectives**. The degree to which these objectives are achieved is an important **measure of success**.

There are different types of consultants. **Management consultants** analyse and propose ways to improve an organisation's structure, efficiency and/or profits. **Technology consultants** provide **implementation, support, training** and **strategic planning services**. **Web consultants** provide assistance with websites, which may include **setting goals, optimising** search engines and designing the site.

Consultants can offer the most **cost-effective** solution to a company's needs by providing **specialised expertise; overload assistance** during a peak period, as consultants can **absorb workloads** from permanent employees; **impartial analysis** (providing an **objective point of view**); **innovation** and **training**. Consultants may also carry out the work themselves.

Many business leaders, however, have a **love-hate relationship** with consultants, as **advisory services** are expensive and organisations have become more dependent than ever upon **bought-in advice**. Consulting expert, Fiona Czerniawska says that cases such as Enron have **tarnished the reputation** of the industry and reinforced clients' concerns that consulting projects are likely to go wrong when they involve **end-to-end** or **bundled services**; that there is insufficient objective information available to clients; and that **aggressive selling** compromises the ability of firms to offer the best possible advice or assistance.

Companies should not **retain** consultants without understanding how to capture the desired **return on investment (ROI).** There are different ways of getting the most benefit from working with a consultant.

If a company wants to **streamline business processes** or **increase profitability**, they should choose a specialist in **tactical matters**. This type of consultant should have **real-world experience** in the same industry as the client. **Competitors' benchmarks**, as well as **cause-and-effect analysis** and **cost-benefit analysis** should form part of the consultant's methodology for a tactical project.

If a company is looking to enter new markets, increase sales from existing clients or acquire another business, they should choose a consultant who excels in **big-picture thinking**. **Scenario planning, forecasting** and **risk analysis** are required for this type of strategic advice. A client sometimes decides to **retain a consultant** as a **coach**.

When choosing a **consultancy firm**, check the consultancy's **references** and whether the consultant has advised clients in the same type of business, at the same point in the company's **life cycle**. It is also necessary to understand the **potential conflicts of interest**. Is the advice truly objective?

Communication is another key factor when selecting consultants. The advisor's answers need to be clearly explained. A good working relationship on a personal level is also essential: the client needs to work with the consultant with **trust**, often revealing **confidential information.**

Where cost and contract are concerned, if the consultant **bills by the hour,** both parties need to agree on exactly where and when the work will take place. The contract should **detail precisely** what the consultant is paid to do. It should include details on how to **handle issues** that are not anticipated. The **contractual arrangement** should also include a **confidentiality agreement** or **non-disclosure agreement** that prevents the consultant from revealing the company's business to anyone else.

Finally, there will be no return on investment when hiring a consultant unless the company's managers **buy in**, or agree, to the proposed changes. This is best achieved before the consultant begins the work, so that managers and other staff will be **co-operative** in providing necessary information to the consultant.

Business brief

Consultancy and your students

In-work students will be able to describe projects or tasks that have been or could be outsourced to consultants. Some students may also have had first-hand experience working alongside consultants. Pre-work students will be able to talk about whether they could be interested in a career in consulting. All students will probably have world knowledge of some of the major consultancy firms.

Read on

Mick Cope: *The seven Cs of consulting: the definitive guide to the consulting process,* Financial Times Prentice Hall, 2003

Fiona Czerniawska and Paul May: *Management consulting in practice: award-winning international case studies,* Kogan Page, 2004

Calvert Markham: *The top consultant: developing your skills for greater effectiveness,* Kogan Page, 2004

Lesson notes

Warmer

- Ask SS to brainstorm some names of consultancy firms and the kind of consulting they do (e.g. McKinsey & Company, BCG (Boston Consulting Group), Bain & Company and Booz Allen Hamilton were the top four US firms in management and strategy consulting in 2005, whereas IBM, CSC and Accenture are leading companies in IT consulting).

- Write SS's ideas up on the board. Then ask in-work SS:
  What kind of consultancy firms have you worked with in your company or organisation?
  Why did the company need to recruit them?
  Was the consultancy project/assignment successful? Why (not)?

- Ask SS to focus on the positive aspects of working with consultants in this section, as Exercise F in Listening and discussion deals with criticisms of using consultants.

- Alternatively, ask SS to give a definition of a consultant – see the Business brief on page 93.

Overview

- Tell SS that they will be looking at using consultants in this unit.

- Go through the overview panel at the beginning of the unit, pointing out the sections that SS will be looking at.

Quotation

- Get SS to look at the quotation and ask them what they think it means. (The idea is that when you are too involved with a problem or in a crisis, it's best to ask an outsider for advice, as they will see the problem objectively in a different light. Alternatively, the quote could also imply that the work of experts or consultants is redundant, as they may state the obvious, i.e. tell a company what it already knows.)

Discussion: Consultants

SS discuss the benefits of taking on external consultants and appropriate steps for recruiting a consultant.

- Ask SS to brainstorm possible reasons why companies might take on an external consultant or advisor. Write SS's ideas up on the board (e.g. specialised expertise; assistance during a busy period, as consultants can temporarily take on the work of employees; analysis, providing an objective point of view; for innovation purposes as well as providing training. Consultants may also carry out the implementation work of a project or task themselves without long-term commitments to the client company).

- Then ask SS to work in pairs to discuss questions 2 and 3. Set a three-minute time limit for this. Then get SS's feedback as a whole class. Explain any difficult vocabulary, although much of this vocabulary features in the Listening section and follow-up vocabulary work (e.g. *brief, milestones, timescale, deliverables,* etc.).

Listening: Radio interview on recruiting consultants

SS listen to business advisor Michelle Geraghty. In the first part of the interview, she talks about the different stages of recruiting consultants. In the second part, she talks about managing consultancies during an assignment or project.

(B) 8.1

- Play the first part of the interview; SS compare their answers to the previous exercise.

- SS compare answers in pairs. It should not be necessary to play this section a second time for this exercise.

---

1 To provide advice or a service to make the business more successful. Consultants usually help with specific problem or tasks when your company doesn't have the know-how or the resources, e.g. controlling project costs, training, improving managerial performance; they may also manage specialist projects.

2 Choose one that has experience of businesses of your size, that understands your industry, and is a member of a professional body like the Institute of Management Consultancy.

3 Order for recruiting a consultant:
  c) Define the problem, project or task.
  e) Write a brief for the consultant.
  f) Make a shortlist of possible consultants.
  d) The consultant submits a written proposal.
  b) Negotiate contracts, terms and conditions for the consultancy.
  a) Recruit the consultant.

Ⓒ 🎧 **8.1**

◎ SS listen to the first part of the interview in more detail. Play the recording a second time, pausing in sections to allow SS time to write notes. Play any difficult sections a third time if necessary.

◎ SS check their answers in pairs. Circulate and deal with any queries SS have. If you can see that all SS have the correct answers, you may decide not to go through all the answers in open class, simply confirm that everyone has the correct answers and deal with the problem questions. This saves class time.

---

1 Five principles of SMART: is it (the project or task) **s**pecific, **m**easurable, **a**chievable, **r**elevant and **t**ime-limited?

2 The brief should include: (i) a description of the organisation – what it does and its size and structure; (ii) an explanation of the problem; (iii) what you want to achieve.

3 The consultant's proposal should include: (i) their understanding of the problem; (ii) any relevant experience of the consultancy firm; (iii) a work plan and schedule; (iv) the reports and any systems that will be supplied; (v) any input required by you / the client company.

4 A written contract should include (i) objectives; (ii) a brief; (iii) how and for how long the consultancy will be managed; (iv) fees; and (v) the deliverables (the consultant's report and any systems required by the client).

5 T&M (time and materials) contracts or fixed-price contracts.

6 If you are not happy with any aspects of the proposal, don't take them on. 'Make sure the chemistry is right.'

◎ You may want to refer SS to the audio script on page 169. It's often very useful for SS to listen and read the script. You may want to just listen to one part of the interview again, depending on the time available and SS's needs. Then ask SS to pick out a language area, such as ten words relating to consulting and projects. Don't spend too long going over the script in detail.

Ⓓ 🎧 **8.2**

◎ Ask SS to discuss the questions in pairs before listening.

◎ Play the second part of the recording, pausing in sections to allow time for SS to write their answers.

◎ SS compare their answers in pairs. Circulate and monitor, helping where necessary with vocabulary.

◎ Play the recording a second time for SS to check their answers.

◎ Go through the answers with the whole class, playing difficult sections a third time, if necessary.

---

1 You have to agree on several things: tasks to be done by your staff: short-term goals, milestones or long-term goals, deliverables, also regular meetings to discuss progress, problems, or whether the client's situation has changed.

2 So that they are informed about what the consultant is doing. It's crucial they feel they're part of the process.

3 In a report and followed by a presentation.
Ask the consultant to produce a first a draft of the report, and then discuss it with colleagues before the final report is written. The final report should contain no surprises. If there are very confidential issues, they can always be put in a private letter.

◎ You may want to refer SS to the audio script on page 169 before they do the next exercise.

Vocabulary: Managing consultancies

SS look at managing consultancy projects and use related vocabulary in context.

Ⓔ

◎ As a lead-in to the exercise, ask SS which of the words refer to (i) deadlines (*milestones*); (ii) what the consultancy has to hand over to the client (*deliverables*); and (iii) the project calendar schedule (*timescale*).

◎ Drill pronunciation of these terms, if necessary, highlighting word stress on the board. Elicit the first answer.

◎ Get SS to do the exercise individually before comparing in pairs. Tell SS them may look at the audio script on page 169 to check their answers, if they didn't do so at the end of the previous exercise.

◎ Circulate and monitor, helping where necessary with vocabulary.

◎ Bring the class together and go through the answers with the whole class. Deal with any questions SS may have.

---

1 specialist tasks; managerial performance   2 brief; fees
3 T&M   4 timescale   5 short-term; milestones
6 communication   7 deliverable

Discussion: Disadvantages of consultancies

SS talk about some of the disadvantages and criticisms of hiring consultants.

Ⓕ

◎ Encourage SS to make a connection between the line quoted in the first question and the opening quote for the unit.

◎ Get SS to discuss the questions in pairs or small groups.

◎ Circulate and monitor, encouraging SS particularly to talk about any personal experience of consultancy firms they may have. Make a note of five or six points for correction and points for praise.

◎ Call the class to order and go through the correction work and praise examples of good use of the language.

Suggested answers for question 3

1 Some consultants may talk using a lot of management buzzwords and clichés, but may not have the specialist knowledge the company is looking for. The consultant may be inexperienced in the industry/sector.

2 Despite being costly, the consultant's fees are not usually based on the success of the project; there is little or no guarantee the consultancy will be successful, depending on the contract negotiated and which party is assuming most risk.

3 The report is the most tangible deliverable, and the fee will not involve implementation unless it has been previously negotiated and included in the contract.

4 With so many consultancies in the market and increased competition, it is sometimes difficult to see how they differ from each other or what a consultancy's unique selling points or 'added value' may be. More prestigious consultancies may offer the same advice and services as cheaper, lesser-known ones.

5 Consultancies are given work based on the premise there is a problem with the company or the company requires a specialist service or task that they are unable to do in-house. Consultants are unlikely to turn down a possible contract, or they may find a problem in the way a company works, even if one does not exist in reality.

Discussion: Using consultants

SS discuss the use of consultancy firms and business sectors that spend the most money on consultants.

◎ Have SS do the exercise as a whole-class activity.

◎ Do not spend too long on the first question, as this forms part of the reading task.

◎ For the second question, you may like to ask SS to provide examples of popular consultancy firms in their country.

◎ For the third question, you may like to give SS the following information on consultancy spending in the UK:

In the UK in 2004, the spending on consultants was highest in the financial sector, closely followed by the public sector, then the communications industry. In fourth place was the utilities sector. Spending on consultancy by the retail industry increased and saw it become the fifth largest sector, closely followed by manufacturing. Once one of the most important sectors for consultants, manufacturing is no longer considered to be a major market.

Reading: *Could it be you when they need an expert?*

SS read an article on the benefits and drawbacks of becoming a consultant and the consultancy industry in general.

◎ As a lead-in to the article, ask SS:
Would you be interested in having a career in consultancy? Why (not)? (pre-work SS)
Would you be interested in working as consultants as a side-line to your present job? Why (not)? (in-work SS)

◎ You may also like to ask SS:
Do you think you would make a good consultant? Why (not)?
If so, what type of consultant would you be?

◎ Alternatively, see the Resource bank on page 227 as a warmer for this reading section.

◎ Get SS to read the whole article. Explain that the idea is to scan the article quickly for topics a–h. Tell SS they should ignore any words or phrases they don't know at this stage and focus on the task. In order to make this a quicker reading exercise, set a time limit. As a guideline, read through the text quickly, do the task and time yourself. Allow your SS about twice the time you needed to read and do the task – probably about four to five minutes.

◎ Ask SS for their initial reactions to the points made in the article before checking the answers to the questions. Did they predict correctly in question 1 of Exercise A?

◎ Go through the answers with the whole class.

---

a) Paragraph 5   b) Paragraphs 1, 3   c) Paragraph 3
d) Paragraphs 4, 6   e) Paragraphs 2, 8   f) Paragraph 9
g) Paragraph 8   h) Paragraphs 2, 6

◎ Ask SS follow-up questions, such as:
What other problems might consultancy firms sometimes have with clients? (The client might not take the advice of the consultant or might implement their recommendations incorrectly; there may be lack of support from the rest of management and resentment from other staff, etc.)
What do you understand by the expression 'high maintenance' in paragraph 4? (The client is very demanding.)

◎ Ask SS to give examples of successful or failed consultancy projects in their company:
Why do you think it was (un)successful?
What should your company do differently next time?
What should/shouldn't the consultant(s) have done?

©

◎ SS do the exercise individually, then compare in pairs.

◎ Alternatively, if time is short, or SS don't want to read the whole article again, then write the jumbled answers on the board along with a few distractors and get SS to complete the exercise using the words you have given them.

◎ Go through the answers with the whole class.

> 1 leading player(s)   2 money spinner(s)   3 back office
> 4 keep up with   5 fee   6 tout(ing) for   7 take/taking on
> 8 pare(d) back   9 in-house   10 get (got) off the ground

◎ As a follow-up exercise, ask SS for synonyms and words that are similar in meaning to some of the vocabulary items, e.g. *leading player* (key player/market leaders), *take on* (recruit or hire), *pare back* (cut back/down-sized/cut costs), *in-house* (in-company), *get off the ground* (start a venture or project). This is a good way for SS to extend and recycle their vocabulary.

Language review: Negation using prefixes/Conditionals

SS look at negation using prefixes (in the context of the reading) and conditionals (as an optional activity in the Grammar reference).

Ⓓ

◎ As a lead-in to this section, refer SS to Exercise D and paragraph 5 of the article. Do this question with the whole class.

◎ Write the sentence on the board and highlight the answers.

> unregulated, inexperienced, substandard

◎ Ask SS which other negative prefixes they know and ask for examples of adjectives using prefixes for negation (e.g. *illegal, imperfect, dissatisfied, misleading, irregular, overqualified,* etc.). Elicit from SS possible spelling patterns: that with certain prefixes, double consonants may occur, e.g. *illegal, irregular, dissatisfied,* etc. Point out that hyphens are not usually used with most adjectives, verbs and nouns, although they may be used with some prefixes, e.g. *misconduct, deregulation,* but *anti-riot police* and *non-executive director*.

Ⓔ

◎ Get SS to read the short extract on psychometric testing and get their initial reactions to the text.

◎ Ask SS to do the exercise individually. Circulate and confirm answers where SS are having difficulties.

◎ Get early finishers to compare their answers with a partner.

◎ Go through the answers with the whole class.

> 1 overused; unnecessary   2 inaccurate; misleading
> 3 incompetent   4 irrelevant; impossible   5 unreliable

◎ As a follow-up, ask SS to write five sentences using adjectives with negative prefixes.

 Grammar reference: Negation using prefixes page 127; Conditionals page 128

◎ For further practice on negation using prefixes, refer SS to the Grammar reference on page 128.

> 1 misinformed   2 dissatisfied   3 inconvenient
> 4 misused   5 non-core   6 discontinued
> 7 misinterpreted   8 unloading   9 illegible
> 10 incompatible   11 misleading   12 deregulated

◎ For revision of conditional forms, refer SS to the Grammar reference on page 129.

> 1 e   Third conditional, describing a hypothetical situation in the past
> 2 a   Second conditional, making a polite request
> 3 f   Second conditional with inversion, emphasising that something is unlikely to happen
> 4 d   Third conditional with inversion, expressing complaint or criticism about a past action or event
> 5 b   First conditional, stating a necessary condition
> 6 c   First conditional, giving a warning

Negotiating sales

SS listen to a sales manager giving a training session on sales negotiations, look at some negotiating tips for making concessions and do a role-play to negotiate a car deal for their company.

Ⓐ

◎ As a lead-in to this section, use this quote.
My father said: 'You must never try to make all the money that's in a ....[1]. Let the other fellow make some ....[2] too, because if you have a reputation for always ....[3] all the money, you won't have many ....[4].'
(J. Paul Getty)

◎ Write the quote with the gaps on the board and ask SS to guess the words that are missing.

> 1 deal   2 money   3 making   4 deals

◎ Then ask SS's initial reaction to the quote. Alternatively, ask SS about situations when they need to negotiate. Pre-work SS may talk about situations at home, with friends or family, etc.
What do you negotiate? Where? Who with?
In what situations do you negotiate in English?
Do you enjoy negotiating? Why (not)?
Have you ever done any training in negotiating? What did you learn? Was it useful?
Have you ever read any books on negotiation? If so, which ones? Would you recommend them?

◎ Get SS to look at the cartoon on page 74. Ask SS which grammar structure we often use when negotiating (conditionals). Ask SS to identify the conditional in the caption (the first conditional).

◎ Do Exercise A as a quick-fire activity with the whole class.

> **1** c **2** d **3** a **4** b

◎ Go through initial reactions to the sentences with the whole class. Ask SS if they are aware of any other negotiating skills or techniques (e.g. bluffing or pretending; checking facts and figures etc.).

Ⓑ 🎧 8.3

◎ Get SS to read the tips and say whether they think they are true or false before they listen.

◎ Play the recording once and get SS to mark their answers individually, pausing in sections, if necessary.

◎ SS compare answers in pairs. It shouldn't be necessary to play the recording a second time at this stage.

◎ Go through the answers with the whole class.

> **1** False **2** False **3** True **4** False **5** True **6** True **7** True

◎ Refer SS to the audio script on pages 169–170. You may like to play the recording a second time whilst SS read the script, underlining or noting the terms and expressions used in the exercise.

Ⓒ

◎ Refer SS to the expressions used in the box in Exercise C.

◎ Get SS to complete the tips for making concessions without listening to the recording again.

◎ SS compare their answers in pairs.

◎ Go through the answers with the whole class.

> **1** big concession **2** one by one **3** some sort of compensation **4** understands its full value **5** you are giving one **6** willing to make concessions **7** 'take-it-or-leave-it'; ill-will **8** walk away from the negotiation

◎ As a follow-up activity, get SS to discuss their reactions to these tips in groups of three or four. Ask SS:
Do you find theses tips useful? Why (not)?
What other tips would you like to add?

◎ Go through feedback with the whole class. There are no right or wrong answers to this activity, and SS's reactions will depend on their professional experience and cultural background. Be aware that some SS may feel uncomfortable with the 'aggressive' techniques of American-style negotiating.

Ⓓ

◎ As a lead-in to this activity, ask SS the following questions:
When was the last time you bought something which you had to bargain for (e.g. a house or flat, an antique or painting, food produce in a local market, or a holiday souvenir)?
What happened? How much did you pay? Was it a good price?

Who ended up making most concessions? You or the seller? Did you or the seller use any of the previous negotiating techniques?

◎ Explain to SS that they are going to do a role-play, using some of the techniques from the previous exercise. You may want to refer SS to the previous negotiating expressions on page 26 of the Course Book (Exercise B).

◎ Divide SS into pairs. SS A and SS B look at their corresponding information on pages 146 and 153. Ask SS to take notes before they start the role-play. This preparation time is very important if SS are to perform the task successfully.

◎ Monitor and circulate round the class as SS act out the role-plays. Make a note of SS who carry out the task successfully, any useful language used and five or six language points for correction, including pronunciation. Write up any errors on the board.

◎ Earlier finishers can be referred to the board to see if they can correct the errors.

◎ Time permitting, ask SS to repeat the task, swapping role-play information and, possibly, with different partners.

◎ Go through feedback with the whole class, praising appropriate language for negotiating and techniques used. Note there are no right/wrong outcomes for this activity, but a good measure for a successful negotiation is the 'win-win' scenario. Are both parties happy with the outcome? If not, and if peer correction is appropriate in your setting, you may like SS to repeat the negotiation, with another pair observing and making notes. Be aware, however, that SS in-work may have their own preferred style of negotiation. Drill pronunciation of any difficult expressions if necessary. Write up any language points that need further work on the board.

◎ For follow-up practice, go to the Resource bank on page 227.

◎ If SS are interested in finding out more on negotiation, refer them to this reading list:
Roger Fisher, William Ury, Bruce Patton: *Getting to yes: the secret to successful negotiation*, Random House Business Books, 2003
Howard Raiffa: *The art and science of negotiation*, Harvard University Press, 1985
Michael Watkins: *Negotiation,* Harvard Business Essentials, Harvard Business School Press, 2003

Writing: Terms and conditions

SS write up the terms and conditions agreed in the previous sales negotiation.

Ⓔ

◎ As a lead-in to this writing section, ask SS what kind of written terms and conditions they generally receive or write.

◎ Refer SS to the Useful language box. Deal with any questions they may have.

- SS write the e-mails confirming the terms and conditions agreed upon according to the previous role-play. Circulate and monitor, helping SS whilst they write with language used for confirming terms and conditions. Make a note of any useful expressions used and five or six points for correction on the board.

 Writing file page 137

- Earlier finishers can be referred to the board to see if they know all the expressions and if they can correct the errors.
- Alternatively, this writing task could be set for homework.

(F)

- SS compare their e-mails in pairs. Were the terms and conditions described the same? Were there any differences? Were any points omitted? What phrases did they both use?
- If peer correction is appropriate in your setting, SS could also be asked to proofread each others' writing task and point out any spelling mistakes or grammatical errors they spot. Be on hand to help with this if necessary, but leave most of the feedback and discussion to SS. If necessary, change the pairs around and repeat the process.
- Go through feedback with the whole class, praising good examples of language and style and pointing out five or six areas that need further work.

Case study: Mobi-net: it's their call

SS study proposals from two consultancy firms for Mobi-net, a mobile service provider based in Austria that needs to keep a lead in the competitive mobile-phone market. SS negotiate with both consultancies and write a summary of the terms agreed with the preferred consultancy.

- In class, pay particular attention to clearly breaking down the case study into the different tasks and making sure that SS understand and follow the structure of what you are doing.

Background

- Get SS to focus on the photo of the skier. As a lead-in, ask SS:
  What is she doing? (texting on a mobile phone from a ski station)
  How dependent are you on your mobile phone?
  What mobile service providers do you use?
  Which are the main mobile phone companies in your country?
  Which one(s) offer the best services and deals for customers?
  Which ones have the most aggressive sales tactics (e.g. phoning potential customers, door-to-door sales people, etc.)?

- It is not necessary to spend a long time on this discussion, but use it to highlight the competition in the industry.
- Get SS to study the background information in the Course Book.
- Write the following headings from the left-hand column of the table and elicit information from SS to complete the right-hand column. Deal with any questions they may have.

Company	Mobi-net
Purpose	Mobile service provider
Industry	Mobile/telecommunications
Markets	Austria, Slovenia and Croatia
Problem	Increased competition, demand for convergence of Internet and mobile industries; needs to keep the lead in the Austrian market.
Task	Find a consultancy with mobile and IT know-how to improve processes and services to Mobi-net's customers; maintain position as a market leader.

Task 1

- Refer SS to Task 1. Explain they will first have to study two proposals from competing consultancy firms. Ask SS to note the differences, making a list of each of the consultancy's strengths and the recommendations they propose.
- Write up on the board the name of each consultancy and a subheading for each for its strengths and recommendations.
- SS A look at the proposal from Performance Consulting on page 77, and SS B study the proposal from Unicorn Consulting on page 154. With larger classes, SS may work in pairs and exchange information in groups of four.
- Get SS's initial reaction to the proposals.
- Ask SS to summarise in their own words the proposals they have read and listen to the summary that their partner gives. SS make a note of the strengths and recommendations of the competing consultancies. Circulate and monitor, helping SS with the task, pointing out relevant sections in the texts, where necessary.
- Go through the answers with the whole class, writing up the strengths and recommendations of each consultancy on the board.

Lesson notes

Suggested answers

Performance Consulting (UK firm)

Strengths

◎ Is a more established consultancy with ten years' experience.

◎ Specialises in strategy and mobile telecommunications.

◎ Is a member of the Association of Management Consultancy (AMC).

Recommendations

◎ 'Family and friends' pricing package for subscribers.

◎ Centralisation of the call centre.

◎ Training for both customer service staff and management.

Unicorn Consulting (US-Austrian firm)

Strengths

◎ Is a US-Austrian firm and should therefore know the market well.

◎ Is a young consultancy with only five years' experience.

◎ Specialises in IT consulting.

◎ Offers quality and 'fair prices'.

Recommendations

◎ Installing a unified desktop/interface in the call centre.

◎ Competitive pricing package designed for young people (12–18-year-olds).

◎ A strategic alliance with an Eastern European partner.

◎ Ask SS which consultancy they think should win the contract with Mobi-net. A quick show of hands should be enough. There is no right answer to this question at this stage. SS may or may not reach a consensus about the best proposal. Use any discussion of the questions as a lead-in to the listening section.

Listening 🎧 8.4

◎ Refer SS to the listening task. Ask them to try and predict some of the problems the mobile phone company is experiencing. SS should be able to predict from having read the background that Mobi-net is looking for a consultancy with knowledge of the mobile industry and with IT expertise; that they are looking to improve their processes and services; and that they want to maintain their position as a leader in the Austrian market, as competition in the industry is tough. Don't reject any ideas at this stage or give the answers away before SS listen.

◎ SS listen. In pairs, they compare ideas. If necessary, play the recording a second time. Go through the points with the whole class.

◎ Discuss their initial reactions to the problem. Do they think Performance Consulting is a suitable candidate? Why (not)? SS may argue that Andrew from Performance Consulting doesn't convince Cristoph Kahnwald of Mobi-net that theirs is the best consultancy, as the MD thinks they charge too much, and Andrew hasn't looked into possible partners yet for Mobi-net. SS might also add that the MD sounds stressed out and that Mobi-net could be a 'high-maintenance' customer.

◎ Go through the answers with the whole class, referring SS to the audio script on page 170, if necessary.

1 Mobi-net wishes to maintain its position in the market (by differentiation); mobile services must remain distinctive.

2 Mobi-net needs to maintain its reputation for customer problem-solving, although customer service needs to be more efficient and cost-effective.

3 Mobi-net is looking for a strategic alliance / partner or acquisition (in order to develop their product portfolio).

4 Mobi-net also wants a consultancy with the right expertise and know-how in IT.

Task 2

◎ Divide SS in groups of three or four. Explain that in this role-play, Mobi-net has to negotiate the best deal with one of the consultancies. Get SS to look at their role-play information in the Activity file (pages 147, 154 and 157). Make sure SS have time to make notes and deal with any questions they may have before they begin the negotiation. Tell SS representing Mobi-net that they will have to negotiate the best deal for their company, which includes the consultancy's solution, fees and terms and conditions. Write these three points up on the board, if necessary.

◎ If SS are working in groups of four, Student A negotiates with Student C, and Student B negotiates with a different Student C. After the task, both SS C, who represent Mobi-net, will discuss which is the best deal for the company.

◎ If SS are working in groups of three, one of them takes the role of a consultant (A) and the other two SS the role of Mobi-net (C). SS then repeat the task with one of the SS taking the role of Student B.

◎ Circulate and monitor, checking SS are carrying out the task correctly. Make a note of any good negotiating expressions being used and five or six common errors for correction, including pronunciation, for later feedback.

◎ Bring the class to order.

◎ If SS are working in groups of four, ask SS C to discuss which is the best consultancy and give reasons for their choice. SS A and B meanwhile can compare what they negotiated with the client.

◎ If SS are working in groups of three, ask both SS C to confer and choose the best deal. The other student (A/B) may listen and take notes.

◎ Circulate and monitor, checking SS are completing the task correctly. Make a note of useful expressions being used and write up some common errors for correction on the board for later feedback.

◎ Early finishers may correct the errors on the board.

◎ When SS have finished the second part of the task, bring the whole class to order.

Feedback

◎ Ask for a quick show of hands to find out which consultancy was chosen by the majority of SS representing Mobi-net. Ask one or two groups to say what happened in their groups and to give reasons for their choice.

◎ Praise the strong language points and work on five or six points that need improvement, especially in relation to language used for negotiating and consulting.

◎ To round off the activity, you may want to read out or photocopy the following information for SS.

Mobi-net's choice of consultancy

Performance Consulting has the necessary strategic experience and a more established reputation. Although they are more expensive, they can offer junior consultants at a reduced rate, but will need four months for the project. Their proposal for staff training may not appeal to Mobi-net, as the client has already spent money in this area. However, their recommendation to centralise the call centre may be an effective solution to their customer-service problem, despite possible resistance from the Head of Customer Service.

Unicorn Consulting is a less established firm, but is probably cheaper and seems to have more IT know-how. Their proposal for a unified desktop/interface for the call centre sounds like a practical IT solution. They may have less experienced consultants, but the firm can start immediately. They also appear to have more knowledge of the Eastern European markets than Performance Consulting, which may prove valuable when finding potential partners.

◎ There is no right answer to the negotiation, as Mobi-net's final choice will depend on the deal (the consultancy's solution, fees and conditions) that SS managed to negotiate. However, Unicorn Consulting is possibly the best option for Mobi-net because of their IT expertise, their knowledge of the Eastern European market and because their prices may be lower.

Writing

◎ Refer SS to the writing task and deal with any questions they may have.

◎ Brainstorm the information that should go in the e-mail and put these points on the board. All this information has come up in listening and role-plays in Tasks 1 and 2.

◎ Write up on the board the following four points to consider when writing the summary:

◎ Project brief (the needs of the client)
◎ Consultancy's proposal (the solution and recommendations)
◎ Terms and conditions of the project (contractual agreement, milestones and timescale)
◎ Consultancy's fees

◎ Ask SS to look at the Useful language box on page 75 again.

◎ Get SS to write in pairs or individually, depending on how the role-play was conducted.

Writing file page 137

◎ Circulate and monitor, checking SS are completing the task correctly.

◎ This could probably be quite a long summary if SS include all the points agreed upon in the negotiation. Alternatively, set this summary writing task for homework.

◎ For early finishers, or as an extra activity, SS compare each others' summaries to check if they contain all the main points agreed upon in the negotiation.

---

1 to 1

◎ Go through the information in the Course Book with your student. Explain any difficulties. In Task 1, you and your student are SS A and B. Don't dominate the conversation in this task, but say enough to keep it going and allow your student to summarise the proposal and ask you questions.

◎ In Task 2, you are Student A and take the role of a consultant from Performance Consulting, and your student is Student C and represents Mobi-net. Then repeat Task 2: you are now Student B, taking the role of a consultant from Unicorn Consulting, and your student is still Student C. Your student then decides on the best deal negotiated.

◎ At the same time, monitor the language that your student is using. Note down any good examples of language and points for error correction or improvement. Come back to these later.

◎ Praise any good examples of language used and go over any errors, including pronunciation. Record the role-play on cassette or video, if desirable, as this increases the challenge for the student and is useful for giving intensive feedback on your student's particular strengths and weaknesses.

Strategy

At a glance

	Classwork – Course Book	Further work
Lesson 1: **Listening and discussion** (page 78–79) *Each lesson is about 60–75 minutes. This time does not include administration and time spent going through homework in any lessons.*	**Discussion: Company strategy** SS are encouraged to discuss the concepts of strategy, vision and mission and to talk about the strategy process in (their) companies. **Listening: 'Fast fashion' and the challenges of long-term strategies** Josep Valor-Sabatier from IESE Business School in Barcelona talks about the strategy of clothing retailers such as Zara, then describes the measures of success and the challenges for companies of implementing their long-term strategies. **Vocabulary: Strategy and growth** SS look at and use vocabulary related to strategy and growth in context. **Discussion: Quotes on strategy** SS talk about companies who are 'successful imitators' and discuss some quotes on the strategies of some successful companies.	**Practice File** Word power (pages 52–53)
Lesson 2: **Reading and language** (page 80–81) *Each lesson is about 60–75 minutes.*	**Reading: *Growth mode*** SS read about the challenges for companies of finding new growth opportunities and give examples of growth strategies that went wrong. **Vocabulary: Market growth** SS look at and use vocabulary related to growth in context. **Discussion: Growth crisis** SS discuss the growth crisis, core business and adjacencies. **Language review: Idioms for giving examples** SS look at idioms for giving examples.	**Text bank** (TRB pages 188–191) **Grammar reference and practice** (CB page 130) **Practice File** Text and grammar (pages 54–55)
Lesson 3: **Business skills** (page 82–83) *Each lesson is about 75–90 minutes.*	**Brainstorming and creativity** SS discuss some quotes on creativity in the context of business ideas, listen to a trainer discussing brainstorming techniques, then brainstorm marketing strategies for a clothing retailer that is experiencing difficulties. **Writing: Mission statements** SS brainstorm ideas and write a mission statement for their company or organisation.	**Resource bank** (TRB page 228) **Writing file** (CB page 140) **Practice File** Skills and pronunciation (pages 56–57)
Lesson 4: **Case study** (page 84–85) *Each lesson is about 75–90 minutes.*	**The company makeover** Hazel is a multinational seller of cosmetic and beauty products that is in need of an overhaul. Hazel's sales are declining and its products have little appeal for younger women. SS listen to a presentation from the new CEO, hold a meeting to devise a new strategic vision in order to boost growth and write a summary of their proposals.	**Writing file** (CB pages 138–139)

For a fast route through the unit, focusing mainly on speaking skills, just use the underlined sections.

For one-to-one situations, most parts of the unit lend themselves, with minimal adaptation, to use with individual students. Where this is not the case, alternative procedures are given.

Business brief

Strategy is an outline of how a business intends to achieve its **goals**. The goals are the **objective**; the strategy sets out the **route** to that objective. In the early stages, business objectives are usually fairly simple: to **survive** and to achieve **growth targets**. Strategies are correspondingly simple, and are often not even committed to paper; it is enough that everyone in the company understands where it is going and how it will get there. But as the business grows, so does the need for co-ordination. Everyone in the business contributes to the execution of the strategy in some way.

Many managers believe that the key to successful leadership (and a successful strategy) is articulating a long-term **vision**, sometimes known as a **'mission statement'**, **'strategic intent'** or **'corporate purpose'**. This is a long-term view of what a company should be doing and where it should be going.

The mission statement should be clear and understood by everyone in the organisation. Professor Donald Sull from the London Business School suggests these three steps for setting out a company's vision:

1   Specify the **industry domain**: a long-term vision should define where the company competes. This helps managers and employees to sort opportunities in their domain from those that distract them from their **core business**.
2   Specify **geographic scope**: does a company consider itself local, national, regional or global?
3   Set **aspirations**: many companies state this in terms of **global leadership** or **excellence**. The problem, of course, is that most companies aspire to 'being number one or number two'.

Long-term visions offer certain advantages. They give an organisation a **shared sense of direction** and can motivate people to achieve the vision. Professor Sull, however, believes that too much vision can result in managers becoming fixated on a long-term goal rather than concentrating on the here and now. Take, for example, Microsoft's early vision of a world with 'a computer on every desk and in every home, running Microsoft software'. It was a vision that blinded the company to the early potential of the Internet.

Management thinkers tend to fall into one of two camps, according to Simon London of the *Financial Times*: **strategists**, who believe that most companies fail because they try to sell the wrong products to the wrong customers at the wrong price; and **pragmatists**, who see business failure as mainly the result of **poor execution**: **missed sales targets**, **poor-quality products** and **tactical errors**. The best managers have the mental agility to deal with both the **strategic** and **operational issues**.

Experts also say that television and Internet media have allowed advertisers to address **precise market segments**. This can actually reduce competition between companies by enabling them to concentrate on distinct **sub-markets**. Yet **fragmentation** increases the complexity of advertising. It also makes it necessary for companies to think hard about their **value proposition,** which is the essence of strategy.

Nicholas Carr, author at the *Harvard Business Review*, looks at **competitive advantage** from the viewpoint of information technology. He argues that IT has become so diffused through the economy that it is no longer a **source of differentiation**; technology is now a cost of doing business. This challenges managers to think again about **adding value** in ways that are difficult for competitors to replicate.

Strategy and your students

In-work students will be able to discuss strategy and growth, vision and mission statements in the context of their own companies and organisations and competitors. Pre-work students may have knowledge of strategies concerning marketing, pricing and 'fast fashion' of high-street retailers such as Zara, Benetton, Gap, etc. They can also talk about the vision and purpose of the organisations where they study.

All students will have general world experience of successful and unsuccessful companies, and what makes the most successful companies different from their competitors. It may also be appropriate for both types of student to discuss the ideas of certain influential management writers, such as those listed here.

Read on

Jim Collins: *Good to great*, Random House Business Books, 2001

Peter Drucker: *The essential Drucker: the best of sixty years of Peter Drucker's essential writings on management*, HarperCollins, 2003

Henry Mintzberg: *The rise and fall of strategic planning*, Financial Times Prentice Hall, 2000

Henry Mintzberg, Bruce Ahlstrand, Joseph B. Lampel: *Strategy bites back*, Financial Times Prentice Hall, 2004

Kevan Scholes, Gerry Johnson, Richard Whittington: *Exploring corporate strategy: text and cases*, FT Prentice Hall, 2004

Lesson notes

Warmer

- Ask SS to brainstorm some very successful companies and write SS's ideas up on the board. Then ask SS to discuss in pairs or small groups why they think these companies have been so successful and what were their differentiating factors compared to other companies in their industry or sector. SS's answers will depend on the companies they choose, but they may come up with some of the following factors: innovation, new technologies, corporate values, leadership, pricing/marketing/growth/organisational strategies, etc. Go through feedback with the whole class.

- Alternatively, ask SS what they understand by the title of the unit, 'Strategy' (a plan or series of plans for achieving an aim, especially success in business, or the best way for an organisation to develop in the future, *Longman Business English Dictionary*; see the Text bank reading, 'Plan to think strategically' on page 188 for an alternative definition).

- As always, with more complex topics such as this one, or with pre-work SS, you may choose to give SS the Business brief on page 103, getting them to look at it for homework before the first class on this unit.

Overview

- Tell SS that they will be looking at strategy and growth in this unit.

- Go through the overview panel at the beginning of the unit, pointing out the sections that SS will be looking at.

Quotation

- Get SS to look at the quotation and ask them what they think it means. (The idea is that it is easy to predict something is going to happen or needs to happen, but the issue is how you are going to make this happen. Or, in a business context, it is obvious that a company needs to survive and achieve its growth targets but the question is *how* it is going to achieve these goals.)

Discussion: Company strategy

SS are encouraged to discuss the concepts of strategy, vision and mission and talk about the strategy process in (their) companies.

- SS work in pairs to discuss the questions. Set a three-minute time limit for this. Then get SS's feedback as a whole class. Help them with vocabulary on strategy in English (see the Business brief on page 103). It is not necessary to spend too long on this, as it forms part of the listening section.

Suggested answers

1 It's very important to look beyond immediate circumstances, clarifying where the company wants to be in the future. The mission and vision of the company are part of its overall strategy, as is getting to know customers, the market and the competition.

2 Strategic meetings for multinationals may be as often as every quarter. Microsoft have come up with an innovative solution. They have used a sort of 'strategy slam' process to make sure strategies get mapped and adapted quickly. They identify a group of 20 or 30 people most capable of contributing to the strategy of a new initiative and literally lock them in a room for 48 hours with a skilled facilitator. The only ground rule: a comprehensive strategy and detailed action plan that the entire team will endorse must be delivered on the 48th hour.

3 Strategic goals are generally developed by top management, but increasingly the responsibility is being shared by lower-level management and operations people, i.e. people closest to the market. Some might argue it is best if the CEO or company chairman is not present at meetings where strategic goals are being discussed or reviewed, so that participants feel less inhibited.

4 If a company wants to enter new markets, it may come up with completely new products/services, and innovation will be a key factor. However, if its products/services are very similar to those of its competitors, it will need to distinguish itself with differentiation factors such as quality, pricing or customer service, and 'adding value' will be key. A company may gain a competitive advantage by becoming a fast copier/follower, imitating the market leaders (see Listening), usually at a much lower price.

Listening: 'Fast fashion' and the challenges of long-term strategies

SS listen to Josep Valor-Sabatier from IESE Business School in Barcelona. In the first part of the interview, he talks about the 'fast fashion' strategy of clothing retailers such as Zara (Inditex group). In the second part, he describes the measures of success and the challenges for companies of implementing their long-term strategies.

(B) 🎧 9.1

- Ask SS if they are familiar with the Spanish retailer Zara.

- Get SS to work in pairs, look through the questions and try to predict the correct answers before they listen.

- Play the first part of the interview, pausing in sections, if necessary.

◎ SS check their answers in pairs; replay any difficult sections for them, referring them to the audio script on page 170.

◎ SS check their answers in pairs. Circulate and deal with any queries SS have. If you can see that they all have the correct answers, you may decide not to go through all the answers in open class; simply confirm for the class that everyone has the correct answers and deal with any problems.

---

1 b   **2** a   **3** a   **4** b   **5** b

◎ As a follow-up, and if SS are interested in fashion retail, you could ask the SS whether they buy from Zara, Benetton, H&M or similar fashion retailers in their country, and how these companies differentiate from each other in quality and design of product, price, target markets, e.g. teenagers or older customers, location of stores, etc. The Swedish retailer H&M, for example, sells at very low prices, but have occasionally employed well-known designers, like Stella McCartney to create designer collections at affordable prices. These collections have sold out within an hour of the stores opening and have helped to improve the company's image.

◎ Ask SS if their home country fashion retailers mass-produce in China or similar countries.

Ⓒ 🎧 9.2

◎ Get SS to look through the questions individually. Explain that they will have to listen to the general meaning of the interview, rather than listening for specific words and phrases.

◎ Play the second part of the interview, pausing in sections to give SS time to write their answers.

◎ After listening, SS compare notes in pairs. Circulate and monitor, helping SS where necessary. Point out that sometimes more than one answer is possible, as with questions 2 and 4.

◎ Replay the recording.

◎ Go through the answers with the whole class, playing the recording a third time in sections, if necessary.

Suggested answers
1 The success of a company can be measured either by its **sales and profits or (profit) margins.**
2 According to Professor Valor-Sabatier, companies need to concentrate on both **mission and vision and defining the measures of success / long-term and short-term goals.**
3 When implementing long-term strategies, it's easier to **convince an owner than to convince the stock market.**
4 When measuring success, the stock market tends to focus more on **short-term goals and profitability / quarterly profits.**
5 It's very difficult to change a company's strategies because of the conflict between **short-term gains and long-term goals.**
6 Good strategic management consists of taking a company in the right direction for the future, whilst **maintaining short-term profitability.**

◎ You may want to refer SS to the audio script on page 170. It's often very useful for SS to listen and read the script. You may want to just listen to one part of the interview again, depending on the time available and SS's needs. Don't spend too long going over the script in detail, as this forms part of the next exercise.

Vocabulary: Strategy and growth

SS look at and use vocabulary related to strategy and growth in context.

Ⓓ

◎ Elicit the answer to the first question as an example, then get SS to do the rest of the exercise individually, referring to the audio scripts on pages 170–171 where necessary.

◎ SS check their answers in pairs.

◎ Go through the answers with the whole class.

---

1 reinvented   **2** newcomer   **3** mass-produce
4 market follower   **5** innovate   **6** bottom line   **7** margin
8 profitability

◎ Deal with any other vocabulary questions the SS had on reading the audio scripts.

Discussion: Quotes on strategy

SS talk about companies who are 'successful imitators' and discuss some quotes on the strategies of some successful companies.

Ⓔ

◎ Refer SS to the cartoon on page 79 and ask the SS what it means. (The idea is that although companies and their marketing departments may collect a great deal of data about their customers, they may not know what to do with this information; the big question after market research and analysis is, How do you implement the right strategies to ensure further sales and growth?)

◎ Get SS to discuss the questions in pairs or small groups. SS's answers will largely depend on their experience of and personal interest in the companies mentioned. SS may say that:
– the computer manufacturer Dell has achieved growth through its system of direct sales and emphasis on customer service;
– Airbus has a track record for quality and safety as well as profitability;
– Campbell's has also developed worldwide brand recognition since 1869 as the world's largest soup manufacturer, with a presence in 120 countries, despite competition from, often cheaper, competitors;
– McDonald's is another prime example of globalisation, despite criticism of American fast-food nutritional content, especially for children, and controversy surrounding BSC ('mad cow disease'), as it has managed to enter emerging markets such as Brazil, Russia, India and China.

◉ Circulate and monitor, helping where necessary with vocabulary. Make a note of any useful language used and three or four points for correction.

◉ For early finishers, or as a follow-up question to question 2, you may want to ask SS: To what extent do you think innovation is more or less important than other aspects of strategy? As a follow-up to question 3, you may like to ask SS: How important is 'business genius' and courage when it comes to making a company successful?

◉ You may also like to make reference at some point in the discussion to some well-known world business leaders, for example Jack Welsh (General Electric), Bill Gates (Microsoft), Carlos Ghosn (Nissan/Renault), Steve Jobs (Apple), John Browne (BP), Hiroshi Okuda (former chairman of Toyota), Lindsay Owen-Jones (L'Oréal), Dieter Zetsche (Mercedes), Heinrich von Pierer (Siemens), Michael O'Leary (Ryanair), José María Castellanos (former vice president of Inditex/Zara) and up-and-coming leaders such as Zhang Ruimin (Haier) in China.

◉ Bring the class together and encourage SS particularly to talk about the (un)successful strategies of companies they know. Go through feedback with the whole class, praising appropriate language for talking about strategy. Write up any points that need further work on the board.

◉ If appropriate in your setting, you could encourage SS to research all or some of the companies mentioned in question 2 on the Internet. Alternatively, if SS are interested in finding out more about these companies, refer them to the following websites:
www.airbus.com/en
www.dell.com
www.campbellsoup.com
www.mcdonalds.com

Reading: *Growth mode*

SS read about the challenges for companies of finding new growth opportunities and give examples of growth strategies that went wrong.

◉ Write the names of all or some of these companies on the board: GE (General Electric), Microsoft, Coca-Cola, Nissan, BA, McDonald's, IBM, Apple.

◉ Tell SS these companies have been commended for their turnaround ability and successful strategies.

◉ Ask SS to match the companies to the following comments. Do this as a quick-fire activity. Read out the comments, while SS match the companies. SS may either say the names or write them down.
  1 The best turnaround in the car industry, with constant cost reductions and restructuring.
  2 Constant innovation and their success of iPod and iTunes.
  3 A perfect transformation from selling computers to selling services.
  4 Quality of products and handling of the transition from long-serving leader, Jack Welch, to its current chief executive.

5 Its market dominance: a very innovative company that touches almost everything in our lives with a strong base and employee satisfaction.
6 Turning a loss into a profit; they hit a bad time and pulled together.
7 Its ability to attract customers through its effective commercials and strong brand power.
8 Reacting fast in the war around fat consumption.

◉ Go through the answers with the whole class.

---

1 Nissan   **2** Apple   **3** IBM   **4** GE   **5** Microsoft   **6** BA
7 Coca-Cola   **8** McDonald's

◉ You may like to tell SS that these comments came from a report by the *Financial Times* on the Most Respected Companies in 2005 and that Nissan, Apple and IBM were the top three in the turnaround category.

◉ As a follow-up activity, divide SS into pairs or small groups. SS discuss the attributes of the various companies, then compile their own list of companies they admire most, either using the companies given, or other companies they know.

Ⓐ

◉ As a warmer for this section, get SS to look at the photos. Ask them to identify the company logos and tell you what they know about the companies (Giorgio Armani, the designer clothes label, and Swissair, an airline). Don't reject any ideas about further details of the companies at this stage, as this forms part of the reading task.

◉ As a lead-in to the article, ask SS what is meant by the sub-heading, *Finding new ways to grow a company in today's tough climate isn't easy* (it's difficult to expand a company or achieve growth targets because of fierce competition/the state of the economy etc. in the business world today).

◉ Ask SS to do the exercise individually and say whether the companies are examples of a successful or failed growth strategy. Explain that the idea is to scan the article quickly for this information. Tell SS they should ignore any words or phrases they don't know at this stage and focus on the task. In order to make this a quicker reading exercise, set a time limit. As a guideline, read through the text quickly, do the task and time yourself. Then allow your SS about twice the time you needed to read and do the task. SS will probably need about four or five minutes.

◉ Go through the answers with the whole class. Ask SS for their initial reactions to the points made in the article before doing Exercise B.

Logitech: a mouse and computer peripheral manufacturer (successful growth strategy)

Giorgio Armani: a designer clothes label (successful growth strategy)

Accor: a budget hotel chain (successful growth strategy)

Swissair: an airline (failed growth strategy)

Marconi: a defence and electronics conglomerate (failed growth strategy)

(B)

◎ Get SS to read the whole article again, pointing out that the paragraphs are numbered.

◎ If someone asks a question, throw it open to the whole class to find out if someone else can provide an explanation. If not, explain where necessary.

◎ Circulate and confirm answers or indicate in which sentence a word or expression occurs where SS are having difficulties. Get early finishers to compare their answers.

◎ If short of time, divide the class into pairs and ask SS A to do items 1–4 (paragraphs 1–4) and SS B, items 5–9 (paragraphs 5–9). SS then exchange answers.

◎ Go through the answers with the whole class.

---

1 the usual methods of achieving growth are almost exhausted
2 most companies' growth levels are unlikely to reach 10%
3 growth of twice their industry rate and earnings four times higher
4 Logitech, Armani, Accor
5 their ability to move into sectors adjacent to their core business
6 buying smaller airlines, an airline caterer and an airline retailer
7 the company's financial problems
8 to go into the telecoms industry
9 the company serious financial problems (which it hasn't fully recovered from today)

◎ Ask SS the follow-up question: Which other national companies in your country are doing well or are experiencing difficulty with growth at the moment? Encourage SS to talk about different business sectors, as in the article.

Vocabulary: Market growth

SS look at and use vocabulary related to growth in context.

(C)

◎ Explain the following two exercises will deal with vocabulary related to growth.

◎ Get SS to do Exercise C individually.

◎ Circulate and confirm answers or indicate in which sentence a word or expression occurs where SS are having difficulties. Get early finishers to compare their answers.

◎ Go through the answers with the whole class. Drill pronunciation of these words, if necessary highlighting word stress on the board. Elicit the first answer.

◎ Go through SS's ideas with the whole class, asking everyone to give their explanations of the meanings and find out if the rest of the class agrees.

---

1 f   2 d   3 e   4 g   5 b   6 j   7 i   8 c   9 a   10 h

(D)

◎ Ask SS for the answer to item 1, then get them to do the rest of the exercise individually. SS compare in pairs, then go through the answers with the whole class.

◎ Alternatively, if time is short, write the jumbled answers on the board along with a few distractors (e.g. *adjacency* and *wholesaler*) and get SS to complete the exercise using the words you have given them.

---

1 toehold   2 booming   3 spree   4 venture   5 Revenue
6 targets   7 core business   8 range

Discussion: Growth crisis

SS discuss the growth crisis, core business and adjacencies.

(E)

◎ Get SS to discuss the questions in pairs or threes. Circulate and monitor, helping where necessary with vocabulary.

◎ Bring the class together and encourage SS particularly to talk about how the growth crisis affects/may affect globally as well as nationally (e.g. lack of investment, unemployment, recession, etc.). Encourage SS to be as creative or absurd as possible when brainstorming the possible adjacencies – see the Business skills section for further work on brainstorming techniques.

◎ As a follow-up activity, ask SS to vote on the various ideas with a show of hands and assess whether they would be good business propositions.

Suggested answers
1 It is clearer that some parts of the world, notably emerging markets like China, are experiencing massive growth, whereas the more mature economies in the US and Western Europe have definitely slowed down in terms of growth.
2 Possible adjacencies:
Publisher of children's books: toys and children's clothes, child-friendly café chain, ball-parks for young children, children's CDs and DVDs, books for all ages.
Restaurant: cookbook library, cookery classes, cookbook publishing, branded food labels (e.g. soup, ready meals), specialist food stores, catering service.
Bicycle manufacturer: sportswear, adventure sports equipment, cycling and other sporting holidays, running sporting events.
Supermarket chain: café, cake shop, other domestic services provided at the supermarket, e.g. dry cleaning/laundry service, key-cutting/shoe repair service, Internet shopping, own-label goods, small, local 'one-stop' 24-hour shops.
Mobile-phone company: other electronic equipment, TV channel and radio station, Internet provider, etc.

Language review: Idioms for giving examples

SS look at idioms for giving examples.

 Grammar reference: Idioms for giving examples page 130

> **1** a case in point is Burger Max **2** such as British Airways and Iberia **3** Alitalia for one **4** cars alone **5** A good example is Tesco's 'Finest' **6** Take, for instance, Arnott's **7** like Lindt and Sprüngli **8** Halls, to name a few

Brainstorming and creativity

SS discuss some quotes on creativity in the context of business ideas, listen to a trainer discussing brainstorming techniques, then brainstorm marketing strategies for a clothing retailer that is experiencing difficulties.

◎ You may like to use this quote on strategy as a warmer:
SWOTed by strategy models? Crunched by analysis? Strategy doesn't have to be this way. Strategy is really all about being different.
(From *Strategy bites back* by Henry Mintzberg, Bruce Ahlstrand, Joseph B. Lampel – see the Read on section (page 103) for details)

(A)

◎ As a lead-in to this section, ask SS what they understand by the terms *brainstorming* (a way of developing new ideas and solving problems by having a meeting where everyone makes suggestions and these are discussed); and *creativity* (producing or using new and interesting ideas; also used in marketing, relating to producing advertisements, etc.). Then ask SS the following questions:
In what situations do/would you need to brainstorm at work? Who with?
Do you enjoy brainstorming? Why (not)?
How could it be useful in business?
In what situations is it useful to be creative at work? Why?

◎ There are no right or wrong answers for these questions, but SS may think of brainstorming and creativity as marketing and advertising skills, when they are also useful in terms of product innovation and design, as well as being a useful management skills for problem-solving and strategy – see Warmer quote.

◎ Get SS to look at the photo of Albert Einstein and elicit from SS that he was a great creative thinker.

◎ Get SS to discuss the questions in pairs or small groups.

◎ Go through initial reactions with the whole class.

(B) 🎧 9.3

◎ Ask SS to try to predict the brainstorming tips before they listen.

◎ Play the recording once without stopping. Get SS to answer both sections on brainstorming tips and the principles of Koinonia.

◎ SS check their answers in pairs. Replay the recording if SS ask to, referring them to the audio script on page 171 if necessary.

◎ Go through the answers with the whole class.

> *Brainstorming tips*
> **1** ideas **2** eight or ten people **3** Write down **4** discussing any one item **5** uncritical **6** contributions **7** problem or task **8** Study and evaluate
>
> *Seven principles of Koinonia*
> **1** dialogue **2** ideas **3** argue **4** interrupt **5** carefully **6** thinking **7** honest

◎ As a follow-up, ask SS if they are familiar with any other brainstorming techniques or tips (e.g. writing down ideas on different coloured Post-its and putting them on a board).

◎ Refer SS to the Useful language box on page 83, where there is a summary of some of the expressions used. Ask them if they can think of any more expressions that they use for brainstorming or suggesting and reacting to ideas. Try to sensitise SS to English sentence stress, linking and intonation. Don't get SS to repeat all the expressions, just one or two from each section that might be difficult in terms of pronunciation (e.g. *Would anyone like to get the ball rolling?*).

(C)

◎ Explain that SS are going to brainstorm some marketing strategies for a company in order to turn it around.

◎ SS read the information about the retailer, Rose & Frankwright. (This is a fictitious company, loosely based on the British retailer Marks & Spencer.) Deal with any vocabulary questions they have. Make sure to give SS preparation time to make notes before brainstorming any marketing ideas, as this will improve the quality and length of their contributions.

◎ Divide SS into pairs or small groups. Tell SS that one person in each group will need to take notes during this task. Tell pre-work SS they should all take notes during this task, as they will come in useful later (see Exercise F, writing mission statements).

◎ Monitor and circulate round the class as SS do the task. Make a note of SS who contribute ideas, any useful language used and five or six language points for correction, including pronunciation. Write these errors on the board.

◎ Get early finishers to correct the errors on the board.

◎ When SS have finished, bring the class together.

◎ Go through feedback with the whole class, praising appropriate language for brainstorming. Write up any points that need further work on the board.

◎ There are no right or wrong answers for this task. Do not reject ideas during feedback, as the idea was to encourage SS to be as creative as possible.

SS may suggest some of the following:
1 Diversification into other market segments, e.g. younger customers.
2 Product development of best-selling products or brands and/or developing other lines.
3 Competitive pricing with lower range products. (SS may also suggest cost-cutting measures, including lowering production costs, although this is not strictly a marketing strategy.)
4 Entering new markets, e.g. opening more stores abroad and marketing the idea of 'British quality products'.
5 Creating adjacencies, e.g. food products to complement the core business.
6 Promotional marketing and advertising campaigns with a new slogan.

◎ As a possible follow-up activity, and time permitting, ask SS to evaluate the ideas for Rose & Frankwright and choose the best ones. You may also like to take the opportunity to ask SS to give presentations to the rest of the class for this activity.

◎ For follow-up practice, go to the Resource bank on page 228.

Writing: Mission statements

SS brainstorm ideas and write a mission statement for their company or organisation.

◎ As a lead-in to this writing section, ask SS what is meant as a mission statement (see the definitions at the beginning of the unit (CB page 78) and the Business brief (TRB page 103). Ask them if they are familiar with the mission statement of their company or organisation. If there is Internet access in the classroom, you may like to ask SS to find one on a company website. Otherwise, keep a copy of the statement to compare with their own mission statement once they have completed the writing task.

◎ SS do the exercise and check their answers in pairs.

◎ Go through the answers with the whole class.

1 c	2 e	3 b	4 d	5 a

◎ Ask SS to discuss the follow-up questions in pairs.

◎ Go through their answers with the whole class.

◎ You may like to read out extracts from the mission statements of three of the companies, or refer SS to their websites for further reading:
1 We will ensure a stress-free car rental experience by providing superior services that cater to our customers' individual needs ... always conveying the 'We Try Harder®' spirit with knowledge, caring and a passion for excellence. (www.avis.com)
2 www.avoncompany.com
3 www.kodak.com

4 ICRC is an impartial, neutral and independent organisation whose exclusively humanitarian mission is to protect the lives and dignity of victims of war and internal violence and to provide them with assistance. It directs and co-ordinates the international relief activities conducted by the Movement in situations of conflict. It also endeavours to prevent suffering by promoting and strengthening humanitarian law and universal humanitarian principles. (www.icrc.org)
5 The World Bank Group's mission is to fight poverty and improve the living standards of people in the developing world. It is a development bank which provides loans, policy advice, technical assistance and knowledge-sharing services to low and middle income countries to reduce poverty. The bank promotes growth to create jobs and to empower poor people to take advantage of these opportunities. (web.worldbank.org)

◎ For further reading on mission statements see the Text bank of this book.

E

◎ Ask SS to read the text on writing mission statements and make a note of the four criteria.

◎ Go through the answers with the whole class.

An effective mission statement should:
1 define the purpose of the organisation;
2 say what we want to be remembered for;
3 be short and sharply focused;
4 be clear and simple / easily understood.

◎ You may also like to tell SS (or dictate) these additional tips not mentioned in the text but suggested by Peter Ducker. SS may then number the seven criteria in order of importance:
5 provide direction for doing the right things
6 match the organisation's competence
7 inspire commitment among members in the organisation

F

◎ Explain to SS that they are going to write a mission statement for their company or organisation in pairs or small groups. In the case of pre-work SS, they may either write a statement for their place of study or one for Rose & Frankwright (see Exercise C) using the notes they took during the brainstorming task.

◎ Get SS to brainstorm ideas before they write. This task may take longer than the actual writing of the mission, as it is important that SS reach a consensus on the vision and mission of the company.

◉ Circulate, monitor and help SS whilst they write, referring SS to the writing tips on page 27 and the Writing file. Alternatively, with more confident SS, you may like to show them the example mission statement after they have completed the writing task, so that they do not copy from it directly.

 Writing file page 140

◉ Make a note of any useful expressions used and five or six points for correction on the board. Although the mission statement may be quite short, it will be necessary to revise it and write a couple of drafts before SS are completely satisfied with the final version.

◉ Early finishers can be referred to the board to see if they know all the expressions and if they can correct the errors.

◉ After completing the task, SS may compare mission statements with other pairs or groups, referring to the four criteria discussed previously. Does it include the purpose of the organisation? Does it say what the company can be remembered for? Is it the right length and focused? Is the mission clear?

◉ If peer correction is appropriate in your setting, SS could also be asked to proofread each others' writing task. What expressions did both pairs/groups use? How could it be improved? Are there any spelling mistakes or grammatical errors? Tell SS accuracy is extremely important in this kind of writing, as the mission statement would normally appear in company literature and/or be diffused on the Internet and therefore read by many people. Be on hand to help with this, if necessary, but leave most of the feedback and discussion to SS. If necessary, change the pairs around and repeat the process.

◉ Go through any common errors and the useful vocabulary and phrases on the board to round off the activity.

◉ Alternatively, this writing task could also be set for homework, but it is obviously preferable for SS to do the brainstorming as a group activity in class in order to generate more ideas.

◉ As an alternative to writing mission statements, or as an additional writing activity on strategy, you may like to use this anecdote on the Mini and pricing as a 'dictogloss'. Tell SS you are going to read them a text and they should concentrate on understanding the general sense of it, and not focus on every word. Before you read, write the proper names on the board and tell SS these names are mentioned in the text (i.e. Tony Cram, Ashridge, Austin Martin).

◉ Read out the text at normal speed. SS take notes while you read and then compare their notes in pairs. Read the text a second time, at normal speed again. SS then reconstruct the text in pairs. Explain to SS the important thing is that the content should be accurate and their writing should be grammatically correct, but they do not need to reproduce the text word for word.

◉ If peer correction is appropriate, SS compare each others texts. Go through feedback with the whole class, showing SS the original text as an overhead slide.

Tony Cram of Ashridge Business School argues that pricing, the fourth of the 'four Ps' in marketing, has been sorely neglected. He reminds us that a one-per-cent increase in the selling price of products usually has a greater impact on profits than a one-per-cent improvement in volume, fixed or variable costs. The launch price of new products is often set too low, leading to high volumes but low margins. Among his examples is the Austin Mini, an almost immediate sales success that earned no profits for the company because the launch price was cut at the last minute to below £500. He might have added that BMW has avoided making the same mistake with its modern reincarnation of the iconic small car. The German company's decision to price the new Mini as a premium compact car broke new ground in the US market and has meant high profits on every sale.

(Adapted from the FT Summer School series, *Return to classroom for business leaders*, by Simon London, published 30 July 2004)

Case study: The company makeover

Hazel is a multinational seller of cosmetic and beauty products that is in need of an overhaul. Hazel's sales are declining, and its products have little appeal for younger women. SS listen to a presentation from the new CEO, hold a meeting to devise a new strategic vision in order to boost growth and write a summary of their proposals.

◉ In class, pay particular attention to clearly breaking down the case study into the different tasks and making sure that SS understand and follow the structure of what you are doing.

Background

◉ Get SS to focus on the photos of cosmetics. As a lead-in, ask female SS whether they would buy these kinds of cosmetics. Why (not)? (Younger students may say the colours are too old-fashioned.) Alternatively, ask SS to give examples of successful CFT (cosmetics, fragrances and toiletries) companies, e.g. L'Oréal, whose chairman, Lindsay Owen-Jones, is a well-respected business leader.

◉ Write the following headings from the left-hand column of the table on the board.

◉ Get SS to study the background information in the Course Book and the three pie charts.

◉ Elicit information from SS to complete the right-hand column of the table.

Company	Hazel
Purpose	Direct seller of cosmetic and beauty products
Industry	Cosmetics, fragrances and toiletries (CFT)
Markets	US, South America, Western Europe and Asia Pacific
Experience in the industry	50 years
Problem	Only modest revenue in the last ten years; now has annual sales growth of less than 1.5%
Task for CEO	Devise a new strategic vision
Direct sales as a % of the total CFT market	7%
Top five sectors for Hazel's sales (%)	fragrances (19%), cosmetics (16%), hair care (16%), skin care (15%), bath and shower products (14%)

Reading

◎ Refer SS to the world market overview on cosmetics and toiletries.

◎ Ask SS to write on the board or dictate the following questions on the key market trends:
  1 *Which specific consumer groups in CFT are manufacturers now targeting?*
  2 *Which markets and products are doing particularly well?*
  3 *What are the reasons for this?*

◎ Get SS to compare their answers in pairs.

◎ Go through the answers with the whole class.

---

1 People with sensitive skin, 'older' people, and teens/pre-teens.
2 Anti-ageing products, which account for almost 2% annual growth in the CFT industry; teens and pre-teens, especially skin care.
3 There is demand products that counter the visible effects of ageing, and 80% of teenage girls use skincare products on a daily basis.

Listening 🎧 9.4

◎ Get SS to read the listening task. Write the two headings (Customer problems and Sales reps' problems) on the board.

◎ Ask SS to try and predict some of the CEO's findings. SS may be able to predict from reading the background that customers may complain Hazel has an outdated image or that there is a lack of interesting new product lines. Don't reject any ideas at this stage or give the answers away.

◎ Play the recording once. SS compare ideas in pairs.

◎ Ask SS If they would like to read the audio script on page 171 and listen to the recording again. Deal with any questions. Go through points with the whole class.

a) Customer problems	b) Sales reps' problems
◎ outdated image ◎ unattractive catalogues ◎ too many products ◎ poor quality of products ◎ lack of interesting new lines	◎ not being able to reorder popular items ◎ not receiving correct items ◎ old-fashioned/complicated/slow/cumbersome ordering system

◎ Discuss SS's initial reactions to the problem. What do they think takes priority in terms of dealing with these complaints and why? What kind of strategy might be needed? There is no right answer to this question, but do not spend too long on it at this stage as it forms part of the main task.

Task

◎ Divide the SS into pairs or small groups. Tell them they will be the management team during this role-play. With larger groups, it may be appropriate to give SS different manager roles, e.g. Finance, Production, Marketing and Sales, R&D and Customer Service, depending on SS's interests.

◎ Refer SS to the SWOT analysis. Explain that this is a common framework for analysing a company's problems and devising initial strategies.

◎ SS brainstorm the new vision for Hazel. Tell SS to be as creative and innovative as possible at this stage.

◎ Circulate and monitor, checking SS are completing the task correctly. Make a note of any key language being used and five or six common errors for correction, including pronunciation, for later feedback.

◎ Early finishers may write up their ideas on the board.

Feedback

◎ When SS have finished the task, bring the whole class to order.

◎ Ask one or two groups to say what happened in their groups and summarise their ideas of a strategic vision.

◎ Praise the strong language points and work on five or six points that need improvement, especially in relation to language used for brainstorming, strategy and growth.

◎ During feedback, highlight some of SS's best ideas and those that were common to most groups.

◎ Alternatively, or if you choose to omit the following writing task, ask SS to present their ideas formally to the rest of the class as the management team. Make sure SS have enough preparation time to do this and preferably refer to graphic information like the pie charts on page 84.

◎ This case study is based on Avon. You may like to photocopy the following information for SS so that they can compare their proposals with the real case.

This case study is based on the world's leading direct sellers of cosmetics and beauty products, Avon. Andrea Jung became Avon's CEO in November 1999. This is the strategy execution and business results under CEO Andrea Jung and President and Chief Operations Officer Susan Kropf.

Business process re-engineering: The heart of Avon's strategy implementation efforts was its ability to eliminate the costs of low value-added activities from its value chain. Much of Kropf's re-engineering had to do with improving the company's manufacturing and distribution systems.

Sales representatives: The recruitment and retention of sales reps was a strategic objective that led to the implementation of Jung's Sales Leadership program.

E-commerce and the Internet: Jung and Kropf saw the Internet as the driver of transformation in the relationships between representatives, customers and the company's marketing and supply-chain operations.

Image enhancement: The transformation of Avon's image called for new products, new packaging, celebrity endorsements, stylish new catalogues and new advertising campaigns.

Product development: In 2000, Avon's R&D team responded to Jung's challenge to develop a blockbuster product within two years by introducing Anew Retroactive anti-ageing skin cream.

International: Avon pushed its innovative new products like Anew Retroactive into emerging markets like China, Poland, Russia, Hungary and Slovakia; redesigned catalogues to illustrate the glamour of the Avon brand; and allocated up to 7 per cent of sales to advertising in each country market.

Writing

- Tell SS they are going to evaluate their ideas in the previous task and summarise their proposals in the form of a report for the company's board of directors.
- Get SS to look at the rubric for the Writing task and deal with any questions they may have.
- Brainstorm the information that should go in the proposal and put these points on the board. All this information has come up in the listening and main task.
- Ask SS to look again at the writing tips for report writing on pages 138–139; you may also want to refer SS to proposal writing on page 39 if necessary.
- Get SS to write in pairs or individually, as this is a detailed proposal.

Writing file pages 138–139

- Circulate and monitor, checking SS are completing the task correctly.
- Get SS to write the final proposal either as a class activity or for homework. This could probably be quite a long proposal if SS include the background information, the CEO's findings and the strategic plan for the company.
- Alternatively, ask SS to write a new mission statement for Hazel in pairs or small groups. Tell SS that they need to make sure they reach a consensus on the vision for the company before they start writing. Refer SS to the Writing file (page 140) for this alternative writing task.

1 to 1

- Go through the information in the Course Book with your student. Explain any difficulties. In the main task, you and your student are senior management team members (the CEO and one of the other directors, e.g. of Marketing and Sales). Don't dominate the conversation in this task, but say enough to keep it going and allow your student to ask and answer questions.
- At the same time, monitor the language that your student is using. Note down any good examples of language and points for error correction or improvement. Come back to these later.
- Praise any good examples of language used and go over any errors, including pronunciation. Then repeat the task, swapping roles or taking on the role of different directors (e.g. Finance and Customer Service or R&D). Record the role-play on cassette or video, if desirable, for intensive correction work.

Revision

This unit revises and reinforces some of the key language points from Units 7–9, and links with those units are clearly shown. This revision unit, like Revision units A, B and D, concentrates on reading and writing activities. Some of the exercise types are similar to those in the Reading and Writing section of the Business English Certificate examination (Higher level) organised by the University of Cambridge ESOL Examinations (Cambridge ESOL).

For more speaking practice, see the Resource bank section of this book beginning on page 211. The exercises in this unit can be done in class, individually or collaboratively, or for homework.

7 Finance and banking

Vocabulary

◎ This exercise gives SS further practice in using the language of banking, finance and growth, following the vocabulary sections on pages 62 and 65. Point out the rubric and explain that SS have to find one word which does *not* collocate.

> **1** equity **2** interest **3** shareholder **4** an ATM **5** accounting **6** price **7** fixed
> **8** bankruptcy **9** assets **10** flow

Business skills: presentations

◎ This exercise gives SS further practice in introducing a presentation following the Business skills section on pages 66–67.

> **1** c **2** f **3** d **4** e **5** a **6** b

Describing financial performance

◎ This exercise gives SS further practice in describing financial performance following the Business skills section (pages 66–67).

> **1** consecutive quarter **2** net loss **3** reducing costs **4** the next four years **5** the same
> period last year **6** higher steel costs **7** poor results **8** dragged CH shares down
> **9** recovery plan **10** recorded a profit

Writing: introduction to a presentation

◎ SS write an introduction to a presentation describing the company performance of CH Autos as mentioned in the previous exercise.

> **Sample answer**
>
> ### Introduction to a presentation
>
> **Company performance for CH Autos**
>
> Good morning. My name's …, I'm the Finance Director for CH Autos. I'm very pleased to welcome you all here this morning. I'm here today to tell you, our shareholders, about the bright future ahead for our company. Let me take this opportunity to say that, despite recent losses as a result of challenges we have faced in the industry, such as higher steel costs, we firmly believe that CH Autos will recover fully from these temporary setbacks and we hope to significantly increase our output in the next year. I'll start my talk by reporting on last year's financial results. Then I'll talk about our recent performance and the results of our recovery plan in the last quarter. Finally, we'll look at the company's plans for further reduction of costs and our projected forecast. I'm sure you'll agree that our European operation, which recorded a profit of $37m this year, is growing from strength to strength. There'll be an opportunity at the end of my presentation to deal with any questions you might have.
>
> (180 words)

8 Consultants

Vocabulary: word-building

◎ This exercise gives SS further practice in word-building associated with consulting vocabulary, following the listening and vocabulary sections on pages 70–72.

> **1** expertise **2** reputable **3** consultancy/consulting **4** allocation **5** deliverables
> **6** proposal **7** achievable **8** recruitment/recruiting

Grammar: conditionals

◎ SS practise conditional forms when negotiating, following work on conditionals in the Grammar reference on pages 128–129.

> **1** b (2nd) **2** e (3rd) **3** f (mixed: 2nd and 3rd) **4** a (1st) **5** c (1st) **6** d (1st)

Business skills: negotiating

◎ This exercise gives SS further practice in negotiating from the Business skills section on pages 74–75. SS may then role-play the dialogue with a partner as an optional speaking activity.

> Suggested answers
> **1** To be honest, we think six months would be a more realistic timescale.
> **2** You need to bear in mind that we charge more for senior consultants. / All of our consultants are experienced, but we prefer to use both junior and senior consultants on projects.
> **3** Actually, we were looking at fees paid according to hourly rates, but I'm sure we can come to a satisfactory agreement.
> **4** Let me just say that having access to company information is very important for us. It ensures good communication and the success of the project.
> **5** That's fine, but we would need to negotiate any implementation work separately, as it will obviously increase our fees. What did you have in mind?
> **6** I'm sure you are aware that other firms don't have our reputation, although I admit they may be cheaper, largely due to the fact that they take on inexperienced consultants. If you take a look at our proposal in more detail, you'll see we can really offer you the best solutions.

Writing: putting it in writing

◎ SS correct a letter of a contractual agreement between a consultancy and a client, practising summarising terms and conditions (page 75). If SS have not done this type of exercise before, draw their attention to the rubric and point out there isn't an error on every line. You may also like to tell SS there are seven errors in total.

> **1** ✓ **2** ✓ **3** an **4** for **5** high **6** ✓ **7** within **8** pay **9** If/should **10** to **11** ✓ **12** ✓

9 Strategy

Marketing strategies

◎ This exercise gives SS practice in the language of marketing strategies following the exercise on Rose & Frankwright in the Business skills section on page 82.

> **1** develop their products or services **2** integrating them both at an early stage **3** adapting their products or services **4** downscaling their operations **5** more responsive and flexible

Reading: communicating the brand

◎ SS are given practice in vocabulary related to communicating brands following the exercise on Rose & Frankwright in the Business skills section on page 82.

> **1** advertising **2** communicating **3** advertisements **4** innovative **5** brand **6** leveraging
> **7** differentiating **8** core values **9** creative **10** competitors

Vocabulary: strategy

◉ SS are given further practice in vocabulary associated with strategy following the listening section on pages 78–79.

---

1 market position   **2** customers and suppliers   **3** significant impact   **4** entering the market
5 future competitor   **6** change the rules   **7** management systems   **8** goals and objectives
9 planning systems   **10** the same vision

Writing: mission statements

◉ SS are given practice in mission statements by writing a press release, outlining the new strategy of a British retailer (pages 82–83).

Sample answer

Press release

Rose & Frankwright: new vision

We aim to be the number-one store in British fashion offering down-to-earth prices, while continuing to provide excellent service and quality of design to our customers. We have developed an exciting vision at R&F, with new lines for young adults. Visit our new-look stores where you will love our 'Designer Discovery' collection. This special collection has been inspired by our Designer of the Year award in the search for talented, young designers who understand what's happening on the high street and can make designer clothing accessible to R&F customers.

(94 words)

Doing business online

At a glance

	Classwork – Course Book	Further work
Lesson 1: **Listening and discussion** (pages 90–91) *Each lesson is about 60–75 minutes. This time does not include administration and time spent going through homework in any lessons.*	**Discussion: Online shopping 1** SS are encouraged to talk about online shopping. **Listening 1: Three types of online shopping** SS listen to three people talk about shopping online. **Vocabulary: Online shopping** SS look at vocabulary related to the Internet and e-business. **Listening 2: Interview with Maija Pesola** SS listen to Maija Pesola, the IT correspondent for the *Financial Times*. In the first part of the interview, she talks about the dot-com crash in 2000. In the second part, she talks about trends in online business today. **Discussion: Online shopping 2** SS discuss Internet security, cyber crime and online business.	**Practice File** Word power (pages 58–59)
Lesson 2: **Reading and language** (pages 92–93) *Each lesson is about 60–75 minutes.*	**Reading: *Net gains on the shop front*** SS read about the successes and failures of online companies. **Vocabulary: Word partnerships** SS look at word partnerships for online sales and use related vocabulary in context. **Language review: Cleft sentences** SS look at cleft sentences and use them in context.	**Text bank** (TRB pages 192–195) **Practice File** Text and grammar (pages 60–61) **Grammar reference and practice** (CB pages 130–131)
Lesson 3: **Business skills** (pages 94–95) *Each lesson is about 75–90 minutes.*	**Presentations: Summarising and dealing with questions** SS discuss websites they often use and the concept of usability; listen to a website expert summarise her presentation and deal with questions; practise dealing with difficult questions related to the Internet, summarise a short presentation on a topic of their choice and deal with questions from the audience; discuss how to present information on a website on the topic of doing business online. **Writing: Presenting information on a website** SS look at tips for writing web pages and write up the main points of their presentations for a site.	**Resource bank** (TRB page 229) **Practice File** Skills and pronunciation (pages 62–63) **Writing file** (CB page 141)
Lesson 4: **Case study** (pages 96–97) *Each lesson is about 75–90 minutes.*	**Improving the online experience** Audio Wire is a manufacturer of electronic equipment that wants to improve its online sales. It has hired the web design company, Online Experience, to analyse sales data, improve the website and overall sales of the earphones section, where they sell directly to consumers. SS listen to a meeting with the team at Online Experience, analyse the website data, write up a proposal for redesigning the website and present their recommendations to the client company.	**Writing file** (CB pages 138–139)

For a fast route through the unit, focusing mainly on speaking skills, just use the underlined sections.

For one-to-one situations, most parts of the unit lend themselves, with minimal adaptation, to use with individual students. Where this is not the case, alternative procedures are given.

Business brief

Ever since Jeff Bezos set up amazon.com, the world's largest bookseller, the Internet has opened up a **massive consumer market** for **e-tailers** (online retailers). The experts advise building **e-business** into any business plan, although smaller retailers are still nervous about **e-tailing**, as they often see it as a risk. **Online shoppers** have the idea that delivery should be immediate, apart from being extremely convenient, so if companies don't deliver until a week later, they won't get **returning customers**.

On an **e-commerce site**, where customers may **browse stock**, **select items** to fill a **shopping basket** or **cart** and then go to a **virtual checkout** to pay for goods. The main difference between this and a brochure site that simply displays products and company information is **interactivity**. When a customer is making choices on the website, this requires a more sophisticated website. Many ISPs (**Internet Service Providers**) have packages that can enable small businesses to **host a website**.

Web metrics are the numbers that tell managers what is happening in their site. Success on the web essentially means getting people to do what you want when they visit the site. This is called the **target action,** which is usually buying something or filling in a form. Another important consideration is whether the site's design makes it easy for people to **engage** in the target action. **Ease of navigation** is one of common complaints people have about **web design**.

The key **performance indicator** in e-business is the **conversion rate**: the percentage of visitors who engage in the target action, which can either be the percentage of visitors who **submit a form** or who buy online. The average conversion rate is 2 per cent, whereas Amazon are said to have the highest rate at about 9 per cent. However, these sites have very high **brand recognition**, which means people already know what the site is selling before they visit.

The most important area in online shopping is the **credit-card payment page**. Between viewing **product pages** and completing the target action, the visitor ideally does something: fill in a form and **hit the submit button**, or submit a credit-card page. People who don't submit are said to have '**abandoned**'. Each form therefore has an **abandonment rate**.

The basic rule for **reducing abandonment** is to ask fewer questions. The form is primarily for having a record of potential customers so the sales team can contact them. Many companies treat contact forms as an opportunity for **market research**. They ask questions like 'Where did you find our site?' These types of questions will be a reason for someone to **disengage with the site**, or '**click off**'. Many potential customers will also have second thoughts about buying online when they are asked to enter credit-card information.

When a visitor first arrives on a website, they quickly **scan** it to see if it has what they are looking for. At this time, they are a **scanning visitor**. **Web designers** also talk about the '**eight-second rule**', that is, most people will allow no more than eight seconds to review a site before making a decision. Research indicates, however, that 30 seconds is more the norm. In either case, an e-tailer should make sure the **core offering** of its site can be conveyed in this short time.

Committed visitors are those who read more than one page or spend more than one minute. Getting **first-time visitors** to stop scanning and start reading requires different design elements from selling. Successful sites will have **landing pages** to switch visitors from scanning to reading. A company can also analyse its web metrics results to determine the **ROI (return on investment)** for **online advertising**. A good rule of thumb is to multiply the conversion rate for visitors coming from each ad by the cost per visitor. That is the **cost per acquisition** (CPA). Ultimately, a business should ask itself if it can afford to spend that much to attract **e-tail consumers** and get online sales.

Doing business online and your students

In-work students will be able to talk about their company's website and will possibly have experience of doing e-business and analysing data from online customers. Pre-work students will probably have their own ideas about what makes an effective website. They can also talk about writing for web pages or contributing to their organisation's website.

Most students will have experience of using the Internet and buying goods or services online.

Read on

Nicholas G. Carr: *Does IT matter? Information technology and the corrosion of competitive advantage,* Harvard Business School Press, 2004

John Cassidy: *Dot.con: the real story of why the Internet bubble burst,* Penguin Books, 2005

Dave Chaffey: E-*business and e-commerce management,* FT Prentice Hall, 2003

Ravi Damani, Chetan Damani, Neil Sait: *7 habits of successful e-commerce companies: give yourself a real competitive advantage. Read this book. Study it. Practice it,* Imano Plc, 2004

Lesson notes

Warmer

◉ Ask SS to brainstorm some successful online companies (e.g. mass retailers such as amazon.com, eBay, buy.com, sears.com or specialised retailers such as easy-jet.com, dell.com, gap.com, Discoverystore.com, etc.).

◉ Write SS's ideas up on the board. Then ask them if they thought that these companies would do so well when they first started. Why (not)? SS may say that they didn't think certain products would sell on the Internet, that people get irritated by online advertisements or that they did indeed foresee the potential for online selling. Don't spend too long on this, as it forms part of the first exercise.

◉ Alternatively, ask SS what they understand by the title of the unit, 'Doing business online'.

Overview

◉ Tell SS that they will be looking at doing business online and e-business.

◉ Go through the overview panel at the beginning of the unit, pointing out the sections that SS will be looking at.

Quotation

◉ Get SS to look at the quotation and ask them what they think it means. (The idea is that human errors are minor compared to the catastrophes that computers and IT systems can cause, although SS may also argue that most computer errors are in fact human errors, such as not saving documents, deleting files, not knowing how to use software programmes correctly or forwarding viruses unintentionally.)

Discussion: Online shopping 1

SS are encouraged to talk about online shopping.

◉ As a lead-in to this activity, ask SS if they shop online and ask for a show of hands. If SS are reluctant to put up their hands, ask the questions:
Have you ever bought something on the Internet?
If so, what did you buy?

◉ Get SS to work in pairs to discuss the questions. Set a three-minute time limit for this. If SS don't have many ideas, refer them to the symbols showing the types of products and services you can buy online on page 90. Help SS with online or computer vocabulary in English by putting up some words and expressions on the board as they do the activity. Note that some of this vocabulary will be dealt with in Exercise C.

◉ Get SS's feedback as a whole class. They may say that they don't usually shop online, but may in fact realise that at some point they have bought books, CDs, DVDs, software, electronic equipment or done their supermarket shopping online, and booked cinema/theatre/concert tickets, flights, holidays or hotel accommodation. SS may also mention that they wouldn't buy certain products online, such as fresh food, clothes and shoes, or furniture. If SS mention the dot-com crash in 2000, do not spend too long discussing this, as it forms part of the listening section.

Listening 1: Three types of online shopping

SS listen to three people talk about shopping online.

 10.1

◉ Explain briefly SS are going to listening to three people. To increase the challenge with larger classes, you may like SS to raise their hands as soon as they know what type of online shopping is being described. Alternatively, SS may write down their answers and then check in pairs after listening to the three speakers.

◉ Play the first recording once, then pause and check the answer. Repeat the procedure for the next two speakers. If SS get the answer early on in the recording, pause it and ask them to note down the words they heard that helped them, then play the rest of the recording (e.g. Speaker 1: *hand luggage, terminal, boarding pass, departure lounge*; Speaker 2: *download, Internet, update my anti-virus scan, spyware remover*; Speaker 3: *plot summaries, readers' reviewers*).

◉ Only play the recording(s) a second time if SS have not understood what type of online shopping is being described. It should not be necessary for SS to refer to the audio script on page 171, as this Listening section is not the main listening task. If SS need to refer to the script, do not spend a long time going through it in detail, although you may like to draw SS's attention to the colloquial use of language in the third recording: *it's always been a **hassle** (= problem) posting **stuff** (= things) to people.*

◉ If SS have noted down vocabulary they heard, go through their answers, and write up words related to the Internet from the second recording on the board, checking that SS know what they mean.

---

1 buying airline tickets / checking in for flights   **2** buying software   **3** buying books

---

◉ As a follow-up question, you could ask the SS to guess the nationality of the different speakers after playing each recording (speaker 1: Australian; speaker 2: Indian; speaker 3: British).

Vocabulary: Online shopping

SS look at vocabulary related to the Internet and e-business.

Ⓒ

◎ This exercise deals with vocabulary which features in the next listening section.

◎ Ask SS to do the exercise individually, then check their answers in pairs. Circulate and monitor, while SS check their answers, helping them with language for the Internet and online business, where necessary.

◎ Go through the answers with the whole class.

1 d	**2** h	**3** j	**4** e	**5** g	**6** i	**7** f	**8** b	**9** a	**10** c

◎ Drill pronunciation of some of the words and expressions, highlighting stress on the board if necessary. This is particularly important, even with SS with a background in IT: although SS may be familiar with the written word and its meaning, they sometimes do not pronounce technical words correctly in English, but say them as they would in their mother tongue.

Listening 2: Interview with Maija Pesola

SS listen to Maija Pesola, the IT correspondent for the *Financial Times*. In the first part of the interview, she talks about the dot-com crash in 2000. In the second part, she talks about trends in online business today.

Ⓓ 🎧 10.2

◎ Do the question in the rubric as a quick-fire activity with the whole class. (i.e. a lot of companies and individuals invested in dot-coms, then lost a lot of money / got their fingers burnt).

◎ Play the first part of the interview without stopping.

◎ Play it a second time, pausing in sections if necessary to give SS time to note down the errors.

◎ After listening, SS compare notes in pairs and discuss the answers with the whole class.

> The problem was that there was too much investment money coming into the market too quickly. Therefore funding was given to dot-com companies that didn't have particularly **well-thought-out** business plans and didn't necessarily have the **back-end systems** to carry out their plans. Another factor was that the market wasn't ready for Internet shopping in the way that it is today, and in 2000, not many people had **broadband connections**. The positive outcome of the dot-com collapse is that it's **weeded out** some of the weaker companies, and those companies that are still in existence today have refined their **business models**.

◎ You may want to refer SS to the audio script on page 171 to highlight the differences between the text on page 91 and the correct answers. With SS who are not very familiar with this language area, you may ask them to pick out five or six words and collocations (e.g. adjective + noun, adverb + verb, etc.) relating to online business in the audio script (*back-end systems, Internet browsing, broadband connections, online shopping, bubble burst*). Don't spend too long going over the script in detail.

Ⓔ 🎧 10.3

◎ Get SS to read the questions before they listen.

◎ Play the second part of the interview without stopping.

◎ SS compare their answers in pairs.

◎ Play the recording a second time, pausing in sections if necessary to allow SS time to complete their answers.

◎ After listening, SS compare notes in pairs.

◎ Get SS's initial reaction by asking them whether they predicted correctly, then discuss the answers with the whole class.

> **1** Banner ads, which were very similar to putting an advert in a newspaper. However, companies found that they weren't getting a lot of response from them.
> **2** Consumers were annoyed by pop-up ads.
> **3** Advertising that's related to search results when people use search engines.
> **4** Companies are happy to pay for this because they see higher response rates from these targeted ads, and it's easier to measure how many times the ad has come up.
> **5** Products that are very easy to ship, such as books or music and to some extent wine, sell well. Another category that has done well is travel, for similar reasons; also because booking travel on the Internet adds something genuinely different to the experience. Clothing tends to be difficult because these are examples of goods that people would like to see, feel and try on before buying.

◎ You may want to refer SS to the audio script on pages 171–172, but don't spend too long going over it in detail, as SS need time to discuss the questions in the next exercise.

◎ As a follow-up activity, you may like to refer SS to the Internet to find recent articles on e-business either by Maija Pesola or other IT correspondents. These articles can serve as background reading before going on to the reading section.

Discussion: Online shopping 2

SS discuss Internet security, cyber crime and e-business.

(F)

◎ Get SS to discuss their answers in pairs or threes. Circulate and monitor, helping with vocabulary, where necessary.

◎ Bring the class together and encourage SS particularly to talk about e-business and online security issues. In question 3 on cyber crime, SS may say that while some fears about the misuse of credits cards have been allayed by banks and government measures, they might resurface again, e.g. due to newspaper reports about hackers getting into online bank accounts. In question 4 on data collection, SS may talk about 'data mining' (analysing large amounts of data about customers held on computer in order to get information about them that is not immediately available) and the way that online retailers and marketing departments try to collect as information on online visitors via cookies, etc. as part of their market research (see the Business brief (page 119) on filling out online contact forms). Regarding question 6, the benefits of doing business online are enormous, and online sales are expected to increase, despite ongoing price wars with high-street retailers. For many consumers, price has long ceased to be the primary reason for shopping online, says Maija Pesola, primarily because research shows convenience is the main factor (delivery was the second). However, e-retailers still need to ensure they have the necessary back-end systems to cope with orders and guarantee prompt delivery (see the Reading section of this unit).

Reading: *Net gains on the shop front*

SS read about the successes and failures of online companies.

(A)

◎ As a lead-in for this section, write the following sentences with gaps on the board. They are taken from Kelkoo.com, the price-comparison website. Ask SS to guess which items are missing.

Electronic goods such as c…………[1], d………… c…………[2] and M………… p…………[3] continue to dominate as the most popular items for online shoppers. However, increasing numbers of shoppers are also moving to buying c…………[4] over the Internet.

> **1** computers   **2** digital cameras   **3** MP3 players
> **4** clothes

◎ Refer SS to the exercise and get them to number the four factors for good e-retailers in order of importance (1 = most important) individually. Then get SS to discuss their lists in pairs and give reasons for their choices.

◎ Go through SS's answers with the whole class. Do not reject any ideas at this stage, as this forms part of the Reading section.

◎ Alternatively, do the exercise as a quick-fire activity with the whole class.

◎ Get SS to look at the cartoon. Ask them what it means. (The idea is that employees spend a lot of time playing on the computer, e-mailing friends, searching on the Internet, etc. when they look like they're working, and they use problems with technology as an excuse.)

(B)

◎ Ask SS what they think the title of the article – 'Net gains on the shop front' – means (the idea is that profits can be made from online business).

◎ Get SS to read only the first part of the article and do the exercise individually. Explain that the idea is to scan the article quickly for this information. Tell SS they should ignore any words or phrases they don't know at this stage and focus on the task. In order to make this a quicker reading exercise, set a time limit. SS will probably need two or three minutes for each part of the reading.

◎ After reading, SS compare their answers in pairs.

◎ Ask SS for their initial reactions to the points made in the article before checking the answers to the questions. Do their lists in Exercise A coincide with the writer's opinion?

◎ Go through the answers with the whole class.

> The article suggests that customer service and delivering orders as promised are the deciding factors for online success. Features such as a user-friendly website are expected as the norm, and low prices are important, but not as important as order fulfilment and customer service.

◎ Ask SS follow-up questions about success and failure for other online companies they are familiar with. You may also like to ask about other factors that may influence e-tailing. (SS may mention the convenience factor; that people can buy from the comfort of their home and at any time of the day; also access to goods that are not usually available locally, e.g. foreign films, books, food and wine.)

(C)

◎ Get SS to read the first part of the article again, pointing out that the paragraphs are numbered. Alternatively, if time is short, or SS don't want to read the first part of the article again, do the exercise as a quick-fire activity with the whole class. If someone asks a question, throw it open to the whole class to find out if someone else can provide an explanation. If not, explain where necessary.

◎ Circulate and confirm answers or indicate in which sentence a word or expression occurs where SS are having difficulties. Get early finishers to compare their answers in pairs.

◎ Go through the answers with the whole class, asking SS to give their explanations of the meanings and find out if the rest of the class agrees.

1 now offer (paragraphs 1 and 2)   **2** have mixed feelings (paragraph 2)   **3** repercussions for the company's good name (paragraph 3)   **4** no longer impressed (paragraph 4)   **5** unlikely to be cost effective (paragraph 5)

D

◉ Refer SS to the photo and ask them if they would buy the product online. (The photo shows some women's scarves or shawls from the White Company, mentioned in the article. You may like to tell SS that this e-tailer is based in London and sells a variety of products including bed linen, bathroom accessories, adult and children's clothes, gifts and furniture.)

◉ Get SS to read the second part of the article. Circulate and monitor, pointing out relevant sections from the text helping where necessary, as SS do the exercise individually.

◉ Get early finishers to compare their answers.

◉ Go through answers with the whole class, asking SS to explain which part of the text confirms their answers.

1 False   *Rather than the website being a separate, self-contained part of the business, e-tail needs to be fully integrated into the support systems and infrastructure that drive every other part of the business … If it [the website] can't be fitted into the existing framework, then the framework needs to change to fit the website.* (paragraph 6)

2 True   *If your website says one thing and the stock room another, they are not going to invest their time with you again.* (paragraph 7)

3 True   *Overall growth is about 40 per cent, but the online side is up 86 per cent on last year.* (paragraph 8)

4 True   *… when an item is sold, whether through a shop or mail order, the website is automatically updated.* (paragraph 9)

◉ If SS are interested in finding out more, hand out the reading list in the Read on section (page 119) and the website www.thewhitecompany.com

Vocabulary: Word partnerships

SS look at word partnerships for online sales and use related vocabulary in context.

E

◉ Explain this is an exercise on word partnerships with vocabulary related to online sales and retail in general. Go through the first question with the whole class.

◉ Get SS to do the rest of the exercise individually.

◉ Early finishers can compare their answers in pairs.

◉ Go through the answers with the whole class, dealing with any vocabulary questions the SS may have, highlighting the pronunciation and stress of some of the more difficult words and expressions (e.g. *flashy, fickle, fulfil, fulfilment*).

1 ~ come rolling in; part with ~   **2** flashy ~; user-friendly ~; up-to-date ~   **3** demanding ~; (un)forgiving ~; fickle ~; (good old-fashioned) ~ service   **4** meet and manage (customer) ~; high(er) ~   **5** to (not) be in ~; ~ is stored; ~ control; ~ availability; ~ room; ~ management; ~ orders   **6** take an ~; fulfil an ~; process an ~; pick an ~

F

◉ Get SS to complete the sentences.

◉ Early finishers may check their answers in pairs.

◉ Go through the answers with the whole class.

1 part with   **2** fulfil/process   **3** high   **4** be in **5** flashy; up-to-date   **6** fickle; service

Language review: Cleft sentences

SS look at cleft sentences and use them in context.

 Grammar reference: Cleft sentences, page 131

◉ As a lead-in to this language review section, dictate the following information to SS. Alternatively, write it up on the board. (Note this dictation is an alterative explanation to the full Grammar reference on page 131 of the Course Book.)

◉ SS compare their dictations in pairs.

Cleft sentences
When we want to give new information, contrast ideas, clarify, summarise or simply emphasise something, we can use a cleft sentence. The thing about cleft sentences is that they have two clauses, each with their own main verb. Different expressions can be used with these types of sentences. Here are some examples:
1   *The thing about online shopping is (that) it's really convenient.*
2   *What I like most about e-tailers is the fact that they deliver to your home.*
3   *The White Company moved on to the web six years ago. What they did next was move on to the high street.*
It's not only for emphasis that cleft sentences can be used. The great thing about cleft sentences is they can be used for a variety of business situations, such as meetings, negotiations, writing reports, for training purposes and presentations.

Lesson notes

- Ask SS to identify six cleft sentences in the dictation and underline the main verbs and expressions used to introduce them. Do the first one as an example with the whole class.
- While SS do the task, circulate and monitor, referring SS to the Grammar reference on page 131 and helping them to identify the different parts of the cleft sentences, where necessary.
- Get SS to compare their answers in pairs.
- Go through the answers with the whole class, highlighting the main verbs and expressions used in cleft sentences, if possible on a slide or on the board. There are six cleft sentences in total, including the three examples.
- Refer SS to paragraph 10 of the article and ask them to identify two cleft sentences.

It is not taking the orders online that causes the problems for e-tailers, **it is** the operational costs of fulfilling those orders.

It is meeting the higher expectation levels of the e-tail consumer **where it gets** tricky.

- Alternatively, or if time is short, omit the dictation activity and simple write the two sentences from the text up on the board, pointing out that information in these kinds of sentences is divided in two clauses, each with its own main verb.
- Refer SS to the exercise in the Grammar reference on page 131 of the Course Book.

---

1 It is meeting the expectation of online shoppers that is very difficult.
2 What has had a huge impact on e-commerce is the rapid spread of broadband Internet access.
3 Why / The reason why they contracted Amazon was to help them improve their online sales.
4 All they (have to) do is print off the orders and deal with them manually.
5 It was delays in delivery that damaged the company's reputation and sales.
6 The thing we like most is the simplicity of the online ordering process.

Presentations: Summarising and dealing with questions

SS discuss websites they often use and the concept of usability; listen to a website expert summarise her presentation and deal with questions; practise dealing with difficult questions related to the Internet, summarise a short presentation on a topic of their choice and deal with questions from the audience; discuss how to present information on a website on the topic of doing business online.

- As a lead-in to this section, ask SS what makes an effective website. SS will probably mention some of the factors that were discussed in the previous reading section, i.e. that it should be easy to navigate, user-friendly, visually attractive and up to date, etc.). SS may also add that it depends what the website sets out do, e.g. simply inform and offer information, or sell. Ask SS what they understand by the term *usability* in relation to web pages. Do not reject any ideas at this stage, as they will form part of the next task.
- Get SS to look at the definition of the website extract on usability and see if they were correct. Deal with any questions they may have. Ask SS whether they think the intentions of designers are in conflict with the needs of the users. SS may say that photos or images can take a long time to download, or that if there are too many 'flashy' pages, images or adverts to click through to find what you are looking for, users will leave the site.
- Get SS to discuss the questions in pairs.
- Go through initial reactions with the whole class, making a note of some of SS's favourite websites on the board and how they rate the usability factors. SS may or may not reach a consensus on this.
- As a follow-up, ask SS if they have designed or created web pages, either for their company or their own personal sites. Ask them whether they think they were successful or not. You may also like to mention the three Ws in web page design: write the following questions on the board, leaving out the first *wh-* question word and get SS to complete them:
  Why do you want to have a website in the first place?
  What do you want to achieve?
  Who are the audience and what do they want to do or find out on your site?

B 🎧 10.4

- Tell SS they are going to hear the summary of a presentation on the topic of creating web pages.
- Get SS to read the statements. You may also like to ask them to note down the four things Sophie is asked about. (SS do not need to write down the questions word for word, as Exercise C deals with the exact phrasing of the questions.)
- Play the recording once, getting SS to mark their answers individually and pausing after each of the speaker's responses if necessary.
- Get SS to compare their answers in pairs.
- Play the recording a second time, then go through the answers with the whole class. Do not refer SS to the audio script at this stage if possible, as this is dealt with in the following exercise.

---

1 c, d (differences between government websites and the private business sector)
2 c, d (how a company can improve its online sales)
3 a (copy writing; language that works well on a website)
4 b (language to be avoided when writing for websites)

◎ Get SS's initial reaction to the recording of Sophie's talk about her advice for web page design and how she dealt with the Q&A session (e.g. she sounds authoritative and confident, although she admits she's not an expert in online sales and refers the audience to her colleague when asked about this).

◎ Ask SS some of the following follow-up questions: *— what kind of pros do you have you given?*
What do you find most difficult about summarising presentations?
What do you find most difficult about dealing with, or asking questions, in these kinds of situations?
SS may say that they have usually rehearsed the start of their presentation, but have not practised the conclusion, or that they often run out of time at the end and have to hurry through the summary. They may also say that they do not feel confident about either asking or dealing with questions in public, and end up avoiding the Q&A if they are presenting because they are afraid of tricky questions.

◎ Ask SS in work if they have any tips for dealing with the Q&A. Explain to SS that it is always best to anticipate questions people may ask them, but that there are certain expressions they can use to sound more positive or play for time.

© 🎧 10.4   MATCH PHRASES

◎ Refer SS to the Useful language box on page 94 where there is a summary of the expressions used for summarising a talk and the Q&A. Explain to SS they will be dealing with questions in this exercise. Ask them if they can think of any more expressions that they use for these purposes. Drill pronunciation of the expressions, highlighting sentence stress and, especially, intonation when asking questions on the board. Don't get SS to repeat all the expressions, just one or two from each section that might be difficult in terms of sentence stress and intonation (e.g. *I was just wondering what you thought about ...*).

◎ Refer SS to Exercise C. Play the recording a second time, pausing in sections to give SS time to write their answers.

◎ Get SS to compare their answers in pairs.

◎ Circulate and monitor, helping SS where necessary and pointing out these are indirect questions that are used to sound polite.

◎ Go through the answers with the whole class.

> 1   I was just wondering what you thought ...
> 2   I'd like to know ...
> 3   I'd be interested to know more ...; I mean to say, could you tell us ...
> 4   Yes, but I was wondering ...

◎ As a follow-up activity, you may like to ask SS what the direct forms of these questions are. (**1** *What are the main differences ...?* **2** *How can a company actually improve ...?* **3** *What kind of language do you think works well ...?* **4** *Is there any kind of language you would ...?*)

◎ Refer SS to the audio script on page 172. Play the recording a third time if necessary, whilst SS read the dialogues and underline or note the expressions used for summarising, asking questions politely and dealing with questions.

◎ Alternatively, you may like to refer SS to the audio script and ask them to practise the dialogue in pairs, using the correct intonation.

◎ For further practice, go to the Resource bank on page 229 of this book.

Ⓓ

◎ Explain to SS they are going to do a role-play as Internet/IT experts, practising dealing with difficult questions related to the Internet and using some of the expressions in the Useful language box.

◎ Divide SS into pairs. SS A and B look at their corresponding information on pages 147 and 155. Ask SS to take notes before they start the role-play, referring to other sections in the Course Book where necessary. This is important if SS are going to do the task successfully. Help them, if necessary, to formulate the additional questions on the topic (e.g. *I was wondering what kind of software you would recommend for creating my own website? Could I ask you what sort of dot-com companies you think have done well in recent years? I'd be interested to know your opinion of the eight-second rule in web page design.*). Point out to SS that the questions do not have to relate only to e-business, but can be general questions on the Internet and other IT issues, depending on SS's interests. Explain that in the role-play, it is acceptable for them to admit they are not an expert, but they should try to give a general opinion and refer their partner to some other source or person for more information.

◎ Monitor and circulate round the class as SS act out the role-plays, encouraging them to ask follow-up questions. Make a note of SS who carry out the task successfully, any useful language used and five or six language points for correction, including pronunciation.

◎ Go through the correct question forms with the whole class.

> **Suggested answers**
> **Student A**
> 1   I was (just) wondering what you thought about university and higher education exams being administered online.
> 2   I'd be interested to know how access and use of the Internet can be improved in developing countries.
> 3   I'd like to know if/whether you think there should be stricter control of the Internet regarding security.
>
> **Student B**
> 1   I was (just) wondering how company websites might encourage consumers to shop more online.
> 2   Could you tell me what the government can do to reduce online credit-card fraud?
> 3   I'd like to know whether children under five should use computers for educational purposes.

◎ As a follow-up, you may like to ask a couple of SS to ask / deal with a question for the rest of the class. Alternatively, get SS to ask you some difficult questions.

◎ Go through feedback with the whole class, praising appropriate language for dealing with difficult questions. Write up any points that need further work on the board.

◎ For further practice, go to the Resource bank on page 229 of this book.

 E

◎ Explain to SS they are going to summarise a short presentation on a topic of their choice, but related to online business, the Internet or IT, and that they will need to use some of the expressions in the Useful language box. The presentations need only be three to five minutes long.

◎ Ask SS to look at the possible topics on page 161. Ask SS to take notes and give them enough time to prepare the summary or conclusion of their presentation. This is important if SS are going to do the task successfully. Monitor and circulate as SS do this, helping where necessary. Point out that SS should also anticipate questions they may be asked by the audience. Explain that in the role-play, it is acceptable for them to admit they are not an expert, but they should try to give a general opinion and refer their partner to some other source or person for more information.

◎ SS give their presentations to the rest of the class. Encourage the other SS to ask follow-up questions. In one-to-one classes, ask the questions yourself. Make a note of SS who gave effective presentations, the key language used and five or six language points for correction, including pronunciation.

◎ Go through feedback with the whole class, praising appropriate language for dealing with difficult questions. Write up any points that need further work on the board.

◎ You may like to ask SS to give their presentations and do the following writing exercise in the next class in order to give SS more time to prepare and use slides, handouts or other visual aids. It may also be appropriate to record SS on cassette or video during this task for intensive correction work.

Writing: Presenting information on a website

SS look at tips for writing web pages and write up the main points of their presentations for a site.

F

◎ Explain to SS they are going to look at presenting information about doing online business on a website.

◎ Get SS to look at the information on page 161 first individually and ask SS to take notes before they start discussing in a group.

◎ Divide the class into groups of threes or fours. SS talk about how they could present this information in the best way. Explain to SS they do not need to rewrite the information, only discuss and take notes as to how they would set out the information on the web.

◎ Monitor and circulate, encouraging SS to discuss various ways of writing for web pages and highlighting that in this task, the organisation of the material is more important than the 'copy' (the actual language used). Make a note of SS who carry out the task successfully, any useful language used and five or six language points for correction.

◎ Go through feedback with the whole class, summarising some of the best ideas and praising appropriate language used for talking about online business and web writing. Write up any points that need further work on the board.

◎ Refer SS to the writing tips at the bottom of the page and the example web page on page 141 and get SS to compare their ideas with the latter. Note there is not right or wrong answer for this task, but SS may mention some of the following points.

Suggested answers

1 Use/non-use of white space and colour: too much text on one page.

2 Organisation of text: divide the text over 2–3 web pages? Re-write the introduction into a shorter paragraph? Reduce the existing text for the different points, adding bullet points?

3 Headings and sub-headings: Issues and Solutions are perhaps confusing sitting next to each other in two columns.

4 Key words and expressions in the text need highlighting.

There are, however, short, clear sentences in the introduction and bullet-style points under each sub-heading. A direct and informal style of web writing has also been used.

 Writing file page 141

 G

◎ As a lead-in to this writing section, ask SS whether they have ever written information for web pages for their company or organisation or for a personal website.

◎ Get SS to read the tips on Writing for web pages.

◎ Set out a template for a web page on the board, much like the one on page 141. Alternatively, if you have computer access in your classroom, refer SS to their company or organisation's website. Ask SS to comment on the organisation of the web page, e.g. use of headings and subheadings, white space, menus, etc.

◎ Refer SS to Exercise G. If they have given a presentation recently, they can base their writing on that. If not, they can use the one they did in Exercise E.

Lesson notes

◎ Circulate, monitor and help SS whilst they write up their presentations. Explain that this summary should fit on approximately three web pages. SS may tend to use more formal language, as this is a writing task, but explain that for web pages, a more informal style is usually used. Make a note of any useful expressions used on the board and any common errors.

◎ Early finishers can be referred to the board to see if they know all the expressions and if they can correct the errors.

Writing file page 141

◎ After completing the task, and if peer correction is appropriate in your setting, SS may compare their web writing in pairs. Were the pages short and simple? Was there one idea per paragraph? Did they use an objective and informal style that would be direct and clear for a web visitor? Did they use headings and sub-headings and highlight key words or expressions? What could be improved?

◎ To help SS be more aware of the impact their writing has on the reader, put each pair of SS with another pair. They exchange and read each others' web pages, etc. If they spot any words and expressions they don't know, they can ask their colleagues who wrote it about the meaning.

◎ Go through feedback with the whole class, praising good examples of web language and style and pointing out five or six areas that need further work.

◎ Alternatively, this writing task could also be set for homework. You may like to encourage SS to write up the main points of their presentations on slides to present in the following class.

Case study: Improving the online experience

Audio Wire is a manufacturer of electronic equipment that wants to improve its online sales. It has hired the web design company, Online Experience, to analyse sales data, improve the website and overall sales of the earphones section, where they sell directly to consumers. SS listen to a meeting with the team at Online Experience, analyse the website data, write up a proposal for redesigning the website and present their recommendations to the client company.

◎ In class, pay particular attention to clearly breaking down the case study into the different tasks and making sure that SS understand and follow the structure of what you are doing.

◎ As with other units involving specific vocabulary, it is a good idea for SS to have looked at the Business brief (page 119) as background reading before doing this case study in class.

Background

◎ Get SS to focus on the Audio Wire web page. As a lead-in to the case study, ask SS to discuss in pairs for a minute or two what they think of the web page. Is it effective for online shoppers?

◎ Go through feedback with the whole class, writing up SS's ideas on the board. (SS may say that there is not enough information/text, no prices are given, the image of the earphones is too large and the menu on the left takes up too much space; you cannot tell from this page whether the product is available or not; they may also mention that the background is too dark and 'busy' and that it makes it difficult to read the main text.)

◎ Write the following headings from the left-hand column of the table on the board. Refer SS to the background information and elicit information from SS to complete the right-hand column. Deal with any questions SS may have (e.g. conversion rates are explained beneath the background information – see also the Business brief for this unit (page 119)).

Company	Audio Wire Incorporated
Purpose	Manufacturer and seller of professional microphones, earphones, etc.
Industry	Audio electronics
Based in	New York, USA
Task	Improve sales of the earphones section of AudioWire.com
Solution	Improve its online business and website; increase conversion rates and overall sales by 100%
Consultants	Online Experience, a web design company
Deliverables required	Analysis of Audio Wire's website usability; analysis of online sales data (web metrics); recommendations for redesign.

Listening 🎧 10.5

◎ Get SS's initial reactions to the pie chart showing conversation rates for Audio Wire. SS will probably say that abandonment rates (see the Business brief on page 119) are high at 49% and that there are few returning customers (17%).

◎ Refer SS to the rubric for the listening.

◎ Establish with SS what the team members are responsible for and write this up on the board (i.e. Ed = MD; Larry = Online Sales Analyst; Kirstie = Designer and Copywriter). Also write up on the board the following three headings:
Problems with Audio Wire.com
Recommendations
Deliverables

◎ Play the recording once without stopping.

◎ After listening SS compare ideas in pairs. If necessary, play it a second time.

◎ Go through the answers with the whole class. Note that much of this information has already come up in the background or is apparent from the image of the website.

Lesson notes

Problems with Audio Wire.com

Bad sales-conversion rates, very few users are returning to purchase; high shopping-cart abandonment rates (49%); problems with the checkout process, which is too long and requires registration; confusing navigation; content and design – images too large; not enough information about the products.

Recommendations

Redesign and relaunch the website: Audio Wire needs a single functional web page to view all their product selections, pricing, delivery and payment information. Make images smaller. Rewrite copy for the web page.

Deliverables

1 A file showing screenshots of the current site and their recommendations. They recommend improving navigation and content for every page in the buying process, from the earphones home page through to checkout.

2 Rewrite the copy / web text with exact wording for one of Audio Wire's products in the earphones range.

◎ As a follow-up, refer SS to the audio script on page 172. Deal with any questions they may have regarding colloquial American words and spoken expressions, e.g. *like* (used as a filler while you are thinking of what to say next, also British English); *just way too big* (= *much too/extremely*, informal, spoken); *Yup* or *Yep* (= *Yeah/Yes*, informal and spoken); *Some of it really sucks* (= *is awful/very bad*, spoken). Do not spend too long going through the audio script at this stage.

Task 1

◎ As a lead-in to the task, get SS to focus on the Online Experience web page. Ask SS to read it quickly and ask them the following questions:
What's the name of the client company mentioned? (DTV Television Networks)
What kind of an increase in sales conversion rates did they achieve for DTV? (50%)
What kind of improvements do they usually achieve in sales conversion rates? (40%–150%)

◎ Remind SS that Audio Wire has asked for a 100% increase in online sales and they are going to have to live up to their reputation of experienced web consultants in the following task.

◎ Divide SS in small groups of three or four. Explain that in this role-play they meet as members of the team at Online Experience to discuss improvements and recommendations for the relaunch of Audio Wire. Note that the client originally asked for improvements to the earphones section, but has now agreed to a relaunch of the site. Ask SS to take notes on the different points to consider and deal with any questions SS may have before they begin the task. You may also want to ask SS to take on the three roles of the MD (Ed), the Online Sales Analyst (Larry) and the Designer and Copywriter (Kirstie).

◎ Circulate and monitor, checking SS are carrying out the task correctly. Make a note of any key language and expressions being used and common errors for correction on the board, including pronunciation, for later feedback.

◎ Early finishers can try to correct the errors on the board, or summarise their recommendations for improvements.

◎ Bring the class to order. Quickly summarise some of the best ideas that were mentioned and go on to the next task.

Task 2

◎ SS continue working in the same groups as in Task 1.

◎ Ask them to review their recommendations and prepare to present them in the form of a summary. Explain that they will now present their recommendations for Audio Wire management. SS should divide the presentation into equal parts between them and anticipate any questions they may be asked. Make sure SS have sufficient preparation time at this stage so that they can carry out the task successfully.

◎ SS give their group presentations. Get other SS to ask questions at the end of each presentation. Make a note of useful language being used for summarising presentations and dealing with questions, and five or six points for correction, including pronunciation, for later feedback.

◎ Alternatively, if short of time, or SS are not willing to give presentations, ask SS to compare their recommendations for Audio Wire with another group.

Feedback

◎ When SS have finished, bring the whole class together.

◎ Ask one or two groups to say what happened in their groups and whether they think their recommendations will result in 100% improvement in online sales for Audio Wire.

◎ Praise the strong language points and work on five or six points that need improvement, especially in relation to language used for presentations and the Q&A. Make sure you highlight some of the SS best ideas and praise those SS who gave effective presentations or asked/dealt with questions appropriately.

Writing

◎ Get SS to look at the rubric for the Writing task and deal with any questions they have.

◎ Brainstorm the information that should go in the proposal and put these points on the board. All this information has come up in the listening and role-plays in Tasks 1 and 2.

◎ Get SS to write in pairs or individually, and look again at the section on proposal writing on page 39 of the Course Book, as well as the section on report writing in the Writing file.

 Writing file pages 138–139

◎ Circulate and monitor, checking SS are completing the task correctly.

◎ Alternatively, this writing task could be done for homework.

1 to 1

◉ Go through the information in the Course Book with your student. Explain any difficulties. In Task 1, you and your student are members of the team at Online Experience. Don't dominate the conversation in this task, but say enough to keep it going and allow your student to ask and answer questions. In Task 2, your student gives the presentation summary, and you represent Audio Wire.

◉ At the same time, monitor the language that your student is using. Note down any good examples of language and points for error correction or improvement. Come back to these later.

◉ Praise any good examples of language used and go over any errors, including pronunciation. Record the presentation on cassette or video, if desirable, for intensive correction work.

New business

At a glance

	Classwork – Course Book	Further work
Lesson 1: **Listening and discussion** (pages 98–99) *Each lesson is about 60–75 minutes. This time does not include administration and time spent going through homework in any lessons.*	**Discussion: Starting your own business** SS discuss their views about running their own business. **Listening: Interview with a consultant** SS listen to Max Benson, a director of Everywoman, a UK consultancy that provides advice to women running their own businesses. **Discussion: The difficulties of starting up** SS discuss the challenges involved in starting a business. **Vocabulary: Starting a new business** SS look at expressions relating to starting a new business.	**Practice File** Word power (pages 64–65)
Lesson 2: **Reading and language** (pages 100–101) *Each lesson is about 60–75 minutes.*	**Discussion: Opinions on start-ups** SS look at different opinions about starting a new business. **Reading: *The bruises of the bandwagon*** SS read about the qualities that distinguish successful entrepreneurs. **Language review: Noun phrases** SS look at noun phrases and practise using them in context. **Discussion: Entrepreneurs** SS talk about the qualities of leading entrepreneurs.	**Text bank** (TRB pages 196–199) **Grammar reference and practice** (page 132) **Practice File** Text and grammar (pages 66–67)
Lesson 3: **Business skills** (pages 102–103) *Each lesson is about 75–90 minutes.*	**Telephone strategies** SS look at tips and useful expressions for dealing with customers and suppliers on the telephone. **Chasing payment** SS look at useful phrases for chasing payment, then role-play a phone call about an outstanding payment. **Writing: A letter chasing payment** SS write a letter chasing payment.	**Resource bank** (TRB page 230) **Practice File** Skills and pronunciation (pages 68–69)
Lesson 4: **Case study** (pages 104–105) *Each lesson is about 75–90 minutes.*	**Copisistem: the next step** SS look at Copisistem, a DVD copying and printing company, and try to resolve a number of problems and constraints in order to manage the company's strong growth.	

For a fast route through the unit, focusing mainly on speaking skills, just use the underlined sections.

For one-to-one situations, most parts of the unit lend themselves, with minimal adaptation, to use with individual students. Where this is not the case, alternative procedures are given.

Business brief

Many people are attracted to the idea of running their own business. However, there is no blueprint for becoming a successful **entrepreneur,** and the reality is that more than half of all **start-ups** in the UK alone **go out of business** within the first 12 months. While the fundamental principles of starting a business are not complex, in practice there are many pitfalls on the path to success.

The hallmark of any entrepreneur is a **drive** and **determination** to succeed. Yet the **founder** of a business can ruin it if he or she lacks ability to think quickly and make good judgements. This **commercial acumen** is often only arrived at through years of experience and, very often, by learning the hard way.

Every entrepreneurial **venture** needs to have the fundamentals in place: a superior product or service that has been rigorously tested; extensive **market research**, an efficient **supply chain**, a **motivated team** and **adequate funding** are the basics without which no business can survive for long.

Entrepreneurs also need a receptive business environment. Many **small and medium-sized business (SME)** owners complain that government **red tape** is one of their biggest headaches. Bank financing is often expensive, and banks and other financial institutions are generally risk-averse. Businesses can sometimes **raise finance** from **venture capitalists**. These range from **business angels** to very large venture capital institutions, often specialising in particular fields such as biotechnology.

Another vital ingredient is skilful **team-building**. An entrepreneur may be personally capable of doing some tasks, such as finding clients or potential **backers**. But it is rare for one person to be able to carry out all of the tasks that are essential for success. It is possible to build an entrepreneurial team by hiring **top talent,** but this is usually unaffordable for a cash-starved start-up. Another approach is to hire younger, energetic workers and trust their vitality and commitment to overcome the inevitable hurdles. However, financiers are generally more reluctant to **back** a **management team** of enthusiastic novices.

In a rapidly changing world, change creates new **niches** that large corporations are often slow to exploit. Entrepreneurial competitors can move more quickly on ideas. The pace of innovation is increasing, with more new ideas coming on to the market more quickly than ever before. Those companies that start up on the back of successful **product or process innovation** are sooner or later faced with the problem of how to maintain the advantage that innovation has given them.

A few **critical success factors** (CSFs) tend to account for much of the difference in performance from one company to another within an industry. The essential questions are: Which decisions or activities are the ones that, if carried out wrong, will have crippling effects on **company performance**? Second, which decisions or activities, done right, will have a disproportionately positive effect on performance?

In retailing, for example, industry veterans have said that the CSFs are location, location and location. Retailers in top locations can get many things wrong and still perform very well. But those in poor locations, however many things they do right, will probably struggle to survive.

Businesses that do survive the first two years have probably survived because they have built up a good **customer base**, are adequately funded and have a strong management team. The first objective, survival, has been met. This is a good time for the founder entrepreneurs to consider explicitly what the goals of the business are and how it needs to be expanded. Do they plan to **go into partnership** with a rival company, **float the company** on the stock exchange or do they wish to keep it private? However quickly the company grows and whatever new form it takes, expansion inevitably means a change in culture. No one feels this cultural change more than the entrepreneurs who founded the business.

New business and your students

Both pre-work and in-work students will be able to talk about the pros and cons of being a business owner and whether they have any aspirations to run their own business. Some of them may have relatives who run a family business and know people who work for themselves or have a small business. In-work students may even have experience of running their own businesses. All students will have some knowledge of the new businesses that are doing well in their country.

Read on

Rachel Bridge: *How I made it: 40 successful entrepreneurs reveal all*, Kogan Page, 2004

Peter F. Drucker: *Innovation and entrepreneurship,* Butterworth Heinemann, 1999

Rita Gunter McGrath and Ian C. MacMillan: *The entrepreneurial mindset,* Harvard Business School Press, 2000

Steve Parks: *Start your business: week by week*, Prentice Hall, 2004

Howard Schultz: *Pour your heart into it: how Starbucks built a company one cup at a time*, Hyperion, 1999

Lesson notes

Warmer

◉ Put the following names on the board: Richard Branson, Thomas Edison, Bill Gates, Ted Turner, Anita Roddick. Ask SS what these five people have in common. (They are/were all successful entrepreneurs of one type or another.)

◉ Ask SS if they have heard of any or all of them and elicit what they know about them. Do this as a quick-fire activity. Alternatively, if SS are interested and you have Internet facilities, split the class into five groups and get each group to research one of these people on the Internet. Tell them their task is to come back and give a five-minute presentation on her/him.

◉ Give SS a copy of these five quotations or read them out and ask SS if they know which entrepreneur said what. Do this as a quick-fire activity.

◉ Finally, ask SS what they think about these views.

Business opportunities are like buses, there's always another one coming.
(Richard Branson, founder of Virgin Enterprises)

I never perfected an invention that I did not think about in terms of the service it might give others … I find out what the world needs, then I proceed to invent.
(Thomas Edison (1847–1931), inventor)

We were young, but we had good advice and good ideas and lots of enthusiasm.
(Bill Gates, founder of Microsoft Corporation)

My son is now an 'entrepreneur'. That's what you're called when you don't have a job.
(Ted Turner, broadcasting entrepreneur)

Nobody talks about entrepreneurship as survival, but that's exactly what it is and what nurtures creative thinking. Running that first shop taught me business is not financial science; it's about trading: buying and selling.
(Anita Roddick, founder of The Body Shop)

Source: http://entrepreneurs.about.com/od/famous entrepreneurs/a/quotations.htm

---

Overview

◉ Tell SS they will be looking at the subject of new business in this unit.

◉ Go through the overview panel at the beginning of the unit, pointing out the sections that SS will be looking at.

Quotation

◉ Get SS to look at the quotation and ask them if they've heard of Peter Drucker and what they know about him. (Peter Drucker (1910–2005) was a writer, management consultant and university professor. He wrote more than a dozen titles dealing with management, such as the landmark books *The practice of management* and *The effective executive*. He is regarded as the founding father of the study of management.)

◉ Ask SS what they think the quotation means, specifically, what type of 'courageous decisions' are needed to start a business. Don't reject any ideas, allow SS to brainstorm their ideas. They may choose to refer to the lives of the five entrepreneurs they looked at in the warmer, e.g. *Bill Gates dropped out of Harvard Business School to set up Microsoft.*

◉ If SS are interested, you could also give them these quotations from Drucker to discuss:
For the first four years, no new enterprise produces profits. Even Mozart didn't start writing music until he was four.
(Peter Drucker on the importance of entrepreneurship and innovation)
Everybody has accepted by now that change is unavoidable. But that still implies that change is like death and taxes – it should be postponed as long as possible and no change would be vastly preferable. But in a period of upheaval, such as the one we are living in, change is the norm. (Peter Drucker, *Management challenges for the 21st century*, 1999)

Discussion: Starting your own business

SS discuss their views about running their own business.

Ⓐ

◉ SS work in pairs to discuss the questions. Set a five-minute time limit for this. Then get feedback as a whole class, identifying the business sectors that attracted most SS, any hobbies that SS have that could be made into a business, and brainstorming the qualities of a start-up entrepreneur.

◉ Get SS to identify the top five qualities that they think an entrepreneur needs. Let them discuss their ideas for a few minutes, but it isn't necessary for them to come to a final conclusion if they don't agree. Lead and moderate the discussion and bring it to a close after a few minutes.

---

3 Business Angel Robert Drew includes in his list of qualities a willingness to succeed above all else, a lot of energy and total focus. He says, 'It's got to be a pleasure, not an irritation, when a customer calls you with a problem in the dead of night when you're on holiday.'
Other suggested answers: strong leadership qualities, creative ideas, hardworking.

Listening: Interview with a consultant

SS listen to Max Benson, a director of Everywoman, a UK consultancy that provides advice to women running their own businesses.

 B

- Get SS, in pairs, to read through the description of the work Everywoman does and try to predict the missing words and expressions. Deal with any questions, but don't tell SS the correct answers at this stage.
- Call the class together and compare SS's ideas.

Ⓒ 🎧 11.1

- Play the first part of the interview.
- Get SS to check their answers in pairs.
- Play the recording again if necessary. Ask SS if they would prefer you to pause the recording after each section or play the whole recording through again without stopping.
- Go through the answers with the whole class.

> **1** business skills   **2** qualified   **3** networking opportunities   **4** challenges   **5** barriers   **6** offline   **7** face to face   **8** workshops   **9** previous job   **10** workplace

Ⓓ 🎧 11.2

- Discuss the question in the rubric with the whole class as a quick-fire activity.
- Get SS to read through the summary before playing the recording. Deal with any questions.
- Play the recording; SS listen and correct the summary.
- Get SS to compare their corrections to the summary in pairs. If you think SS need extra help, tell them that there are five words to change in the summary. Ask them if they have found all five.
- Play the recording again if not all the SS have finished.
- Go through the answers with the whole class. One way to do this is to look at one sentence at a time and ask SS if it is correct or not.

> Research has shown that there are **five** specific barriers that women face when starting a new business. Firstly, they don't know how get access to **finance**. Secondly, a lot of business networks are set up and dominated by men. Another major barrier is their lack of **confidence**. Furthermore, women are not reaching high positions in corporations and they therefore lack the range of **skills** of many men starting their own businesses. It also appears that women are slow to adopt **technologies** that can be used to help a business to grow.

Ⓔ 🎧 11.3

- Ask SS to look at the list and brainstorm some examples of businesses in each category. Deal with any questions.

- Get them to predict which of these business sectors probably attracted women entrepreneurs in the UK.
- Listen to the recording once. It should be enough for SS to get the answers. Get SS to compare their ideas in pairs, and ask SS if they need to hear all or part of the recording again.
- Go through the answers with the whole class.

> Two main types of businesses:
> - Health and personal care, e.g. alternative therapists
> - Training and development, e.g. coaches and trainers in business skills

Ⓕ 🎧 11.4

- Ask SS to look at the question and brainstorm some possible problems people face when starting their own businesses. Don't spend long on this; just generate a few ideas before listening.
- Listen to the recording once. It may be enough for SS to get both answers. Get SS to compare their ideas in pairs. Ask SS if they need to hear all or part of the recording again.
- Go through the answers with the whole class.

> Two main problems:
> - Underestimating how much money they're going to need to borrow in their business plans.
> - Underestimating how long it's going to take until the money starts coming in.

- As a final listening activity, you may want to refer SS to the audio scripts for recordings 11.1–11.4 on pages 172–173. It's often very useful for SS to listen and read the script both for pronunciation purposes and in terms of the language structures and vocabulary used in the recording.
- Ask SS to pick out a language area, such as words or expressions relating to new business or ten words/expressions they'd like to know the meaning of. Don't spend too long going over the script in detail.

Discussion: The difficulties of starting up

SS discuss the challenges involved in starting a business.

 Ⓖ

- Get SS to discuss their answers in groups of three or four. Circulate and monitor, helping where necessary with vocabulary.
- Bring the class together and encourage SS particularly to talk about some of the problems and risks facing small businesses starting up today.
- Alternatively, you may want to allow some time to research some of these questions (e.g. on the Internet and in management books and magazines) and then discuss their findings.

Lesson notes

Vocabulary: Starting a new business

SS look at expressions relating to starting a new business.

- Get SS to look at the words and expressions in the box. Tell them to look up any words they don't know in their dictionaries. The *Longman Business English Dictionary* is a good monolingual source of business vocabulary.
- Get SS to work in pairs to do the exercise.
- Bring the class together and go through the answers, checking that SS know what the words mean and drawing their attention to collocations, e.g. *go into partnership*, *go out of business*, *offer business grants*, *government red tape*.

1 partnership	**2** out of business	**3** business grants
4 red tape	**5** Venture capital	**6** franchise

Discussion: Opinions on start-ups

SS look at different opinions about starting a new business.

- Tell SS to do the exercise individually. Deal with any questions (e.g. A 'mature market' is one where growth is relatively low and there are fewer competitors than before).
- Get SS to compare and discuss their answers in groups of three or four.

Reading: *The bruises of the bandwagon*

SS read about the qualities that distinguish successful entrepreneurs.

- Refer SS to the title of the article. Ask them what they think *The bruises of the bandwagon* means (the painful experiences of being a start-up entrepreneur). Explain that *to jump/climb/get/scramble on the bandwagon* means 'to start doing or saying the things that a lot of people are already doing/saying'. Ask SS what they imagine some of these 'bruises' might be (e.g. losing a lot of money) and how they think these bruises might be beneficial for an entrepreneur (e.g. learning from experience).
- Get SS to look at the cartoon in the article. Ask them how it relates to the title of the article. (A 'small' business man is trying to chase the success of a 'big' business man.)
- Divide SS into two groups. Tell Group A to read paragraphs 1–5, and Group B to read paragraphs 6–10, and review their answers to Exercise A, with Group A focusing on statements 1–4 and Group B on statements 5–8. Tell SS to ignore any words or phrases they don't know at this stage and focus on the task.

- When the SS have had time to read and discuss their answers, put SS into A+B pairs to tell each other about the part of the article they've read and to review their answers to Exercise A together.
- Call the class together and go through statements 1–8 in Exercise A. Get SS to say if the article agrees (A) or disagrees (D) with the statements and where this information is found in the article.
- Ask SS if they were surprised by, or disagreed with, any of the points made in the article.

---

1 D *Venture capitalists and business angels have always been more inclined to back a great team with a mediocre idea than a mediocre team with a great idea.* (paragraph 2)

2 D Both are important. *Ultimately, the success of a business idea rests on the ability of the entrepreneur. They must have basic business skills or acquire them via personal development or hiring. They must also have leadership qualities …* (paragraph 3)

3 D *… their chances of success will also improve in proportion to the level of relevant knowledge they bring to their chosen market … for example, where an engineer takes the knowledge he gains at a large company and uses it to set up a rival.* (paragraph 3)

4 A *Herbert Simon … suggests this process is intuitive: a good business idea stems from the creative linking, or cross-association, of know-how and contacts.* (paragraph 5)

5 A *Innovation – whether in the form of a new product type, production method or marketing medium – is a temporary source of market power that erodes the profits and position of old companies.* (paragraph 6)

6 A *'Early entry during the growth phase helps survival, but is disadvantageous during the mature phase' … In other words, jumping on a bandwagon is almost always a bad idea.* (paragraph 7)

7 D *Entrepreneurs should, in fact, be encouraged when they find there is very little data available about their chosen market. '[It] is frequently inversely related to the real potential of an opportunity,' says Jeffry Timmons* (paragraph 7)

8 A *Meeting these more focused consumer needs gives small firms greater competitive advantage over their larger counterparts.* (paragraph 8)

Language review: Noun phrases

SS look at noun phrases and practise using them in context.

- Do the first item together as an example with the whole class. SS should get this answer immediately, as the title of the article was discussed in the previous exercise.
- Get SS to work individually on the remaining vocabulary items, reading the whole text through this time. Circulate and tell SS if their answers are right or wrong at this stage.

Lesson notes

- Alternatively, if time is limited, divide the class into pairs and ask SS A to find items 2–6 (paragraphs 2–5) and SS B, items 7–10 (paragraphs 6–9); then SS exchange answers.

- Go through the answers with the whole class.

- If SS would like further practice with this vocabulary, get them, in pairs, to write three example sentences using some of the words or expressions. Circulate and check that SS are completing the task correctly.

---

1 scrambling on to the bandwagon / jumping on a bandwagon   **2** venture capitalists   **3** assets   **4** cashflow   **5** spin-outs   **6** know-how   **7** radicalism   **8** oligopolies   **9** ventures   **10** ground-breaking

---

- Refer SS to the Grammar reference section (page 132). Get them to read the explanation.

- Return to pages 100–101. Tell SS to identify both noun phrases and prepositional phrases in the relevant paragraphs.

- Get SS to compare their answers in pairs. Monitor and check if SS have identified all the noun and prepositional phrases correctly.

- Go through the answers with the whole class if necessary. If you can see that all the SS have the correct answers, tell them so and avoid the need to check everything in open class.

- paragraph 2
  ... have always been more inclined to back **a great team (with a mediocre idea)** *than* **a mediocre team (with a great idea).**
  Both noun phrases (+ prepositional phrase)
- paragraph 3
  Ultimately, **the success of a business idea** *rests on* **the ability of the entrepreneur.**
  Noun phrase + prepositional phrase; noun + prepositional phrase
- paragraph 4
  Research led by Dr Rajshree Agarwal, **associate professor of strategic management at the University of Illinois,** *suggests ...*
  Noun phrase + prepositional phrase + prepositional phrase
- paragraph 5
  ... a good business idea stems from the **creative linking,** *or* **cross-association, of know-how and contacts.**
  Noun phrase + prepositional phrase
- paragraph 7
  Subsequent research by Dr Agarwal, in collaboration with Professor Michael Gort, *has shown that ...*
  Noun phrase + prepositional phrase + prepositional phrase

- For further practice, get SS to do the extra exercises on page 132.

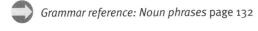

Grammar reference: Noun phrases page 132

---

1 **1** b   **2** f; a   **3** e   **4** c; g   **5** d
2 **1** e   **2** c   **3** b   **4** a   **5** d   **6** h   **7** j   **8** i   **9** f   **10** g
3 **1** prize money   **2** space flight   **3** zero-gravity   **4** space station   **5** 21st-century version   **6** ticket sales   **7** video games   **8** home computers   **9** reality TV show   **10** Aeronautics engineers

---

Discussion: Entrepreneurs

SS talk about the qualities of leading entrepreneurs.

Ⓔ

- Get SS to work in small groups of three or four to discuss the questions for a few minutes.

- Call the SS together and get feedback from each group's discussion.

- Add two further questions for discussion with the whole class:
  - *How can smaller companies have a competitive advantage over larger ones?*
  - *The American management guru, Peter Drucker, who said the opening quotation, also said: 'Few technical innovations can compete in terms of impact with such social innovations as the newspaper or insurance.' What innovations have entrepreneurs come up with in the last 25 years that have had a major impact on society?*

Telephone strategies

SS look at tips and useful expressions for dealing with customers and suppliers on the telephone.

Ⓐ

- As a lead-in to this section, ask SS if they ever have to deal with customers and suppliers. How often? What about? What form of communication do they usually use? Brainstorm some of the problems when dealing with customers and suppliers on the phone (e.g. misunderstanding, difficulties getting them to agree to do something).

- Split the class into two groups. Group A turns to page 147 and Group B looks at the telephone tip box on page 102. Tell SS to read the tips and try to predict the missing words.

- Explain that the other group has the missing information they need to complete the tips and they have to write questions to ask the other group.

- Circulate while SS prepare their questions and help where necessary.

- Put SS into A+B pairs to ask and answer questions and complete the tips.

- Ask SS for their initial reactions to the telephoning tips. Are there any points they agree or disagree with or more tips they would add?

Suggested answers

Student A

1 What should you (always) use? (*the other person's name*)
2 What should you quote? (*any relevant account/customer/invoice numbers*)
3 How should you connect with the other person? (*by apologising or empathising as appropriate*)
5 What should you confirm? (*the follow-up action*)

Student B

1 What does it (giving your name and using the other person's name) help to establish? (*a good working relationship*)
2 What should you have to hand? (*the paperwork*)
4 Why should you restate the details you are given? (*to check that you understand what's been said*)
6 What should you set? (*a deadline for follow-up action*)

(B) 🎧 **11.5**

◎ Refer SS to the picture of the kitchenware on the left. Ask them if they can identify any of the objects in the photo. Do this as a quick-fire activity as a lead-in to the listening.

◎ Get SS to listen to the recording and identify what the call is about (a mistake with an invoice; 12 units were ordered and delivered, but 16 were billed for).

◎ Get SS to listen again and say what techniques each speaker used that were good or could be improved on.

◎ SS compare their ideas in pairs, then go through the answers with the whole class.

Suggested answers

1 Both speakers state their names and use each other's names.
2 Darren doesn't have all the paperwork in front of him and seems disorganised.
3 Wendy shows she is listening closely by restating and checking the details, but she doesn't apologise or empathise with Darren's problem.
4 At the end of the conversation, the speakers are clear about the follow-up action and have set a time limit for it.

◎ As a follow up, if there is time, refer SS to the audio script on page 173 and ask them to work in pairs to write an improved version of the dialogue. Circulate and monitor, helping where necessary.

◎ Call the class together and get one or two pairs to do their dialogue in open class. Draw SS's attention to any useful language used.

(C) 🎧 **11.6**

◎ Ask SS the name of the two people (Wendy Taylor and Darren Bailey) and the two companies (Fenwick Plastics and Dyson Kitchenware) in the previous recording. Put the information on the board if necessary to remind SS. Ask who the supplier is (Fenwick Plastics) and who the customer is (Dyson Kitchenware). Explain that they have to phone each other regularly.

◎ Get SS to read the instructions and elicit from them what the phone call is about on this occasion (Fenwick are chasing Dyson for payment). Brainstorm the type of information SS can expect to hear (e.g. invoice numbers, dates, amounts).

◎ Get SS to listen and make a note of the outstanding payments and the follow-up action mentioned.

◎ SS compare ideas in pairs and listen again if necessary.

◎ Go through the answers with the whole class.

◎ There are two overdue payments: invoices 16987 dated 28 May and 17124 dated 8 June.
◎ Darren agrees to settle the invoice for 28 May this week. He also agrees to pay the other invoice within 15 days. Wendy will contact Darren again on 30 July if she hasn't received both payments.

◎ Get SS to look at the Useful language box on page 102. Drill one or two of the phrases from each section that might be difficult in terms of pronunciation.

◎ SS look at the audio script on page 173 and underline any useful expressions from the language box and noting any more useful expressions.

◎ Get SS in pairs to practise the dialogue, paying attention to the intonation, linking and stress patterns.

Suggested answers

This is Wendy Taylor from Fenwick Plastics.
Could you give me the invoice number?
Could you tell me when that will be?
I'm sorry, but we'd expect payment sooner.
We'd have to consider withdrawing credit terms …
Would that be acceptable?
We would prefer payment …
I think we can work with that.
OK, Darren. I'll get back to you on …

Chasing payment

SS look at useful phrases for chasing payment, then role-play a phone call about an outstanding payment.

(D)

◎ Ask SS if late payment is a problem for companies in their country and how long companies can usually expect to wait for payment.

- Get SS to look at the words in the box. Deal with any questions.
- Get SS in pairs to complete the sentences.
- Go through the answers with the whole class.

> **1** debt recovery   **2** account/invoice   **3** payment terms
> **4** delivery notes   **5** recipient   **6** deadline   **7** reminder
> letter   **8** withholding payment

(E)

- Explain that SS are going to do a role-play, using some of the expressions in the Useful language box.
- Get SS to work in the same pairs again. Student A reads the information on page 103 and Student B reads the role card on page 155. Deal with any questions. Allow SS a few minutes to prepare what they are going to say and remind them to try to incorporate some expressions from the Useful language box. One way to encourage this is to give each student cards with two or three expressions written on. They should try to get the expressions on their cards into the conversation.
- During the role-play, circulate and monitor SS. Make a note of five or six points for correction and points for praise, focusing particularly on how SS use the telephoning language.
- Call the class to order and go through the correction work and praise examples of good use of the language.
- Ask SS about the outcome of their phone calls. Did they get what they wanted? Get feedback from each pair, or if time is limited, get feedback from one or two pairs of SS only.

Writing: A letter chasing payment

SS write a letter chasing payment.

(F)

- As a lead-in to this writing section, ask in-work SS what kind of difficult correspondence they generally have to write. Ask pre-work SS what kind of difficult correspondence a supplier might have to write. If necessary, remind them of the phone call chasing payment in Exercise C and their own role-play in Exercise E.
- Get SS to read the information and deal with any questions.
- Copy and give SS the following useful expressions. Alternatively, give SS the headings and ask them to classify the expressions. Or write these headings and expressions on the board.

> **Useful expressions for difficult correspondence**
>
> *Establishing the specifics*
> We are writing to inform/remind/advise you that …
>
> *Supporting documents*
> Please find enclosed/attached a copy of …
>
> *Making concessions*
> In view of our good commercial relationship to date / in the past, …
> Other than on this occasion, we have always found your service/products to be excellent.
>
> *Firm request*
> We ask that you …
> Please contact us immediately should / if / in the event that …
> We'd be grateful if you could give this matter your urgent attention.
>
> *Consequences of not complying*
> In the event that we don't receive payment within ten days, we shall …
> Should you fail to settle this account, we will …
> Unless payment is received by this date, we may have no alternative but to …

- SS work in pairs to write the letter. Tell them to try to incorporate some of the useful language in their letters.
- Circulate, monitor and help SS whilst they write. Make a note of any more useful expressions used and any common errors (e.g. spelling, vocabulary) on the board.
- Earlier finishers can be referred to the board to see if they know all the words and if they can correct the errors.
- To help SS become more aware of the impact their writing has on the reader, and if peer correction is appropriate in your setting, put each pair of SS with another pair. They exchange and read each others' letters. If they spot any words and expressions they don't know, they can ask their colleagues who wrote it about the meaning. SS could also be asked to proofread each others' writing task and point out any spelling mistake or grammatical error they spot. Be on hand to help with this, if necessary, but leave most of the feedback and discussion to SS. If necessary, change the pairs around and repeat the process.
- Go through any common errors and the useful vocabulary and phrases on the board.
- To round off the activity, give SS copies of the model letter to compare with their versions.
- This writing task could also be set for homework.

Sample letter

Dear Mr Bailey,

Final Payment Reminder Invoices No. 17289 and 17356

I am writing to inform you that, despite earlier requests for payment, invoices no. 17289, dated 15 June, for €2,915 and 17356, dated 22 June, for €2,675 are now overdue. Please find enclosed copies of the invoices for your information. I'd like to remind you that, under our terms and conditions of trade, payment is due 30 days from the date of invoice. In view of the situation, I have to inform you that we will not dispatch further orders until we receive payment in full. We ask that you settle this account within seven working days.

Should you fail to pay these invoices by this date, then we may have no alternative but to reduce Dyson Kitchenware's credit limit to €6,000.

In the event that you have already paid these invoices, please ignore this reminder.

Yours sincerely,

Wendy Taylor
Accounts Manager
(153 words)

Case study: Copisistem: the next step

SS look at Copisistem, a DVD copying and printing company, and try to resolve a number of problems and constraints in order to manage the company's strong growth.

Background

- As a lead-in to the case study, ask SS whether they would like to run their own business and, if so, who they would like to run it with.

- Put the following table on the board. Write the following headings from the left-hand column of the table. Get SS to study the background information in the Course Book and to complete the right-hand column.

Company/organisation	Copisistem
Industry	DVD copying and printing
Based in	Valencia, Spain
Started	ten years ago
Owners	Doug Halliwell and José Ramón García
First clients and orders	Wildlife documentaries for a major publisher and DVDs for a national newspaper.
Initial problem	Turnover was low as few people had DVD players.
Initial success	Good margins and managed to capture some of the biggest clients in the country.

- Ask SS in pairs to look at the financial information and make statements about it, with possible explanations for the changes over the last three years. Invite comments and encourage brief discussion.

Suggested answers
- Assets have increased in value, which suggests that the company may have bought more data-duplication equipment and/or property. Note that this is a simplified description of the company's financial position and depreciation has not been included.
- Shareholder equity has also risen each year, suggesting that the owners have reinvested profits from the previous years in the company.
- Although sales have almost tripled over the three-year period, profits have not risen by the same level. This suggests that while the volume of sales has increased, the company is working for lower prices. Clients are increasing the size of their orders, but also may be negotiating lower prices in return for repeat business and large orders. There may also be cashflow problems while the company awaits payment on big orders. The company is therefore working with very tight profit margins.
- The strong sales growth obliges the company to have a lot of fixed costs (e.g. staff salaries, rent, energy bills) and assets (e.g. expensive machinery and stocks, which will be depreciating in value). All this leads one to suspect that although the company is doing very well, it will need external sources of revenue (e.g. bank loans) to help finance growth. This is a very common problem for new businesses which are successful.

Listening 🎧 11.7

- Get SS to read the listening task. Ask them to try and predict some of the information. SS may be able to guess from reading the background and the financial information that the number of staff, turnover and competition have all increased. They may also imagine, given its success so far, that the company wants to expand.

- SS listen. In pairs, they compare ideas. If necessary, play the recording a second time, pausing at the relevant points.

- Go through points with the whole class, referring to the audio script on page 173 if necessary.

Staffing

Started out with the two owners employing three people on production, two in dispatch, two in administration and José Ramón's cousin Pilar doing accounts one morning a week.

Now there are eight more operators, a chief technician, a couple of people now working on sales, and Pilar is now the full-time company accountant. There are also three more people working in the admin and customer service.

Turnover

Three years ago, turnover was around six million euros. Last year, it was almost 16 million.

Threats and competition

Now one of the leading companies in this sector, but there's heavy competition from start-ups and companies that have switched from VHS duplication.

Future plans

- To expand, particularly into other European markets.
- To be ready when something comes along to replace DVD.

Reading

- Get SS to read the e-mail, the Post-it note and the problems facing the company. Deal with any questions.
- Get SS to discuss their initial reactions to the problem in pairs.

Task 1

- Put SS into pairs. Student A turns to page 148, Student B turns to page 155. Tell SS they have to read the information and summarise it for their partner. Deal with any questions as SS read the texts.
- SS give their partners an oral summary of what they've read, referring back to the information briefly if they need help.
- Ask SS to discuss the pros and cons of Copisistem's owners going to a venture capital firm for finance.

Suggested answers
They can get much-needed investment money.
The interest rate on the loan is higher than a bank loan.
They could lose control of the company.
The company would probably be floated on the stock market within three to seven years.

Task 2

- Divide SS into small groups to discuss the issues.
- Circulate and monitor, checking SS are completing the task correctly. Make a note of good language and expressions being used and five or six common errors, including pronunciation, for later correction.

Possible solutions to consider
1 Subcontract some of the work to cope with demand.
2 Apply to venture capital firms for more finance and try to negotiate on interest rates, ownership and control issues.
3 Run the expensive machinery for more hours so that they recoup their investment before this asset depreciates in value and even becomes obsolete as another technology replaces DVD.
4 Appoint a Sales Director with experience of other European markets.

Feedback

- When SS have finished the task, bring the whole class together.
- Praise the strong language points and work on five or six points that need improvement.
- To round off the activity, ask one or two groups to say what decisions they came to. Also highlight some of the SS's best ideas.
- Ask SS what they think will replace DVD and how soon. SS might like to investigate this topic on the internet to see what companies like Sony are researching at the moment.

Writing

- As a lead-in, ask SS which publications and websites they would go to for job adverts if they were looking for work. You may also like to bring in examples of job adverts in English from the press or get SS to look at adverts on the Internet.
- Get SS to look at the rubric for the writing task and read the checklist. Deal with any questions they may have.
- Brainstorm the type of jobs that Copisistem might need to advertise (e.g. Sales Director, Marketing Director, Human Resources Manager).
- Get SS to work in pairs or individually to write their advertisements.
- Circulate and monitor, checking SS are completing the task correctly and helping where necessary.
- Get SS to read each others' adverts and say which job they would most like to apply for and why.

1 to 1

- Go through the information in the Course Book with your student. Explain any difficulties. In Task 1, you and your student read one of the texts each and exchange information. In Task 2, you and your student are the two directors of Copisistem. Don't dominate the conversation in this task, but say enough to keep it going and allow your student to propose solutions and respond to your ideas.
- At the same time, monitor the language that your student is using. Note down any good examples of language and points for error correction or improvement. Come back to these later.
- Praise any good examples of language used and go over any errors, including pronunciation. Record the role-play on cassette or video, if possible, for more intensive correction work.

Project management

At a glance

	Classwork – Course Book	Further work
Lesson 1: **Listening and discussion** (pages 106–107) *Each lesson is about 60–75 minutes. This time does not include administration and time spent going through homework in any lessons.*	**Discussion: What makes a good project team?** SS do a quiz on project teams and discuss their answers. **Listening: Interviews with two project managers** SS will hear two project managers giving their opinions about different aspects of a project. **Vocabulary: Project management** SS look at words related to projects and use the vocabulary in context.	**Practice File** Word power (pages 70–71)
Lesson 2: **Reading and language** (pages 108–109) *Each lesson is about 60–75 minutes.*	**Discussion: Job ratings** SS rank different jobs according to the level of difficulty and discuss their views. **Reading: *Not enough good project managers?*** SS read an article from a website about the difficulties that project managers face. **Language review: Cohesion** SS look at cohesion and referencing in texts. **Discussion: Project managers** SS discuss their views on some issues arising from the article.	**Text bank** (TRB pages 200–203) **Grammar reference and practice** (CB page 133) **Practice File** Text and grammar (pages 72–73)
Lesson 3: **Business skills** (pages 110–111) *Each lesson is about 75–90 minutes.*	**Writing: Briefing multinational teams** SS listen to three people talking about aspects of their own cultures, read tips for working with multinational teams and then write a brief. **Teleconferencing** SS listen to teleconference calls, look at some advice and role-play a teleconference.	**Resource bank** (TRB pages 231–232) **Writing file** (CB pages 138–139) **Practice File** Skills and pronunciation (pages 74–75)
Lesson 4: **Case study** (pages 112–113) *Each lesson is about 75–90 minutes.*	**Leatty Shanghai: a construction project** A Canadian developer has a major construction project in Shanghai. The team is multinational and based in three continents. A new project manager has to deal with delays and cost overrun.	**Writing file** (CB pages 138–139)

For a fast route through the unit, focusing mainly on speaking skills, just use the underlined sections.

For one-to-one situations, most parts of the unit lend themselves, with minimal adaptation, to use with individual students. Where this is not the case, alternative procedures are given.

Business brief

Project management has evolved from the engineering, construction and defence/aerospace industries in the last 50 years and is now found in all industries and organisations. For instance, the top industries now represented by the Project Management Institute's membership are information and computer technologies, telecommunications, business management and financial services.*

Project management is becoming more closely linked, through **project portfolio management**, to the strategic goals of organisations. Senior managers inevitably find themselves running projects as well as doing their day-to-day managerial role, and the principles and practices of project management are now an important part of every executive's responsibilities in project-driven industries.

A project manager (PM) has many responsibilities and has to **juggle priorities** and know how to **multi-task**. This includes the ability to assemble the right team, work out a realistic schedule, estimate the resources needed and manage the project as it progresses. A PM also has to get results when he/she doesn't have direct authority over team members, know how to handle differing **departmental agendas**, and how to combine his /her regular work with additional project management or participation responsibilities.

To ensure effective teamwork, certain conditions are necessary. Team members must understand the project objectives and have clearly defined roles and responsibilities. The project schedule should be achievable. Everyone must be aware of the team rules (e.g. communication channels), and these must be reasonable. The PM must have good leadership, conflict-resolution and team-building skills.
It is generally accepted that there are four broad project stages: **initiation, definition, implementation** and **completion,** although different terms exist to describe each of these stages. When designing a **project lifecycle** process, it's important to set out the project **objectives** clearly, to identify and define the number of **phases** and **sub-phases** of the project and to know which of these are **sequential** and which will be **overlapping**. Various **graphic tools** and systems exist to help with project planning, such as **flow charts** and **Gantt charts**.

It is then essential to identify the **deliverables** for each phase, i.e. what produce or result will be produced. These deliverables could be documents or physical objects. Key decision points (**milestones** or **events**) occur at the start and end of each phase or sub-phase. Depending on how the project is progressing, these decision points may include the need to revise the objectives or scope of the project, to **put it on hold**, to repeat a phase or to even end the project.

Advances in information technologies and the Internet have had a significant impact on project management in recent years. **Web-enabled project management** allows project information to be updated 24 hours a day from any location. Companies have been able to build **virtual project teams** with people located all over the world. It also makes it easier for PMs to react more rapidly to changes such as **schedule slippages, cost overruns** or other **risk factors,** and makes it easier to spot opportunities for improvements.

When evaluating the success of a project, there are **hard criteria** which are **measurable**, the most frequent being to do with time, cost, resources, safety levels and technical standards. It is less easy to measure **soft criteria** such as the levels of stakeholder and client satisfaction and the effectiveness of the team.

*Source: *Project management state of the art 2004* by Russell D. Archibald
http://www.maxwideman.com/guests/stateofart/intro.htm

Project management and your students

Your in-work students may be able to talk about their experiences of working on projects for their companies or for external clients. They may also have attended team-building training sessions as part of their staff training.

Pre-work students may have experience of working on projects and assignments with their colleagues and have views on the pros and cons of team-working.
Both in-work and pre-work SS may also have experience of team sports and can talk about how it compares to working in project teams.

Read on

http://www.pmforum.org/ PMFORUM is a not for profit resource that gives information on international project management affairs.

Russell D. Archibald: *State of the art of project management,*
http://www.pmforum.org/library/papers/2004/StateArtofPM2003Part1.pdf, 2003

A. Bruce and K. Langdon: *Project management*, Dorling Kindersley, 2000

Sebastian Nokes: *The definitive guide to project management,* Financial Times Prentice Hall, 2003

Stanley Portney: *Project management for dummies*, Hungry Minds Inc., 2001

Lesson notes

Warmer

- Write some, or all, of these sentence stems (in bold) on the board or dictate them to SS. Deal with any questions. Then ask SS how they could complete the sentences. Do this as a quick-fire activity.

- Read out the second half of the quotes and ask SS to match them with the correct stems. Write the answers on the board one at a time and/or get SS to complete the sentence stems they have written down.
  A two-year project will take three years, a three-year project will never finish.
  Any project can be estimated accurately once it's been completed.
  If it wasn't for the 'last minute', nothing would get done.
  The more ridiculous the deadline, the more money will be wasted trying to meet it.
  The sooner you get behind schedule, the more time you have to make it up.
  What is not on paper has not been said.
  When all's said and done, a lot more is said than done.
  Everyone asks for a strong project manager – when they get one, they don't want her.
  (Quote source: http://en.wikiquote.org/wiki/Project_management)

- Ask SS for their reactions to the quotes. Do they think there is an element of truth in any of these or not? What has been their own experience of working to deadlines? What tasks do they tend to leave until the last minute?

Overview

- Tell SS they will be looking at project management in this unit.

- Go through the overview panel at the beginning of the unit, pointing out the sections that SS will be looking at.

Quotation

- Get SS to look at the quotation and ask them what they think it means. Deal with any questions SS have about the vocabulary.

- Ask SS if they think it is true and brainstorm some of the reasons why a project might take longer than anticipated or cost more than budgeted for (e.g. poor project planning to begin with, people are too busy working on other things, experienced people aren't available or leave the project, work gets duplicated, work has to be redone because specifications change, staff sickness, computer viruses, testing throws up problems, cost of materials increase, more materials needed than expected, things get broken or lost, bad weather conditions, other unforeseen risk factors, etc.). Do this as a quick-fire activity.

Discussion: What makes a good project team?

SS do a quiz on project teams and discuss their answers.

(A)

- Get SS to read the quiz and deal with any questions. SS work in small groups of three or four to discuss their opinions. Set a five-minute time limit for this. Then get SS's feedback as a whole class.

- There are no clear-cut right and wrong answers to this quiz. The aim is to compare ideas and to highlight some of the issues associated with project management.

> Suggested answers
> 1 c A project manager can't be too easy-going if they want to get things done.
> 2 b It may be impossible to get total consensus, or take a very long time, so a) isn't likely to be the best solution.
> 3 b Being too rigid about schedules isn't likely to prove successful, as work may get done on time but done badly. If projects always take much longer than expected, then they haven't been planned or organised well.
> 4 c All these factors could be causing problems, but c) is possibly the most serious to overcome.

- As a follow-up activity, ask SS to say what they think makes a good project manager. Do this as a quick-fire activity and don't reject any ideas at this stage. Tell SS that they will be listening to two experts giving their opinions in the recording.

Listening: Interviews with two project managers

SS listen to two different types of project managers. Michael Sawyer is VP of Supply Chain and Purchasing for the Sara Lee Bakery Group. He deals with internal efficiency projects for his company. Rob Jackson is Operations Manager for the French construction firm Bachy Soletanche and he works on projects for external clients. In the first part of the interview, they talk about the qualities of a good project manager. In the second part, they talk about problems that can arise and measures of success.

(B) 🎧 12.1

- Explain briefly that Michael Sawyer deals with internal efficiency projects for his company, while Rob Jackson works on construction projects for external clients.

- Get SS to look through the characteristics and deal with any questions.

- Point out that Michael is the first speaker. Play recording 12.1 once.
- Get SS to check their answers in pairs, then play the recording again, without stopping.
- SS check their answers in pairs again. Then check the answers with the whole class.

		Michael	Rob
1	has good communication skills	✓	
2	clarifies people's roles on the team	✓	
3	knows how to organise and motivate people	✓	✓
4	avoids acting like a boss	✓	
5	includes members of the team in decisions	✓	
6	knows how to delegate work		✓
7	can deal with many tasks at the same time		✓
8	is able to take a global view of the project		✓
9	ensures everyone is clear about the project aims		✓

Ⓒ 🎧 12.2

- Explain briefly that in this second part of the interviews, Michael talks about sources of conflict in his projects and the role of the project sponsor in his company, while Rob Jackson talks about what he does when a project isn't going on track.
- Get SS to read the notes before they listen. Deal with any questions.
- Get SS, in pairs, to predict the missing words or phrases.
- Play the second part of the interviews. Pause briefly after the first speaker to allow SS time to finish writing.
- Play the recording a second time.
- After listening, SS compare notes in pairs.
- Go through the answers with the whole class. Deal with any questions (e.g. a milestone is an important accomplishment/event. In a project, a date is scheduled for each milestone).

> **1** help and resources   **2** the team up   **3** milestones
> **4** monthly progress   **5** moderator   **6** major   **7** minor
> **8** the client or the sponsor   **9** working with / reassessing and redirecting

Ⓓ 🎧 12.3

- Get SS to read the notes before they listen. Deal with any questions.
- Get SS, in pairs, to predict the missing words or phrases.
- Play the third part of the interviews. Pause briefly after the first speaker to allow SS time to finish writing.
- Play the recording a second time.
- After listening, SS compare notes in pairs.
- Go through the answers with the whole class.

> **1** set goals / set specific targets and deadlines   **2** tracking measures   **3** relationship between the members
> **4** programme and milestones   **5** budget   **6** make a profit
> **7** safety   **8** repeat business

- Ask SS to identify the similarities and differences between the projects that Rob and Michael manage and which job seems more difficult to them.

> **Suggested answers**
> Rob has an external client and needs to ensure they get repeat business. Michael has a senior manager in his company as a sponsor rather than an external client. SS may decide that both jobs are difficult but for different reasons.

- You may want to refer SS to all or some of the audio scripts on page 174 for Exercises B, C and D. SS listen again and read the scripts. Then ask SS to focus on a language area, such as finding and underlining ten words or expressions relating to project management (e.g. *goals*, *delegate*, *multi-tasking*, *project sponsor*, *resources*, *set up a team*, *milestones*, *going on track*, *remove obstacles*, *redirect team*, *targets*, *deadlines*, *tracking measures*, *costs*, *budget*, *safe systems*).
- Go through the ideas as a whole class, writing key words on the board so that SS build up a lexical set relating to projects.
- Deal with any questions related to the target language and don't spend too long going over all the other vocabulary in the scripts in detail.

Vocabulary: Project management

SS look at words related to projects and use the vocabulary in context.

Ⓔ

- Get SS to look at the phrases in the box. Most of these should now be familiar to SS from the previous exercises and the recordings. Deal with any questions.
- Get SS to work in pairs to complete the weblog. Circulate and monitor, helping where necessary.
- Bring the class together and check the answers with the whole class.

> **1** take on a project   **2** have a strong sponsor
> **3** renegotiate budgets and timescales   **4** face setbacks
> **5** celebrate the major milestones   **6** miss a deadline
> **7** reach a consensus   **8** get a quick progress report

Lesson notes

Discussion: Job ratings

SS rank different jobs according to the level of difficulty and discuss their views.

Ⓐ

- Get SS to look at the jobs and deal with any questions. They then do the exercise individually.
- Get SS to compare their ideas in groups of three or four, giving reasons for their choices.
- Go through the answers with the whole class to find out if there was any consensus of opinion. Ask SS to provide examples of the difficulties of each job and ask them for examples of other jobs they think are very challenging.

Reading: *Not enough good project managers?*

SS read an article from a website about the difficulties that project managers face.

Ⓑ

- Get SS to read the first paragraph of the article quickly.
- Brainstorm some of the reasons why SS think these firms might not have enough good project managers with the whole class (e.g. low pay, lack of training, stressful work). Don't reject any suggestions at this stage.
- Get SS to read sections 2–4 of the article for the information. Tell SS to ignore any words or phrases they don't know for the moment and focus on the task.
- Ask SS in small groups to compare their answers before checking the questions with the whole class.
- Go through the answers with the whole class. Start with all the points in section 2, then look at sections 3 and 4 in turn.
- Ask SS follow-up questions about which of these factors they would find the hardest to deal with.

Suggested answers
There are not enough good project managers because …

Section 2
- it's a tough role;
- you may get responsibility for completing a job you didn't start;
- the budget for the project may be low;
- the client could be impossible to please;
- the job you are assigned to manage may be one of ten jobs that you are responsible for managing (i.e. work overload and the problem of having to wear 'different hats');
- inefficient computer system;
- there just isn't enough time, money, or manpower to do the job properly (lack of resources).

Section 3
- lack of appreciation from your firm; lack of control of external factors (*budgets are routinely exceeded, deliverables late or quality lacking for any number of reasons … The fact that many, if not all, of these things were not/are not under the control of the PM …*)

Section 4
- intrusion of work time into personal time; need for constant connectedness (*The need for rapid-fire response requires that the cellphone be turned on and e-mail be constantly checked.*)

Ⓒ

- Get SS to read through the section headings first to check vocabulary. If someone asks a vocabulary question, throw it open to the whole class to find out if someone else can provide an explanation. If not, explain where necessary.
- Point out that there is one heading that is not needed.
- Get SS to read the whole text this time and match the headings to the sections. Explain that this is a skim-reading exercise and set a time limit of five to six minutes, approximately double the time you would need to do the task. Circulate and check answers, clarify any doubts and confirm correct answers.
- Get SS to compare answers in pairs.
- If necessary, check answers with the whole class. If not, then confirm that SS have matched the headings and sections correctly.

> **1** f **2** d **3** g **4** a **5** c **6** e (Distractor: b)

Ⓓ

- Do the first item with the whole class as an example. Deal with any questions.
- Get SS to do the exercise individually and then compare their ideas in pairs. Circulate and monitor, helping where necessary. Encourage SS to try to work out the answers by using the word form (e.g. is it a verb, noun phrase, etc.) and context.

◎ Call the class together and go through the answers with the whole class.

> **1** low performers **2** universally lauded **3** griping about (informal) **4** tremendously gratifying **5** intrusion **6** connectedness **7** real-world **8** restrictive

Language review: Cohesion

SS look at cohesion and referencing in texts.

 E

◎ Do the first item with the whole class as an example. Ask SS what *it* on line 5 of the text refers to (*a firm*). Ask SS if the *it* refers to something previously mentioned in the text ('anaphoric reference'), something yet to come in the text ('cataphoric reference') or something external to the text ('exophoric reference') (*previously mentioned*).

◎ Get SS to work in pairs to do the task. Circulate and monitor, helping where necessary.

◎ Call the class together and go through the answers with the whole class.

> **1** My theory is that no firm is completely happy with how **it** handles project management. = *no firm* (anaphoric reference)
>
> **2** There's no doubt about **it** – being a PM is a tough role. = *being a PM is a tough role* (cataphoric reference)
>
> **3** Your computer system may not support moving the work around the firm to get **it** completed by those best qualified to do **it**. = *the work* (in both cases anaphoric reference)
>
> **4** As the lead person handling the project from the architectural, engineering or environmental firm, **they** are also in the best position to see the firm's successes … = *project managers* (anaphoric reference)
>
> **5** … project managers probably face more of **this** than anyone else. = *intrusion of work time into personal time* (anaphoric reference)
>
> **6** The reasons for **that** are many. = … *the skills that are essential to being a good project manager … (which) are not emphasised in the typical engineering, architecture or science education* (anaphoric reference)
>
> **7** If **we** want to solve the problem of not enough good project managers in our firms, **we** are going to have to do some things differently. = *business leaders / management* (exophoric reference)
>
> **8** … not allowing **them** to go on with a dysfunctional idea that it is less important than the technical stuff they do = *the project mangers* (anaphoric reference)
>
> **9** … not allowing them to go on with a dysfunctional idea that it is less important than the technical **stuff** they do = *work that PMs do* (exophoric reference)
>
> **10** … not allowing them to go on with a dysfunctional idea that it is less important than the technical stuff **they** do = *PMs* (anaphoric reference)

 Grammar reference: Cohesion page 133

◎ As further practice to this language review section, refer SS to the exercise on page 133.

> reasons = *omit word*
> in an intercultural setting = *omit phrase*
> team members = they
> of living and working in a different culture = *omit phrase*
> All of these … mean that = This is why
> project managers = they
> cultures = ones
> Distractors: it, those

Discussion: Project managers

SS discuss their views on some issues arising from the article.

 F

◎ Get SS to discuss the questions in small groups.

◎ Circulate and monitor the discussions. Make a note of any useful language used and five or six language points for correction, including pronunciation. Put these on the board and get early finishers to start work on these.

◎ Call the class together and praise any good use of language. Then do the corrections with the whole class, eliciting the correct forms from SS wherever possible.

◎ Get some SS feedback from the task, such as some of the positive aspects of project work and their views on the need for praise.

Writing: Briefing multinational teams

SS listen to three people talking about aspects of their own cultures, read tips for working with multinational teams and then write a brief.

 A 🎧 12.4

◎ Tell SS to listen to the three speakers and try to identify where they are from based on what they say about their culture.

◎ Play the recording, then allow SS time to compare their ideas in pairs.

◎ Play the recording again.

◎ If SS have no idea, put the three nationalities on the board and add one or two distractors.

◎ Go through the answers with the whole class, eliciting some of the key information that each speaker gave. Highlight speaker one's explanation of 'loss of face / to lose face', meaning 'to stop having the respect of other people'. It is also 'to lose prestige', and therefore to feel humiliated or discredited.

Lesson notes

1 Chinese: 'loss of face' and 'saving face' are vital issues.
2 American: very direct and frank style of communication, not afraid to disagree
3 Russian: business culture is changing rapidly, don't have western 'good manners', don't smile much, direct style of communication

◎ SS might like to read the audio script on page 174 and listen at the same time. Deal with any vocabulary questions.

◎ Discuss the second question about misunderstandings with the whole class. At this stage, SS will mention their own culture's views on loss of face, frankness in communication and so on. If this is a multicultural group, allow an opportunity for at least one person from each national group to give their opinion. You may well find that even in a monolingual/monocultural group, there are differences of opinion about national characteristics, and people will argue there are differences between regions. To finish the discussion, ask SS if it is possible for people to be truly objective about their own culture and other cultures.

(B)

◎ Get SS to study the phrases in the box. Deal with any questions, in the first instance by asking the other SS if they can answer the question.

◎ Get SS to work in pairs to complete the tips. Circulate and monitor, confirming SS answers and helping where necessary.

◎ Call the class together and go through the questions with the whole class.

1 perceptions   2 working practices   3 sticking to deadlines   4 senior staff   5 frank and direct   6 sharing information   7 loss of face

(C)

◎ Tell SS that they are going to write a brief for a multinational team, explaining the working procedures in their country. This brief should take the form of a report.

◎ Look at the model report on pages 138–139 to remind SS of some of the features of a report. Alternatively, elicit the structure of a report from SS and develop a template with headings and sub-headings on the board. The sub-heading could be the items in the third tip, i.e. Time, Relationships, Communication, Social Values and Meetings.

◎ SS can work in twos or threes to discuss their ideas and prepare a report. If you have a multicultural class, group the SS according to nationality. Circulate and monitor, helping and correcting where necessary and making a note of good language used, and five or six common errors for later correction with the whole class.

◎ Alternatively, if an overhead projector is available, you could get SS to write their reports on transparencies and then present it to the whole class. You can then do correction work from the transparencies as well.

◎ Call the class together and ask one person from each group to present the ideas in their report. If time is limited, just do this feedback with one or two groups. In a multinational class in particular, SS might want to ask each other follow-up questions about the issues mentioned in the reports. Alternatively, in a monocultural class, get SS to swap their reports with another group and to read and feedback on each others' reports, pointing out any errors, if appropriate, and noting any good points that were mentioned and which they could have included in their own reports.

 Writing file pages 138–139

Teleconferencing

SS listen to teleconference calls, look at some advice and role-play a teleconference.

(D) 🎧 12.5

◎ Get SS in groups to discuss the four questions. SS who are in work may have experience of teleconferencing and therefore will have more to say on this subject. Find out how often SS have teleconferences, what the meetings are about, how many people attend, where the participants are based and what type of problems SS have had with teleconferences (both technical and language problems).

◎ If your SS are pre-work and have little or no knowledge of the subject, use the answer key as a 'live listening' comprehension task, i.e. tell the SS to listen while you read out (some or all of) the information and take notes to answer the first three questions.

◎ Call the class together and go through their answers, adding points from the answer key as appropriate.

Suggested answers

1 Options available:
   Dial-in
   The chairperson of the conference advises all participants of the date and time of the meeting, and then provides them with the phone number and access code for the call.

   Dial-out
   The chairperson (or operator, if requested) dials participants and connects them to the teleconference. This eliminates the need to get phone-number and access-code information to the participants before the call can take place. The participant simply answers the phone if he or she is available, and is immediately connected to the call.

   Operator assisted
   An operator greets participants when they call in, and that operator usually performs the roll call for the meeting (otherwise the chairperson is responsible for roll call). The operator also remains available throughout the call.

Lecture/broadcast teleconference
This feature allows a single person to speak or lecture for part or all of the conference without interruption. All other participants are placed in listen-only mode, their lines muted so there is no background noise or interruption from them.

Question-and-answer sessions
This feature is popular for shareholder presentations. During the conference, each participant, other than the presenter, is placed in listen-only mode. If a participant has a question, they indicate it by pressing a key on the phone, such as the hash key (#). The chairperson can then place them into speak mode. The chairperson is usually given the ability to field questions before they are addressed to the group, cutting down on unnecessary interruptions and keeping the meeting running smoothly.

2 Pros and cons
Pros: enables quick decision-making, problems can be handled quickly, it's cheap, saves time and money on travelling and setting up meetings, and allows you to be in contact with people anywhere in the world.
Cons: no visual communication or help (e.g. facial expressions, body language), easier to get distracted, people may be less communicative than in a face-to-face meeting, could be interruptions, background noise.

3 Advance planning
◎ Make a list of all attendees and check their availability on the date and time planned.
◎ Decide on what options you will use for your call. Will it be dial-in or dial-out? Will you want it recorded?
◎ Contact all participants and give them the date and time of the teleconference. Be sure to specify which time zone you are referring to.
◎ Include a written agenda for the teleconference.
◎ If you're going to provide handouts and supplementary material to participants, send it early enough so that it arrives before the teleconference and participants have time to read it and generally prepare for the meeting.
◎ Short biographical information on the participants is a nice addition, especially when people aren't familiar with each other.
◎ Remind participants of the telephone number and access code the day prior to the meeting, as they frequently mislay it and can't find it when needed.

◎ Tell SS they are going to listen to three conference calls and have to decide what the problem is.
◎ Play all three recordings and allow SS time to compare their ideas before playing the recordings again.
◎ Go through the answers with the whole class asking SS to say what they heard which helped them to decide.

Suggested problems
1 The first speaker is talking about an issue that isn't on the agenda for discussion.
2 Someone arrives late, giving her apologies and interrupting someone at an inappropriate moment when he is giving a presentation.
3 Gerry uses an in-joke or colloquial language (*a trick up his sleeve*) which is insensitive, as other people who may not understand the joke will feel excluded.

◎ As a follow-up to the listening, ask SS if they have ever had similar problems. SS often complain that native English speakers use a lot of jargon, slang and jokes that they don't understand, which can lead to SS feeling frustrated.

E

◎ Explain that SS have to complete the sentences stems (1–7) and then match them with the second part (a–g).
◎ Get SS to study the phrases in the box and deal with any questions, initially by throwing the question open to the class.
◎ Do the first item together as an example, then get SS to work individually on the rest of the exercise. Circulate and monitor, helping where necessary.
◎ Get SS to compare their ideas in pairs before going through the answers with the whole class.

> **1** g) take a roll call   **2** a) the agenda   **3** b) basic rules
> **4** c) an eye on   **5** d) keep track of   **6** f) get feedback
> **7** e) go over what was discussed

◎ As a follow-up, ask SS who do have telecons if they do these things, whether they agree with all the advice and if they would add any more suggestions of their own.

F

◎ Tell SS that they are going to role-play a teleconference, using some of telecon expressions in the Useful language box.
◎ Go through the expressions in the box with the whole class. Ask them if they can think of any more expressions that they use for these purposes. Drill pronunciation of some expressions, highlighting sentence stress, linking features and intonation on the board, if necessary. Don't get SS to repeat all the expressions, just one or two from each section that might be difficult in terms of pronunciation.
◎ Get SS to look at the background information about Archibald Food Group and look at the photo of some of its products. Deal with any questions. Ask SS how they think the company might have to adapt the products for the Chinese market (e.g. make the biscuits sweeter to suit the Chinese palate).
◎ Divide SS into groups of three. SS A, SS B and SS C look at their corresponding information on pages 148, 156 and 158. Make sure all the SS know who they are in the role-play. Get SS to take notes and prepare for a few minutes before they start the role-play. Deal with any questions. When there is a class with only two students, or a one-to-one class, the Student B (Francesca Russo) and Student C (Gao Shan) roles could be combined. With bigger groups, a fourth student could listen and evaluate how well the others do according to the tips in Exercise E.
◎ Circulate and monitor as SS do the role-plays. Make a note of SS who carry out the task successfully, any useful language used, and five or six language points for correction, including pronunciation.

- Call the class together when it seems that most groups have completed the task. Go through feedback with the whole class, praising appropriate techniques and language used for telecons.

- Write up any points that need correction on the board. Elicit the correct forms and pronunciation from SS where possible

- Feedback could then be in the form of action minutes. Elicit the decisions made from the SS discussion, the person responsible and the date for action. Alternatively, for further writing practice, SS could write action minutes from the telecon themselves. Remind them of the structure of action minutes by referring to page 136 of the Writing file.

- For follow-up practice, go to the Resource bank on pages 231–232.

Case study: Leatty Shanghai: a construction project

A Canadian developer has a major construction project in Shanghai. The team is multinational and based in three continents. A new project manager has to deal with delays and cost overrun.

Background

- Get SS to focus on the opening photo. As a lead-in to the case study, ask SS what they can see and where they think this picture was taken (e.g. building workers in hard hats, scaffolding, skyscrapers in Shanghai, China).

- Write the following headings from the left-hand column of the table on the board.

- Get SS to read the background information. Deal with any questions they may have and elicit information from SS to complete the right-hand column.

Project developer / client	Leatty
Industry	Property development
Based in	Canada
Location of project	Shanghai, China
Project description	three-phase housing development with shops and leisure centre
Location of team members	Architects in Germany, structural engineers and building contractors in China.
Problems at nine-month stage of project	16% over budget, two months behind schedule
Why a new project manager (PM) has been appointed	to rescue the troubled project

Report

- Ask SS to look at the milestones set at the start of the project on page 112. Deal with any questions.

- Ask SS to predict why a building project might be two months behind schedule. Don't reject any ideas at this brainstorming stage.

- Tell SS to read the report about the delays on page 113 to see if any of their predictions were correct and to find out what caused the delays.

- Deal with any questions SS have by throwing the question open to the whole class in the first instance.

- Get SS, in pairs, to compare their answers, summarising and retelling what they've read using their own words.

- Call the class together and go through the answers with the whole class.

> Suggested answers
> - The developers wanted the designs changed, and the architects took three weeks to do this.
> - There was delayed road access to the site for some equipment.
> - A building sub-contractor couldn't start on time because they had financial problems and they were delayed on another project.
> - Delivery of steel had to be delayed as there was nowhere to store it. The cost of steel subsequently went up.
> - A heatwave meant it wasn't possible to work the around the clock in the summer.

- Finally, ask SS to imagine they were the PM on the project. Get them to work in small groups to brainstorm some solutions to the problems as they arise.

- Call the class together and get feedback from the groups. If time is limited, ask only one or two groups to feedback.

Listening 🎧 12.6–12.9

- As a lead-in to the listening, get SS to look at the World Clock Meeting Planner and decide when the best time for teleconferences would be for a team based in these three locations. (There's no right answer to this question. Clearly when it's morning in Toronto and early evening in Berlin, it's late at night in Shanghai. One solution would be to rotate the meeting time.)

- Ask the SS where each of these groups is based. (The property developers are in Toronto, Canada; the architects are in Berlin, Germany; the building contractors are in Shanghai, China, as are the structural engineers for the project.)

- Ask SS to predict why team morale might be at 'rock bottom'. Don't reject any ideas at this stage.

- Tell SS to listen and note down the problems one representative from each group makes.

- Get SS to compare their ideas in pairs and play the recording again.

- Go through the answers with the whole class.

- After checking the answers, ask SS if they would like to read the audio scripts on page 175 and listen to the recordings again. Deal with any questions.

The developers

◎ Not everyone knows how to use the Internet-based application correctly. But some people are not familiar with the software.

◎ It's causing problems with communication. Some people in Germany and China are using e-mail, telephone and paper-based systems instead. It's therefore difficult to keep track and work is duplicated or missed.

◎ The developer wants people to be more task-driven and deadline-oriented, but contractors and consultants in China and Germany focus on maintaining a very high quality. The developer wants a 'good enough' approach.

The architects

◎ There's no face-to-face communication, and it's more difficult to exchange information and solve problems. No sense of working towards a common goal. More telecon meetings would help for status and progress reports.

◎ Not enough time allocated for quality design and revisions to the plans.

The building contractor

◎ Time differences make teleconferences difficult. The meeting times are set at the Canadian team's convenience. Everyone in China is tired when meetings are held.

◎ Contractor doesn't like speaking at telecon meetings and feels he's confronting the client by discussing delays in the schedule. This causes misunderstandings.

The structural engineers

◎ The feedback from the client is negative. They have achieved a lot in nine months,

◎ The engineering team is working 60-hour weeks. There's no time to enjoy their work as the work schedules are unrealistic and aggressive. There's a danger of burn-out.

◎ There's no clear idea when this phase of the project will be finished.

◎ Get SS's initial reactions to the problems mentioned. Don't spend long on this, as SS will have an opportunity to discuss their ideas in more detail as part of the main task.

Task

◎ Divide the SS into small groups of three or four. Get SS to look at the task and deal with any questions SS may have before they begin.

◎ Ask SS who they think the project sponsor would be in this case (i.e. someone in a senior management position in Leatty, the property development firm, but not the PM's immediate line manager. The PM works for the main building contractor overseeing the project in China).

◎ Circulate and monitor, checking SS are carrying out the task correctly. Make a note of any useful language being used and common errors for correction, including pronunciation, for later feedback.

Feedback

◎ When most of the groups have wound down their discussions, bring the class together.

◎ Praise any examples of good use of language and ask SS to provide corrections to the common errors wherever possible.

◎ Go through each of the points quickly with the whole class. Ask one or two groups for their solutions and ask the other groups if they had any different solutions. Ask SS to decide what the best solutions were.

◎ To round off the activity, summarise the discussion, highlighting some of the SS best ideas.

Writing

◎ Get SS to look at the rubric for the Writing task and deal with any questions they may have. Brainstorm the information that should go in the report and put these points on the board.

◎ Ask SS to look again at the report about delays on page 113 and to note features such as the structure (e.g. headings and sub-headings) and language used (e.g. passive forms, no contractions, linkers). Also get SS to look at the model report on pages 138–139 of the Writing file.

◎ Get SS to write in pairs or individually to produce the report.

 Writing file pages 138–139

◎ Circulate and monitor, checking SS are completing the task correctly.

◎ Get SS to write the final report either as a class activity in pairs or for homework.

---

1 to 1

◎ Go through the information in the Course Book with your student. Explain any difficulties. In the task, you are the project sponsor and your student is the project manager. Don't dominate the conversation in this task, but say enough to keep it going and allow your student to ask and answer questions.

◎ At the same time, monitor the language that your student is using. Note down any good examples of language and points for error correction or improvement. Come back to these points later. Praise any good examples of language used and go over any errors, including pronunciation. Record the role-play on cassette or video, if desirable, for intensive correction work.

Revision

This unit revises and reinforces some of the key language points from Units 10–12, and links with those units are clearly shown. This revision unit, like Revision units A, B and C, concentrates on reading and writing activities. Some of the exercise types are similar to those in the Reading and Writing section of the Business English Certificate examination (Higher level) organised by the University of Cambridge ESOL Examinations (Cambridge ESOL).

For more speaking practice, see the Resource bank section of this book beginning on page 211. The exercises in this unit can be done in class, individually or collaboratively, or for homework.

10 Doing business online

Reading

◎ This exercise gives SS further practice in using the language of online business, following the vocabulary and listening on pages 90–91.

> **1** b **2** c **3** d **4** a **5** a **6** b **7** c **8** d **9** b **10** c

Vocabulary: e-commerce

◎ This exercise gives SS further practice in using e-commerce vocabulary following the reading on pages 92–93. Point out the rubric and explain that SS have to find one word which does *not* collocate.

> **1** fickle **2** time **3** flashy **4** back-end **5** store **6** order **7** website **8** selling
> **9** price **10** a mistake

Cleft sentences

◎ This exercise gives SS further practice in using cleft sentences, following the language work in the Grammar reference on page 131.

> **1** It is the increased   **2** was their poor   **3** The thing that   **4** What has   **5** Queuing
> **6** is that it's

Presentations: summarising and dealing with questions

◎ SS work on expressions for summarising and dealing with questions in presentations (page 94).

> **1** c **2** f **3** b **4** e **5** a **6** g **7** d

Writing

◎ SS write a report which gives further practice in using the language of online business following the case study on pages 96–97.

Sample answer

Report
Audio Wire's Online Sales

Introduction

Audio Wire launched its website ten years ago. The site was initially used solely for advertising purposes. It was felt that it was not viable at this early stage to introduce the option to buy our products online for two main reasons. Firstly, the cost of integrating the online purchasing process with back-end systems was high. Secondly, the general public were more wary about buying goods and services online at the time.

Shopping cart

A shopping cart was added to the website five years ago. Over a three-year period, we monitored sales conversion rates, that is the percentage of people who visit our site and decide to make a purchase online. It was found that user abandonment during registration and purchasing was high, at around 49%. Some 23% of visitors only browsed the site, 17% were repeat online customers and 11% were one-off customers.

Redesigned website

Given the fact that only 28% of visitors actually made a purchase online, the consultants Online Experience were hired to evaluate and redesign our website with the aim of increasing conversion rates.

Online sales since the relaunch

The website was relaunched on July 15 last year, and the first 12 months have seen a marked improvement. User abandonment has fallen to 41%, while the percentage of visitors who only browse the site has also dipped slightly to 22%. Returning customers now represent 24% of visitors and one-off customers 13%.

Conclusion

The streamlined registration and purchasing process and the more user-friendly interface have clearly had a positive impact on conversion rates.

(262 words)

11 New business

Reading

◎ This exercise gives SS further practice in using the language of new business, following the vocabulary on page 99.

1 an entrepreneur **2** going into **3** franchising **4** red tape **5** running **6** business plan
7 grants **8** loan **9** Venture capital **10** go out of business

Telephone language

◎ SS work on expressions for dealing with customers and suppliers on the telephone (page 102).

1 d **2** c **3** b **4** e **5** a

Chasing payment

◎ SS correct a letter by identifying the extra word that appears on some, but not all, of the lines. Draw SS's attention to the rubric and the fact that some of the lines are correct.

1 ✓ **2** ✓ **3** you **4** ✓ **5** the **6** have **7** to **8** been **9** that **10** ✓ **11** not **12** do

Presentation

◎ SS write a short presentation. This task follows on from the context of the case study on pages 104–105.

Sample answer

It is my great pleasure to make this presentation on behalf of Copisistem today. My name's Doug Halliwell, and I am joint-owner of the company with my colleague here, José Ramón García.

I'd like to start by telling you about our great management team at Copisistem. Then I'll outline the risks and opportunities of investing in our company. I'd also like to talk briefly about a recent joint venture and our plans to expand our team. Finally, I'll give you the financial details. If you have any questions during my presentation, please feel free to ask me.

José Ramón and I started Copisistem ten years ago. Between us, we have 20 years' technical and managerial experience working for electronics corporations. We have a great team working with us, most of whom have been with us from the start of this venture.

We were one of the first companies to offer DVD copying services and we have managed to capture some of the biggest clients in the country, making us the leading company in this field. It is true that there is strong competition. However, we believe that our commitment to high quality, competitive pricing, timely order processing and constant innovation continue to give us the edge.

There has been a major development this year. We have formed a strategic alliance with a rival DVD company in order to deal with the increase volume of orders. We are also planning to recruit a Sales Manager with experience of other European markets to help expand our business.

I'd now like to turn your attention to some figures. As you can see from page 3 of the handout, our turnover has almost tripled in the last three years, from 5.8 million to 15.7 million euros. What's more, our projections show steady growth for the next two to three years at least.

You can also see that this high volume has also meant the need to invest in equipment and staff, and our running costs are therefore high. We estimate that we need a capital investment of 10 million euros to take our company to the next level. This injection of cash will allow us to set up a factory in Slovakia as part of our strategy to break into the European market. If you look at page 5 of my report, you'll see a breakdown of costs for this project.

Thank you for your attention. I'm sure you'll agree that Copisistem has the potential to be one of Europe's leading DVD duplication services.

(420 words)

---

12 Project management

Vocabulary

◎ This exercise gives SS further practice in using the language of project management, following the listening and vocabulary on page 107.

1 deadline　**2** reach a consensus　**3** setbacks　**4** over budget　**5** safety　**6** multi-task
7 on track　**8** sponsor

Cohesion

◎ SS work on cohesive devices following the language work on pages 108 and 133.

1 It　**2** it　**3** By then　**4** they　**5** the other　**6** both parties　**7** the project　**8** this
9 them　**10** this

Reading

◎ SS are given further practice in vocabulary related to working with international project teams following the Business skills section on page 110.

1 speak up　**2** confronting　**3** overruns　**4** direct style　**5** milestones and deliverables
6 face-to-face　**7** around the clock　**8** meeting times　**9** telecon　**10** teamwork

Writing

◉ SS write an e-mail giving cultural advice, based on the information they have read in the previous exercise.

Sample answer

Subject: Your new project
From: Sandra Winterbottom
To: Enrique Martínez

Hi Enrique,

Congratulations on your new project. It sounds very exciting. I'd be glad to help you prepare for working with your Indian and American colleagues. As you know, I've worked in Chicago and I spent a month in India on my last project.

The first thing to bear in mind is that Americans may seem a bit argumentative, but it's just their direct style of communication. Don't be offended, it's nothing personal and you like a lively discussion anyway. Indian people, on the other hand, are more indirect in the way they speak and they won't usually say 'yes' or 'no' outright. Make sure you always confirm what's been agreed and write down all the targets and deliverables for everyone to see. I use a flipchart or whiteboard for that purpose in meetings and then send action minutes afterwards.

I expect you'll have lots of teleconferences and you won't have many face-to-face meetings after the initial phase of the project. You may find that your Indian colleagues don't like contributing much to telecons. It's best to ask them a question directly to encourage participation and always thank them for their contribution. Also, I'd suggest you rotate the telecon times so it isn't always set in the daytime here in the States and at unsocial hours in India.

That's all that occurs to me for the moment. I hope it's useful. If I think of anything else, I'll let you know.

All the best
Sandra

(255 words)

⊚ SS are given further practice in writing action minutes and a short report following the teleconference role-play on page 111. The status report can be in the form of an email.

Sample answers

Action minutes
'Toto in China' project

Date: 25 November 2006
Present: Bob Frasier, Gao Shan and Francesca Russo

		Action	By
1	**Next round of trials** Fran reported on the success of the last round of product trials with the new improved biscuit flavour. Fran is going to Guangzhou next week to work with Gao on two days of further trials.	FR and GS	2 Dec
2	**Product labelling** The packaging department has solved the problem with the labels. Sample labels will now be available in Chinese and English by mid-December.	FR	15 Dec
3	**Production capacity** Gao Shan is still working on options to increase capacity. He's expecting a quote for new machinery in the next few days and will contact Bob if the cost is more than 7% over what was budgeted for.	GS	28 Nov
4	**Consumer testing** The Marketing department will start consumer testing after the next set of trials in China next week.	BF	9 Dec

---

Subject: Toto in China Status Report
To: Rachel Stevens
From: Bob Frasier

Hello Rachel,

I've just had a teleconference with Fran Russo from R&D and Gao Shan, our Head of Production, to discuss the status of the TIC project.

You'll be pleased to know that the biscuit flavour was improved in the last round of trials. Fran and Gao are doing more trials next week in Guangzhou, and then we can start consumer testing soon afterwards. I've now scheduled that for the week beginning 9 December, so the slippage there isn't looking bad at this stage, about two weeks.

Gao will also get back to me next week about the new machinery they're installing to boost production capacity. I'll let you know if there is likely to be any delay or major cost overrun on that front by the end of the month.

That's all for now. We've agreed to hold another telecon after the trials, so I'll send you an update next week.

Best regards
Bob
(167 words)

Text bank

Teacher's notes

Introduction

The Text bank contains articles relating to the units in the Course Book. These articles extend and develop the themes in those units. You can choose the articles that are of most interest to your students. They can be done in class or as homework. You have permission to make photocopies of these articles for your students.

Before you read

Before each article, there is an exercise to use as a warmer that allows students to focus on the vocabulary of the article and prepares them for it. This can be done in pairs or small groups, with each group reporting its answers to the whole class.

Reading

If using the articles in class, it is a good idea to treat different sections in different ways, for example reading the first paragraph with the whole class, then getting students to work in pairs on the following paragraphs. If you're short of time, get different pairs to read different sections of the article simultaneously. You can circulate, monitor and give help where necessary. Students then report back to the whole group with a succinct summary and/or their answers to the questions for that section. A full answer key follows the articles (starting on page 204).

Discussion

In the Over to you section(s) following the exercises, there are discussion points. These can be dealt with by the whole class, or the class can be divided, with different groups discussing different points. During discussion, circulate, monitor and give help where necessary. Students then report back to the whole class. Praise good language production and work on areas for improvement in the usual way.

Writing

The discussion points can also form the basis for short pieces of written work. Students will find this easier if they have already discussed the points in class, but you can ask students to read the article and write about the discussion points as homework.

Networking

Text bank

Before you read

Why do people 'network'? Do you think networking is useful? Why (not)?

Reading

Read this article from the *Financial Times* and answer the questions.

I refuse to hobnob for advantage

by Lucy Kellaway

1 At some point on Tuesday, 1,000 of the world's leading businessmen will get on aircraft and hurtle across the sky to Davos to attend the World Economic Forum. In their briefcases they will have a fat stack of business cards and a collection of glossy invitations. Every hour of the day for five days there will be a different social engagement to key into their personal digital assistants.

2 On Tuesday, I will be on the 8.38 a.m. to Moorgate Station as usual. I am not going to Davos this year. I did not go last year, either. In fact, I have never been. 'Never been to Davos?' people say, eyes wide with amazement. 'You must go. You'd love it. You'd get to meet so many people.' I always nod, but actually the prospect of the biggest networkathon in the world appeals to me even less than the prospect of going skiing – which appeals not at all. Having to make conversation with strangers while squinting at their name tags and trying to work out if you should have heard of them is a wretched way to spend an evening; doing it for days on end must be pure torture.

3 The whole networking process defeats me, in particular the business cards. I keep my own at the bottom of my handbag, and they are usually a bit grubby on the rare occasions I am required to produce one. Other people's cards go back into my bag, and get fished out whenever I spring clean it. They then sit on my desk for a while before eventually going into the bin.

4 Networking may not be all it is cracked up to be. Last week, I had lunch with a man who was a famous UK entrepreneur in the 1980s and now has many fingers in many pies. The previous night he had been invited to a drinks party in a grand London hotel. The great and the good of British industry were there, along with all the biggest brokers, lawyers and accountants touting for business and laughing just a touch too loudly.

5 He checked in his briefcase and went into the heaving ballroom, smiling and catching the eyes of the people he knew. Suddenly he felt tired by the whole thing. He did not see the point of being there. So he collected his briefcase, regretting the £2 he had paid to the cloakroom attendant for five minutes' custody, and went home to watch the cricket on television.

6 It had taken him 60-plus years to realise that networking was a waste of time. He could not remember one business deal or one person he had ever hired on the strength of a meeting at this sort of occasion. So why did he go on turning up? As a younger man, he had simply liked seeing and being seen. It had tickled his vanity, but that day he discovered that his ageing vanity was no longer in need of tickling, or at least not in this way.

7 The more I think about it, the odder I find the whole networking process. The very word is off-putting: it sounds so pushy and calculating. The point of networking is to meet someone more important than you are. But if everyone goes to a party determined to network, the whole exercise becomes self-defeating. It also offends against the idea that we work in a meritocracy, where talent will out, eventually. In true life, of course, talent does not always out. The smarmiest have an annoying way of getting to the top. But it does not follow that the collecting of business cards at drinks parties is a good use of time. Ah yes, networkers say. Theirs is an art, and you have to learn to do it well. Hence the success of volumes called *Non-Stop Networking*, *Networking Magic* or *The Networking Survival Guide*.

FINANCIAL TIMES

UNIT 1   Being international

1 Read the whole article and match these headings to the paragraphs they relate to.
   a) A recent networking event in London
   b) One entrepreneur's reaction to the London event
   c) The entrepreneur's new-found feelings about networking
   d) A description of an international networking event
   e) Why Lucy Kellaway criticises the networking process
   f) The reasons why Lucy Kellaway isn't going to Davos
   g) Lucy Kellaway's policy towards business cards

2 Match these adjectives from paragraph 1 (1–5) with the noun they describe (a–e).
1	leading	**a)**	digital assistants
2	business	**b)**	cards
3	glossy	**c)**	businessmen
4	social	**d)**	engagement
5	personal	**e)**	invitations

3 Match each of these nouns with the adjective from Exercise 2 it commonly goes with. More than one combination may be possible.
   a) brochure   **b)** lunch   **c)** brand   **d)** computer   **e)** occasion

4 Read paragraphs 2 and 3 and say whether these statements are true or false.
   Lucy Kellaway …
   a) goes to work by train.
   b) has always been interested in attending the World Economic Forum.
   c) doesn't like talking to strangers at networking events.
   d) can neither understand nor deal with networking.
   e) finds her business cards don't stay very clean in her handbag.
   f) often has to give people her business card.
   g) regularly searches through her handbag to find cards.
   h) keeps all the business cards she receives from contacts.

5 Read paragraphs 4 and 5. Choose the correct alternative to explain the words and expressions in *italics*.
   a) 'Networking may *not be all it is cracked up to be*.' This means it isn't as …
      i) difficult as it seems at first.
      ii) crazy as it looks.
      iii) good as people say it is.
   b) … *has many fingers in many pies* means that someone …
      i) suffers from an eating disorder.
      ii) is influential and involved in many activities.
      iii) is the owner of a famous chain of restaurants.
   c) *The great and the good* means people who are …
      i) respected for their charitable works.
      ii) considered important.
      iii) members of a secret organisation.
   d) *Touting for business* means they were …
      i) trying to persuade people to buy what they were offering.
      ii) praising something to convince others that it's important.
      iii) trying to buy and sell tickets for sports event or concert.

   e) 'He *checked in* his briefcase' here means he …
      i) looked inside it.
      ii) left it at the airport check-in desk.
      iii) left it in the hotel cloakroom.
   f) '… and went into the heaving ballroom, smiling and *catching the eyes of the people he knew*.' This means he was …
      i) trying to get the attention of influential people.
      ii) looking at acquaintances as they looked at him.
      iii) wanted to avoid eye contact with people he knew.
   g) 'He *did not see the point of being there*' means that he …
      i) felt there was no good reason to be there.
      ii) felt lost because he didn't know anybody.
      iii) didn't understand why the event had been organised.

6 Read paragraph 6 and correct these sentences where necessary.
   The entrepreneur …
   a) had only recently come to think that networking was not a good way to spend his time.
   b) thought he had made a lot of useful business deals while networking.
   c) had employed only one person he had met while networking.
   d) found he enjoyed networking more as he got older.
   e) had networked to help him feel good about himself when he was younger.

7 Find adjectives in paragraph 7 to match these definitions.
   a) appearing unattractive or causing dislike
   b) doing everything you can to get what you want from other people
   c) thinking carefully about how to get exactly what you want, without caring about anyone else
   d) causing problems that you are trying to prevent
   e) making you feel slightly angry

Over to you 1

- **What are the advantages and disadvantages of networking, according to the article? Do you agree with some or any of the points made?**
- **Can you add any more examples of advantages and disadvantages?**
- **What is the best way to go about networking in your profession or company? What organisations are useful to join? What events are worth attending?**

Over to you 2

Do you think you live in a meritocracy where the highest social positions are occupied by people with the most ability? Why (not)?

UNIT 1   Being international

Relocating

Level of difficulty: ● ● ○

Before you read

Would you consider relocating to another region or country for work? Why (not)?

Reading

Read this article from the *Financial Times* and answer the questions.

It's a brave new world out there …
so should you relocate?

by Henry Tricks

1   Relocation agents like to say their business is shockproof. When times are good, business people move around the world with the fluidity of cross-cultural commuters. When times are tough, they head back home again. One way or another, they are always on the move. However, the business of relocation agents is changing. These days, when executives are given their marching orders, it is a brave new world they are entering. In decline are the expat ghettos, the lavish rental allowances and the monocultural schools. Instead, expatriates are increasingly wanting to blend into their surroundings.

2   The habits of this well-heeled human traffic have big implications for property markets around the world; expatriates have long been a mainstay of the luxury rental sector. In central London, some 40 per cent of tenants work in the financial sector, and three-quarters traditionally come from overseas.

3   Landlords in the most exclusive expatriate neighbourhoods – St John's Wood for Americans, Kensington and Chelsea for Europeans – have been forced to take lower rents on the chin. They have also had to invest heavily to stand out in a saturated marketplace, ripping out old carpets to put in wooden floors, radiators to fit underfloor heating, and baths to make way for power showers. Horror of horrors, they have also been forced to compete with lower rental locations attractive to expatriates outside of London.

4   The change is felt just as keenly in other parts of the world. According to Stephan Branch of Sirva Inc., the worldwide relocation specialists, landlords in Hong Kong have been offering businesses free accommodation for up to 18 months of a three-year lease to secure their tenure. He says even expat-friendly Singapore, home to 80,000 foreigners working in white-collar professions, has begun to play second fiddle to Chinese cities such as Shanghai, where rents are lower, and the infrastructure and schools are improving immeasurably.

5   So, what are the changes to the typical expat way of life? Cris Collie, executive vice president of Worldwide ERC, a global relocation association, says Americans, for example, are likely to travel less, with more US companies moving employees locally, rather than across continents. 'It's not just going to be the typical American expat working for a US company any more. They've built up cadres of professionals all over the world. The talent is much more global.' That means shuffling more Europeans around Europe, and Asians around Asia. When they do travel, American assignments are likely to be shorter: to train local employees, for example, then head home. The days of compound living are also in abeyance, he believes: 'We're clearly moving to a more homogeneous world.'

6   Fons Trompenarrs, a Dutch cross-cultural academic and author of a pioneering book on the subject Riding the Waves of Culture, believes the old expatriate lifestyle is dying out. 'You now see many more nomads, who stay not years in a country, but days, and jump from country to country.'

7   The hotel industry has already adapted to the strain of such a lifestyle, offering fitness rooms, healthier food and better communication links – in short, more home comforts. Increasingly, however, executives will demand from their companies homes away from home, he believes, in the form of serviced apartments peppered around the world. These might be owned on a fractional basis: available for a number of weeks a year. But they will often come with concierge services and tailored facilities, so your favourite wine is stored for you, your own paintings are on the wall, and there are tickets to your favourite show when you arrive.

8   That means there is less need to uproot families, disrupting the children's education and putting strains on a marriage. It does mean, however, that some of the pungent flavour of living abroad will be lost. Which is a shame. Because it's a wonderful world out there, and exploring its neighbourhoods – and the people who live in them – should be one of the most fulfilling career moves a business executive can ever make.

FINANCIAL TIMES

UNIT 1 Being international

1 Read the article and put these points in the order they appear in the article. There are two that do not appear.

a) Executives' families do not have to relocate as often as in the past.

b) People now want a different type of accommodation when they relocate.

c) Cultural differences put stress on business people who relocate.

d) Executives are no longer working abroad for long periods of time.

e) Relocation agencies believe that they will always have lots of business.

f) Serviced apartments may become a more popular alternative to hotels.

g) More Asians and Europeans are relocating to America.

h) There is a downward pressure on luxury rents in many key locations.

2 Use the correct form of an expression in paragraph 1 to complete these statements.

a) A person or thing that is strong and resilient after being in a difficult situation is ....

b) If someone returns to a particular place, they .... there.

c) A person who travels a long distance to work every day is a ....

d) To be constantly travelling is to be ....

e) When a person is ordered to leave somewhere, they are ....

f) A situation that is new and exciting and expected to improve one's life is known as a ....

g) Part of a city where people of a particular group or class are concentrated is known as a ....

h) A generous sum of money given to someone for accommodation is a ....

i) A person who lives in a foreign country is an .... , or an .... for short.

j) If you want to appear similar to people around you and not be noticed, you try to .... the group.

3 Read paragraphs 2 and 3 and find words and expressions which match these definitions and descriptions.

a) informal word meaning 'rich'

b) the activity of buying, selling and renting buildings

c) important part of something that makes it possible for it to continue to exist

d) people or organisations that pay rent to work or live somewhere

e) people or organisation that own land or buildings

f) expensive parts of town where foreigners live

g) accept a difficult situation without complaining

h) be really much better than the rest

i) when there are more people selling than buying

j) make it possible for something newer or better to be built

4 Read paragraph 4 and say whether these statements are true or false.

a) Some landlords offer three years' free accommodation to businesses in Hong Kong.

b) It's possible to get a rent-free period for signing a three-year agreement in Hong Kong.

c) There are 80,000 foreign office workers living in Singapore.

d) Singapore is more popular than Chinese cities with people who relocate.

e) The infrastructure in Shanghai is gradually getting better.

5 Match the two parts of these phrases from paragraphs 5 and 6.

1	executive	**a)**	relocation association
2	global	**b)**	lifestyle
3	local	**c)**	academic
4	compound	**d)**	world
5	homogeneous	**e)**	book
6	cross-cultural	**f)**	living
7	pioneering	**g)**	employees
8	old expatriate	**h)**	vice president

6 Read paragraphs 7 and 8 and use the correct form of the verbs to replace the words in *italics*.

a) Hotels *provide* many new facilities for business travellers.

b) Serviced apartments are *in many different locations* around the world.

c) Serviced apartments will *have* concierge services and tailored facilities.

d) Families won't have to *leave their homes for a new place* as often.

e) Relocation can *adversely affect* a couple's relationship.

Over to you 1

- **What are the most exclusive neighbourhoods in your city or town? Do many expats live in them? What nationalities are they?**
- **What would be the most important factors for you in terms of relocating to another country?**

Over to you 2

What hotel facilities and services do you think are essential when you travel abroad for work?

UNIT 2   Training

Business ideology

Level of difficulty: ●●○

Before you read

Why do you think many MBA students choose to study abroad? Would you study business in an emerging economy such as China, India, Brazil or Russia? What would be the advantages and disadvantages?

Reading

Read this article from the FT.com website and answer the questions.

Goodbye to old-fashioned ideology

by Della Bradshaw

1 Earlier this year, the Chinese government took one of its most significant steps to date in ditching old-style business and education ideology. It licensed China's first privately owned business school to run MBA programmes. This ultra-capitalist move was a sign that China intends to become a world player in management education and that it will adopt US-style education policies to do so. The move comes just 14 years after the government licensed its first MBA programme.

2 The school in question is the Cheung Kong business school, established with money from one of China's richest men, Li Ka-Shing, two-and-a-half years ago. Already it has become a notable participant in the nascent Chinese market. Bing Xiang, the dean, believes the government is using his school as a pilot. Clearly others will follow, but meanwhile the school has to pioneer ways of running programmes in the traditional Chinese environment.

3 The Chinese university system's application procedure is very different from those in the US or Europe. Applicants can only apply to one school, and instead of the GMAT test – widely used in the rest of the world – they must sit a locally developed test known as GRK, which is written in Chinese. With Professor Xiang aspiring to attract overseas students to his programme, which is taught in English, the Chinese education department has agreed that, although all MBA participants must sit the test, there is no minimum score required.

4 If infectious enthusiasm were all it took, then the school would already be a world leader in business education. It is easy to see why Professor Xiang, an accounting professor by training, is so keen. Since its inception, the Cheung Kong business school – the name means 'Yangzte River' – has graduated its first MBA students, launched a range of executive programmes and is contemplating a doctoral degree programme. That the school has come so far so quickly is thanks not only to Professor Xiang, but to the remarkable changes happening in China and the thirst for knowledge that exists for the region.

5 The school's policy is to aim big. Its executive MBA (EMBA) programme – an MBA for working managers – is the most expensive in China, costing Rmb 288,000 ($35,500). Some 68 per cent of the participants are chief executives or directors. Getting the right faculty is more difficult. At the moment, there is just a handful of professors, but Professor Xiang intends to attract 80 faculty in the next ten years. As with the top traditional Chinese universities – Fudan, Beijing and Tsinghua – top of the hit list are Chinese professors who have studied and taught abroad. Academic associate dean Jeongwen Chiang was a marketing professor at the University of Rochester, and strategy professor Ming Zeng taught at Insead, for example. Both were seduced by the idea of conducting research in China.

6 'You really have to be here,' says Professor Zeng. 'If you are going to live in an e-world, using e-mails, it's really not going to happen.

Companies are eager to learn from you, the professors. China is changing every day.' The EMBA alumni network is extremely powerful, he says. 'We can get into companies, we can get information not through the formal channels.'

7 Professor Xiang believes the Cheung Kong school is a bridge between western academic research and Chinese knowledge. He says: 'People like myself have this view and vision. We don't want to regurgitate what we learnt in the US.' The school has written up to 80 case studies of local companies, and the dean believes this is a significant bartering chip when negotiating with overseas business schools to run joint programmes in the region. The school has organised a three-week programme with Insead and the Wharton School of the University of Pennsylvania for March, with one week taught on each campus. 'Our connections are getting better every day,' says Professor Xiang. 'We want to look at top-ranked business schools in the US and Europe. We will be complementary to each other.'

8 The Li Ka-Shing foundation is committed to keeping the school afloat for ten years, but Professor Xiang believes the school will be able to raise additional funds from individuals in the next few years. He believes the school has to consolidate its position in China, but does not intend to stop there. 'Our ambition is to go way beyond China,' he says.

FINANCIAL TIMES

UNIT 2   Training

1 Read through the whole article to find these people or things.
 a) the dean of Cheung Kong business school
 b) the university test used in the US and Europe
 c) the type of course the school offers
 d) the price of the school's MBA programme
 e) the number of teaching staff the school hopes to acquire
 f) two foreign schools that are collaborating with the Chinese MBA

2 Correct these statements about paragraphs 1 and 2 where necessary.
 a) The Chinese government set up China's first privately owned business school.
 b) China hopes to ban US-style education in management education.
 c) The new school was set up with money from Li Ka-Shing and Bing Xiang.
 d) The new business school belongs to Bing Xiang.
 e) The school is a model for future Chinese business schools.

3 Find words and expressions in paragraphs 3–5 that mean the following.
 a) system of requesting a university place
 b) do an exam
 c) the number of points required to pass a test
 d) the start of an organisation or institution
 e) a university qualification of the highest level
 f) a strong desire for information or to learn
 g) university teaching staff
 h) the head of a university or university department

4 Read paragraphs 3–7 and say whether these statements are true or false.
 a) The school's MBA is taught in various Chinese languages.
 b) The school's policy is to attract more professors from the US.
 c) Professor Chiang and Professor Zeng both prefer teaching in China.
 d) Contacts with ex-students means they can conduct research more easily.
 e) They want to implement an American ideology in the school.

5 Look at paragraphs 6 and 7 and choose the best alternative to replace the words in *italics* in the context of the article.
 a) *alumni network* (paragraph 6)
   i) contact with former students
   ii) meetings between former students
 b) *a bridge between* (paragraph 7)
   i) a transition from ... to ...
   ii) a way to get rid of differences between
 c) *regurgitate* (paragraph 7)
   i) reproduce exactly without thinking
   ii) memorise effectively

 d) *a significant bartering chip* (paragraph 7)
   i) a factor other than money used in negotiating
   ii) a concession used in exchange of goods and services
 e) *run joint programmes* (paragraph 7)
   i) give courses simultaneously
   ii) organise courses with other institutions
 f) *on (each) campus* (paragraph 7)
   i) online
   ii) on the university or business-school site
 g) *connections* (paragraph 7)
   i) relationships with other business schools
   ii) communication with foreign institutions
 h) *top-ranked* (paragraph 7)
   i) most expensive
   ii) most prestigious

6 Match each expression (1–6) with the verb that it goes with in the article (a–f).
 1 *pioneer* (paragraph 2)   a) *keeping* the school *afloat*
 2 *aspiring* (paragraph 3)   b) has *come so far*
 3 If infectious enthusiasm   c) *get into* companies
    (paragraph 4)   d) were *all it took ...*
 4 the school (paragraph 4)   e) ways of *running* programmes
 5 We can (paragraph 6)   f) *to* attract overseas students
 6 committed to (paragraph 8)

7 Match the words in *italics* in Exercise 6 to these meanings.
 a) having enough money to operate
 b) the only thing required
 c) organising or managing
 d) done very well in the circumstances
 e) have significant access to
 f) be the first to do something
 g) hoping to be successful in

Over to you 1

- **What are the benefits and drawbacks of working and studying at the same time?**
- **Which business schools are considered to be the top business schools in your country?**
- **How necessary is it to have an MBA in order to further your career in your country or sector/line of business?**

Over to you 2

Find out about three business schools or universities on the web. Compare the fees, the faculty and the kind of courses they offer. Which school would you prefer to attend, which course offers best value for money and why? Report your findings back to your class.

Professional development

Level of difficulty: ● ● ○

Before you read

What are the arguments for and against companies spending money on training and professional development for their employees?

Reading

Read this article from the FT.com website and answer the questions.

Emphasis should be skills investment

by Gill Plimmer

1 Ask any question about the problems facing an ailing economy and the answer is likely to include the skills shortage. Yet, while the diagnosis may be correct, the prescription is all too often wrong. Instead of developing existing staff, companies poach the best from their competitors or from overseas.

2 Rather than organising work-based educational programmes, employees are sent on generalist courses in 'management' or its new incarnation, 'leadership'. 'Companies are often failing to hit the target,' says Jim Hinds of Marakon Associates, a consultancy that advises FTSE 100 companies on the issues that most drive their performance and long-term value. 'They are not investing enough in training, and what they are investing is often directed at the wrong places.'

3 A competitive labour market and a shortage of skilled professionals should give more weight to the old credo that 'people are your finest asset'. But a gaping gulf has emerged between rhetoric and reality. On the one hand, professional development – broadly described as the systematic development of knowledge and skills – is receiving more attention from policy gurus than ever before; on the other hand, companies have become increasingly reluctant to invest in training, leaving the job to the regulators, individual employees or the professional associations they have formed.

4 Exact figures are hard to pin down, but Saratoga, an arm of accountancy firm PwC, estimates that expenditure on formal, off-the-job training has decreased by 10 per cent during the past two years. This could be masked by the rise in online learning, but is still a fall big enough to cause concern. So long as employees are likely to change jobs at any time, employers will question whether they should be picking up the tab for training. But the simple answer is that companies cannot afford not to.

5 'A good employer is not necessarily one who pays the highest rate, but is one who helps keep their staff's skills and hence their employability up to date,' says Richard Phelps, partner at Saratoga. Mr Phelps says that training is often the last item to be added to a company's budget and the first to go because it is hard to demonstrate the return on investment. 'Companies have failed to take training as seriously as they should because it is hard to demonstrate exactly how much impact it has on the bottom line,' he adds.

6 However, the changing nature of work – with downsized, flatter organisations, the end of the 'job for life' and the rise of the 'player manager' – has also made companies aware that to be competitive, they need to get more out of their people. 'Companies have downsized, right-sized, reorganised, but they now cannot cut or reorganise any further. So, where do they focus next as a way of getting an advantage over their competitors? The most obvious place has to be their people,' says Mr Hinds.

7 Consultancies, training providers and business universities all point to a near doubling in the number of customised education programmes as a result. 'Most companies are looking for training that will have the biggest impact. They are beginning to invest again, but they are being much more discriminatory,' says Bill Shedden, director of customised executive development at Cranfield University.

8 Certainly, the increase in regulation is starting to push some companies to put their money where their mouth is. Continuing professional development (CPD) has become compulsory in most core accountancy disciplines. However, much of the burden has fallen on individuals who have been forced to foot the bill for training themselves. Jonathan Harris, chairman of the Institute of Continuing Professional Development, says employees are much like athletes, 'engaged in a process of permanent and endless training. They plan their route, exercise and, as soon as they hit one goal, there is a new one.'

9 Professional associations are forcing the many organisations that compete for members within each industry to pay more attention to CPD. The Financial Services Authority now requires employers to be responsible for keeping their staff's competence up to date, with those that fail liable to stinging fines. Proposals put forward as part of the Operating and Financial Review in the UK have put pressure on companies to increase transparency and to demonstrate to shareholders the impact of human-resource policies.

10 'Once companies have worked out a way of measuring and demonstrating clearly to stakeholders the contribution that training makes to the company, they will find it easier to make room for it in their budgets,' says Mr Phelps. In business terms, this could mean that the sums on training finally add up. Or, as Derek Bok, the Harvard president, once said: 'If you think training is expensive, try ignorance.'

FINANCIAL TIMES

Photocopiable

UNIT 2   Training

1 Complete the sentences (1–8) with the appropriate expressions (a–h), then re-read the article to check your answers.

1 According to the article, companies should invest more ....

2 According to one consultancy, ... are not the answer to the problem.

3 Despite recognition of its importance, money allocated to .... has diminished in recent years.

4 Employers are .... training, knowing that their people may leave at any time.

5 Organisations need to provide regular skills training for their staff ....

6 One current trend is the .... of executive training programmes.

7 Some professional bodies are making it obligatory for ....

8 Richard Phelps says that it will be easier to increase spending on CPD once companies are able to measure ....

a) in order to remain competitive in the marketplace
b) in the professional development of their employees
c) companies to keep staff skills up to date
d) off-the-job training
e) reluctant to pay for
f) customisation or tailoring
g) return on investment
h) generalised courses on management or leadership

2 Read the first three paragraphs and match the words (1–8) with their definitions (a–h).

1 ailing (paragraph 1)
2 prescription (paragraph 1)
3 poach (paragraph 1)
4 incarnation (paragraph 2)
5 credo (paragraph 3)
6 gaping (paragraph 3)
7 gulf (paragraph 3)
8 rhetoric (paragraph 3)

a) take unfairly or illegally
b) impressive language used to influence people
c) great difference or lack of understanding
d) very wide and open
e) sickly or unhealthy
f) formal statement of beliefs
g) latest version or reinvention
h) medicine or treatment ordered by a doctor

3 Match the adjectives (1–7) with the nouns (a–g) to form word partnerships from paragraphs 4–8.

1 off-the-job
2 bottom
3 flatter
4 business
5 customised
6 professional
7 online

a) universities
b) programmes
c) organisations
d) learning
e) development
f) training
g) line

4 Choose the correct meaning of these multiword verbs as they are used in paragraphs 9–10.

a) keep up to date (paragraph 9)
 i) make something continue
 ii) continue to learn and know about the most recent facts
 iii) continue to practise a skill so that you don't lose it

b) put forward (paragraph 9)
 i) suggest a plan for others to consider or discuss
 ii) suggest formally that someone should be considered for a job
 iii) arrange for an event to start at an earlier time

c) work out (paragraph 10)
 i) exercise or train
 ii) think carefully about how to do something
 iii) work very hard

d) add up (paragraph 10)
 i) say more about something
 ii) give a particular quality to something
 iii) come to an acceptable total within a given budget

5 Replace the idiomatic expressions in *italics* in these sentences (1–6) with the definitions (a–f).

1 companies *poach the best* from their competitors (paragraph 1)

2 Companies are often failing to *hit the target* (paragraph 2)

3 they should be *picking up the tab* for training. (paragraph 4)

4 training is often the last item ... and the first *to go* (paragraph 5)

5 end of the *'job for life'* (paragraph 6)

6 push some companies to *put their money where their mouth is* (paragraph 8)

a) paying for something when it's not your responsibility
b) take the most qualified and experienced people unfairly
c) to be given up readily
d) successfully find the exact answer or solution
e) long-term employment with the same company
f) do what they say they will do

Over to you 1

What kind of training do you think is required at your company or organisation? Who do you think should foot the bill for professional development? Employers, staff or professional bodies? Should professional training always take place during work hours? Why (not)?

Over to you 2

Find out about two or three organisations on the web that provide professional development training for your sector of business. Which company would you prefer to provide you or your company with training? Bear in mind cost, programme content and return on investment. Give reasons for your choice.

UNIT 3 Partnerships

Toll systems

Level of difficulty: ● ● ○

Before you read

What are the arguments in favour of paying tolls on roads?

Reading

Read this article from the FT.com website and answer the questions.

An Italian job takes its toll on Austrian roads

by Adrian Michaels

1 Sometimes a marriage of technology and government policy pays off very quickly. Just ask the Austrian government. In 2002, its revenues from drivers on Austrian roads in tolls and taxes were €642m. In 2004, the figure rose by 79 per cent to €1.14bn. The change is down to the introduction of Europpass, a tolling system for heavy commercial vehicles on Austria's 2,000km of motorways that were designed and built by Autostrade of Italy. The government has told Autostrade that it will take up an option to buy the whole system, and the two sides are negotiating on the worth of the project.

2 Europpass's advantage is that, compared with other toll systems, it is simple, works smoothly and is cheap to install. It is 'free-flow', meaning that truck drivers do not have to pull over, queue for toll booths or look for loose change or wallets. The tolls are paid automatically as vehicles pass under 800 gantries across carriageways on motorways. The gantries read data from small, microwave-emitting boxes that are installed in the trucks. The boxes can be installed in seconds and cost just €5. Autostrade says an equivalent system in Germany, based on satellite technology and costing €300 per truck, suffered start-up problems and the units take four hours to install.

3 The gantries detect trucks in the time it takes for a vehicle to pass underneath. The system is enforced by 30 roving inspectors and a central office that receives reports on vehicles without data boxes or those that have opted for pre-payment but have not paid sufficient funds. The toll system cost €300m and was fully financed by Autostrade. The Italian company carried the risk because, at the time of installation, the system was untried. For now, it receives a share of tolls paid.

4 But, while other governments might be tempted by the success of the scheme, Austria is a special case because of its position as a transit country. Only one-quarter of the signal boxes have been fitted in Austrian trucks, the rest have gone to vehicles merely passing through the country. It is also mountainous terrain, offering few options for those who want to use other roads to evade fees. Nonetheless, Autostrade says it is in talks with authorities in the Czech Republic and Slovakia on similar schemes. Furthermore, Antonio Marano, Autostrade's corporate development executive, says the company has suddenly attracted competition. 'As it seems to be a very attractive business, there has been a new set of players.'

5 Back in Italy, where tolls have operated on motorways since the early 1960s, the technology is less advanced. However, there is a clear trend away from cash towards easier means of payment such as credit cards or passes. Five years ago, says Autostrade, more than half of Italian drivers paid tolls in cash. Now 65 per cent pay with credit cards or Telepass, a system that makes vehicles stop temporarily while data is transferred and a gate opens.

6 The company, which is controlled by the Benetton family, sees technology as crucial to increased efficiency and lower costs. Some 1 per cent of revenues – about €30m – goes on research and development. Of its almost €3bn revenues in 2004, 85 per cent came from tolls. Part of the remainder comes from royalties from motorway service areas, many of which are run by Autogrill, a company that is also controlled by the Benettons.

7 Autostrade directly controls 60 per cent of the Italian tolled network and acts as a clearing house for the non-cash revenue received on another 20 per cent of the toll roads. Autostrade has installed about 1,000 cameras on motorways, and the accompanying sensors can relay information on traffic and weather to units such as media outlets or screens in service stations. The next stop is to send information to mobile telephones. Autostrade is discussing a venture with 3, the telecommunications company, that will see free and paid-for services available on mobiles.

8 Piero Bergamini, an employee in the company's technology division, says drivers' phones can be located by readings taken from the mobile phone network. But there are still problems to overcome. Mr Bergamini says tracking the exact location of vehicles, and speed and direction of travel are not yet precise enough. 'If you want personal information, you want information that is tailored for you, not for someone who is near you.'

FINANCIAL TIMES

UNIT 3 Partnerships

1 Read the whole article and chose the correct options in this summary.

Autostrade has developed a new toll system called Europpass for **a)** *Austrian /Italian* motorways, making motorway driving easier for commercial drivers. The tolls are paid automatically as vehicles pass under toll **b)** *booths /gantries* on the motorway. Drivers therefore do not need to stop when crossing tolls or waste time looking for **c)** *cash /driving licences* or credit cards. The system, which is cheap **d)** *but difficult /and easy* to install, is monitored by **e)** *inspectors /roving attendants* and a central office that can pick up information regarding pre-payment and non-payment of tolls. The project cost **f)** *the Austrian government /Autostrade* €300m; they also carried the risk of the partnership because **g)** *the system was untried /of its position as a transit country*. There are plans for a similar project both abroad and in Italy, where 65% of drivers pay by Telepass or **h)** *credit card /cash* and where Autostrade controls **i)** *20% /60%* of the Italian tolled network. The company is currently looking into using telecommunication technology to locate drivers so that driving becomes even more convenient for **j)** *mobile-phone users /truck drivers*.

2 Choose the best definition for these multiword expressions in *italics* as they are used in paragraphs 1 and 2.

a) ... government policy *pays off* very quickly (paragraph 1)
  i) pay all the money you owe a company or person
  ii) pay someone in order to stop them from making trouble
  iii) when a particular plan or project gets a good result or is successful

b) ... it will *take up* an option (paragraph 1)
  i) decide to go ahead with an idea or suggestion
  ii) start a new job or position
  iii) use a particular amount of time or space

c) ... truck drivers do not have to *pull over* (paragraph 2)
  i) overtake other vehicles
  ii) wear warm winter clothing
  iii) drive to the side of the road and stop

d) ... *pass under* 800 gantries (paragraph 2)
  i) go through without stopping
  ii) go below or underneath something
  iii) drive past a landmark

3 Match these words to form partnerships that occur in paragraphs 1 and 2.

1	government	**a)**	technology
2	loose	**b)**	problems
3	truck	**c)**	booths
4	start-up	**d)**	vehicles
5	satellite	**e)**	drivers
6	toll	**f)**	change
7	commercial	**g)**	policy

4 Complete these sentences with a suitable expression from Exercise 3 in the correct form. Two are not used.

a) .... can save a lot of time if they don't have to pull up or queue at .... on motorways.

b) It's really annoying when you stop at a motorway toll and discover you don't have enough .... to pay.

c) Europpass, the Italian toll system, was introduced for the purposes of easing the journeys of .... on Austria's extensive motorway network.

d) Although similar gantries in Germany use .... , they are more expensive than their Austrian counterparts and take longer to install.

5 What or who do these figures refer to in paragraphs 5, 6 and 7?
a) 1960s **b)** 5 **c)** 65 **d)** 30m **e)** 85 **f)** 60 **g)** 20 **h)** 1,000 **i)** 3

6 Read paragraphs 7 and 8 and say whether these statements are true or false.

a) Information about traffic and weather conditions can be communicated to the media and petrol stations via sensors on Autostrade's cameras.

b) A joint venture between Autostrade and a telecommunications company will mean toll systems will be free for mobile users.

c) As a result of Autostrade's new technology, vehicles can be located using their drivers' mobiles.

d) However, this new technology for locating drivers needs to be developed further.

e) Mr Bergamini says this high-tech tracking information needs to be tailored to meet Autostrade's specific requirements.

Over to you 1

- **What are the arguments in favour of paying tolls on roads? What measures would you take to improve your national roads, motorways and service stations? What can be done to reduce traffic jams during peak periods on busy roads?**

- **What percentage of roads and motorways in your country are controlled by the government and by public companies? Do you know of any existing or future projects for improving your country's roads or motorways by way of private-public partnerships?**

Over to you 2

Find out about existing tolls or future plans for motorway tolls in your country using the Internet. How much do drivers have to pay and how do they pay? What kind of technology is/will be used? What are the installation costs compared to other countries like Austria or Italy?

Text bank

UNIT 3 Partnerships

Partnerships with NGOs

Level of difficulty: ● ● ●

Before you read

What role do you think campaigning groups have in business, if any?

Reading

Read this article from the FT.com website and answer the questions.

Partnerships: Campaigners use peace as a weapon

by Sarah Murray

1 When Peter Melchett, head of Greenpeace, accepted a position as an adviser at Burson-Marsteller, the corporate communications company, his move angered many environmental campaigners. Lord Melchett, however, insisted that he could achieve more working with companies than in opposition to them. Today, a growing number of campaign and advocacy organisations are taking a similar stance.

2 The Rainforest Alliance, the conservation group, works with companies such as Chiquita, the US banana giant that has been heavily criticised for its poor record on the environment and labour rights, to alter their business practices. Greenpeace, too, has embarked on alliances, joining companies such as NPower, the UK electricity supplier, and Unilever, the consumer goods group.

3 Divisions remain between those in non-governmental organisations and campaign groups who believe in opposing the corporate sector, and those who see engagement as the way forward. However, some organisations manage to do both at the same time. Greenpeace, for example, supported Unilever's introduction of environmentally friendly Greenfreeze technology for fridges but has attacked the company on other issues, such as mercury pollution from a Hindustan Lever factory in Tamil Nadu, India. Stephen Tindale, executive director of Greenpeace, says that, at a personal level, this can create tensions. 'But at the strategic level, companies understand that when they go into a joint venture with us, this is an occupational hazard.'

4 For companies that are keen to win public trust, such tensions are a small negative factor in a relationship that they see as giving them a way to build credibility and demonstrate transparency. At the same time, campaign groups are able to harness the scale and efficiency of the corporate sector to further their aims. 'We need companies, because companies are in a position to deliver the solutions. And when they engage, they can move faster and be more dynamic and creative than government can,' says Mr Tindale. 'With the right company, it enables you to get things done that you could never possibly do on your own.'

5 Auret van Heerden, executive director of the Fair Labor Association, believes the rapprochement between the corporations and campaigners will continue. 'Initially the campaign groups were only exposing and shaming,' he says. 'But slowly the campaign groups have realised that exposés only take you so far, and you need to be willing to engage if you want to promote long-term change.'

6 The FLA, a US-based monitoring organisation, works more closely with companies than many organisations whose mission is to improve corporate behaviour in areas such as human rights or environmental protection. The FLA has, for example, both companies and non-governmental organisations on its board.

7 However, to maintain its independence and credibility, the organisation lays down strict rules of engagement. All businesses co-operating with the FLA must agree to give it unimpeded and unannounced access to their factories, and none of the companies has any control over what the FLA publishes in its reports about the labour conditions in their supply chains. 'It's warts and all,' says Mr van Heerden. 'And we've specified the ground rules precisely because we feel we can only do our job properly if we have independence.'

8 Maintaining this independence is crucial for organisations that do not want to be seen to provide 'greenwashing' – a veneer of credibility – for their partners. For this reason, Greenpeace does not take any money from companies. And, says Mr Tindale, all joint projects must be based around something concrete and clearly defensible, such as the partnership with NPower that has led to construction of an offshore wind farm. 'If anyone says this is greenwash, we just point to the 30 turbines in the sea and say "that's what it's delivered",' he says.

9 'This delivery of results is something organisations need to keep in mind when contemplating joint projects to tackle social and environmental problems,' says Ros Tennyson, co-director of the Partnering Initiative at the International Business Leaders Forum. 'The key question is whether the collaboration is allowing the campaigning NGO to achieve its primary mission more effectively or not,' she says.

10 As campaign groups recognise that confrontation is only part of the process of change, alliances with companies are likely to increase. 'We seek things where we can co-operate because people don't just want to hear about what's going wrong. They want to know what the solutions are,' says Mr Tindale. 'That's a very important part of where environmentalism is at now. People know there are big problems. We need to be able to convey the message that there are reasons for optimism.'

FINANCIAL TIMES

UNIT 3   Partnerships

1 Read the article quickly. Who are these people / What are these organisations?

   a) Lord Melchett   **f)** Unilever

   b) Burston-Marsteller   **g)** Stephen Tindale

   c) The Rainforest Alliance   **h)** Auret van Heerden

   d) Chiquita   **i)** Fair Labor Association

   e) NPower   **j)** Ros Tennyson

2 Read paragraphs 1 and 2 and correct these sentences.

   a) Peter Melchett angered many environmentalists when he became head of Burston-Marsteller.

   b) Peter Melchett argued that he could achieve more working with environmental campaigners than in opposition to them.

   c) Few non-governmental organisations are currently doing the same as Greenpeace and the Rainforest Alliance.

   d) The Rainforest Alliance has come under severe criticism for its poor record on environmental and labour issues.

   e) Greenpeace has embarked on joint ventures to improve working practices in companies such as Chiquita, NPower and Unilever.

3 Choose the best definition for these words in *italics* from paragraphs 4 and 5.

   a) ... are able to *harness* the scale and efficiency ...

      i) control and use the natural force or power of something

      ii) fasten two animals together

      iii) hold in place or stop from falling using leather bands

   b) ... to *further* their aims

      i) become successful

      ii) achieve or obtain

      iii) promote or help something progress to be successful

   c) And when they *engage*, they can move faster ...

      i) attract someone's attention and keep them interested

      ii) get involved with other people and their ideas in order to understand them

      iii) arrange to employ someone or pay someone to do something

   d) ... the *rapprochement* between the corporations and campaigners ...

      i) establishment of a good relationship between two groups after unfriendly relations

      ii) conflictive or unpleasant situation between two opposing parties

      iii) mutual understanding and co-operation between two groups or countries

   e) ... campaign groups were only exposing and *shaming*

      i) be so much better than someone else

      ii) making someone feel ashamed or embarrassed

      iii) pretending to be upset or ill to gain sympathy or an advantage

   f) ... exposés only *take you so far* ...

      i) achieve limited or temporary results

      ii) achieve negative results

      iii) attract a lot of attention from the public

4 Read paragraphs 6 and 7 and say whether these statements are true or false.

   a) The FLA works with other non-governmental organisations on global issues such as human rights and environmental concerns.

   b) The FLA applies strict rules so that it is not influenced by any one dominant company or organisation.

   c) Member companies of the FLA have to undergo lengthy inspections of their factories which are arranged well in advance.

   d) Member companies of the FLA have some influence on the reports into their working practices and suppliers.

   e) The organisation publishes the real facts about companies, however unpleasant or embarrassing they may be.

   f) Mr van Heerden states the FLA can only be effective if it remains independent.

5 Read paragraphs 8, 9 and 10, then match the beginnings of the sentence summaries (1–6) with the endings (a–f).

   1 'Greenwashing' is giving the appearance ...

   2 Greenpeace does not accept company money ...

   3 Greenpeace's joint projects have to be specific and tangible, ...

   4 According to Ros Tennyson, any joint ventures with businesses should ...

   5 Stephen Tindale says campaign groups need to collaborate with companies ...

   6 Mr Tindale states that the public is well aware of environmental problems ...

   a) such as the construction of a wind farm in the sea.

   b) that a company has a good record on environmental issues.

   c) in order to maintain its credibility.

   d) and wants to see some positive solutions.

   e) and not just criticise them.

   f) help toward achieving the long-term aims of the NGO.

Over to you 1

- Do you think campaigning groups interfere too much with the business of multinationals? Why (not)?
- The FLA monitors companies on issues such as human rights and the environment. What other areas of corporate business do you think need to be monitored closely? Why? How can non-governmental groups help solve some of these problems?

Over to you 2

Find out on the web about a joint venture or partnership in your country. What is the problem and the proposed solution? What are the benefits of the project to society? What kind of image does the company hope to project with their involvement in the partnership?

Text bank

India's energy needs

Level of difficulty: ● ● ●

Before you read

Do you know which five countries are the biggest energy consumers in the world? How might that change over the next 20 years?

Reading

Read this article from the *Financial Times* and answer the questions.

India and its energy needs: Demand is rising but lags rest of the world

by Kevin Morrison

1   India, a sleeping giant in the energy world, may have finally awoken, with energy consumption projected to grow by the second fastest rate during the next 25 years, putting it just behind China, its bigger neighbour. Future energy usage, however, will still fall well short of consumption rates in the developed world. India's population of about 1 billion represents about 16 per cent of the world's population, but accounts for less than 2 per cent of its energy consumption.

2   Even if the country achieves the forecast growth rate of 2.3 per cent for energy use during the next 25 years, each person would still be using less than half of the energy used by the average person in the developed world by 2030. Nevertheless, the growth in energy consumption in India is expected to result in a doubling of greenhouse gas emissions over the next 25 years, according to the International Energy Agency (IEA), the energy watchdog for the developed world.

3   'The increased amount of CO_2 emissions to come out of India and China, will negate whatever we are trying to do in the West in attempting to reduce emissions,' says John Waterlow, an energy

analyst at Wood Mackenzie. 'This is the conundrum,' he says. 'How can the West tell the developing world that it must limit the amount of emissions it can emit, which, in turn, affects the development of their economies?' In spite of the increase in emissions in India and China, developed countries will have far higher per capita emissions than in India. This is largely due to India's wide use of wood and cow dung in rural areas for cooking and heating.

4   Biomass and waste accounts for more than 50 per cent of India's total energy use. Although its share is expected to decline during the next 25 years as India's consumption of oil, gas and coal increase, it will still remain the most common fuel for residential energy consumption, the IEA said in its World Energy Outlook report. The IEA forecasts that Indian oil demand will rise to 5.4m barrels a day by 2030, with more than 90 per cent of this consumption to be supplied by imports. This growth may push India into the top tier of oil consumers in the world, but still puts it well behind China.

5   India's low level of car ownership is the main reason for the relatively low use of oil. Even if the car ownership increases in

the next decade from the present nine cars per 1,000 people to 24 cars per 1,000, it is still lower than China's growth rates and a fraction of the levels of car ownership in Europe, where one in two own a car. 'India will never be able to have the same rate of car ownership as the West because there is simply not enough oil in the world,' says Mr Waterlow.

6   The IEA's projected strong economic growth rates of more than 4 per cent a year on average over the next 25 years will stimulate gas demand among industrial users in India. Despite a recent significant gas discovery, this will not be enough to meet future demand. Therefore a substantial increase in gas imports is forecast, mainly through shipments of liquefied natural gas (LNG). India has signed a $40bn deal to import LNG from Iran and is also negotiating with Bangladesh and Burma about building pipelines to import gas. Nevertheless, coal will remain the preferred energy for industrial users. The IEA projects Indian coal demand to rise at similar rates to total growth rates of energy use in the country during the next 25 years.

FINANCIAL TIMES

UNIT 4   Energy

1 Read the whole article. How many types of energy are referred to, and what is expected to happen to India's consumption of each over the coming years?

2 Read paragraphs 1 and 2 and find the meanings of the words in *italics* as they are used in this context.

  a) ... energy consumption *projected* to grow by the second fastest rate ...
  - i) made a picture or film appear on a large screen
  - ii) calculated to be in the future
  - iii) stuck out beyond an edge or surface

  b) ... energy usage, however, will still *fall well short of* consumption rates ...
  - i) be a clear equivalent to
  - ii) be a lot more than
  - iii) be much less than

  c) ... 1 billion *represents* about 16 per cent of the world's population ...
  - i) officially speak or take action for other people
  - ii) is equal to
  - iii) be a symbol of

  d) Even if the country achieves the *forecast* growth rate ...
  - i) prediction of the weather
  - ii) what is happening now
  - iii) what is expected to happen in the future

  e) Even if the country achieves the forecast *growth rate* ...
  - i) speed at which something increases in size
  - ii) payment fixed according to a standard scale
  - iii) percentage charged for borrowing money

  f) ... half of the energy used by the *average* person ...
  - i) not unusually big or small
  - ii) typical of most of the people (or things) in a group
  - iii) usual standard, level or amount

  g) ... is expected to *result in* a doubling of greenhouse gas emissions ...
  - i) cause to happen
  - ii) success or achievement of something
  - iii) profit or loss made by a company over a period of time

3 Use the correct form of the words and expressions from Exercise 2 to complete these sentences.

  a) China has a strong economic .... which is expected to last for several decades.

  b) Energy savings last year were only €50,000, which .... the €90,000 target.

  c) The over 50s .... the majority of our clients.

  d) Falling share prices .... calls for the CEO's resignation.

  e) The .... is for more oil price rises.

  f) Our sales are .... to grow by 4% a year.

  g) The .... worker in Spain earns €1,200 a month.

4 Look at paragraph 3 and find the words and expressions which mean the following.

  a) cause something to have no effect

  b) confusing and difficult problem

  c) industrialised countries *(2 expressions)*

  d) countries that are changing their economic system to one based on industry

  e) as a result

  f) when a country or region increases its wealth, for example by changing the economic system

  g) for each person

  h) by many people and in many places

5 What do these numbers refer to in paragraphs 4 and 5?

  a) 50   **b)** 25   **c)** 5.4   **d)** 90   **e)** nine   **f)** one in two

6 Read paragraph 6 and say whether these statements are true or false.

In India ...

  a) the economy is expected to grow annually by over 4%.

  b) the demand for gas is expected to increase in the industrial sector.

  c) large deposits of gas have been found.

  d) there will be sufficient locally produced gas to meet the needs of industry.

  e) the government is in negotiations with three countries to import gas via pipelines.

  f) gas is the most common energy source with industrial users.

  g) the demand for coal is expected to remain stable.

Over to you 1

What is the West doing to reduce CO_2 emissions? How could some of the world's largest energy users reduce their consumption? Why might they resist reducing their consumption?

Over to you 2

Use the Internet to help you find out about the economic growth rate in highly industrialised countries and compare it to the growth rate in fast-growing economies like China and India. What are the implications of this?

UNIT 4 — Energy

Nuclear energy

Level of difficulty: ● ● ●

Before you read

What are some of the arguments for and against using nuclear power?

Reading

Read this article from the *Financial Times* and answer the questions.

Nuclear energy: Come-back kid or ugly duckling?

by Fiona Harvey

1 For environmentalists, it is thinking the unthinkable. Nuclear power, once the target of protests and demonstrations, has been transformed into the unexpected darling of some sections of the green lobby. The reason is simple: nuclear energy offers the hope of producing power on a large scale without burning fossil fuel. That would solve what many regard as the biggest threat the planet faces: global warming, caused by a dramatic rise in the level of carbon dioxide since industrialisation.

2 As people still want the benefits of industrialisation, and as developing nations pursue economic development – leading to predictions that our energy consumption and thus levels of atmospheric carbon could more than double – some experts depict the once-maligned nuclear industry as the best solution. The nuclear industry has itself assisted this transformation, through the development of new technologies designed to make nuclear power safer and to deal with long-term problems such as the disposal of waste.

3 But critics argue that the technology still suffers from problems. For instance, any nuclear reactor takes a long time to build and to produce energy. Safety concerns have also been heightened by the escalation in terrorist threats. Not only is there the possibility of a terrorist attack on a nuclear installation, but the creation of nuclear material for use in reactors and the waste generated provides terrorists with opportunities to steal valuable nuclear materials for use in nuclear bombs, or 'dirty' bombs.

4 Another question is whether nuclear energy would be economically viable. The upfront costs are discouragingly high at an estimated \$1,300 to \$1,500 per kilowatt to build a nuclear plant, which works out as roughly twice what it costs to build a gas-fired power station. However, proponents claim that over the life of a nuclear plant, it can generate energy at a cost comparable to or even cheaper than that of conventional fossil-fuel power.

5 Detractors counter that the industry has been subsidised by the public purse in so many ways, from research and development to clear-up operations, that the energy is much more expensive than the sector admits. For all these reasons, though some green lobbyists support a nuclear future, most remain opposed. They argue that alternatives, from better energy conservation and natural sources such as wind, to technologies such as hydrogen fuel cells, are more realistic and less risky.

6 Eileen Claussen, president of the Pew Centre on Global Climate Change, believes there may be a role for nuclear energy, but only when certain conditions have been met. 'You have to make sure you have enough safeguards and that you don't have nuclear proliferation.' Some governments also remain opposed to the idea. Sweden recently confirmed plans to shut down one of its 11 nuclear reactors, to reduce its dependence on nuclear power.

7 By contrast, Sweden's neighbour Finland has heartily embraced nuclear power. The Finnish parliament recently ratified a decision to build a final spent-nuclear-fuel storage facility and approved a new nuclear reactor. France generates three-quarters of its energy from nuclear sources, and President George W. Bush has indicated his support for new nuclear reactors in the US.

8 Perhaps the most important government in the debate is China, whose appetite for energy requires sweeping solutions. It plans to build as many as 30 nuclear plants, and to generate as much as 300 gigawatts from nuclear means by 2050. This has made other governments nervous. The development of a problem-free alternative, nuclear fusion, is as far as 50 years away. Long before then, governments and the public will have to decide what part they want nuclear power to play in energy production.

FINANCIAL TIMES

UNIT 4   Energy

1   Read the whole article. Which paragraph(s) contain the following information?
   a) Countries that favour using nuclear energy   ....
   b) A country committed to lessening its reliance on nuclear energy   ......
   c) Why some environmentalists now support nuclear energy   ....
   d) Improvements being made within the nuclear industry   ......
   e) Recent concerns about nuclear power and waste products   ......
   f) The hidden costs of nuclear power   ......
   g) Comparative costs of coal and nuclear power stations   ......

2   Read paragraphs 1 and 2. Then replace the word(s) in *italics* in these sentences with the correct form of a word or expression from the paragraphs, keeping the same meaning.
   a) There were *at some time in the past* plans to build a new nuclear reactor.
   b) The company is *the subject of criticism by* safety inspectors because of its accident record.
   c) Solar energy is *very popular with* many environmental groups.
   d) The use of *gas, coal and oil* increases the levels of carbon dioxide in the atmosphere.
   e) The Swedish government is *trying to achieve* its plan to reduce dependence on nuclear energy.
   f) A major problem with nuclear energy is *throwing away the unwanted substances produced.*

3   Read paragraph 3. Which of these disadvantages of nuclear power are NOT mentioned?
   a) Fears of nuclear waste falling into the wrong hands
   b) The preparation time before any energy can be produced
   c) Concerns about possible attacks on nuclear installations
   d) Risk of accidents at a nuclear plant
   e) Contamination of the local environment
   f) The time it takes to construct a nuclear installation

4   Match the word partnerships from paragraphs 4 and 5.
   1 upfront   a) plant
   2 nuclear   b) purse
   3 gas-fired   c) lobbyists
   4 the public   d) operations
   5 clear-up   e) power station
   6 green   f) costs

5   Complete these sentences using one of the word partnerships from Exercise 4.
   a) If money is provided by the government, it is said to come from ....
   b) A factory that generates energy using nuclear material is called a ....
   c) An activity or activities which are planned to deal with a problem are ....

   d) People who try to persuade the government to act on environmental issues are ....
   e) When money is paid as soon as a project starts or a deal is signed, this is known as ....
   f) A factory that generates energy using gas is described as a ....

6   Read paragraphs 6 and 7, then replace the verbs in *italics* in the sentences below (a–f) with a verb or phrase from the box with a similar meaning (1–6).

1	signed (an official agreement)
2	eagerly accepted
3	made clear
4	satisfy
5	said that it's definitely true there are
6	continue to be

   a) The nuclear industry must *meet* certain conditions.
   b) The Dutch and Swedish governments *remain* opposed to nuclear power.
   c) The Chinese government recently *confirmed* plans to build many new plants.
   d) France *embraced* nuclear power as its main source of energy many years ago.
   e) India has *ratified* a plan to build a gas pipeline from Burma.
   f) The green lobby has *indicated* its opposition to plans for a nuclear waste facility.

7   Read paragraph 8. Why is China's nuclear policy so important?
   A Because it will be the first country to use nuclear fusion, which is more dangerous than existing nuclear reactors.
   B Because it plans to build a large number of nuclear power stations in a relatively short period of time.
   C Because other governments are worried about the competition from China's nuclear industry.

Over to you 1

   • **Has the article changed your opinion of nuclear energy?**
   • **Would you be happy to live near a nuclear power station? Why (not)?**

Over to you 2

   • **Which countries have the highest dependence on nuclear energy in the world?**
   • **What is your country's energy policy? What percentage of your country's energy is produced by nuclear power? What other forms energy are used in your country?**

UNIT 5 | Employment trends

Offshoring

Level of difficulty: ● ● ○

Before you read

Outsourcing is a process, offshoring is a location.
What do you understand by this quote? What are the advantages and disadvantages for companies when outsourcing work to low-cost labour markets?

Reading

Read this article from the *Financial Times* and answer the questions.

Offshoring: A loss of jobs or a gain in profits?

by Brian Groom

1 The bitter US-inspired debate about offshoring, the transfer of jobs to low-cost labour markets, is spreading to the non-English-speaking world. The issue is rising up the political register in countries such as France, Germany and Spain. While it often arouses emotion out of proportion to the jobs involved, the underlying questions go to the heart of Europe's competitiveness. To the French, the phenomenon is 'delocalisation'. In Germany, it merges into a longer-running debate about de-industrialisation or the 'bazaar economy' – in which goods made elsewhere are sold on through the world.

2 West Europeans are as worried about losing jobs to Eastern Europe as to India or China. Increasingly, these are white-collar and skilled technology posts as well as the manufacturing jobs that have been moving for more than a decade. The European Union's enlargement gave the argument fresh impetus. Cheap and often highly skilled workers can be found in countries such as Slovakia, Russia, Croatia or Bulgaria.

3 Germany's Chancellor denounced offshoring as 'unpatriotic' after Ludwig Georg Braun, head of the chambers of commerce, urged businesses to take advantage of possibilities afforded by EU expansion. Siemens, Volkswagen, Continental and SAP are among companies that have shifted activities abroad, and now financial institutions such as Commerzbank and Deutsche Bank are looking at relocating back-office work. Medium-sized Mittelstand companies are joining the exodus.

4 At first, Berlin responded by saying Germany must improve its own skill levels. Recently, however, it has shown more protectionist impulses by

joining France in calling for new member states to be denied EU regional aid unless they raise company tax levels. Nicolas Sarkozy, France's finance minister, is proposing tax incentives to persuade companies to stay at home and encourage others to return. In Spain, trade unions say nearly 40 foreign multinationals have left in the past three years, creating a challenge for the government.

5 What impact is offshoring having? The evidence is patchy, which has helped fears to grow. A recent survey, by the United Nations Conference on Trade and Development and Munich-based Roland Berger Strategy Consultants, found nearly half of European companies planned to shift more services offshore. UK companies accounted for 61 per cent of the total of jobs moved, followed by Germany and the Benelux countries with 14 per cent each. It was not a one-way street, though. Asia was top destination, with 37 per cent of projects, but western Europe itself benefited with 29 per cent – the favoured locations being the UK, Ireland, Spain and Portugal – and Eastern Europe with 22 per cent.

6 Forrester Research forecasts 1.2m European information technology and service jobs will move offshore over the next ten years, nearly three-quarters from the UK. It sees continental countries as slower to outsource, whether because of management caution, tight labour laws or union resistance, and argues that Germany, Italy, France and the Netherlands will lose by being less competitive as a result.

7 However, Forrester's definition of offshoring – use of service providers based at least 500 miles away – ignores Eastern Europe. On that issue, a study of German and Austrian companies by Dalia Marin, professor at the University of Munich, found

surprisingly limited negative impact. While German multinationals created 460,000 jobs and Austrian ones 201,000 in Eastern Europe between 1990 and 2001, the result was a direct loss of only 90,000 jobs in Germany and 22,000 in Austria – partly because of productivity differences.

8 What drove many companies east was the search for skilled employees because of a shortage at home, where there was a 'human capital crisis'. Ms Marin's remedies include better education and looser immigration rules to import skilled workers. In France, a finance ministry study found the negative impact of 'delocalisation' greatly exaggerated. Only 4 per cent of French foreign investment was production moved offshore in order to re-import goods into France.

9 That still leaves governments wrestling with the problem of how to act. Tax breaks to encourage companies to stay seem likely to have only a limited effect. More fruitful would be a determined effort to reform labour, product and capital markets as promised under the EU's Lisbon agenda. A report by McKinsey Global Institute found that every dollar of corporate spending shifted offshore generates up to $1.14 in US wealth. But when a German company invests a euro in a cheaper place, its home economy is on average 20 cents worse off. The main difference is that displaced workers in the US quickly find replacement jobs. In Germany, because of labour laws and slow growth, they do not.

10 Companies can benefit from outsourcing if it makes them more competitive. Increased profits can then translate into higher investment and more employment at home – but governments must first create conditions for job creation to thrive.

FINANCIAL TIMES

UNIT 5   Employment trends

1 Read the whole article and number these items in the order they appear.
   a) The advantages of outsourcing.
   b) Countries that are resistant to outsourcing may fall behind others that are not.
   c) Pressure on newer EU member states to raise taxes in order to reduce offshoring.
   d) Results of research into job losses as a consequence of offshoring
   e) Countries which are becoming a source of cheap and highly skilled workers
   f) Alternative terms for the phenomenon of 'offshoring'
   g) German companies that have transferred jobs to low-cost labour markets
   h) Possible solutions for increasing the number of skilled workers in western Europe

2 Read paragraphs 1–4 again. Are these points true of Germany, France or both?
   a) The issue of offshoring is becoming increasingly controversial.
   b) Some call offshoring a form of 'de-industrialisation' or a bazaar economy.
   c) Others refer to outsourcing or relocating abroad as 'delocalisation'.
   d) Some countries are worried about losing jobs to Eastern Europe, as well as Asian economies.
   e) There is disagreement between business institutions and politicians concerning outsourcing work abroad.
   f) One minister is giving financial incentives to encourage companies to stay at home.

3 Read paragraph 5 and say whether these statements are true or false.
   a) There isn't much evidence to demonstrate the real effects of offshoring.
   b) According to one survey, 61% of European companies aim to move services abroad.
   c) Germany and the Netherlands are the countries that use offshoring most.
   d) The UK, Ireland, Spain and Portugal are the top destinations in Europe for offshoring.
   e) Eastern Europe is currently the most popular location for outsourcing work abroad.

4 What do these figures in paragraphs 6 and 7 refer to?
   a) 1.2   b) $\frac{3}{4}$ c) 500   d) 460,000   e) 201,000   f) 90,000

5 Read paragraphs 8 and 9. Match the words and phrases in italics in sentences a–h to their correct definitions from the box (1–8).

---

   1 productive or with better results
   2 less strictly controlled
   3 try to understand or solve
   4 people and their skills considered as a production factor
   5 made to seem better, larger or worse than it really is
   6 similar
   7 force someone to do or go somewhere
   8 incentives given as encouragement

   a) What *drove* many companies east was …
   b) a '*human capital* crisis'
   c) *looser* immigration rules
   d) … found the negative impact of 'delocalisation' greatly *exaggerated*
   e) with wage levels *comparable* to France's
   f) That still leaves governments *wrestling with* the problem …
   g) Tax *breaks* to encourage companies …
   h) More *fruitful* would be …

6 Read paragraphs 9 and 10. What do the words in *italics* refer to?
   a) *its* home economy is on average 20 cents worse off.
   b) … *they* do not.
   c) if *it* makes *them* more competitive.

Over to you 1

Do you think that companies should be given financial incentives or encouraged by governments to stay at home? Do you agree that certain countries should increase company tax rates in order to stop them from being more attractive propositions for companies? Why (not)? Why are those companies that outsource work more competitive than ones that do not?

Over to you 2

What kind of work is usually outsourced abroad? Is your country one of the popular destinations of multinationals for offshoring or outsourcing? Why do you think that is? To what extent does offshoring benefit your country's economy?

Text bank

UNIT 5 Employment trends

Older people

Level of difficulty: ● ● ○

Before you read

According to the one forecast, by the year 2050, the number of people in the world aged over 60 will rise from 600m to 2bn. What do you think will be the implications of this trend in terms of employment?

Reading

Read this article from the *Financial Times* and answer the questions.

Older people: Age and experience

by Sarah Murray

1 Demographics usually proves a powerful force for change in the business world, and the rapidly ageing world population looks likely to continue the pattern. By the year 2050, according to the International Labour Organisation, the number of people aged over 60 will rise from 600m to 2bn. In less than 50 years, for the first time in history, there will be more people in the world over the age of 60 than under the age of 15. All this has profound implications for employers and, says the ILO, should provide an incentive for companies to fight age discrimination and accommodate older workers, creating challenging careers to persuade them to stay in their jobs longer.

2 However, changing demographics alone are unlikely to spark drastic changes in corporate policies and practices towards older workers. John Atkinson, who runs the Unemployment and Labour Market Disadvantage programme at the Institute for Employment Studies, says legislation is likely to provide a sharper stick with which to prod companies into action. In the UK, for example, the government is committed to implementing age legislation under the European Directive on Equal Treatment.

3 The exact form the new rules will take is not yet clear, but it is thought likely that it will be similar to existing legislation on race and gender. 'It wasn't until the law came in that most employers pulled their socks up and started to take it seriously,' says Mr Atkinson. 'So the best employers are thinking about their policies and practices towards age, but the vast majority are not.'

4 And yet, as savvy companies have realised, positive policies and practices on age diversity make good business sense. Because of the nature of its business, B&Q, the British DIY retailer, has found that having older workers on its staff has enhanced sales and customer loyalty. Older employees often have a basic knowledge of DIY, and customers, who tend to associate older people with this knowledge, feel comfortable asking their advice.

5 And for sectors such as financial services, the age profile of customers means it makes business sense to increase the average age of sales teams. Changing demographics was part of the reason that Halifax Bank of Scotland (HBOS) re-evaluated its diversity programmes. An ageing population was driving a need to put a greater focus on savings and retirement plans and the release of capital tied up in property – and at least half of the bank's customers are now over the age of 50. In response, the HBOS group policy was altered to allow people to work beyond the traditional retirement age of 60 or 62.

6 But permitting employees to work beyond traditional retirement age is one thing. It is quite another to persuade them to remain in work – particularly when private pensions and savings and the possibility of buying a house in the south of France provide a tempting alternative. Indeed, many workers, rather than staying on, are retiring early – either through desire or because of poor health.

7 At the same time, changing demographics present another challenge for employers that hope to persuade their staff to remain with the company for longer. In a world where a higher proportion of employees are older, there will no longer be a sufficient supply of the sort of senior management positions that were once the goal of many in the workforce.

8 'People tend to look at older employees when they talk about age,' says Michael Stuber, founder of Mist Consulting, the Cologne-based diversity consultancy. 'What they often ignore is that the main clientele are people who are today 38 to 45. They are growing older and they have made their careers with an idea that they should be at a director's rank by the age of 43, otherwise they won't make it. And now it's obvious that, particularly in times of lean management, they cannot all be promoted to director level.'

9 With rates of promotion slowing and pay growth declining from about 35 onwards, working longer looks far less attractive than it did a couple of decades ago. 'What used to be a manual worker's earnings pattern – they earned their most at their fittest, and their earnings declined as they got worn out – has become the pattern for everyone,' says Mr Atkinson. Given such trends, simply abolishing the formal retirement age and removing age specifications from recruitment advertisements remain cosmetic initiatives. They fail to address a deeper underlying problem. That is the need to create an appealing working life for those growing older in a world where career structures, rather than being vertical, will look increasingly horizontal.

FINANCIAL TIMES

UNIT 5   Employment trends

1 Read the article quickly. Who are these people and organisations?
   a) ILO
   b) John Atkinson
   c) B&Q
   d) HBOS
   e) Michael Stuber
   f) Mist Consulting

2 Read paragraphs 1 and 2 again and correct these sentences.
   a) The Institute for Employment Studies says that, by the year 2050, the number of people over 60 will increase from 600m to 2bn.
   b) In 50 years' time, it is predicted there will be more over-60s than teenagers in the world.
   c) Employers should deal with race discrimination at work and provide incentives for senior workers to agree to early retirement.
   d) John Atkinson from the ILO says changes in demographics will force companies to take action.
   e) The British government is hesitant about implementing age legislation under the European Directive on Equal Treatment.

3 Choose the best alternatives to replace the words in *italics*, according to the context of paragraphs 3 and 4.
   a) It wasn't until the law *came in* ... (paragraph 3)
      i) was involved in a plan or deal
      ii) came into effect
      iii) became fashionable or popular
   b) ... most employers *pulled their socks up* (paragraph 3)
      i) made more of an effort
      ii) criticised someone or something
      iii) showed disapproval
   c) ... *savvy* companies (paragraph 4)
      i) smart and wise
      ii) ignorant or lacking in ability
      iii) high-tech and up-to-date
   d) ... enhanced sales and *customer loyalty* (paragraph 4)
      i) the length of time customers stay with a company
      ii) the act of consumers refusing to change their purchasing habits
      iii) the degree to which people buy a brand or use a company's services

4 Read paragraphs 4 and 5 again and complete these sentences (a–h) using the expressions in the box (1–8).
   a) For many supermarket chains, it .... to employ older people as checkout attendants.
   b) B&Q prefers more experienced workers .... , as they can explain their products more effectively.
   c) If you .... of something, you understand the main principles behind it, but you are certainly not an expert.
   d) I didn't .... applying for that job, as I didn't think I had the necessary skills.
   e) .... should ensure that a variety of people of different race, age and background are recruited by a company.
   f) What is really .... to employ older people for longer is the change in demographics in the world.
   g) He had always put money towards .... in case he was suddenly made redundant.

h) The business had gone bankrupt, but managed to pay off its workers, as it had money .... in property.

1	because of the nature of its business
2	diversity programmes
3	driving a need
4	feel comfortable about
5	have a basic knowledge
6	makes good business sense
7	savings and retirement plans
8	tied up

5 Match the words and expressions (1–6) from paragraphs 7–9 with the correct definitions (a–f).
   1 demographics (paragraph 7)
   2 workforce (paragraph 7)
   3 lean (paragraph 8)
   4 earnings (paragraph 9)
   5 abolish (paragraph 9)
   6 recruitment (paragraph 9)

   a) all the people who work in a country, industry or factory
   b) money a person receives for work for a particular period
   c) using the most effective methods and the fewest possible employees
   d) process of finding new people to work for an organisation
   e) officially end a law, system or organisation
   f) details concerning age, sex and income of a particular group of people

6 Read paragraph 9 again and choose the best summary.

A Working longer is now more appealing than it was in the past, and all workers now earn most when they are in their forties. A change in legislation is not the answer. There is a need to create a more attractive working life for older employees whose careers are more likely to develop horizontally, rather than going up the career ladder.

B Working longer is now less appealing than it was in the past, and all workers now earn most when they are in their physical prime. Changing the retirement age and not mentioning age requirements in job advertisements are only minor changes. We need to find ways of working for longer and accept that careers may develop horizontally.

Over to you

- **Do you agree with the formal retirement age in your country? Why (not)?**
- **At what age would *you* expect to retire?**
- **Do you think older employees should earn more or less or the same as younger workers? Why (not)?**

Text bank

UNIT 6 Business ethics

Business responsibilities

Level of difficulty: ●●○

Before you read

What do you understand by the term 'corporate social responsibility'? Is CSR an important issue for companies in your sector or country?

Reading

Read this article from the *Financial Times* and answer the questions.

Business bows to growing pressures

by Alison Maitland

1 The language of responsibility has spread so rapidly in business that it is now turning up in some surprising places. Messages such the small print in drinks advertisements that urge customers to enjoy alcohol 'responsibly' are not directed at the public so much as governments, regulators, investors and employees. A decade ago, few companies with social and environmental programmes were willing to speak out about them for fear of attracting closer scrutiny, and possibly shouts of 'hypocrisy', from campaign groups. Today, many companies feel they cannot afford not to talk about what they are doing, even if this does make them more vulnerable to attack.

2 Rising expectations of business are being given extra impetus by continuing revelations of corporate malpractice, particularly in the US. Companies that find themselves subject to greatest scrutiny include those with dominant market positions, such as former state-owned utilities; those dealing directly with consumers, such as banks and retailers; those producing essentials such as food or drugs; and those exploiting natural resources or depending on supply chains in low-income countries, such as oil producers and clothing manufacturers.

3 Trust and responsibility have become valued additions to the CEO lexicon. Some talk of responsibility as a moral obligation. Mervyn Davies, chief executive of Standard Chartered Bank, which does business in more than 50 developing economies, says that the pursuit of profit is not enough; companies need principles, and employees want to see those principles in action. 'I don't think companies can just go about doing their business and ignore what's happening around them and not make a contribution,' he says.

4 Others justify it on business grounds. 'We know very clearly that companies which adopt and embrace corporate responsibility are more likely to create wealth and shareholder value than those that do not,' says Michael Fairey, deputy chief executive of Lloyds TSB. 'The business case revolves around the creation of employee motivation, customer satisfaction and brand loyalty.' Is there clear evidence that responsible business boosts financial returns? Many studies have examined whether there is a link. Those that have established a connection easily outnumber those that have found no link or a negative correlation, according to Risk, Returns and Responsibility, a report by the Association of British Insurers that reviews the evidence.

5 The biggest incentive for companies to behave properly is the damage caused when they do not. Take Citigroup, the world's largest financial services company, which saw its share price dragged down by a series of legal and regulatory problems that have cost it billions of dollars. The image of Chuck Prince, Citigroup chief executive, apologising for banking-law violations in Japan is a powerful one. Mr Prince has been trying to instil ethical behaviour in the group since his appointment.

6 The damage caused by corporate malpractice can be both immediate and enduring. 'CEOs are talking more about [corporate responsibility]. Are they taking responsibility? Some are. Some are not,' says Robert Davies, chief executive of the International Business Leaders Forum (IBLF), which has been promoting responsible business practices for 14 years. 'The tragedy is that, so often, they have to be hit by a crisis.'

7 Institutional investors are increasingly concerned about this type of crisis and the ethical, social and environmental risks that companies run. Big investors see the way that companies handle issues such as obesity or human rights as a measure of the overall quality of their management, says Mr Davies. For growing numbers of companies in the supply chain, responsible practices are no longer a matter of choice. Vodafone, for example, requires its suppliers to comply with its new code of ethical purchasing, designed to provide safe and fair working conditions. Vodafone says terminating a contract with a supplier would be an act of last resort, but the threat is there.

8 Greater government regulation to enforce corporate responsibility is one of the demands of non-governmental organisations. They can be expected to continue to lobby for it as long as they perceive a mismatch between the rhetoric and the way some companies behave. For multinationals in particular, it requires unrelenting effort to ensure high standards by every employee at every site in every country in which they operate. But unless they do, their credentials will be jeopardised. Witness the way that the reserves scandal at Royal Dutch/Shell has undermined its pretensions to leadership as a 'sustainable' oil company. Companies that fail to make all the connections on corporate responsibility increase the risk of damage to shareholder value and fuel cynicism among the public and campaigners.

FINANCIAL TIMES

UNIT 6   Business ethics

1 Read the whole article and number these items in the order they appear.
  a) A scandal at a financial company
  b) The expectations of major investors
  c) The views of a CEO and a deputy CEO
  d) Types of companies that are under most pressure
  e) Use of product advertising to promote a CSR message
  f) A company putting demands on suppliers
  g) A crisis at a major oil company

2 Read paragraph 1 and find the meanings of the words in *italics* as they are used in this context.
  a) The language of responsibility has *spread* ...
    i) share work, responsibility or money among several people
    ii) become widely used or known about
    iii) pay for something gradually over a period of time
  b) ... it is now *turning up* in some surprising places.
    i) being found
    ii) arriving unexpectedly
    iii) operating a switch to increase temperature, volume, etc.
  c) ... for fear of *attracting closer scrutiny* ...
    i) causing people to like or admire someone or something
    ii) moving towards another person or thing
    iii) creating interest in examining something carefully
  d) ... many companies feel they *cannot afford not to talk* about ...
    i) must talk because there could be serious problems if they didn't
    ii) do not have enough money or time to talk
    iii) must not talk because it could cause serious consequences

3 Match the word partnerships from paragraph 2.
  1 corporate   a) manufacturers
  2 dominant   b) countries
  3 state-owned   c) utilities
  4 supply   d) malpractice
  5 low-income   e) market positions
  6 clothing   f) chains

4 Complete the sentences below using the word pairs from Exercise 3 in the correct form.
  a) The series of organisations that are involved in passing products from manufacturers to the public is known as the ....
  b) Examples of .... are usually water, gas and electricity, although these companies have been privatised in many countries.
  c) .... are often criticised for their use of non-biodegradable synthetics such as nylon and polyester.
  d) The company has a .... , as its brands now have over 60% of combined market share.
  e) When companies break the law to gain some advantage for themselves, this is referred to as ....
  f) Many call centres have been outsourced to .... in a move to economise on employee salaries.

5 Read paragraphs 3 and 4. Are these points made by Mervyn Davies, Michael Fairey or the Association of British Insurers?
  a) People continue to buy a company's goods or services if it acts responsibility.
  b) Companies can't just concentrate on making money.
  c) Clients are happier if the company is more responsible.
  d) Most research suggests that companies gain financially from responsible business.
  e) Staff feel that companies have a moral duty to society.

6 Find words in paragraphs 5 and 6 which have a similar meaning to these phrases.
  a) actions that break the law, an agreement or principle
  b) teach people to think, behave or feel in a particular way
  c) being chosen for a job or position
  d) continuing for a very long time
  e) accepting
  f) trying to persuade people to support

7 Use the words from Exercise 6 in the correct form to complete these sentences.
  a) Since her .... as CEO, she has announced plans to make 5,000 people redundant.
  b) Jeans have an .... appeal with people of all ages and social classes.
  c) The government has announced a campaign to .... healthy eating habits.
  d) The sale of these animal skins is a .... of international law.
  e) The manager has worked hard to .... discipline in the department.
  f) Although he was head of the project, he let his deputy .... the blame for the financial mismanagement.

8 Read paragraphs 7 and 8. Match the verb-noun collocations as they appear in the text.
  1 handle   a) credentials
  2 terminate   b) cynicism
  3 ensure   c) issues
  4 jeopardise   d) a contract
  5 fuel   e) high standards

Over to you

Should CEOs and senior management be held legally responsible for actions taken by other members of staff? What penalties should there be for companies that commit the following violations?
- polluting the environment
- employing child labour
- not providing a safe working environment
- lying to shareholders about the financial position of the company
- selling unsafe products to consumers
- fixing prices

Business models

Level of difficulty: ● ● ○

Before you read

Do you think multinational companies operating in poor or developing countries have a duty to improve the quality of people's lives in these countries? Why (not)?

Reading

Read this article from the *Financial Times* and answer the questions.

Take a good look at the local issues

by Sarah Murray

1 Because business has access to financial resources and modern management methods, it might seem a logical candidate to contribute to the development of poor communities in the countries in which it operates. With social responsibility on corporate minds, the will to participate certainly exists. However, since companies are not experts in health or education, and many lack staff equipped to manage social programmes, they need to tread extremely carefully to ensure that those programmes do not backfire.

2 The issue is most contentious in the extractive industries, whose companies create vast footprints wherever they invest and whose operations are often located in countries run by oppressive and corrupt regimes. Here, the thorniest issue is defining the limits of responsibility. If an oil company builds hospitals and schools for communities immediately surrounding its operations, conflicts can arise with neighbouring villages that feel left out. Yet if companies do nothing, they will be operating in what Richard Sandbrook, special adviser to the United Nations Development Programme, calls 'an oasis of affluence in a desert of need'.

3 Another danger is that, by improving life for those around their operations, multinationals can create a culture of dependence. The question then arises as to what happens to the programmes companies have funded or the townships they have built when a mine needs to be closed or conflict forces investments to be withdrawn. In recent years, however, many have become better equipped to deal with such issues. Big mining companies, which often work in remote areas populated by indigenous people, now employ sociologists and anthropologists.

4 Multinationals have learned to work with local governments, unions and non-governmental organisations (NGOs) in rolling out social programmes, and many conduct social-impact studies before even embarking on an investment. 'The large mining companies I've dealt with have become so experienced at this that they have community plans, closure plans for their mines and the whole thing is done on a basis that is so much more thorough than it used to be,' says Mr Sandbrook. 'But there are still plenty of companies that do just abandon a place and leave a mess.'

5 Even for less controversial businesses working in more stable parts of the world, community investments or philanthropic programmes must be approached in a measured way. 'The first thing is to understand the local conditions,' says Adrian Hodges, managing director of International Business Leaders Forum. 'Then you must be clear about what it is you have to offer – and cash is probably not the answer.'

6 Such resources include technology, office space and business expertise. Accenture, the technology and consulting company, for example, offers its services to NGOs in developing countries at an affordable price via Accenture Development Partnerships, a non-profit group. When companies offer their own skills or services, however, transparency is essential. A software company partnering with an education establishment to promote better schooling, for example, may be also selling software to that institution. 'The danger is that it's seen as self serving,' says John Kline, professor in international business diplomacy at Georgetown University. 'So it's important that there is a partner group that's separate from the company so there's credibility to it.'

7 Often, companies' day-to-day business has unforeseen benefits. Pfizer, the pharmaceuticals company, is trying to map what it calls 'value transfer' throughout the business. Nancy Nielsen, Pfizer's senior director of corporate citizenship, cites the example of construction sites where the company has imposed safety standards requiring, for example, workers to wear hard hats and shoes, a practice that has subsequently been adopted elsewhere.

8 If organisations focus on spreading the benefits of their investment outwards – through, for example, local sourcing – they can make substantial contributions. 'Unilever in Vietnam employs about 4,500 people directly, but has created 800 to 1,000 small businesses in support as well – so the numbers get really quite big,' says Mr Sandbrook. 'In the past 15 years, everything has been concentrated on the environmental story and to some degree on the social story, rather forgetting that actually the biggest contribution companies can make to development is the economic story. Rightly, the pendulum is now swinging back towards that one.'

FINANCIAL TIMES

UNIT 6 Business ethics

1 Read the whole article. According to the article, which industries and companies have done the following?
  a) provided health and education facilities for the local community
  b) built homes for their workers
  c) worked with specialists in isolated indigenous populations
  d) done research into the impact of their operations on the community
  e) offered their services to non-profit organisations at a reduced price
  f) created safer working environments
  g) given contracts to local businesses

2 Read paragraphs 1 and 2. Find the words and expressions which mean the following.
  a) don't have enough
  b) plans to improve the quality of people's lives
  c) be very cautious about what is done in a difficult situation
  d) have the opposite effect to the one intended
  e) causing a lot of disagreement between people
  f) companies obtaining raw materials, such as oil and coal, from under the ground
  g) have an enormous impact
  h) the most complicated and difficult problem
  i) begin to happen
  j) sense that you are not accepted or included

3 Read paragraphs 3 and 4 and find the verbs which are used with these nouns. Put the verbs in the infinitive.
  a) life
  b) a culture of dependence
  c) (social) programmes *(2 verbs)*
  d) investments/an investment *(2 verbs)*
  e) social-impact studies
  f) a place
  g) a mess

4 Read paragraphs 5 and 6. Find the phrases which have a similar meaning to the following.
  a) done in a careful and controlled manner
  b) providing money for community projects might not be the best solution
  c) it must be clear to everyone that what the company is offering is fair and honest
  d) to help develop improved educational standards
  e) it appears that a company is only doing something to gain some advantage for itself
  f) it can be believed and trusted

5 Read paragraphs 7 and 8 and say whether these statements are true or false.
  a) Pfizer knew that their safety policy would be beneficial outside the company as well.
  b) Unilever works with up to one thousand small businesses in Vietnam.
  c) Richard Sandbrook believes that the most important role of companies is to help countries develop economically.

Over to you 1

What type of information might a mining company want to include in a social-impact study? What impact could the closure of the company have on the local community? What might a closure plan involve?

Over to you 2

What do you think a multinational company working in a developing country should provide for
• its staff;
• its staff's dependents;
• the wider community;
• the country as a whole?

Over to you 3

What type of social programmes are some well-known multinational companies involved with? Use the Internet to help you find out. Which programmes do you like most and why?

UNIT 7   Finance and banking

International banking

Level of difficulty: ● ● ●

Before you read

What are the biggest banks operating in your country?

Reading

Read this article from the *Financial Times* and answer the questions.

Why Deutsche resists national champion status

by Patrick Jenkins

1   Ever since Deutsche Bank discovered that operating abroad – particularly in investment banking – was more profitable than much of its root-and-branch business back home, Germany's biggest bank has had a difficult relationship with the local establishment. For a nation that demands patriotism from its big companies, Deutsche's announcement recently that it would be laying off 6,400 people – even though it had made record profits of €2.5bn – was hard to swallow.

2   Politicians of all parties have accused Josef Ackermann, the bank's affable Swiss-born chief executive, of 'immorality' for putting profits before jobs. Yet politicians – especially those preparing for important regional elections against a background of a record 5 million unemployed – were always likely to criticise Deutsche over its job cuts. For Deutsche, the real trouble is that the German social ethos fits uncomfortably with global shareholder value principles.

3   Deutsche might have made record profits last year. But, when compared with its global peer group, a pre-tax return on equity of 19 per cent and a market capitalisation of barely €35bn put it outside the top 20 – even though, in terms of assets, revenues and investment-bank league-table performance, it

is a top-ten operator. For Mr Ackermann, it is the age-old tussle between what Germany demands and what investors and the analyst community want to hear – namely that he is undertaking serious measures to reach his goal of a 25 per cent pre-tax return on equity, on a par with US rivals.

4   'Deutsche Bank is supposed to be a national champion,' says David Williams, an analyst at Morgan Stanley in London. 'The trouble is that the definition of a national champion differs inside and outside Germany. Deutsche can only really play in the top tier if its profits, share price and market capitalisation are comparable with the best. But inside Germany, all that matters is for a bank to have a big balance sheet, employ a lot of people and lend money to anyone who wants it.'

5   That kind of tension does not only apply to Deutsche Bank, but to any company that pits itself against an international peer group and puts pressure on jobs while being highly profitable. For Deutsche, though, it is more acute, analysts believe. Siemens last year extracted longer hours for no extra pay from several thousand staff in its mobile and networks operations, while BASF said in November it would cut 3,600 jobs despite recording forecast-beating profits. Yet both Siemens and BASF appear to have avoided a political onslaught by being open to compromise.

Siemens abandoned initial plans to shift up to 5,000 jobs overseas, and BASF promised to avoid compulsory redundancies.

6   Deutsche's difficult relationship with the German establishment is long-standing. Despite carrying its nationality in its name, it no longer regards itself as a German bank, and these days employs more people – and makes more money – abroad than at home. To compound matters, Mr Ackermann is not even German. Despite reasonable links to government, advisers say Mr Ackermann is obliged to maintain a degree of distance in his political and corporate networking in order to avoid being drawn into unprofitable patriotic business.

7   Morgan Stanley believes the political outcry over the Deutsche jobs saga carries a resonant message. 'This kind of political interference is derailing capitalism in Germany,' says Mr Williams. 'It is social engineering. And it is delaying much-needed consolidation in German banking. It is a big deterrent for potential acquirers from abroad.' For Deutsche, in particular, senior managers believe the debacle has exacerbated the 'German discount' attached to the share price. That is the last thing Mr Ackermann needs as he tries to play catch-up with his international rivals.

FINANCIAL TIMES

UNIT 7   Finance and banking

1   Read the whole article and complete this summary using BETWEEN ONE AND THREE words from the text in each space.

Deutsche Bank is Germany's **a)** .... bank, but there are increasing tensions between the expectations of German society and the bank's strategy to become a leading player in international banking. German **b)** .... are accusing the bank of giving more priority to making profits rather than saving jobs.

Although the bank made record profits last year, it is not one of the **c)** .... investment banks in the world in terms of share value. For this reason, Josef Ackermann, Deutsche's CEO, needs to increase pre-tax return on **d)** .... from **e)** .... in order to compete with **f)** .... banks.

Two other German companies, **g)** .... , suffered similar pressure when they planned to cut jobs in Germany, and both had to **h)** .... In reality, Deutsche is a German company in name only, since it now employs more people and makes more money abroad. Experts at Morgan Stanley believe that German banking is in need of **i)** .... but that **j)** .... is making this difficult.

2   Read paragraphs 1 and 2, then match the two parts of these word partnerships.

1	investment	**a)**	establishment
2	root-and-branch	**b)**	value
3	local	**c)**	off
4	laying	**d)**	profits
5	record	**e)**	ethos
6	social	**f)**	banking
7	shareholder	**g)**	business

3   Match the expressions from Exercise 2 with the correct definition.
a) set of ideas and moral attitudes that are typical of a particular group
b) highest ever level of money gained from doing business
c) principle which states that the first consideration in business decisions is the interests of people who own company shares
d) group of people in a society who have a lot of power and influence and who are often opposed to any kind of change or new idea
e) the complete network of local offices that are part of the larger organisation
f) activity of buying stocks and shares and then selling them to the public; also offering advice on mergers and takeovers
g) stop employing someone because there is no work for them to do

4   Find the words and expressions in paragraphs 3 and 4 which mean the following.
a) group of companies or products that can be compared because they are similar in a number of ways
b) amount of profit made on an investment
c) capital that a company has from shares

d) total value of a company's shares
e) things belonging to a business that have value or the power to earn money
f) money a company receives from selling goods or services
g) expert who studies financial data and recommends business actions
h) at the same level, value or standard as
i) participate at the highest level
j) document showing a company's financial position and wealth

5   Read paragraph 5. Which statements refer to Siemens, BASF, both or neither?
a) increased working hours without increasing salaries in some divisions
b) introduced longer working hours throughout the company
c) made bigger profits than expected last year
d) planned to reduce the workforce in Germany
e) received the same strong criticism from politicians as Deutsche
f) will transfer about 5,000 jobs outside Germany
g) decided not to move thousands of jobs to other countries
h) agreed to ask which staff want to leave their jobs in return for a payment

6   Read paragraphs 6 and 7 and say whether these statements are true or false.
a) Deutsche was on good terms with the establishment until recently.
b) Mr Ackermann's nationality has helped improve the bank's relationships with the establishment.
c) Mr Ackerman doesn't maintain close ties with the establishment so his company doesn't have to get involved in loss-making businesses.
d) The angry protests about Deutsche's job cuts has a deeper significance in German business.
e) Mr Williams believes that the government is interrupting plans to make German banks stronger.
f) Mr Williams thinks foreign buyers are becoming more interested in German banks.
g) Top management in Deutsche feel that the political situation is helping to increase the bank's share price.

Over to you 1

Do you think the national government and establishment are right to put pressure on national companies? What are the potential risks of this level of political interference? What are the advantages?

Over to you 2

Use the Internet to find three or four of the leading investment banks in the world. Choose one and find out how the firm is organised and what careers are on offer within the company.

Text bank

Corporate recovery

Level of difficulty: ● ● ●

Before you read

If a company is having financial problems, what can it do to help pay its debts?

Reading

Read this article from the *Financial Times* and answer the questions.

Floodgates open to a new style

by Dan Roberts

1 Some years ago at the Plaza Hotel in New York, a group of British clearing banks and officials from the Bank of England were introduced to a new breed of investors who were to revolutionise what happens to companies in trouble around the world. The symposium, organised by PricewaterhouseCoopers (PwC), aimed to acquaint the British bankers with an emerging US style of corporate recovery, led by distressed debt investors and more actively engaged bondholder committees.

2 In the heady days of the late 1990s, bankruptcy was far from the minds of most businessmen, not least among the more traditional lenders in Europe. Of course, soon after, the explosive bursting of the technology bubble was to provide plenty of candidates for this new approach – with entire industries, such as telecommunications, in need of financial restructuring. But it was the more recent arrival of hedge funds and cash-rich private equity firms into the European market that would really open the floodgates to this new style of restructuring.

3 Having seen dramatic and extremely profitable turnarounds in US industries such as steel, coal and utilities, distressed investors are deluging European markets with a flood of money looking for suitably high returns. 'No doubt about it, there has been a significant change in the market,' says Ian Powell, European business recovery leader for PwC. 'US funds are investing big style in European recovery situations.' Their money brings with it both advantages and disadvantages for companies, but most of all it brings far greater complexity and a very fluid set of new stakeholders. 'It used to be just a case of advising local banks; now the people around the table can represent international banks, distressed funds, bondholders and pension trustees,' explains Mr Powell.

4 The results can be seen all over Europe and much of Asia. Lisa Donahue, a New York managing director at Alix Partners, the corporate recovery firm, says the new money can bring much-needed liquidity to companies looking to restructure their debt. While in the past, European companies might have been entirely reliant on a handful of conservative local banks for help, they can now raise fresh capital in a variety of different ways.

5 More liquid debt markets are also creating more flexibility for the banks. Senior lenders are now able to exit at a relatively early stage in a company's financial difficulties, meaning the set of faces around the negotiating table can change very rapidly once a company's credit-worthiness begins to slide. A big challenge for corporate recovery advisers is to make sure that any new capital structure is as liquid as possible, allowing investors to trade freely in and out of restructured debt and equity, rather than finding themselves locked in.

6 But the new faces around the table have also attracted a growing amount of scepticism from seasoned corporate recovery professionals in Europe. David James, a crisis manager, is one of many who fear that the US style of restructuring brings more disadvantages than advantages. 'It has made exit strategies a lot more complicated,' he warns, pointing out that the aggressive new investors are often focused on very short-term objectives rather than worrying necessarily about the long-term health of the company.

7 Even within the same firm, differences of opinion are apparent over this thorny question. Mr Powell at PwC in London is relatively upbeat about the benefits of increased liquidity and tradable debt instruments. 'It is positive in the short term, as there is so much cash entering the market,' he says. 'How long that window is going to stay open is more difficult to assess.' But across the Atlantic, Paul Kirk, who heads PwC's business-recovery practice globally, stresses the other side of the coin. 'Yes, they have added liquidity to the market, but the trading in and out of debt means the goals of the stakeholders are not aligned, and so doing, a successful work-out is much more difficult,' he says.

8 'The US system focuses on keeping the company alive, the rest of the world focuses on keeping the business alive and recognises when a company has no future,' says Mr Kirk. Slowly though, the influx of US investors and turnaround specialists is changing the character of European business recovery. 'The mindset change is pretty fundamental,' says Mr Powell. 'The US approach looks at valuations, in Europe and the UK the emphasis has been on cashflow and the ability to service debt, but that is changing.'

FINANCIAL TIMES

UNIT 7   Finance and banking

1 Read the whole article and match these headings with the correct paragraph.
   a) Comparing approaches to business recovery
   b) Same company, two different expert opinions
   c) An expert's warning about the US approach
   d) British bankers introduced to a new system
   e) Advantages of the US system for big lenders
   f) How the US system helps companies in debt
   g) US distress funds investing in Europe
   h) Changing times brings a need for financial restructuring

2 Read paragraphs 1 and 2 and match the two parts of these financial terms.
   1 distressed   a) funds
   2 bondholder   b) equity
   3 financial   c) restructuring
   4 hedge   d) debt
   5 private   e) committee

3 Choose the correct explanation for each term from Exercise 2.
   a) capital investments made in private companies that are not quoted on a stock market
   b) finance used to buy the bonds of companies that have filed for bankruptcy or appear likely to
   c) making an agreement with lenders to pay debts in a different way to the one agreed originally
   d) money usually used by a small group of rich private investors and institutions to make investments that can often be high risk
   e) group of lenders that has certificates of debt (usually interest bearing) which have been issued by a company to raise money

4 Read paragraph 3 and find words and expressions which have a similar meaning to the following.
   a) change in a company's performance from bad to a very good one
   b) sending a lot of something all at the same time
   c) a large amount
   d) likely to change quickly or often
   e) people considered to be important to an organisation
   f) people that have legal control over someone else's money and the power to invest it

5 Read paragraph 4. Which of these points does Lisa Donahue NOT make?

   New money from US distress funds makes it easier for companies in financial difficulty to ...
   a) pay employees and suppliers and make interest payments to banks.
   b) negotiate with a small number of traditional banks.
   c) find new sources of finance.

6 Read paragraph 5. Choose the correct meaning for the expressions in *italics* in the context of the article.
   a) More *liquid* debt markets are also creating more flexibility for the banks.
      i) free-flowing
      ii) easily converted into cash
      iii) smooth movement
   b) Senior lenders are now able to *exit* at a relatively early stage.
      i) leave the negotiations
      ii) sell their stake in a company
      iii) close down a firm
   c) ... once *a company's credit-worthiness begins to slide*.
      i) It becomes difficult for a firm to pay loans on time.
      ii) A company starts to ask for bigger loans to pay debts.
      iii) A firm's share price begins to decrease over a long period.
   d) ... rather than finding *themselves locked in*.
      i) There are some legal restrictions on ending a contract.
      ii) They are morally obliged to financially support a failing company.
      iii) They have gained something and are certain to keep it.

7 Read paragraphs 6, 7 and 8. Who makes the following points about the new style of corporate recovery? David James (DJ), Ian Powell (IP) or Paul Kirk (PK)? Who seems most in favour of the new style?
   a) The US style of restructuring makes it more difficult to close a company.
   b) A distressed-debt investor may not be interested in helping the company recover in the long term.
   c) It's good that there is more capital available to help companies.
   d) It's not easy to predict if this finance will be available in the future.
   e) Planning a strategy for a company will be harder because the stakeholders' aims are not always the same.
   f) The US system tries to help a company survive.
   g) The European system is becoming influenced by the US system.

Over to you 1

The US system emphasises keeping a company alive. What are some of the arguments for and against this approach?

Over to you 2

Look at the financial press and the Internet to find out about a company that is in trouble. What were the causes of the financial problems and what is the company doing about the situation?

UNIT 8   Consultants

The growth of management consultancy

Level of difficulty: ●●○

Before you read

Has your company or organisation ever employed a consultancy? Why (not)? If so, what kind of consultancy services were provided? Were the assignments successful? Why (not)?

Reading

Read this article from the *Financial Times* and answer the questions.

Advice is once more in demand

by Simon London

1 Reports of the death of management consulting have been greatly exaggerated. The $200bn-a-year business advice industry survived the downturn and dot-com crash. After an extended period of recuperation, it has returned to growth. 'We had a fabulous year last year – strong double-digit growth after several flat years,' says Steve Gunby, head of the Americas region for Boston Consulting Group. Bravado? Excluding information-technology consulting, which remains stagnant, the industry grew by 6.3 per cent last year according to Kennedy Information, the market researcher.

2 But the return to growth does not imply a return to business as usual. The rate of growth over the next few years is likely to be well below the double-digit levels achieved through the 1990s. The strength and pattern of the recovery varies by country, and some sectors remain depressed. Derek Smith, research director at Kennedy Information, points out that the information-technology consulting sector is likely to grow at an average compound rate of little more than 1 per cent. Excluding IT consulting, he expects the wider business advice industry to grow at an annual 7 per cent.

3 The merger and acquisition wave among US public companies helps explain why North America is leading the way. Consultants are often called in to review potential deals and advise on post-merger integration. The return to growth also reflects a familiar, cyclical pattern. The economic boom of the late 1990s led to very strong demand for business advice with which companies struggled to keep pace. Experienced consultants were leaving to work for 'hot' technology companies, and young recruits could not be trained fast enough to fill the gap. The result: raw recruits delivering work of questionable quality to increasingly disillusioned clients.

4 It has taken four years for buyers of business advice to turn again to external advisers. But these companies are wiser for the earlier experience. On average, projects are shorter and less valuable than during the boom years, making it easier for clients to keep track of expenses and objectives. Competitive bidding on engagements is much more frequent.

5 Even once an engagement has been signed, companies are increasingly likely to report to MBA-trained executives in client companies, many of them former consultants. To add value, they must bring to the table more than sharp minds and sharper suits. Experience and perspective are required. The combination of demanding clients and shorter projects is forcing consultancies to take a hard look at how they run their own businesses. Under particular scrutiny is the traditional, pyramid-shaped organisation in which a few senior partners are supported by an army of enthusiastic juniors.

6 The ability to 'leverage' the expertise of senior consultants in this way is central to the economics of the industry. Surveys show a strong correlation between high leverage and high profits per partner. The industry's traditional up-or-out career progression also relies on large annual intakes of raw recruits. Mr Mankins says: 'This is an apprenticeship industry. If you have too few people coming in at the bottom, you end up with not enough managers.'

7 The leverage model works, however, only if clients are willing to pay for bright young MBAs and sign up projects of sufficient duration for them to learn on the job. Increasingly, they are not. 'My sense is that a lot of firms are questioning the traditional business model,' says Betsy Kovacs, AMCF president. Some consultants predict the emergence of 'diamond-shaped' firms, in which partners are supported by more experienced consultants and fewer youngsters. Mr Brown observes: 'People are hiring again, but they are tending to go for the more experienced recruits.'

8 Can consultancies make money if clients decline to support the leverage model? Yes, but only by changing their recruiting patterns and pay practices – and finding new ways to add value. Already, more than half of the AMCF's members are companies whose primary activity is not business advice. Note that the world's largest consulting company is not McKinsey, Bain or Boston Consulting Group – the 'big three' strategy consultants – but IBM, which sells advice alongside IT services, servers and software. Similarly, Bain is now as well known for the exploits of Bain Capital, its private-equity arm, as for strategy consulting.

9 The best that can be said at this juncture is that there will be no single 'right' answer for all consultants. Notwithstanding the disapproval of clients, some will doubtless find ways to maintain the leverage model. Others will evolve into diamond-shaped organisations. Some will remain pure advisers. Others will ally with companies in adjacent industries or develop new sources of income to supplement advisory fees. As consultants are fond of telling clients, the essence of strategy is differentiation.

FINANCIAL TIMES

UNIT 8   Consultants

1 Read the whole article and say whether these statements are true or false.
- **a)** The forecast for the business advice industry depends on country and sector, although IT consulting is expected to do well.
- **b)** American management consultancies have particularly benefited from an increase in the number of mergers and acquisitions.
- **c)** In the past, demand for consultants was high, but clients were often disappointed with the results.
- **d)** Leverage in the management consultancy business involves using a mix of both senior managers together with less experienced and younger consultants.
- **e)** In the 1990s, few apprentice consultants were required, as turnover in the industry was relatively low.
- **f)** A diamond-shaped organisation, where senior consultants are the minority, is predicted to replace the traditional pyramid-shaped consultancy.

2 Read paragraphs 1 and 2 and underline the word or phrase which does NOT collocate in the text with the words in **bold**.
- **a)** IT   management   sector — **consulting**
- **b)** exaggerated   business advice $200bn-a-year — **industry**
- **c)** fabulous   flat   several — **year**
- **d)** recuperation   double-digit   return to — **growth**
- **e)** recovery   IT consulting   depressed — **sector**
- **f)** growth   average compound   sector — **rate**

3 Read paragraphs 3 to 4 and find expressions in the text that mean the same as these phrases.
- **a)** the significant rise in takeovers
- **b)** more successful than others
- **c)** help companies to work together after they have merged
- **d)** time when business activity increases rapidly
- **e)** inexperienced trainees producing poor results
- **f)** different consultancies competing for contracts

4 Choose the best definition for these words and expressions in *italics* from paragraph 5.
- **a)** Even once an *engagement* has been signed ...
  - i) an agreement between companies to merge
  - ii) a consultancy contract
  - iii) an arrangement to meet someone or attend an event
- **b)** To *add value*, they must bring to the table ...
  - i) have other sources of income
  - ii) increase sales and profits
  - iii) offer additional benefits which are not financial
- **c)** ... more than *sharp minds and sharper suits*.
  - i) experience in the retail clothing industry
  - ii) experience and smart appearance
  - iii) intelligence and stylish clothes
- **d)** forcing consultancies to *take a hard look at* ...
  - i) examine something or someone very carefully
  - ii) think about or consider doing something
  - iii) evaluate yourself critically
- **e)** Under particular *scrutiny* is ...
  - i) consideration of an idea, plan or project
  - ii) careful, thorough examination of something/someone
  - iii) close examination of company finances/accounts

- **f)** ... *an army of* enthusiastic juniors.
  - i) those who have already completed their military service
  - ii) a large number of armed forces
  - iii) many people involved in the same activity

5 Add the correct prefix or suffix to these nouns from paragraph 6.
- **a)** lever...
- **b)** expert...
- **c)** ...relation
- **d)** progress...
- **e)** ...takes
- **f)** apprentice...

6 Match the words from Exercise 5 with their definitions.
- **1** the combination of knowledge and special skills a person has in an area of work or study
- **2** the period of time when a person is training for a particular job and is staying with the employer for a specific time
- **3** the numbers of people who join a school or profession at a particular time
- **4** the gradual process of change or development
- **5** being able to improve or enhance your position
- **6** the connection between two ideas or facts, especially when one is the cause of the other

7 Match these words to make word partnerships from paragraphs 7, 8 and 9.
- **1** diamond-shaped
- **2** experienced
- **3** primary
- **4** strategy
- **5** adjacent
- **6** advisory

- **a)** consulting
- **b)** activity
- **c)** firms
- **d)** fees
- **e)** recruits
- **f)** industries

8 Complete these sentences with a suitable expression from Exercise 7.
- **a)** A company's .... is its core business and makes the most money or is the most important.
- **b)** .... are less likely to disappoint clients than younger ones.
- **c)** Recruiting patterns for .... consist of taking on only a small number of junior consultants.
- **d)** We considered taking on a large, international firm, but their .... were very high compared to a local consultancy.
- **e)** As well as selling IT products and services, ... is a major area of the company's business.
- **f)** It is expected that some consultancies will form partnerships with similar or .... to find new sources of income.

Over to you 1

Would you employ the services of a consultancy for business advice? If you needed advice for your company or organisation, how would you go about choosing the best consultancy?

Over to you 2

What are the most well-known consultancy firms in your country? Would you like to work for one of them? Why (not)? Which companies or sectors use their services most?

Text bank

Management consultancy

Level of difficulty: ● ● ○

Before you read

Free advice costs nothing until you act upon it.
What do you think this joke about consultants means?

Reading

Read this article from the *Financial Times* and answer the questions.

A tougher outlook for Britain

by Michael Skapinker

1 American management consultants may be upbeat, but the UK industry has less reason to be cheerful. British consultants' fee income rose only 4 per cent to £10.1bn ($19.2bn) last year, and much of the growth came from outsourcing work rather than the dispensing of advice to senior managers. According to a report by the Management Consultancies Association, about 40 per cent of its members' income now comes from outsourcing. That includes providing advice on how to outsource, but much of the work consists of consultants providing the outsourced service themselves.

2 Many of the consultants not involved in outsourcing are putting together computer systems. Information-technology-related consulting and systems development accounted for about 25 per cent of MCA members' fee income. Traditional management consulting made up only 33 per cent and has fallen for two successive years. The MCA said its members saw fees for traditional consulting fall 8 per cent last year. Not all management consultants are members of the MCA. The association estimates that its members account for 65 per cent of the UK industry's fees. Among the notable absentees are the large strategy consultants. But MCA members make up the majority of UK management consultants, and what happens to them is an indication of wider industry trends.

3 Does it matter that their business has moved away from old-fashioned consulting towards outsourcing and IT? Outsourcing has grown quickly, and consultants would have been foolish not to have grabbed the opportunity to be part of it. The problem is that growth in outsourcing appears to have peaked. The MCA says that outsourcing fee income increased by 18 per cent last year. In 2003, it grew by 46 per cent.

4 Much of the new spending on management consultancy is coming from government rather than from the private sector. The MCA said that its members' fee income from public-sector consulting rose 42 per cent last year, compared with an increase of only 4 per cent from the private sector. Large projects, such as building a modern IT system for the National Health Service, have provided consultants with valuable work. The problem is that many public-sector consulting projects have been controversial, and there is some public and press resistance to the government spending too much on consultancy.

5 What has gone wrong for UK consultants? First, clients are becoming much more sophisticated. They understand the consulting business far better than they did – partly because so many of the client managers are former consultants themselves. Bruce Tindale, chief executive of PA Consulting, says around 30 per cent of the client managers his firm deals with are former consultants.

6 The reason so many consultants now work for client companies should worry the industry: the consultants who leave for clients do so because they find the demands of consulting, and the toll on family life, too heavy. 'There are problems with recruitment and retention,' Mr Tindale says. 'We are noticing pushback from consultants, who are saying: "I'm not prepared to subsume my life any more." We're losing people to clients because clients offer stability.' That has not stopped consultancies from recruiting. MCA member firms employed more than 45,000 people in 2004, an increase of 9 per cent over 2003. At the same time, revenue per consultant fell more steeply last year than in any other recent year – down 11 per cent to £167,000.

7 Fiona Czerniawska, who wrote the MCA report, suggests several reasons why revenue per consultant might have fallen. Changes in MCA membership, particularly the increase in the number of smaller firms, may have depressed the figure, as smaller consultancies tend to charge less. 'It's also possible that the changing mix of services provided by the MCA member firms has had an impact. The growth in outsourcing and IT-related consulting, both of which have lower figures than traditional management consulting services, certainly accounts for part of the drop,' Ms Czerniawska says.

8 But the likeliest explanation for the fall is the increase in the number of consultants. Why have firms been hiring if that has been depressing revenues per head? Because so many consultants, inveterate optimists, believe sales are about to increase. Many consultants over-recruited during the Internet boom at the beginning of the decade, and Ms Czerniawska says: 'Consulting firms have perhaps not entirely learnt the lessons of 2001.'

9 Mr Tindale, who insists his own firm's revenues and profits showed healthy growth last year, says consultants need to provide their clients with a better value-for-money service than they did in the past. 'It's a matter of keeping and sustaining trust among clients. It's very difficult because they look at those bills and say: "What are we getting for this?"'

FINANCIAL TIMES

UNIT 8   Consultants

1. Who said what? The writer of the article, the MCA, Bruce Tindale, Fiona Czerniawska, an anonymous client or an anonymous consultant?
   a) Fees for traditional consulting fell 8 per cent last year.
   b) Does it matter that their business has moved away from old-fashioned consulting towards outsourcing and IT?
   c) The problem is that many public-sector consulting projects have been controversial.
   d) Around 30 per cent of the client managers my firm deals with are former consultants.
   e) I'm not prepared to subsume my life any more.
   f) The increase in the number of smaller firms is one of the reasons why revenue per consultant might have fallen, as smaller consultancies tend to charge less.
   g) Consultants need to provide their clients with a better value-for-money service than they did in the past.
   h) What are we getting for this?

2. Read paragraphs 1 and 2 again. What do these figures refer to?
   a) 19.2   b) 40   c) 25   d) 33   e) 8   f) 65

3. Choose the best definition of these words and expressions in *italics* for the context in paragraphs 3 and 4.
   a) *old-fashioned* consulting
      i) not modern or fashionable
      ii) traditional management consulting
      iii) IT-related and systems consulting
   b) consultants would have been *foolish* ...
      i) silly or unwise
      ii) immature
      iii) taking unnecessary risks
   c) ... not to have *grabbed* the opportunity
      i) taken without asking
      ii) suddenly tried to take hold of
      iii) obtained quickly in a dishonest way
   d) ... outsourcing appears to have *peaked*.
      i) reached the highest point or level
      ii) gone down after reaching a maximum limit
      iii) formed a point above a surface or at the top of something
   e) projects have been *controversial*
      i) discussed in depth and at great length
      ii) shocking or completely unfair and wrong
      iii) causing disagreement as people have strong opinions about the subject

4. Find words in paragraphs 5 and 6 that mean the following in the context of the article.
   a) having knowledge, experience or understanding of complicated subjects
   b) pressure or very bad effect something has over a long period of time
   c) when workers stay with a company instead of taking a job with another employer
   d) resistance or dissatisfaction
   e) treat something as being less important
   f) sharply or dramatically

5. Read paragraph 7 and choose the best summary.
   The author of the MCA report suggests ...
   A there are various reasons why revenue per consultant has fallen recently: the MCA now has new members, especially from smaller consultancies who charge less. She also thinks the change in the type of services consultancies offer is a contributing factor since IT-related consulting and outsourcing both generate less fee income than management services.
   B there are two reasons why revenue per consultant is falling. Many independent consultants have become members of the MCA and charge less, which has significantly reduced the average income of smaller firms. Ms Czerniawska also thinks outsourcing generates less fee income than traditional management consulting services.

6. Say whether these statements about paragraphs 8 and 9 are true or false.
   a) The average consultant fee income has declined mainly due to the rise in the number of consultants.
   b) Consultants are always optimistic and are convinced they will have more work.
   c) Ms Czerniawska thinks that despite consultancies taking on too many new recruits a few years ago, they are making the same mistake again.
   d) Mr Tindale states that consultants generally provide clients with value for money.

Over to you 1

Do you agree with Mr Tindale's opinions in the final paragraph of the article? How can companies justify the expense of consultancy fees? In what ways can consultancies provide their clients with a 'better value-for-money service'?

Over to you 2

Have outsourcing and IT-related consulting become popular forms of consulting service in your sector or country? What do you understand by the term 'traditional management' consulting? Why do you think there has been a reduction in demand for this kind of business advice?

Text bank

What is strategy?

Before you read

How important is it for every business to have a strategy?

Reading

Read this article from the *Financial Times* and answer the questions.

Plan to think strategically

by Morgen Witzel

1 Strategy is, very simply, an outline of how a business intends to achieve its goals. The goals are the objective; the strategy sets out the route to that objective. In the early stages, business objectives are usually fairly simple: to survive and to achieve growth targets. Strategies are correspondingly simple as well, and are often not even committed to paper; it is enough that everyone in the company understands where it is going and how it will get there. But as the business grows, so does the need for co-ordination. Accordingly, there is a need for a mutually agreed and accepted strategy for the business.

2 Some theorists, such as Alfred Chandler, the business historian, would say this is the wrong way to go about it. A strategy should be developed first, and then the organisation tailored to meet the requirements of the strategy. But this is easier said than done. Strategy is also constrained by the company's capabilities. Following privatisation in the 1990s, several British gas and electricity companies branched out into retail operations, selling domestic appliances in high-street shops. Most of these shops quickly closed when it transpired that the companies had no experience or expertise in retailing. This was not a matter of organisation, but of the wrong companies doing the wrong things.

3 Strategy, then, is the art of the possible, and needs to take account of time and resources available. Many managers like to have a formal strategy, a written document to which managers and staff sign up and which sets out everyone's responsibilities in meeting the company's goals. This formal approach has its critics, notably the Canadian guru Henry Mintzberg, who believes that most companies evolve their strategy as they go along. 'Emergent' strategy adapts continuously to changing circumstances and environment.

4 Another possibility is that managers adopt a mixture of both methods, with a formal strategy document creating a framework within which managers respond to events as they arise and make ad-hoc decisions. There is an old adage that 'everything in strategy is very simple, but nothing in strategy is very easy'. One of the first things the novice manager learns is that strategic plans are almost never executed as intended.

5 No matter how careful the planning process has been, there will always be unknown factors and unforeseen events. Known in the jargon as 'turbulence' or 'friction', these build up until they threaten to derail the original plan. This usually means that the original plan must be adapted or, in extreme cases, scrapped and a new plan developed instead. Flexibility is key to good strategic thinking. Is it better to go through obstacles or round them?

6 There is a perception in some quarters that strategy is somehow the preserve of senior managers, who carry out the strategy while everyone else puts their head down and gets on with the job. This is a mistake. Everyone in the business contributes to the execution of the strategy in some way, even if only indirectly. Every department has its role to play – even the cleaning staff and the post room help to contribute to the success of the strategy, by ensuring that offices are clean and communications keep flowing, leading to greater efficiency. If there is a group or department that is not contributing to the strategy, then it is wasting resources and should be dispensed with.

7 Once the company's goals have been established, every ounce of energy should be devoted to carrying out the strategy to reach those goals. This does not mean that the strategy, and indeed the goals themselves, will not change. Change ebbs and flows, and it takes quick and creative thinking to recognise the need for it and adapt the existing strategy accordingly. Ultimately, strategy is not a matter of formal documents and plans, but a way of thinking.

FINANCIAL TIMES

UNIT 9   Strategy

1   Read the whole article and match these headings to the correct paragraphs.
   a) Strategy: a way of thinking
   b) Flexibility is key
   c) What is strategy?
   d) All-round participation and efficiency
   e) A formal or an 'emergent' approach?
   f) Fit the company to the strategy
   g) Have a strategy but be flexible

2   Read paragraph 1 again and say whether these statements are true or false.
   a) Strategy in business is about how you go about achieving your goals or objectives.
   b) Initial business objectives for a company are survival and achieving growth.
   c) Strategies should always be put in writing so that everyone in the organisation understands them.
   d) As a company gets bigger, there is less need to discuss strategies, as everyone should understand where the company is going.

3   Find expressions in paragraph 2 that mean the same as these phrases.
   a) not the correct method to adopt
   b) adapted to the criteria
   c) simple in theory but difficult to put into practice
   d) diversified
   e) a question of

4   Choose the best alternative to complete this summary of paragraph 3.
   Strategy is the art of the possible. Many managers …
   A   … are provided with a written document setting out the company's strategy, although this emergent approach has been criticised by Canadian guru, Henry Mintzberg.
   B   … prefer to have a written document setting out the company's strategy, although this approach has been criticised by those who prefer an 'emergent' strategy which adapts to each situation.
   C   … need to have a written document describing the company's strategy and everyone's responsibilities which all members of staff have to sign. Some business gurus, however, favour an 'emergent' approach which constantly changes depending on the environment.

5   Read paragraph 4 and find words or phrases that are similar in meaning to the following.
   a) set of rules, ideas or beliefs on which decisions are based
   b) happen
   c) not planned, or done only when necessary
   d) proverb or wise saying
   e) new or inexperienced

6   Read paragraphs 6 and 7 and choose the best meaning for the words and expressions in *italics* in the context of the article.
   a) There is a perception *in some quarters* …
      i)   in some areas of a city
      ii) according to some people
      iii) in certain departments
   b) the *preserve* of senior managers
      i)   area of land that is kept for private hunting or fishing
      ii) activity that is only suitable for a particular group of people
      iii) activity of making something without changing it
   c) everyone else *puts their head down*
      i)   lies down or has a rest
      ii) thinks that something is caused by something else
      iii) concentrates or works hard individually
   d) … *gets on with* the job.
      i)   continues doing
      ii) stops doing
      iii) enjoys doing
   e) Change *ebbs and flows* …
      i)   flows away from the shore
      ii) is constantly occurring
      iii) is necessary

7   Match the verbs (1–10) with the phrases (a–j) to make expressions from the text.
      1   achieve (paragraph 1)   a) the original plan
      2   meet (paragraph 2)   b) a mixture of both methods
      3   set out (paragraph 3)   c) ad-hoc decisions
      4   adopt (paragraph 4)   d) everyone's responsibilities
      5   create (paragraph 4)   e) growth targets
      6   make (paragraph 4)   f) obstacles
      7   scrap (paragraph 5)   g) the requirements
      8   go round (paragraph 5)   h) a framework
      9   waste (paragraph 6)   i) those goals
      10 reach (paragraph 7)   j) resources

Over to you 1

'Everything in strategy is simple but nothing in strategy is very easy.' What kind of difficulties do companies experience when trying to put their strategies into practice?

Over to you 2

How would you describe the strategy of the company or organisation where you work or study? Compare it with that of two or three other similar organisations in the sector using the Internet. What are the similarities and how do they differ? Whose is the most/least successful strategy and why?

Mission statements

Level of difficulty: ● ● ○

Before you read

According to the *Longman Business English Dictionary*, a mission statement is a short written declaration made by an organisation, intended to communicate its aims to customers, employees, shareholders and others. Do you think mission statements are useful to these groups? Why (not)?

Reading

Read this article from the *Financial Times* and answer the questions.

Why so many mission statements are mission impossible

by Sathnam Sanghera

1   The woman behind the desk at Avis Rent-A-Car had been chatting freely for some time, but developed a dreadful speech impediment as soon as I queried the bill. 'I'm afraid you're liable for the flat tyre,' she declared, sounding like a robot reciting the small print from a regulatory document. 'It's company policy.' But it was flat when you gave me the car! 'It's company policy.' But I only drove it out of the car park and back!! 'It's company policy.' But I'm a regular customer and a shareholder!!! 'It's company policy.'

2   This treatment continued for a while. Halfway through the encounter – which ended with my threat to sell my shares in Avis Europe, never to use Avis again and to complain about it to everyone I meet for the remainder of my hopefully very long life (have followed through with the first threat, am working on the latter two) – I noticed that Avis's 42-year-old mission statement was emblazoned on surfaces around the office. 'We Try Harder,' it proclaimed. The words haunted me as I stomped off to write a long and ultimately unsuccessful letter of complaint. We Try Harder? Try harder to do what? To irritate our loyal customers? To drive them away?

3   Weeks later, the words were still swilling around my head. So, as an outlet for my rage, I began researching the subject of mission statements, to find out if they are all as annoying as Avis's. Surprisingly, there is a substantial amount of literature available on the subject: tens of books and theses with lively titles such as *Libraries, Mission and Marketing: Writing Mission Statements That Work*. Broadly, the authors fall into two camps: those who think mission statements are not worth the paper, plaster and plastic they are written on, and those who think they are fabulous. Among the critics, it is customary to cite Enron's mission statement, which famously declared that the company was 'open and fair'.

4   Meanwhile, among proponents, it is almost obligatory to craft a mission statement for mission statements: to set out in precise detail the essential ingredients for declarations of company philosophy. One expert insists that there are exactly five things mission statements should cover: the purpose, goals, products, markets and philosophical views of the organisation. Another insists on no less than eight key elements. Yet another insists that the best test of a mission statement is being able to identify the company when one crosses its name off the statement.

5   On reflection, I cannot side with either camp. There is something natural about mission statements – after all, what is the American Declaration of Independence, if not a mission statement? But, at the same time, since the 1982 publication of *In Search of Excellence*, which advised companies to articulate clearer goals, the fad has spread too far.

6   The tiniest businesses are now drafting long statements that bang on tediously about 'passion', 'integrity' and 'excellence'. And a quick Google search reveals that now even individuals and families are getting in on the act. The prospect of the latter is particularly perplexing. Families do not need mission statements. And neither do businesses for that matter: if you have a real raison d'être, as James Collins and Jerry Porras put it in *Built To Last*, 'a visitor could drop into your organisation from another planet and infer the vision without having to read it on paper'. But while businesses do not need them, mission statements need not be a source of irritation, if they are: (1) short, (2) clear and (3) realisable.

7   All the best corporate mission statements adopt this modest approach. Walt Disney's aim 'to make people happy' springs to mind, as does Wal-Mart's aim 'to give ordinary folk the chance to buy the same thing as rich people', 3M's aim 'to solve unsolved problems innovatively' and Google's simple aim 'not to be evil'. As it happens, Avis's 'We Try Harder', which the company describes on its website as its 'rallying cry', fits my criteria perfectly. It is short, memorable and realisable. Indeed, there is no problem with the mission statement at all. The problem, judging from my experience and from Avis's recent lamentable corporate performance, is that the company has given up trying to make its mission statement a reality.

FINANCIAL TIMES

UNIT 9   Strategy

1 Read the whole article and choose the best option.
The writer probably …
   A had had an interest in mission statements before his experience at Avis.
   B has come to dislike all mission statements since his experience at Avis.
   C wrote this article, in part, to complain about his experience at Avis.

2 Read paragraphs 1 and 2 and put the events in the anecdote in order.
   a) The Avis woman told him mechanically that he was *legally responsible* for the cost of repair.
   b) The client *walked away angrily,* imagining that the company was trying hard to *behave in a way that makes* customers *leave.*
   c) The client explained that the car had a flat tyre before he drove it and that he was *someone who used the company's service often.*
   d) Her voice changed when the client *asked a question about the charges.*
   e) The client noticed that the company's mission statement was *clearly visible* on objects around the Avis office.
   f) The Avis woman was *talking in a friendly way* to the client.

3 Find words and expressions in paragraphs 1 and 2 which can replace the phrases in *italics* in Exercise 2.

4 Read Paragraphs 3 and 4 and say whether these statements are true or false.
   The writer of this article …
   a) could not stop thinking about the words the Avis woman had used.
   b) decided to investigate mission statements as a way to deal with his anger.
   c) discovered that some MA and PhD students have written long studies on the subject.
   d) says that a title is 'lively' for humorous effect, because he really believes it's boring.
   e) argues that mission statements can be categorised into two groups.
   f) found experts were remarkably consistent about what makes a good mission statement.

5 Read paragraphs 5 and 6 and choose the best meaning for the words and expressions in *italics* in the context of the article.
   a) On reflection, I cannot *side with* either camp.
      i) agree with
      ii) get angry with
      iii) give an opinion on
   b) … the *fad* has spread too far.
      i) influence of something
      ii) enthusiastic devotion to something
      iii) practice that becomes very popular for a short time

   c) … that *bang on tediously* about 'passion', 'integrity' and 'excellence'.
      i) show that they are confident and happy
      ii) talk continuously about something in a boring way
      iii) express views and opinions in a very loud, forceful way
   d) … individuals and families are *getting in on the act.*
      i) beginning to do something that others are doing
      ii) watching the activities of companies with great interest
      iii) putting pressure on companies to produce mission statements
   e) … a visitor could *drop into* your organisation from another planet
      i) stop doing something
      ii) take something to a place
      iii) visit without arranging a time
   f) … if they are: (1) short, (2) clear and (3) *realisable.*
      i) possible to fulfil
      ii) easy to understand
      iii) dealing with situations in a practical way

6 Read paragraph 7. Match the adjectives (1–6) with the nouns they go with (a–f).
1	modest	a)	problems
2	ordinary	b)	approach
3	unsolved	c)	mission statement
4	rallying	d)	folk
5	memorable	e)	corporate performance
6	lamentable	f)	cry

7 Complete these sentences with the correct adjective from Exercise 6.
   a) It was a truly ………… conference. All the participants said it had been enjoyable and worthwhile.
   b) If something is average, common or usual, it is described as '…………' .
   c) The company encourages all its employees to stay in ………… three-star hotels when they travel for business.
   d) When you can't find an answer or explanation for a mystery, it remains ………… .
   e) The saleswoman's treatment of the customer was ………… , and he left feeling very dissatisfied.
   f) The chairman's ………… speech called on all the staff to support the company's strategy.

Over to you 1

Look at the five mission statements in paragraph 7. Do you agree with the writer's assessment of them? Which do you like most?

Over to you 2

Think of three famous companies and write a mission statement for each. Then check to see on the Internet to see if they already have a mission statement and if your version was similar.

Online groceries

Level of difficulty: ● ● ○

Before you read

If you were going to start up an online business, what kind of products or services would you sell?
What *wouldn't* you sell? Why?

Reading

Read this article from the *Financial Times* and answer the questions.

Groceries by the vanload

by Jonathan Birchall

1   When Andrew Parkinson started his career in online groceries 15 years ago, he was very much an outsider. He and his brother Thomas persuaded Jewel Stores, a Chicago grocer, to take the revolutionary step of allowing some of its customers to place delivery orders via their computers with their start-up, Peapod. But while Peapod's early computer system could take and deliver orders, Andrew and Thomas were not allowed to work from the supermarket that served as their base. Instead, they were confined to a van in the car park. 'By February, it was minus 25 degrees Fahrenheit,' says Andrew. 'They had said they would be surprised if we did more than $1,000 a week in sales, ever. But by then we were doing something like $5,000–$6,000 a week. So they let us inside their store.'

2   Fifteen years and one Internet bubble later, Andrew is still selling online groceries. Peapod is a wholly owned subsidiary of Ahold, the Dutch retail giant. It operates under its own name in the Chicago area, and works with Ahold's Stop & Shop and Giant chains on the east coast, using two distribution warehouses and smaller 'warerooms' at existing store sites. Today, Peapod's service claims about 200,000 regular customers, with an average order of about $145. While Ahold does not produce separate figures, Peapod's sales were estimated to be about $200m last year, making it the biggest online operator in terms of revenue in what is still the comparatively small US market.

3   Peapod's online operation is no longer run from a single Dell computer. But elements of the strategy developed by the brothers remain, Andrew says, starting with the central relationship with a bricks-and-mortar grocer, which now also happens to own them, and its emphasis on software development and customer service. 'We didn't want to be the grocer. So we've always partnered with a retailer. They know how to merchandise.'

4   Peapod's early focus on forming partnerships with supermarkets contrasted with the 'pure play' approach of other Internet bubble-era competitors. Peapod was also guilty of expanding too quickly after the company went public, says Andrew, but formed distribution partnerships with leading super-market chains. Then, when the company's funding crisis hit in 2000, with the sudden collapse of a $120m financing package, Andrew found himself calling retailers in an attempt to sell his company.

5   The takeover by Ahold drama-tically reduced Peapod's sourcing costs. But both Parkinson brothers stayed on, with Andrew becoming chief financial officer. Ahold also kept Peapod's separate identity, he says. 'From the very beginning, we had "the Peapod way", which was to "amaze and delight" the customer, make sure you enjoy your job and don't forget about your family.' Peapod claims that it has achieved far lower turnover of staff than would be usual in a business that combines logistics and retailing, and where the van driver can be the principle point of contact for a customer. It still runs regular employee awards and its 'Broken Promises Index' that monitors its performance in 14 key areas, such as lateness and incomplete orders.

6   Peapod has also continued to draw on its strong background in software. Thomas Parkinson remains chief technology officer and heads web development. The company has developed its own search technology for site users, as well as customised software for planning the routes of its vans, and innovations such as allowing customers to sort products by nutritional content. 'People still want to shop quickly. That's what it comes down to,' he says. 'There are a lot of things we don't even do yet that I hope to do. We can sort, but we can't filter – so if you're a diabetic, in the future you might be able to filter everything out that isn't low sugar.'

7   Despite the transformation under Ahold, Andrew still sees himself as an entrepreneur, saying he still gets to do 'creative things'. But he also faces some distinctly non-entrepreneurial challenges. Com-petition looms with other big supermarket chains that are active online. 'We have competitive plans already in place if they come, and we expect them to come.'

8   Looking back, Andrew sees things he would do differently now. He would not expand so fast, or bring in an outside chief executive to win the confidence of investors, as he did in 2000. He also advises would-be entrepreneurs against listening too closely to their mother's advice. 'We said to her after we developed our business model, what should we start up in ... books or groceries?' Mrs Parkinson, he says, recommended groceries. Jeff Bezos* chose books.

FINANCIAL TIMES

* the founder of amazon.com

UNIT 10   Doing business online

1 Number these events in a logical sequence, then read the whole article and check your answers.
   a) Peapod experiences financial crisis, whilst other dot-coms go bankrupt.
   b) Peapod makes approximately $200m a year and becomes the biggest online operator in the US.
   c) A supermarket allows them to sell to some customers via a computer and a van in the car park.
   d) An outside chief executive is brought in. Andrew becomes chief financial officer, Thomas is in charge of technology and Peapod maintains its company culture.
   e) Peapod makes more than $5,000 a week.
   f) The brothers' mother recommends they start up an online grocery business.
   g) Andrew sells the company to a Dutch retailer.

2 Read paragraphs 1 and 2 and say whether these statements are true or false.
   a) Andrew Parkinson was an experienced grocer when he started Peapod 15 years ago.
   b) A Chicago retailer, Ahold, let Andrew and Thomas sell grocery orders online to its customers.
   c) When the brothers first started the business, they were based outside a supermarket.
   d) Peapod is now completely owned by the well-known Dutch retailer Ahold.
   e) Ahold is probably the largest online operator in US groceries, making approximately $200m a year.

3 Match the words to form partnerships that occur in paragraphs 3 and 4.
   1 online   a) development
   2 bricks-and-mortar b) crisis
   3 software   c) operation
   4 distribution   d) package
   5 funding   e) partnerships
   6 financing   f) grocer

4 Complete these sentences with the expressions from Exercise 3 in the correct form. One word pair is not used.
   a) The most stressful period of his life, admits Andrew Parkinson, was just before the takeover by Ahold when the company was experiencing a crisis, as its .... had collapsed.
   b) One of the keys to Peapod's success was undoubtedly its .... with leading supermarket chains in California, Texas, Ohio and New England.
   c) The main strategy of Peapod was based on a successful mix of customer service and technology, in the form of .... , together with the partnership with Ahold, a ....
   d) The Parkinson brothers' .... has now been profitable in all areas for two years.

5 Read paragraph 5 and say whether these statements are true or false.
   a) The takeover by Ahold was beneficial to Peapod, as it made getting supplies considerably cheaper.
   b) One result of the takeover was that Peapod had to adapt its mission and vision.
   c) Finding the right balance between work and family life is part of Peapod's business ethos.
   d) Peapod's staff are unhappy with the company.
   e) The online grocer gives out various prizes as a way of motivating its workers and ensuring good customer service.

6 Find expressions in paragraph 6 that mean the following.
   a) knowledge and experience
   b) is in charge of
   c) online customers
   d) tailored to specific requirements
   e) the introduction of new ideas or methods
   f) the bottom line or the single most important thing

7 Read paragraphs 7 and 8 and complete this summary using one or two words from the article in each gap.

   Mr Parkinson still thinks like an a) .... , although Peapod is now a subsidiary of a retail giant. He is prepared for future b) .... , namely online competition from other c) .... In retrospect, he would not have expanded so d) .... or brought an e) .... chief executive in to keep the f) .... happy. Neither would he have listened to his g) .... , who recommended the brothers h) .... a grocery business instead of selling i) .... online, as did j) .... , the founder of amazon.com.

Over to you 1

- When the dot-com bubble burst, a lot of Peapod's competitors got their fingers burnt. According to the article, why did Peapod stay in business?
- What do you understand to be the 'pure play' approach of the dot-coms that went bankrupt?
- What do you think will happen to Peapod and other online supermarkets in the future?

Over to you 2

What are the disadvantages of a supermarket selling its goods online? What kinds of business do you think are *not* successful online? Why?

Using a website

Level of difficulty: ● ● ○

Before you read

What are the different possible uses of a commercial website?

Reading

Read this article from the *Financial Times* and answer the questions.

Websites need to have both hard tools and soft touches

by David Bowen

1 Is your website used for marketing, customer service, processing job applications, talking to journalists? Or is it used for brand-building, making your organisation seem like a nice place to work, emphasising its cuddly social side? Both, all and more, you reply. There can be very few large groups (commercial or otherwise) that do not now use their sites in many different ways. The great strength of a website is, after all, that it can do many things at the same time. But it is useful to distinguish between the sets of attributes listed in the first two sentences. They are fundamentally different and represent what I call 'hard web' and 'soft web'.

2 Hard web is the website as a tool. Consumers can buy products or check accounts. B2B customers can place orders. Journalists can find how much money your CEO earned last year. Investors can see how much money they have made out of you. They are all doing something that helps them in their lives or jobs. Soft web is using a site to nudge, to impress, to massage. 'Brochure-ware', where a website reproduces marketing literature created for print, is soft web. So are the look, feel and 'voice' of a site, which transmit messages about the organisation's culture and brand. And the great bulk of corporate social responsibility (CSR) material is soft.

3 Leaving e-commerce aside, the business web has been broadly soft for the last decade. Early elements of hardness came from the HR department, which realised that sites could be used to process applications, and also from investor relations – providing reports online is a hard process, because it saves money. More recently, some companies have been hardening their sites by using them as sales and customer support tools. A good example is the Swedish tools company Sandvik, which uses its site (www.sandvik.com) to replace any number of human beings. Then there are the US companies that are turning their attention to completely new groups of user – Boeing's outplacement areas for redundant employees at www.boeing.com is my current favourite.

4 Does this mean that hard is good, soft is bad? Not at all. One of the best uses for a site is to transmit complex CSR messages. The overall look and feel give off important messages to people who might want to work for you, invest in you or buy from you. The tone of language ('voice') is critical for the same reason. But hard does have one huge advantage over soft. People will make the effort to use hard features, because they save them time, money or whatever. They will not seek out soft features in the same way. Social responsibility material may be admirable and engaging, but apart from that strange new beast – the CSR professional – who will click on a link to find it?

5 Students looking at companies will visit sites to find out facts, and perhaps apply. They will not go there to absorb its look, feel and subtle messages – but having arrived, that is exactly what they will do. The trick is to use hard and soft web in harness. Create as many hard features as you can to get people to your site. At the basic level, make it an essential stopping point for investors, journalists and jobseekers. Think what you can offer customers, B2B or private – interactive calculators to help them choose products, a service reminder perhaps? Back this up with search-engine optimisation, and you will have the right people flowing to your site and staying there. This is when you can bombard them with the soft stuff.

6 The home-page design is critical, but given the likelihood that many people will arrive mid-site from Google, standards must be kept up throughout. Take care to get the 'voice' right, too – companies are increasingly hiring professional writers to produce copy for their sites. The ability to write engaging headlines is a particularly rare and useful skill – and if they can do that, they can write killer labels for links, too. Put those links down the right-hand side of pages. This is where people expect to find routes to related material, and it is the way to get them to content they would otherwise never see – social responsibility material is the obvious example. Siemens (www.siemens.com) scatters links to CSR material throughout its site – it wants everyone to know how virtuous it is, not just those who choose to click the Citizenship or Environment buttons.

7 That's it really. Draw people in with what they want (hard), then feed them what you want (soft). Yes, I know it's obvious; so why don't more companies do it?

FINANCIAL TIMES

UNIT 10   Doing business online

1 Read the whole article and match the following ideas to the paragraphs.
   a) Some tips for writing for web pages
   b) Mixing 'hard' and 'soft' web and making it easier for customers to buy
   c) A parting question
   d) Recent trends in website use and some effective examples of websites
   e) An analysis of the differences between 'hard' and 'soft' web
   f) The many different uses of a website
   g) The look, feel and 'voice' of a website and the main advantage of 'hard' web

2 Read paragraph 1 and find words or expressions which mean the following.
   a) developing a product so that it can be easily recognised by its name or design
   b) soft and friendly
   c) main quality that gives something an advantage
   d) good or useful qualities or features
   e) basically or essentially

3 Read paragraph 2 and say whether these statements are true or false.
   a) Hard web is about doing business or searching for useful information online.
   b) Hard web is only for people who need to work online.
   c) Soft web is about the less tangible features or marketing content of a website that may influence the user.
   d) The way information is communicated about the company and its products or services is also considered to be 'soft' web.
   e) Anything on the web that is related to corporate social responsibility is soft.

4 Choose the correct summary for paragraph 4.
   The writer says …
   A hard web is better than soft web, although soft elements such as overall web-page design or annual reports may influence users. However, people use hard features more often, as they are designed for specific purposes, whereas soft features do not have obvious uses or may only interest a small number of professional users.
   B hard web is not better, but is certainly more useful than soft web, although soft elements, such as a CSR report and the overall tone of a website, are very important. However, people use hard features more often, as they are designed to save time or money, whereas soft features are not obvious to the user or the user may choose not to click on soft links.

5 Find words or expressions in paragraph 5 which mean the following.
   a) technique
   b) together or in combination
   c) destination or visit
   d) a note from a company informing the customer about the benefits of some of its services

e) show that what you are saying is true
f) making the best possible use of something or doing it in the best possible way
g) moving continuously in large numbers
h) give a lot of something, for example information, to someone all at once

6 Match the words to form partnerships that occur in paragraphs 6 and 7.
   1 arrive   a) standards
   2 keep up   b) people in
   3 hire   c) copy
   4 produce   d) people
   5 scatter   e) mid-site
   6 draw   f) writers
   7 feed   g) links

7 Complete these sentences with the expressions from Exercise 6 in the correct form. One of them is *not* used.
   a) If a user .... , he or she may have come to a web page via a link from a search engine.
   b) It's essential to .... throughout the website, as users may not have accessed the site via the home page or the main pages.
   c) The writer recommends .... professional .... who can write good copy, labels and headlines and therefore attract more users to the site.
   d) If .... to citizenship or the environment have been .... throughout the site, there is more of a chance that users will click on them.
   e) .... to a website means attracting users and involves hard web, whereas .... them what you want means communicating your message successfully and entails soft web.

Over to you 1

• According to the article, which of these web pages require 'hard' or 'soft' web? Why?
   – an online job application
   – the Chairman's CSR report
   – a purchasing order
   – the environmental track record of a manufacturer
   – a company's annual financial report
   – a B2B auction
   – the page entitled 'About Us'
• Do you think current trends in web page design favour hard or soft web?

Over to you 2

Look at two or three of the websites mentioned in the article (Sandvik, Boeing and Siemens) on the Internet. Why did the writer recommend them? To what extent do these websites follow the writer's guidelines? What do/don't you like about their websites?

Text bank

Technological innovation

Level of difficulty: ● ● ○

Before you read

What are some of the challenges of setting up your own business?

Reading

Read this article from the *Financial Times* and answer the questions.

Technology that put a shine on a growing business

by Marcus Gibson

1 Three years ago, a young entrepreneur in Leeds risked everything he had to make his business a success. Andrew Ainge's print-technology company, MetalFX, now expects annual revenues in excess of £10m over the next two years. His route to success took him as far afield as China and led him to adopt an innovative technology-licensing model that minimises the operation's overheads while maximising its profits.

2 The technology in question is a new method of printing metallic colours. The system has changed the industry's approach to the use of metallic inks, and the visual results – on brochures, packaging, annual reports and so on – have been stunning. Printers use the CMYK system (combinations of cyan, magenta, yellow and black ink) to create coloured images and text. To print metallic colours, a fifth ink is required. Mr Ainge developed a new kind of ink that enabled the printing of 104 million metallic colours in the same run on a five-colour press. The system allowed millions of metallic colours to be created at once.

3 Once the process was tested and proven, Mr Ainge's first challenge was to convince a global audience of both printers and designers of its benefits. The second was how to maximise revenues. His answer was a strategy that combined innovative marketing of the technology with exploitation of the intellectual property behind the idea. Mr Ainge already ran a design and pre-press agency, so it would have been easy for him to buy a printing press and offer the technique locally. He

foresaw, however, that a much more lucrative strategy would be to license the technology to other printers on a global scale. By late 2002, the product was ready, but there was a problem: Mr Ainge's financial resources were exhausted.

4 By this stage, he had not only built up considerable debts and mortgaged his house, he had even cashed in his pension. He decided to stake everything on a forthcoming print industry exhibition in Shanghai, China. Borrowing £5,500 from a close friend, he bought tickets for himself and his technology manager. 'Then the frenzy started,' he recalls. In only three days, Mr Ainge had collected more than £250,000 in orders for licences. Mr Ainge made access to his technology a carefully controlled process. First, he licensed the rights to manufacture the ink to several of the industry's biggest participants, including Wolstenholme International, a UK printing-ink company. Next, he made sure that designers and printers also gained access to the technology through a software licence that allows them to specify exactly which MetalFX colour they want.

5 Finally, MetalFX put together a sophisticated website, enabling printers around the world to go online and buy a licence. Designers, too, could search the global directory of MetalFX printers to find one closest to them. 'Because the search engine lists all suppliers worldwide, it has created a unique print sector alliance,' Mr Ainge says. 'A MetalFX printer can find a MetalFX designer in their area, or a brand owner can source suppliers to create and print some packaging.' Although the company employs

only nine staff at its Leeds offices, the site gives it an army of 20,000 people around the world who promote MetalFX.

6 Pricing was another issue. MetalFX now licenses its technology for the same price – £1,750 – around the world. The single global price simplifies the licensing process, particularly for a company that sells online and has thousands of distributors and brand owners. Printers who want to buy a licence also have to pass a quality-control test. The marketing strategy has paid dividends, and Mr Ainge claims that the business now enjoys a 92-per-cent profit margin, as well as a worldwide export facility in a market for metallic print worth £100m.

7 He is also branching out in an unexpected direction. Once the technology began to be used to create eye-catching and colourful brochures, posters, packaging and publications, it caught the attention of another group – artists. In response, Mr Ainge set up an art gallery in Ilkley, West Yorkshire, and allowed artists using MetalFX inks to show their work for free.

8 Much of the company's success is down to its efficiency in reaching overseas buyers. At Yorkshire Forward, the regional development agency, Adam Pritchard, head of investment, is well aware of the vital importance of export activity: 'If a business as small as MetalFX can sell to more than 120 countries – using innovative ideas, key trade shows and the power of the Internet – then, frankly, anything is possible.'

FINANCIAL TIMES

UNIT 11 New business

1 Read the whole article and complete this summary with suitable words or expressions from the box. One is not used.

> big break founder intellectual property
> licences nine staff overheads printing-ink
> single price technology manager three days
> trade exhibition

A business model that caught the eye

Andrew Ainge, **a)** .... of MetalFX, a company that licenses technology to print metallic colours for brochures, reports and other publications, had his **b)** .... after travelling to a **c)** .... in China.

Borrowing money from a friend to attend the event with the company's **d)** .... , he found a ready demand among Chinese printers, raising £250,000 in orders for licences in **e)** .... The company employs only **f)** .... and minimises overheads by virtue of a business model that relies on arms-length exploitation of its **g)** ....

Mr Ainge licenses production of his metallic ink to Wolstenholme International, a UK **h)** .... company. Printers around the world then buy licences to use the ink in the printing process, as well as for software that controls the graphic-design process.

For simplicity's sake, Mr Ainge charges a **i)** .... of £1,750 for licences, wherever the purchaser's market. **j)** .... are typically bought through the company website.

2 Read paragraphs 1 and 2 and say whether these statements are true or false.
  a) Andrew Ainge is a young businessman whose company wasn't successful in his hometown of Leeds, but became extremely successful in Asian countries.
  b) MetalFX is a printing-ink company that uses innovative technology and licenses the product so as to reduce the company's overheads and make maximum profits.
  c) The technology has revolutionised the process of printing metallic inks, although the method needs further development.
  d) Cyan and magenta are two of the colours used in the CMYK printing system.
  e) Using Mr Ainge's new system, various metallic colours can be printed simultaneously.

3 Read paragraph 3 and match the adjectives (1–5) with the nouns (a–e).
  1 innovative   **a)** scale
  2 intellectual   **b)** resources
  3 lucrative   **c)** property
  4 global   **d)** marketing
  5 exhausted   **e)** strategy

4 Read paragraph 4 and choose the best meaning for the words and expressions in *italics* in the context of the article.
  a) he had not only *built up* considerable debts ...
    i)   prepared for a particular moment or event
    ii) accumulated
    iii) paid back

  b) ... he had even *cashed in* his pension.
    i)   exchanged for money
    ii) profited from a situation that others considered unfair
    iii) invested in
  c) He decided to *stake* everything *on* ...
    i)   take a big risk
    ii) invest in
    iii) acquire shares in a company
  d) Then the *frenzy* started ...
    i)   difficulties or challenges
    ii) time when people do a lot of things quickly
    iii) great anxiety or excitement in which you cannot control your behaviour
  e) First, he *licensed* the rights ...
    i)   partially sold
    ii) received permission to make something using a patent
    iii) let someone make something using his patent
  f) printers also *gained access to* the technology ...
    i)   managed to enter
    ii) gradually want more of
    iii) obtained or achieved

5 Match these words or expressions from paragraphs 5 and 6 (1–5) with their definitions (a–e).
  1 alliance   **a)** be very useful or bring advantages
  2 brand owner   **b)** an agreement between organisations to work together
  3 source   **c)** difference between the cost of producing all of a company's products and the total sum they are sold for
  4 pay dividends
  5 profit margin   **d)** obtain materials, parts, etc. from a particular place
                      e) individual or company that exclusively produces a recognisable product

6 Read paragraphs 7 and 8 and find expressions that mean the same as the following.
  a) expanding and diversifying
  b) noticeably unusual or attractive
  c) attracted
  d) due to
  e) customers who are purchasing from abroad

Over to you 1

What risks would you or wouldn't you be prepared to take in order to ensure the success of your business?

Over to you 2

The biggest mistake people make in life is not making a living at doing what they most enjoy.
Malcolm S. Forbes (1919–1990), US publisher and editor
Do you agree with the quote? Why (not)?

UNIT 11 New business

Increasing market share

Level of difficulty: ●●○

Before you read

What important factors do you think may help a business make the transition from 'small' to 'big'?

Reading

Read this article from the *Financial Times* and answer the questions.

Assolan's babies battle for market share

by Jonathan Wheatley

1 Defying the laws of gravity is not usually something to attempt every day. But that is how Nelson Mello describes his business model. The Brazilian entrepreneur has launched a succession of products in markets commanded by one or two seemingly unassailable leaders, thanks to a combination of astute strategy and changing market conditions in Brazil.

2 Mr Mello and his team began selling tomato products in 1986 in a market dominated by Unilever. By 2000, one of their products had become a market leader. In 1988, they launched a stock cube to compete with established products, gaining 20 per cent of the market. Other successes include a fruit-flavoured drink that gained a 32-per-cent share against Kraft's Tang, and a mayonnaise that won 19 per cent of a market dominated by the mighty Hellmann's. Then, in 2001, Mr Mello was brought in to head up Assolan, a maker of steel-wool scourers. The giant in the sector was Bombril, with 89 per cent of the market. True to form, Assolan's market share rose from 10 per cent to almost 27 per cent in four years.

3 How did Mr Mello do it? He and his team developed their strategies at Arisco, a foods company that is now case history in Brazilian corporate culture. In 1973, Arisco was a small business in Goiânia, deep in Brazil's interior. Its owners – through their holding company Monte Cristalina – set about making it Brazil's first industrialised condiment company with nationwide distribution. Mr Mello joined in 1978. Twenty years later, Arisco had more than 400 products and had acquired Assolan.

In 2000, Monte Cristalina sold Arisco to Best Foods, and when Best Foods was bought by Unilever, Mr Mello remained head of the Arisco foods portfolio. Yet Assolan languished, and a year later Unilever put it up for sale. The buyer was Monte Cristalina, which bought its old brand and re-hired its old managers.

4 Arisco's success in grabbing market share derives partly from two characteristics of the Brazilian market. First, the course of industrialisation from the 1950s led to each market being dominated by a small number of brands. In the late 1990s, however, conditions began changing. Second, Arisco launched its new brands when Brazilian consumers were becoming aware of a widening choice of products. To exploit these factors, Mr Mello and his team developed what he calls the 'four pillars of success': product, distribution, communications and people.

5 The basic product – the Assolan steel-wool sponge – is barely distinguishable from competitors. Its sales force is also largely ex-Arisco, and distribution is built on the Arisco model, using four logistics contractors, 52 distributors with 2,100 sales representatives. The fact that Assolan products are still made in central Brazil helps greatly with distribution.

6 Yet Mr Mello concedes that Assolan owes much of its success to its marketing nous. 'We set out our strategy based on a seven-year plan,' he says. 'We spend a disproportionate amount on communications at the start. That's the bet: spend much more than normal at the start to reach your targets more quickly.' If the amounts are unusual – about $10m, $12m and $12m in the

past three years – the way they are spent is even more so. For the first year, Assolan used no advertising agency. Instead, Mr Mello met the presenters of 'auditorium' shows that air daily on Brazilian television.

7 Product endorsements on the shows are routine. Mr Mello told presenters that they could improvise at the start and end, but the central message was to be learned by heart. The most powerful opinion formers in Brazil told their admirers about a wonderful steel wool called Assolan. 'We had got across the very simple message that there was a wire wool that was not Bombril,' Mr Mello says. Next, he hired Nizan Guanaes, a star of Brazilian advertising. 'We set two rules,' Mr Mello says. 'One, never mention our competitor. Two, never create expectations beyond what we're selling.'

8 Assolan's advertisements make virtually no claims about the product. Instead they play on changes in Brazilian society, promoting the idea that Assolan is part of a new wave of consumer choice. Bombril is never mentioned, though a version this year notes that nowadays '... letters are by e-mail, cameras are digital, and wire wool is Assolan'. 'We don't mention the competitor, but we make him look old,' says Mr Mello. Other advertisements feature Assolan babies with steel-wool wigs. 'Ads have to create sympathy for the product,' says Mr Mello. Assolan is now launching a range of cleaning products. 'Cleaning is a lot like cooking: there is an emotional element to caring for the family's health,' Mr Mello says. Brand managers of household cleaners would do well to take note.

FINANCIAL TIMES

UNIT 11   New business

1   Read the whole article and tick those factors that helped make the Assolan steel-wool sponge a success.
   a) The application of the Internet and new technologies
   b) An entrepreneurial leader, supported by a good team
   c) Political changes in central Brazil
   d) A change in public awareness of consumer choice
   e) An innovative idea for a brand-new product
   f) A lot of money spent on the launch of the product
   g) Brazilian footballers endorsing the product on television
   h) An emotional element in the advertising campaign

2   Read paragraphs 1 and 2 and find words or expressions in the text that mean the following.
   a) doing the impossible
   b) a series of
   c) apparently unbeatable companies
   d) clever and able to understand things quickly
   e) obtained or achieved
   f) appointed
   g) manage or lead
   h) typically

3   Make word pairs to form expressions from paragraph 3.
   1   case   a) distribution
   2   corporate   b) company
   3   condiment   c) culture
   4   nationwide   d) history

4   Match the verbs (1–4) with the noun phrases (a–d) to form expressions from paragraph 4.
   1   grab   a) conditions
   2   change   b) new brands
   3   launch   c) market share
   4   exploit   d) factors

5   Complete these sentences with suitable expressions from Exercises 3 and 4 in the correct form. Two of the expressions are *not* used.
   a) In the 1980s, Mr Mello and his team .... , such as a stock cube, to compete with established products from Knorr and Maggi.
   b) Due to the remarkable success of the .... , Arisco is regarded as .... by many Brazilian executives.
   c) Over the last two decades, Arisco .... the .... of giants in the industry, such as Kraft and Hellmann's.
   d) One of the factors that greatly helped Arisco sell its steel-wool scourer was .... , as the company is strategically located in central Brazil.
   e) .... in Brazil's economy and industry also played an important part in the rise of the Assolan steel-wool sponge.

6   Read paragraphs 5 and 6 and choose the correct definition of these words and expressions in *italics* in the context they are used in the article.
   a) ... *barely distinguishable from* competitors.
      i)   not very different from
      ii) easily differentiated from
      iii) not very successful compared to

   b) Yet Mr Mello *concedes* ...
      i)   is of the opinion
      ii) admits something is true
      iii) gives up
   c) ... owes much of its success to its marketing *nous*.
      i)   team spirit
      ii) innovations
      iii) know-how or ability
   d) We spend a *disproportionate* amount ...
      i)   relatively large
      ii) exceedingly large
      iii) fairly minor
   e) That's the *bet* ...
      i)   decision to risk money
      ii) justified expense
      iii) an action or situation that is likely to be successful

7   Choose the correct summary of paragraphs 7 and 8.
   A   Nelson Mello told TV presenters to endorse the product by improvising a little but reciting the key message from memory: namely, that Assolan was a fantastic steel-wool scourer. As part of the advertising campaign, presenters could not mention the name of Assolan's competitor or create false expectations of the product. The adverts promoted the idea of change in Brazilian society and the fact that consumers do not have to use the same old brands any more. Another characteristic of Assolan's marketing strategy was playing on people's emotions, such as the use of cute babies in the advertisements.

   B   Nelson Mello told TV celebrities to endorse the wire wool by communicating the key message that Assolan wasn't the only steel-wool sponge on the market. As part of the advertising strategy, presenters could not mention the name of Bombril or create sympathy for the competitor's product. In addition, the advertising promoted the idea of change amongst Brazilian consumers, as well as awareness of the fact that Assolan was launching a new range of cleaning products. Another characteristic of Assolan's marketing was the emotional element, such as the use of babies wearing steel-wool wigs in the advertisements.

Over to you

Think of three food companies whose brands dominate the market in your country. What brands are they? Use the Internet to help you answer these questions:
- How long have they been established leaders?
- What has been the key to their market dominance?
- What kind of marketing and advertising do they employ?
- Are there any newcomers in the sector?

UNIT 12   Project management

Project mediators

Level of difficulty: ● ● ○

Before you read

- What are the possible reasons why technical projects are often 'prone to failure'?
- What is meant by the term *marriage broker* or *marriage guidance counsellor*?

Reading

Read this article from the *Financial Times* and answer the questions.

Advent of the IT marriage broker

by Maija Pesola

1 The chances of large information-technology projects being successful are even more depressing than divorce statistics. While six out of every ten British couples tying the knot can hope to stay married, it is estimated that only about 50 per cent of IT projects will come in on budget, and only about 10 per cent will finish on time. In the worst cases, IT projects fail spectacularly, causing more expense and reputational damage than a trip through the divorce courts. However, estranged clients and providers are now bringing in a new breed of consultant – likened to a marriage guidance counsellor – to help resolve conflicts and put errant projects back on track.

2 To try to prevent relationships breaking down, companies and IT service providers are calling on the services of smaller, third-party consultancies, who can help set up the contract and make sure all parties remain in agreement. 'You can call us marriage counsellors,' says Bob Fawthrop, chief executive of Morgan Chambers, an outsourcing advisory company. 'When a relationship breaks down, it is never totally one party's fault. It is usually a case of people misunderstanding each other. A third party can come in with a more objective view.'

3 Sometimes, to ensure the advice is truly impartial, the client and IT contractor will share advisory fees. 'Ten years ago contracts would merely say that mediation on any contract disputes would be dealt with by senior management,' says Ivor Canavan, European vice-president at Computer Sciences Corporation,

an IT-services company. 'Now, companies are often nominating a third-party mediator from the start. There is more of an expectation that things can get out of shape, and companies are putting in place measures to ensure they can resolve problems quickly,' he says.

4 Mr Fawthrop says Morgan Chambers is being called in frequently to help companies write contracts with their IT suppliers and to mediate when problems arise or the terms of the project need to be changed. The company had about 100 engagements last year, and demand is growing at around 25 per cent each quarter.

5 As well as advising on setting up projects, small consultancy companies are also being called in to oversee them as they progress. 'A lot of projects fail because the parties have different agendas,' says Alistair Clifford-Jones, chief executive of Leadent, an Oxfordshire-based consultancy that does this kind of IT project work. 'Systems integrators may want to make more changes to a project because they make money out of changes. The client may not deliver everything it is supposed to, and the company circumstances might change,' Mr Clifford-Jones says. 'Leadent's job is to keep everyone on track. There is a consulting revolution going on where clients are fed up with the inefficiency and high fees of the big accountancy and consulting companies. People are starting to accept that there needs to be a level of independence driving the project.'

6 A small company that only started operations three years ago, Leadent is already seeing its revenues increasing by 300 per cent a year. It

has worked on a number of projects worth tens of millions of pounds, with customers such as Whitbread, the leisure group, and Anglian Water, the utility company. Sometimes Leadent consultants have been parachuted in to turn round a project that has already run into trouble. But increasingly they are being included at the start.

7 Anglian Water brought in the company as an overseer when it began to plan the launch of a mobile computing system for its workers. Paul Vallely, programme manager at the utility, says, 'Rolling out mobile field services is a new project for both CSC and Anglian Water, and we needed a specialist.' Mr Vallely believes Leadent provides a good counterview to CSC on the requirements of the project. 'We have a good relationship with CSC, but it is good that they can say what is feasible to expect CSC to do, and in what time scale. Leadent are making sure that CSC delivers the specification on time and to cost.'

8 Mr Clifford-Jones says Leadent is also able to flag up problems with the client company more effectively because it is considered to be independent. 'Clients take Leadent's advice seriously because they know the guys aren't there to sell more work,' he says. So far, on the Anglian project, the 'marriage counselling' approach appears to be producing results. The project is expected to finish on schedule next year and is estimated to be running 15 per cent below budget. With a little outside help, it seems, technology providers and their clients can look forward to a long and happy union.

FINANCIAL TIMES

UNIT 12   Project management

1 Read the whole article. Who said what? Bob Fawthrop (BF), Ivor Canavan (IC), Alistair Clifford-Jones (AC), Paul Vallely (PV) or the writer of the article (MP)?

   a) Only about 50 per cent of IT projects will come in on budget, and only about 10 per cent will finish on time.

   b) When a relationship breaks down, it is never totally one party's fault. It is usually a case of people misunderstanding each other.

   c) Companies are putting in place measures to ensure they can resolve problems quickly.

   d) We are being called in frequently to help companies write contracts with their IT suppliers and to mediate when problems arise.

   e) There is a consulting revolution going on where clients are fed up with the inefficiency and high fees.

   f) Leadent consultants have been parachuted in to turn round a project.

   g) We needed a specialist.

   h) We're also able to flag up problems with the client company more effectively because we're considered to be independent.

2 Read paragraph 1. Match the verbs (1–7) with the nouns/adverbs (a–g) to make expressions from the article.

1 tie	**a)** damage
2 come in on	**b)** budget
3 finish	**c)** the knot
4 fail	**d)** track
5 cause	**e)** spectacularly
6 resolve	**f)** on time
7 put back on	**g)** conflicts

3 Read paragraphs 2–4 and say whether these statements are true or false.

   a) Bob Fawthrop, who works in an advisory capacity when business relationships get into trouble, says that one party is never entirely responsible.

   b) Third-party consultancies are compared to marriage counsellors because they give impartial advice and help when communication has broken down.

   c) Only the client pays the advisory consultancy fees when difficulties arise with IT contracts.

   d) Companies are not usually realistic about possible difficulties that may arise in projects.

   e) Morgan Chambers is expecting to have a similar amount of business this year as last year.

4 Read paragraphs 5 and 6 and find expressions in the text that mean the following.

   a) supervise or check an activity is being done correctly

   b) not having the same priorities

   c) all that was agreed or expected

   d) make sure everyone is doing what was agreed

   e) annoyed or irritated

   f) leading or influencing

   g) contracted in an emergency to make a project successful

   h) experienced difficulties

5 Read paragraphs 7 and 8 and choose the best meaning for the words and expressions in *italics* in the context used in the article.

   a) Anglian Water brought in the company as an *overseer* …
      i) financial controller
      ii) project sponsor
      iii) advisory body

   b) Paul Vallely, programme manager at *the utility*, …
      i) CSC
      ii) a mobile computing system
      iii) Anglian Water

   c) *Rolling out* mobile field services …
      i) producing a lot of something in a short space of time
      ii) supplying a new service after it has been tested and marketed
      iii) doing a particular business activity quickly and easily

   d) Leadent provides a good *counterview* …
      i) different agenda
      ii) alternative opinion
      iii) impartial agreement

   e) … making sure that CSC delivers the *specification* on time …
      i) deliverables
      ii) time schedule
      iii) milestones

   f) Leadent is also able to *flag up* problems …
      i) create
      ii) point out
      iii) solve

   g) … because they know the *guys* aren't there to sell …
      i) advisory consultants
      ii) IT suppliers
      iii) client company's management

   h) … look forward to a long and happy *union*.
      i) merger or acquisition
      ii) project
      iii) partnership

Over to you 1

Why do the companies mentioned in the article think it beneficial to employ an advisory or third-party consultancy? What can project managers or project sponsors do to ensure projects are completed on time and come in on budget?

Over to you 2

Have you ever been involved in an IT project? What did it involve and what was your role? Was the final outcome successful? Why (not)? Would an advisory consultancy have helped the project be more successful?

UNIT 12 Project management

Remote management

Level of difficulty: ● ● ○

Before you read

What do you understand by the expression *virtual meetings*?

Reading

Read this article from the *Financial Times* and answer the questions.

People skills still rule in the virtual company

by Jay Conger and Edward Lawler

1 Three weeks ago, the senior management team of a large computer services company met in Manhattan at 7 a.m. on a Sunday. The ten colleagues had not met for several months, which is hardly surprising given their locations. Three are based in California, two in New Jersey, one in Pennsylvania, one in Connecticut, one in London and two in India. They are scattered across the world for a simple reason: their operations and customers are global. Even though the managers do not meet face to face regularly, they communicate daily, making extensive use of e-mail, mobile phones and video conferencing. This company represents an extreme case of how organisations are changing, but it is not unique. It represents what more and more companies will come to look like.

Virtual management

2 Increasingly, managers and those who work for them are no longer in the same location. Gone are the days when managers could supervise the hour-to-hour work of individuals. Managers now need to lead by focusing on the processes shaping performance, along with the results that staff must achieve. This can be done only if managers structure virtual projects, set appropriate goals and milestones, shape behaviour, and develop measures to analyse what progress is being made.

3 Critically, managers must have a deeper understanding of when to use the wide range of communications that are now available. When is a phone call best? A teleconference? A video conference? An e-mail? A face-to-face meeting? Research suggests that face-to-face communication is often the best way to start a virtual project in order to reach an initial agreement on goals, milestones, norms and individual commitments. It helps build a trusting relationship that cannot be built remotely.

4 Once a managerial or team relationship has been established, much can be accomplished with e-mail. That said, it is still important to hold regular meetings, either face to face or by video conference. As a general rule, face-to-face sessions are for intensive, real-time problem-solving, while virtual meetings are for efficient information-sharing and assessing progress.

5 It is also useful to create smaller groups within a virtual team. These smaller groups are held mutually responsible for the successful delivery and integration of their specific task. For the most critical phase of the subgroup's work, they are brought together, often for several weeks. Physical proximity is critical to performance. It allows individuals to respond to ideas immediately, to explore options more deeply, and to be more productive in problem-solving.

Managing without authority

6 Traditional organisations worry about control and reporting relationships. The assumption is that organisations are most effective when there are clear reporting relationships. It is a valid principle when what needs to be done is simple and can be carefully supervised. It is not necessarily a good idea, however, when the product or service is complex and its creation is not easily observed and monitored. Often complex management relationships need to be developed because organisations are trying to produce complex products and services across geographic boundaries.

7 In these circumstances, individual managers need to work with and influence people who are not their subordinates. Among the most important skills to learn are: constructive persuasion, inspirational appeals, exchange of favours and mutual help, coalition-building and consultation. One company that has been highly successful at this is Gore, maker of Gore-Tex fabric. Since 1958, Gore has avoided a traditional hierarchical model, opting instead for a team-based environment that fosters personal initiative, encourages innovation and promotes person-to-person communication.

Shared leadership

8 Because more and more work is being done in cross-functional global teams, leadership increasingly must be shared. One company rotates leadership roles across its project team members at critical phases. Partly this approach to leadership is a result of the fact that team members are now often peers. Partly it is a result of the fact that work is now done in subgroups in different locations. To succeed at shared leadership, managers must start by creating expectations. First, they must explain that sharing leadership is a performance expectation and will be rewarded. Second, team members must accept responsibility for providing as well as responding to peer-based leadership.

9 Managers must select team members who can perform well without strong guidance from a superior. They must encourage team problem-solving and decision-making. This means often deferring critical decisions and managers assuming more of a facilitative rather than directive style. They must be able to demonstrate shared leadership in meetings, turning leadership over to a capable subordinate or peer at the appropriate moment. They must coach and develop their team's individual and collective leadership skills. This may be the most difficult of the new skills to learn, since it requires letting go of direct control. That said, it is becoming a necessity in a world where working relationships are scattered over great distances.

FINANCIAL TIMES

UNIT 12   Project management

1 Read the whole article. Number these ideas in the order they appear in the text.
   a) Managers need to know when it's best to telephone, e-mail or call a teleconference or a virtual meeting.
   b) Global companies nowadays cannot supervise individuals as closely as before.
   c) Managers should encourage team members to share leadership and take responsibility for their actions.
   d) As a result of globalisation, companies will increasingly have to manage teams that work in different parts of the world.
   e) Managers today need to know when to defer decisions, lead, facilitate or coach team members.
   f) Face-to-face meetings are more effective when it comes to complex tasks like problem-solving.
   g) With complex organisations, a manager does not always have the authority to directly ask the team to do something.

2 Match the verbs (1–8) with the expressions (a–h) to make word partnerships from paragraphs 2 and 3 of the text.
1	focus on	**a)**	measures
2	achieve	**b)**	behaviour
3	set	**c)**	processes
4	shape	**d)**	progress
5	develop	**e)**	an initial agreement
6	analyse	**f)**	appropriate goals
7	reach	**g)**	a trusting relationship
8	build	**h)**	results

3 Correct six of the verbs in these sentences, using the verbs from Exercise 2.
   a) Managers now have to lead by setting processes, performance and results.
   b) Staff need to build results.
   c) This can only be done if managers shape appropriate goals and milestones, reach behaviour and develop progress being made.
   d) Face-to-face communication is the best way to start a virtual project in order to analyse an agreement on milestones and commitments.

4 Complete these sentences using expressions from paragraph 4.
   a) Video .... and .... meetings make building relationships more of a challenge, but they are part of today's global business, where managers may be based anywhere in the world.
   b) If a manager wants a group of workers to get the job done effectively, a solid team .... has to exist, and the members will need to meet in .... sessions, particularly at the start of any big project.
   c) Real-time .... in meetings involves building a trusting relationship and should be done face to face, where physical proximity can improve performance, whereas pure .... can be done via teleconference or video conference.

5 Read the section entitled *Managing without authority* (paragraphs 6 and 7) and choose the best meaning for the words and expressions in *italics* in the context of the article.
   a) *The assumption is* that …
      i) something that people think is true although there is no definite proof
      ii) something that everyone knows to be true
      iii) when someone starts to have control or power
   b) … when there are clear *reporting relationships*.
      i) relationships between employees and managers
      ii) working relationships between team members
      iii) management relationships across different countries
   c) The expression *inspirational appeals* refers to …
      i) making public requests for help, money or information
      ii) being creative about motivating staff
      iii) asking staff to do things they do not want to do
   d) *coalition-building* and consultation
      i) organising working groups
      ii) building relationships with people who have a common goal
      iii) building relationships with official bodies or organisations
   e) … a team-based environment that *fosters* personal initiative
      i) requires or makes obligatory
      ii) provides training in a particular skill
      iii) encourages or promotes

6 Read the section entitled *Shared leadership* (paragraphs 8 and 9) and complete this summary with one or two words from the text in each gap.

   Leadership must be **a)** .... due to the development of **b)** .... global teams: team members often work in different **c)** .... and are now regarded as **d)** .... Managers need to convey the idea that sharing leadership is a **e)** .... and that individual members should take **f)** .... for their work. The role of the manager has become less **g)** .... , and team members are also expected to take the initiative. Managers must therefore **h)** .... individual and collective **i)** .... , although this involves letting go of **j)** ....

Over to you 1

What are some of the problems that can arise when communicating with team members from other countries?

Over to you 2

What are the advantages and disadvantages of sharing or rotating leadership in a team?

Text bank

Text bank answer key

Unit 1

Networking

1 1 d 2 f 3 g 4 a 5 b 6 c 7 e
2 1 c 2 b 3 e 4 d 5 a
3 Suggested answers
   a) glossy brochure **b)** business/social lunch
   c) leading brand **d)** personal computer
   e) social occasion
4 **a)** True *On Tuesday, I will be on the 8.38 a.m. to Moorgate Station as usual.* (paragraph 2)
   b) False *... actually the prospect of the biggest networkathon in the world appeals to me even less than the prospect of going skiing – which appeals not at all.* (paragraph 2)
   c) True *Having to make conversation with strangers ... is a wretched way to spend an evening; doing it for days on end must be pure torture.* (paragraph 2)
   d) True *The whole networking process defeats me* (paragraph 3)
   e) True *they are usually a bit grubby* (paragraph 3)
   f) False *on the rare occasions I am required to produce one.* (paragraph 3)
   g) False *... get fished out whenever I spring clean it.* (paragraph 3)
   h) False *They then sit on my desk for a while before eventually going into the bin.* (paragraph 3)
5 **a)** iii **b)** ii **c)** ii **d)** i **e)** iii **f)** ii **g)** i
6 Suggested answers
   a) *correct*
   b) thought he **hadn't made any** useful business deals while networking.
   c) **hadn't employed a single person** he had met while networking.
   d) found he enjoyed networking **less** as he got older.
   e) *correct*
7 **a)** off-putting **b)** pushy **c)** calculating **d)** self-defeating
   e) annoying

Relocating

1 e, b, h, d, f, a
2 **a)** shockproof **b)** head back **c)** commuter **d)** always on the move **e)** given their marching orders **f)** brave new world **g)** ghetto **h)** lavish rental allowance **i)** expatriate; expat **j)** blend into
3 **a)** well-heeled **b)** property market **c)** mainstay **d)** tenants **e)** landlords **f)** exclusive expatriate neighbourhoods **g)** take ... on the chin **h)** stand out **i)** saturated marketplace **j)** make way for
4 **a)** False *landlords in Hong Kong have been offering businesses free accommodation for **up to 18 months** of a three-year lease to secure their tenure.*

   b) True *landlords in Hong Kong have been offering businesses **free accommodation for up to 18 months of a three-year lease** to secure their tenure.*
   c) True *Singapore, home to 80,000 foreigners working in white-collar professions*
   d) False *Singapore ... has begun to **play second fiddle to** Chinese cities such as Shanghai*
   e) True *Shanghai, where rents are lower, and the infrastructure and schools are **improving immeasurably**.*
5 1 h 2 a 3 g 4 f 5 d 6 c 7 e 8 b
6 **a)** Hotels **offer** many new facilities for business travellers.
   b) Serviced apartments are **peppered** around the world.
   c) Serviced apartments will **come with** concierge services and tailored facilities.
   d) Families won't have to **uproot** as often.
   e) Relocation can **put strains on** a couple's relationship.

Unit 2

Business ideology

1 **a)** Bing Xiang **b)** GMAT test **c)** EMBA (executive MBA) **d)** $35,500 (Rmb 288,000) **e)** 80 **f)** Insead and the Wharton School (University of Pennsylvania)
2 Suggested answers
   a) The Chinese government **licensed** China's first privately owned business school.
   b) China hopes to **adopt** US-style education in management education.
   c) The new school was set up with money from Li Ka-Shing ~~and Bing Xiang~~.
   d) The new business school **is run by** Bing Xiang.
   e) *correct*
3 **a)** application procedure (paragraph 3)
   b) sit (a test) (paragraph 3)
   c) minimum score (paragraph 3)
   d) inception (paragraph 4)
   e) doctoral degree (paragraph 4)
   f) thirst for knowledge (paragraph 4)
   g) faculty (paragraph 5)
   h) dean (paragraph 5)
4 **a)** False *Professor Xiang aspiring to attract overseas students to his programme, which is taught in English ...* (paragraph 3)
   b) False *top of the hit list are Chinese professors who have studied and taught abroad.* (paragraph 5)
   c) True *Both were seduced by the idea of conducting research in China.* (paragraph 5)
   d) True *The EMBA alumni network is extremely powerful ... we can get information not through the formal channels.* (paragraph 6)
   e) False *We don't want to regurgitate what we learnt in the US.* (paragraph 7)

5 a) i **b)** ii **c)** i **d)** i **e)** ii **f)** ii **g)** i **h)** ii
6 1 e   2 f   3 d   4 b   5 c   6 a
7 a) keeping ... afloat   **b)** all it took   **c)** running
  d) come so far   **e)** get into   **f)** pioneer   **g)** aspiring to

Professional development

1 1 b   2 h   3 d   4 e   5 a   6 f   7 c   8 g
2 1 e   2 h   3 a   4 g   5 f   6 d   7 c   8 b
3 1 f   2 g   3 c   4 a   5 b   6 e   7 d
4 a) ii   **b)** i   **c)** ii   **d)** iii
5 1 b   2 d   3 a   4 c   5 e   6 f

Unit 3

Toll systems

1 a) Austrian   **b)** gantries   **c)** cash   **d)** and easy
  e) inspectors   **f)** Autostrade   **g)** the system was untried
  h) credit card   **i)** 60%   **j)** mobile-phone users
2 a) iii   **b)** i   **c)** iii   **d)** ii
3 1 g   2 f   3 e   4 b   5 a   6 c   7 d
4 a) Truck drivers; toll booths   **b)** loose change
  c) commercial vehicles   **d)** satellite technology
5 a) period since when tolls have operated on Italian
    motorways
  b) number of years ago when more than half of Italian
    drivers paid tolls in cash
  c) percentage of Italian drivers who pay with credit cards or
    Telepass
  d) amount of money (in euros) spent by Autostrade on
    research and development
  e) percentage of Autostrade's revenue that came from tolls
    in 2004
  f) percentage of the Italian tolled network controlled by
    Autostrade
  g) percentage of Italian toll roads for which Autostrade acts
    as a clearing house for the non-cash revenue
  h) number of cameras installed by Autostrade on
    motorways
  i) name of the telecommunications company with which
    Autostrade is discussing a venture
6 a) True   *the accompanying sensors can relay*
        information on traffic and weather to units such
        as media outlets or screens in service stations.
  b) False   *Autostrade is discussing a venture with 3, the*
        telecommunications company, that will see free
        and paid-for services available on mobiles.
  c) True   *drivers' phones can be located by readings*
        taken from the mobile phone network.
  d) True   *Mr Bergamini says tracking the exact location*
        of vehicles, and speed and direction of travel
        are not yet precise enough.
  e) False   *If you want personal information, you want*
        information that is tailored for you, not for
        someone who is near you. (Here, he is referring
        to personal information for the driver and
        mobile user, not for Autostrade.)

Partnerships with NGOs

1 a) Peter Melchett, head of Greenpeace (paragraph 1)
  b) corporate communications company (paragraph 1)
  c) conservation group (paragraph 2)
  d) US banana giant (paragraph 2)
  e) UK electricity supplier (paragraph 2)
  f) consumer goods group (paragraph 2)
  g) executive director of Greenpeace (paragraph 3)
  h) executive director of the FLA (paragraph 5)
  i) US-based monitoring organisation, working with
    companies and NGOs (paragraph 6)
  j) co-director of the Partnering Initiative at the
    International Business Leaders Forum (paragraph 9)
2 a) Peter Melchett angered many environmentalists when
    he became **an adviser at** Burston-Marsteller.
  b) Peter Melchett argued that he could achieve more
    working with **companies** than in opposition to them.
  c) **A growing number of** non-governmental organisations
    are currently doing the same as Greenpeace and the
    Rainforest Alliance.
  d) **Chiquita** has come under severe criticism for its poor
    record on environmental and labour issues.
  e) Greenpeace has embarked on joint ventures to improve
    working practices in companies such as ~~Chiquita~~,
    NPower and Unilever.
3 a) i   **b)** iii   **c)** ii   **d)** i   **e)** ii   **f)** i
4 a) False   *The FLA ... works more closely with companies*
        than many organisations ... The FLA has, for
        example, both companies and non-
        governmental organisations on its board.
  b) True   *to maintain its independence ... the*
        organisation lays down strict rules of
        engagement.
  c) False   *All businesses co-operating with the FLA must*
        agree to give it unimpeded and unannounced
        access to their factories
  d) False   *none of the companies has any control over*
        what the FLA publishes in its reports about the
        labour conditions in their supply chains.
  e) True   *'It's warts and all,' says Mr van Heerden.*
  f) True   *'... we feel we can only do our job properly if we*
        have independence.'
5 1 b   2 c   3 a   4 f   5 e   6 d

Unit 4

India's energy needs

Before you read
According to the BP Amoco Statistical Review of World Energy
(2000), the top five biggest energy consumers in the world
were as follows:

1 USA   2 China   3 Russia   4 Japan   5 Germany

International Energy Agency forecasts suggest that China will
soon be the top consumer. India is presently the sixth largest
consumer of energy, but will shortly become one of the top
five.

1 Four types of energy:

wood and cow dung (also referred to as biomass and waste)	currently accounts for more than half of the country's total energy use; will remain the main source of energy for domestic energy users
oil	usage currently low due to the low level of car ownership; demand will rise to 5.4m barrels a day by 2030
gas	demand will rise among industrial users
coal	remains the preferred source of energy for industrial users

2 a) ii **b)** iii **c)** ii **d)** iii **e)** i **f)** ii **g)** i
3 a) growth rate **b)** fell well short of **c)** represent
  d) resulted in **e)** forecast **f)** projected (*forecast* used
  as a verb is also possible) **g)** average
4 a) negate **b)** conundrum **c)** the West; developed
  countries **d)** developing world **e)** in turn
  f) development **g)** per capita **h)** wide
5 a) percentage of India's total energy use accounted for by
  biomass and waste
  b) number of years over which the use of biomass is
  expected to decline and use of oil, gas and coal to
  increase
  c) number of million barrels a day of oil India is expected to
  be using by 2030
  d) percentage of oil that will be supplied by importation
  e) number of cars that exist for every 1,000 people today in
  India
  f) number of people that own a car in Europe
6 a) True *strong economic growth rates of more than 4
      per cent a year*
  b) True *will stimulate gas demand among industrial
      users in India.*
  c) True *a recent significant gas discovery*
  d) False *this will not be enough to meet future demand.*
  e) False *India … is also negotiating with Bangladesh
      and Burma about building pipelines to import
      gas.*
  f) False *coal will remain the preferred energy for
      industrial users.*
  g) False *The IEA projects Indian coal demand to rise at
      similar rates to total growth rates of energy use
      in the country during the next 25 years. (similar
      rates refers to 4 per cent a year at the
      beginning of the paragraph.)*

Nuclear energy

1 a) 7, 8 **b)** 6 **c)** 1, 2 **d)** 2 **e)** 3 **f)** 5 **g)** 4
2 a) There were **once** plans to build a new nuclear reactor.
  b) The company is **the target of** safety inspectors because
    of its accident record.
  c) Solar energy is **the darling of** many environmental
    groups.
  d) The use of **fossil fuels** increases the levels of carbon
    dioxide in the atmosphere.

  e) The Swedish government is **pursuing** its plan to reduce
    dependence on nuclear energy.
  f) A major problem with nuclear energy is **the disposal of
    waste**.
3 d, e
4 1 f 2 a 3 e 4 b 5 d 6 c
5 a) the public purse **b)** nuclear plant **c)** clear-up
  operations **d)** green lobbyists **e)** upfront costs
  f) gas-fired power station
6 a) 4 **b)** 6 **c)** 5 **d)** 2 **e)** 1 **f)** 3
7 B

Unit 5

Offshoring

1 f, e, g, c, b, d, h, a
2 a) Both **b)** Germany **c)** France **d)** Both **e)** Germany
  f) France
3 a) True *The evidence is patchy*
  b) False *nearly half of European companies planned to
      shift more services offshore.*
  c) False *UK companies accounted for 61 per cent of the
      total of jobs moved, followed by Germany and
      the Benelux countries with 14 per cent each.*
  d) True *… western Europe itself benefited with 29 per
      cent – the favoured locations being the UK,
      Ireland, Spain and Portugal*
  e) False *Asia was top destination, with 37 per cent*
4 a) the number (in millions) of European information
    technology and service jobs that will move offshore over
    the next ten years (according to Forrester Research)
  b) the proportion of those jobs that will be from the UK
  c) the distance (in miles) used by Forresters to define
    offshoring
  d) the number of jobs created by German multinationals in
    Eastern Europe between 1990 and 2001
  e) the number of jobs created by Austrian multinationals in
    Eastern Europe between 1990 and 2001
  f) the number of jobs lost in Germany as a result
5 a) 7 **b)** 4 **c)** 2 **d)** 5 **e)** 6 **f)** 3 **g)** 8 **h)** 1
6 a) Germany's **b)** displaced German workers
  c) it = outsourcing; them = companies

Older people

1 a) International Labour Organisation
  b) runs the Unemployment and Labour Market
    Disadvantage programme at the Institute for
    Employment Studies
  c) British DIY (do-it-yourself) retailer
  d) Halifax Bank of Scotland
  e) founder of Mist Consulting
  f) a Cologne-based diversity consultancy
2 Suggested answers
  a) The **ILO** says that, by the year 2050, the number of
    people over 60 will increase from 600m to 2bn.
  b) In 50 years' time there will be more over 60s than
    children under 15 in the world.
  c) Employers should deal with **age** discrimination at work
    and provide incentives for senior workers to agree to
    stay in their jobs longer.

d) John Atkinson from the **Institute for Employment Studies** says changes in **legislation** will force companies to take action.

e) The British government is **committed to** implementing age legislation under the European Directive on Equal Treatment.

3 a) ii b) i c) i d) iii
4 a) 6 b) 1 c) 5 d) 4 e) 2 f) 3 g) 7 h) 8
5 1f 2a 3c 4b 5e 6d
6 B

Unit 6

Business responsibilities

1 e, d, c, a, b, f, g
2 a) ii b) i c) iii d) i
3 1d 2e 3c 4f 5b 6a
4 a) supply chain b) state-owned utilities c) Clothing manufacturers d) dominant market position e) corporate malpractice f) low-income countries
5 a) Michael Fairey b) Mervyn Davies c) Michael Fairey d) Association of British Insurers e) Mervyn Davies
6 a) violations b) instil c) appointment d) enduring e) taking f) promoting
7 a) appointment b) enduring c) promote d) violation e) instil f) take
8 1c 2d 3e 4a 5b

Business models

1 a) oil companies b) mining companies c) mining companies d) mining companies e) Accenture Development Partnerships f) Pfizer g) Unilever Vietnam
2 a) lack (para. 1) b) social programmes (para. 1) c) tread extremely carefully (para.1) d) backfire (para. 1) e) contentious (para. 2) f) extractive industries (para. 2) g) create vast footprints (para. 2) h) the thorniest issue (para. 2) i) arise (para. 2) j) feel left out (para. 2)
3 a) improve b) create c) fund; roll out d) withdraw; embark on e) conduct f) abandon g) leave
4 a) approached in a measured way b) cash is probably not the answer c) transparency is essential d) to promote better schooling e) it's seen as self-serving f) there's credibility to it
5 a) False ... has unforeseen benefits.
  b) True ... has created 800 to 1,000 small businesses in support
  c) True the biggest contribution companies can make to development is the economic story.

Unit 7

International banking

1 a) biggest b) politicians c) top 20 d) equity e) 19% (to 25%) f) US g) Siemens and BASF h) compromise i) consolidation j) (political) interference / social engineering
2 1f 2g 3a 4c 5d 6e 7b
3 a) 6e b) 5d c) 7b d) 3a e) 2g f) 1f g) 4c

4 a) peer group b) return c) equity d) (market) capitalisation e) assets f) revenues g) analyst community/analysts h) on a par with i) play in the top tier j) balance sheet
5 a) Siemens b) neither c) BASF d) both e) neither f) neither g) Siemens h) BASF
6 a) False *Deutsche's difficult relationship with the German establishment is long-standing.*
  b) False *To compound matters, Mr Ackermann is not even German.*
  c) True *Mr Ackermann is obliged to maintain a degree of distance in his political and corporate networking in order to avoid being drawn into unprofitable patriotic business.*
  d) True *the political outcry over the Deutsche jobs saga carries a resonant message.*
  e) True *'This kind of political interference is derailing capitalism in Germany,' says Mr Williams. 'It is social engineering. And it is delaying much-needed consolidation in German banking.'*
  f) False *'It is a big deterrent for potential acquirers from abroad.'*
  g) False *For Deutsche, in particular, senior managers believe the debacle has exacerbated the 'German discount' attached to the share price. That is the last thing Mr Ackermann needs as he tries to play catch-up with his international rivals.*

Corporate recovery

1 1d 2h 3g 4f 5e 6c 7b 8a
2 1d 2e 3c 4a 5b
3 a) 5b b) 1d c) 3c d) 4a e) 2e
4 a) (dramatic) turnaround(s) b) deluging ... (markets) c) a flood d) fluid e) stakeholders f) trustees
5 b
6 a) ii b) ii c) i d) i
7 a) DJ b) DJ c) IP d) IP e) PK f) PK g) IP
Ian Powell is most in favour of the new style.

Unit 8

The growth of management consultancy

1 a) False *The strength and pattern of the recovery varies by country, and some sectors remain depressed ... the information-technology consulting sector is likely to grow at an average compound rate of little more than 1 per cent. (paragraph 2)*
  b) True *The merger and acquisition wave among US public companies helps explain why North America is leading the way. Consultants are often called in to review potential deals and advise on post-merger integration. (paragraph 3)*
  c) True *The economic boom of the late 1990s led to very strong demand ... The result: raw recruits delivering work of questionable quality to increasingly disillusioned clients. (paragraph 3)*

d) True   *Under particular scrutiny is the traditional, pyramid-shaped organisation in which a few senior partners are supported by an army of enthusiastic juniors. (paragraph 5)*
The ability to 'leverage' the expertise of senior consultants in this way is central to the economics of the industry. (paragraph 6)

e) False   *Experienced consultants were leaving to work for 'hot' technology companies, and young recruits could not be trained fast enough to fill the gap. (paragraph 3)*
'This is an apprenticeship industry. If you have too few people coming in at the bottom, you end up with not enough managers.' (paragraph 6)

f) False   *Some consultants predict the emergence of 'diamond-shaped' firms, in which partners are supported by more experienced consultants and fewer youngsters (i.e. where senior consultants are in the majority) (paragraph 7)*
… some will doubtless find ways to maintain the leverage model. Others will evolve into diamond-shaped organisations. (paragraph 9)

2 **a)** sector   **b)** exaggerated   **c)** several   **d)** recuperation
   e) recovery   **f)** sector

3 **a)** the merger and acquisition wave   **b)** leading the way
   c) advise on post-merger integration   **d)** economic boom
   e) raw recruits delivering work of questionable quality
   f) competitive bidding on engagements

4 **a)** ii   **b)** iii   **c)** iii   **d)** i   **e)** ii   **f)** iii

5 **a)** leverage   **b)** expertise   **c)** correlation   **d)** progression
   e) intakes   **f)** apprenticeship

6 1 b   2 f   3 e   4 d   5 a   6 c

7 1 c   2 e   3 b   4 a   5 f   6 d

8 **a)** primary activity   **b)** Experienced recruits   **c)** diamond-shaped firms   **d)** advisory fees   **e)** strategy consulting
   f) adjacent industries

Management consultancy

1 **a)** the MCA (para. 2)   **b)** the writer (para. 3)   **c)** the writer (para. 4)   **d)** Bruce Tindale (para. 5)   **e)** anonymous consultant (para. 6)   **f)** Fiona Czerniawska (para. 7)
   g) Bruce Tindale (para. 9)   **h)** anonymous client (para. 9)

2 **a)** amount earned by British consultants last year (in billion dollars)
   b) percentage of members of the MCA whose income comes from outsourcing
   c) percentage of MCA members' fee income accounted for by information-technology-related consulting and systems development
   d) percentage of MCA members' fee income accounted for by traditional management consulting
   e) percentage by which MCA members' fees for traditional consulting fell last year
   f) percentage of the UK consulting industry's fees accounted for by MCA members

3 **a)** ii   **b)** i   **c)** ii   **d)** i   **e)** iii

4 **a)** sophisticated   **b)** toll   **c)** retention   **d)** pushback
   e) subsume   **f)** steeply

5 A is correct. B contains various errors:
   … there are two reasons [*there are various reasons, of which only two are described in this paragraph*] why revenue per consultant is falling. Many independent consultants have become members of the MCA and charge less, which has significantly reduced the average income of smaller firms [*partly true, but not a definite or significant decrease; she says smaller firms may have depressed the figure*]. Ms Czerniawska also thinks outsourcing [*and IT-related consulting*] generate less fee income than traditional management consulting services.

6 **a)** True   *But the likeliest explanation for the fall is the increase in the number of consultants.*

   b) True   *Because so many consultants, inveterate optimists, believe sales are about to increase.*

   c) True   *Many consultants over-recruited during the Internet boom at the beginning of the decade, and Ms Czerniawska says: 'Consulting firms have perhaps not entirely learnt the lessons of 2001.'*

   d) False   *Tindale … says consultants need to provide their clients with a better value-for-money service than they did in the past.*

Unit 9

What is strategy?

1 1 c   2 f   3 e   4 g   5 b   6 d   7 a

2 **a)** True   *Strategy is, very simply, an outline of how a business intends to achieve its goals. The goals are the objective; the strategy sets out the route to that objective.*

   b) True   *In the early stages, business objectives are usually fairly simple: to survive and to achieve growth targets.*

   c) False   *Strategies are correspondingly simple as well, and are often not even committed to paper; it is enough that everyone in the company understands where it is going and how it will get there.*

   d) False   *But as the business grows, so does the need for co-ordination. Accordingly, there is a need for a mutually agreed and accepted strategy for the business.*

3 **a)** the wrong way to go about it   **b)** tailored to meet the requirements   **c)** easier said than done   **d)** branched out
   e) a matter of

4 B

5 **a)** framework   **b)** arise   **c)** ad-hoc   **d)** adage   **e)** novice

6 **a)** ii   **b)** ii   **c)** iii   **d)** i   **e)** ii

7 1 e   2 g   3 d   4 b   5 h   6 c   7 a   8 f   9 j   10 i

Mission statements

1 C
2 f, d, a, c, e, b
3 **a)** liable   **b)** stomped off; drive (customers) away
   c) a regular/loyal customer   **d)** queried the bill   **e)**
   emblazoned   **f)** chatting (freely)
4 **a)** False   The writer says *The words haunted me* and *the
              words were still swilling around my head*, but
              he is referring to Avis's mission statement, not
              to the words of the woman.
   b) True   *as an outlet for my rage, I began researching
              the subject of mission statements*
   c) True   *there is a substantial amount of literature
              available on the subject: … theses* (a thesis is
              an essay written by an MA or PhD student)
   d) True   The writer says … *with lively titles such as
              'Libraries, Mission and Marketing: Writing
              Mission Statements That Work',* but he is being
              ironic.
   e) False   *the authors fall into two camps* (not the
              mission statements)
   f) False   *One expert insists that … Another insists on …
              Yet another insists that …*
5 **a)** i   **b)** iii   **c)** ii   **d)** i   **e)** iii   **f)** i
6 1 b   2 d   3 a   4 f   5 c   6 e
7 **a)** memorable   **b)** ordinary   **c)** modest   **d)** unsolved
   e) lamentable   **f)** rallying

Unit 10

Online groceries

1 f, c, e, a, g, d, b
2 **a)** False   … *he was very much an outsider.* (paragraph 1)
   b) False   *He and his brother Thomas persuaded Jewel
              Stores, a Chicago grocer, to take the
              revolutionary step of allowing some of its
              customers to place delivery orders via their
              computers with their start-up, Peapod.*
              (paragraph 1)
   c) True   *Andrew and Thomas were not allowed to work
              from the supermarket that served as their
              base. Instead, they were confined to a van in
              the car park.* (paragraph 1)
   d) True   *Peapod is a wholly owned subsidiary of Ahold*
              (paragraph 2)
   e) False   … *Peapod's sales were estimated to be about
              $200m last year, making it the biggest online
              operator in terms of revenue in what is still the
              comparatively small US market.* (paragraph 2)
3 1 c   2 f   3 a   4 e   5 b   6 d
4 **a)** financing package   **b)** distribution partnerships
   c) software development; bricks-and-mortar grocer
   d) online operation

5 **a)** True   *The takeover by Ahold dramatically reduced
              Peapod's sourcing costs.*
   b) False   *Ahold also kept Peapod's separate identity, he
              says. 'From the very beginning, we had "the
              Peapod way", which was to "amaze and
              delight" the customer …'*
   c) True   … *make sure you enjoy your job and don't
              forget about your family.*
   d) False   *Peapod claims that it has achieved far lower
              turnover of staff than would be usual in a
              business that combines logistics and retailing*
   e) True   *It still runs regular employee awards and its
              'Broken Promises Index' that monitors its
              performance in 14 key areas, such as lateness
              and incomplete orders.*
6 **a)** (strong) background   **b)** heads   **c)** (site) users
   d) customised   **e)** innovation(s)   **f)** what it comes
   down to
7 **a)** entrepreneur   **b)** challenges   **c)** supermarket chains
   d) fast   **e)** outside   **f)** investors   **g)** mother
   h) start (up)   **i)** books   **j)** Jeff Bezos

Using a website

1 **a)** 6   **b)** 5   **c)** 7   **d)** 3   **e)** 2   **f)** 1   **g)** 4
2 **a)** brand-building   **b)** cuddly   **c)** strength   **d)** attributes
   e) fundamentally
3 **a)** True   *Hard web is the website as a tool. Consumers
              can buy products or check accounts. B2B
              customers can place orders. Journalists can find
              how much money your CEO earned last year.
              Investors can see how much money they have
              made out of you. They are all doing something
              that helps them in their lives or jobs.*
   b) False   *Consumers can buy products or check
              accounts. B2B customers can place orders …
              They are all doing something that helps them
              in their lives **or** jobs.*
   c) True   *Soft web is using a site to nudge, to impress,
              to massage. 'Brochureware', where a website
              reproduces marketing literature created for
              print, is soft web.*
   d) True   *So are the look, feel and 'voice' of a site, which
              transmit messages about the organisation's
              culture and brand.*
   e) False   Most CSR, but not all: ***And the great bulk of
              corporate social responsibility (CSR) material is
              soft.***
4 B
5 **a)** trick   **b)** in harness   **c)** stopping point   **d)** service
   reminder   **e)** back (this) up   **f)** optimisation   **g)** flowing
   h) bombard
6 1 e   2 a   3 f   4 c   5 g   6 b   7 d
7 **a)** arrives / has arrived mid-site   **b)** keep up standards /
   keep standards up   **c)** hiring; writers   **d)** links; scattered
   e) Drawing people in; feeding

Unit 11

Technological innovation

1 **a)** founder **b)** big break **c)** trade exhibition
   d) technology manager **e)** three days **f)** nine staff
   g) intellectual property **h)** printing-ink **i)** single price
   j) Licences

2 **a)** False *Three years ago, a young entrepreneur in*
   Leeds risked everything he had to make his
   business a success … His route to success took
   him as far afield as China … (China is not the
   only country where the company has been
   successful.)

   b) True *Andrew Ainge's print-technology company,*
   MetalFX, … an innovative technology-licensing
   model that minimises the operation's
   overheads while maximising its profits.

   c) False *The system has changed the industry's*
   approach to the use of metallic inks, and the
   visual results – on brochures, packaging,
   annual reports and so on – have been
   stunning. (There is no mention of it needing
   further development.)

   d) True *Printers use the CMYK system (combinations of*
   cyan, magenta, yellow and black ink) to create
   coloured images and text.

   e) True *The system allowed millions of metallic colours*
   to be created at once.

3 1 d 2 c 3 e 4 a 5 b
4 **a)** ii **b)** i **c)** i **d)** ii **e)** iii **f)** iii
5 1 b 2 e 3 d 4 a 5 c
6 **a)** branching out **b)** eye-catching **c)** caught the attention
   of **d)** down to **e)** overseas buyers

Increasing market share

1 b, d, f, h
2 **a)** Defying the laws of gravity **b)** a succession of
   c) seemingly unassailable leaders **d)** astute **e)** gained
   f) brought in **g)** head up **h)** True to form
3 1 d 2 c 3 b 4 a
4 1 c 2 a 3 b 4 d
5 **a)** (had) launched new brands **b)** condiment company;
   case history **c)** has grabbed; market share
   d) nationwide distribution **e)** Changing conditions
6 **a)** i **b)** ii **c)** iii **d)** ii **e)** i
7 A

Unit 12

Project mediators

1 **a)** MP (paragraph 1) **b)** BF (paragraph 2) **c)** IC (paragraph
   3) **d)** BF (paragraph 4) **e)** AC (paragraph 5) **f)** MP
   (paragraph 6) **g)** PV (paragraph 7) **h)** AC (paragraph 8)
2 1 c 2 b 3 f 4 e 5 a 6 g 7 d
3 **a)** True *When a relationship breaks down, it is never*
   totally one party's fault.

   b) True *A third party can come in with a more objective*
   view.

   c) False *Sometimes, to ensure the advice is truly*
   impartial, the client and IT contractor will share
   advisory fees.

   d) False *… companies are often nominating a third-*
   party mediator from the start. There is more of
   an expectation that things can get out of shape

   e) False *The company had about 100 engagements last*
   year, and demand is growing at around 25 per
   cent each quarter.

4 **a)** oversee **b)** have different agendas **c)** everything it is
   supposed to **d)** keep everyone on track **e)** fed up (with)
   f) driving **g)** parachuted in to turn round a project
   h) run into trouble
5 **a)** iii **b)** iii **c)** ii **d)** ii **e)** i **f)** ii **g)** i **h)** iii

Remote management

1 d *They are scattered across the world … their operations*
   and customers are global … It represents what more and
   more companies will come to look like. (paragraph 1)

   b *Gone are the days when managers could supervise the*
   hour-to-hour work of individuals. (paragraph 2)

   a *… managers must have a deeper understanding of when*
   to use the wide range of communications that are now
   available. When is a phone call best? A teleconference?
   A video conference? An e-mail? A face-to-face meeting?
   (paragraph 3)

   f *As a general rule, face-to-face sessions are for intensive,*
   real-time problem-solving (paragraph 4)

   g *… individual managers need to work with and influence*
   people who are not their subordinates. (paragraph 7)

   c *First, they must explain that sharing leadership is a*
   performance expectation and will be rewarded. Second,
   team members must accept responsibility for providing
   as well as responding to peer-based leadership.
   (paragraph 8)

   e *This means often deferring critical decisions … They*
   must be able to demonstrate shared leadership in
   meetings, turning leadership over to a capable
   subordinate or peer at the appropriate moment. They
   must coach and develop their team's individual and
   collective leadership skills. (paragraph 9)

2 1 c 2 h 3 f 4 b 5 a 6 d 7 e 8 g
3 **a)** Managers now have to lead by **focusing on** processes,
   performance and results.
   b) Staff need to **achieve** results.
   c) This can only be done if managers **set** appropriate goals
   and milestones, **shape** behaviour and **analyse** progress
   being made.
   d) Face-to-face communication is the best way to start a
   virtual project in order to **reach** an agreement on
   milestones and commitments.
4 **a)** conferences; virtual **b)** relationship; face-to-face
   c) problem-solving; information-sharing
5 **a)** i **b)** i **c)** ii **d)** ii **e)** iii
6 **a)** shared **b)** cross-functional **c)** locations **d)** peers
   e) performance expectation **f)** responsibility **g)** directive
   h) develop/coach **i)** leadership skills **j)** direct control

Resource bank

Teacher's notes

Introduction

These Resource bank activities are designed to extend and develop the activities in the main Course Book. Each Resource bank unit has between one and three exercises, some of which develop the language points from the Course Book and others which apply this language in role-play activities.

What to give the learners

You have permission to photocopy the Resource bank pages in this book. In some units, you will give SS a copy of the whole page. In others, there are role cards which need to be cut out and given to SS with particular roles. These activities are indicated in the unit-specific notes below.

The **language exercises** can be used to revise language from the main Course Book unit; point out the connection with the Course Book material to SS. In many cases, these activities can be done in a few minutes as a way of focusing SS on the activity that follows.

A typical two-person **role-play** might last ten minutes, followed by five minutes of praise and correction. An animated group discussion might last longer; in this case, drop one of your other planned activities and do it another time, rather than trying to cram it in before the end of the lesson. If you then have five or ten minutes left over, you can always go over some language points from the lesson again, or, better still, get SS to say what they were. One way of doing this is to ask them what they've written in their notebooks during the lesson.

Revising and revisiting

Feel free to do an activity more than once. After one run-through, praise strong points, then work on three or four things that need correcting or improving. Then you can get SS to change roles and do the activity again, or the parts of the activity where these points come up. Obviously, there will come a time when interest wanes, but the usual tendency in language teaching is not to revisit things enough, rather than the reverse.

Fluency and accuracy

Concentrate on different things in different activities. In some role-plays and discussions, you may want to focus on fluency, with SS interacting as spontaneously as possible. In others, you will want to concentrate on accuracy, with SS working on getting specific forms correct. Rather than expect SS to get everything correct, you could pick out, say, three or four forms that you want them to get right, and focus on these.

Clear instructions

Be sure to give complete instructions before getting SS to start. In role-plays, be very clear about who has which role, and give SS time to absorb the information they need. Sometimes there are role cards that you hand out. The activities where this happens are indicated in the notes.

Parallel and public performances

In pair work or small group situations, get all pairs to do the activity at the same time. Go round the class and listen. When SS have finished, praise strong points and deal with three or four problems that you heard, especially problems that more than one group has been having. Then get individual pairs to give public performances so that the whole class can listen. The performers should pay particular attention to the three or four problem areas.

1 to 1

The pair activities can be done one to one, with you taking one of the roles. The activity can be done a second time, reversing the role and getting the student to integrate your suggestions for improvement. (Where there are groups of three, you can take two of the roles, changing your voice for the second role.)

Unit 1 Being international

- ◎ Before the class, photocopy and cut up the role cards for SS A and B. Make as many photocopies as there will be pairs of SS.
- ◎ Tell SS they are going to do a quick social English quiz. Ask SS A and B to look at their respective questions individually, then check their answers with the key given.
- ◎ Get SS to do the quiz in pairs as a speaking/listening exercise. SS A ask questions 1–5. SS B ask questions 6–10.
- ◎ Circulate and help where necessary.
- ◎ After finishing the quiz, ask SS to give each other a score and tell their partner the correct answers.
- ◎ Go through any idiomatic or colloquial expressions that SS didn't understand.
- ◎ One-to-one SS may do all the questions as a quick-fire exercise, setting a time limit of two to three minutes. Alternatively, ask them all the questions.

| 1 b | 2 c | 3 b | 4 b | 5 a | 6 c | 7 c | 8 a | 9 a | 10 c |

B

- Before the class, photocopy and cut up the role cards for SS A and B. Make as many photocopies as there will be pairs of SS.
- Ask the whole class to look again at the expressions in the Useful language box on page 11 of the Course Book and model the intonation of the phrases.
- Tell SS they are networking at an annual conference for their company / organisation / sector. Allow SS a minute or two to highlight or make a note of the expressions they might use before doing the role-play. Tell them they only have five minutes to find out about the items listed.
- Circulate and help where necessary during the role-play, noting down examples of language used, five or six points for correction, including pronunciation and intonation.
- Bring the class to order and go through feedback with the whole class.
- After feedback, SS may repeat the activity, swapping roles.
- With one-to-one students, take on one of the roles.

Unit 2 Training

A

- Ask the whole class to look again at the expressions in the Useful language box on page 18 of the Course Book and model the intonation of the phrases.
- Get the SS to read them with realistic intonation. Do this with the whole class, then repeat in pairs.
- Repeat any phrases that SS had difficulties with.
- Ask SS to close their Course Books and work on this exercise.
- Go through the answers with the whole class.
- Practise the intonation of these phrases.

1 f	2 g	3 e	4 d	5 a	6 c	7 b

B

- Before the class, make as many photocopies of the role cards as there are pairs in the class.
- Explain the scenario set out in the rubric. Divide the class into pairs and hand out the role cards.
- Begin the role-play in parallel pairs. Go round the room and monitor the language being used. Note down strong points and points that need correction or improvement; this can include incorrect structures, vocabulary and pronunciation. Focus particular on clarifying and confirming language. Put these items on the board for later feedback.
- Ask early finishers to look at the board and to attempt the correction work.
- When most pairs have finished, bring the class to order and praise good language points used.

- Refer SS to the board and work on the corrections together, getting SS to provide the correct form, vocabulary and pronunciation if possible.
- If there is time, ask SS to change roles and repeat the role-play, this time being careful to integrate the corrections mentioned.

Unit 3 Partnerships

A

- Before the class, make as many photocopies as there will be pairs of SS in the class and cut up the 'turns'.
- SS work in pairs to rearrange the turns. Tell SS the correct order of the first two utterances to get them started. Circulate and help where necessary.
- SS then read out their conversations.
- When most SS have finished, call the class to order and word on any intonation and pronunciation problems.
- Get SS to concentrate on the last nine lines of the dialogue from *Are you saying you won't be able to deliver this order until the New Year?*
- Get SS to memorise one card each and turn it face down. SS repeat the partially hidden dialogue. Repeat this procedure a few more times, hiding a line each time, until each SS can say their lines from memory. To help them, you can put a few key words on the board from each turn.

B

- Ask the whole class to look again at the expressions in Exercise B on page 26 of the Course Book and model the intonation of the phrases.
- Get the SS to read them with realistic intonation. Do this with the whole class, and then repeat in pairs.
- Repeat any phrases that SS had difficulties with.
- Then ask SS to close their Course Books and work on this exercise.
- Go through the answers with the whole class.
- Practise the intonation of these phrases.

1 We're **looking** at an initial order of two to three thousand.
2 Would you be **willing** to come down a bit on that?
3 Somewhere in the **region** of 500 euros.
4 I think we could work **with** that.
5 Supposing we **were** to make that twelve free samples.
6 **Given** that we are likely to be placing large orders, we'd like a 10% discount.
7 Are you **saying** that you can handle an order of that size each month?
8 **What** would you say to a display of your products in our toy department?
9 **Seeing** that you'd like some free samples, we'd like our logo to be visible.

Resource bank

Ⓒ

◎ Before the class, make as many photocopies of the role cards as there are pairs in the class.

◎ Explain the scenario set out in the rubric. Divide the class into pairs and hand out the role cards.

◎ Begin the role-play in parallel pairs. Go round the room and monitor the language being used. Note down strong points and points that need correction or improvement. This can include incorrect structures, vocabulary and pronunciation. Focus particular on clarifying and confirming language. Put these items on the board for later feedback.

◎ Ask early finishers to look at the board and to attempt the correction work.

◎ When most pairs have finished, bring the class to order and praise good language points used.

◎ Refer SS to the board and work on the corrections together, getting SS to provide the correct form, vocabulary and pronunciation if possible.

◎ If there is time, ask SS to change roles and some of the details on their cards. SS repeat the role-play, this time being careful to integrate the corrections mentioned. Alternatively, ask a strong pair of students to repeat the role-play for the whole class.

Unit 4 Energy

Ⓐ

◎ Get SS, in pairs, to match the expressions and the functions.

◎ Circulate, monitor and help where necessary.

◎ Bring the class together and go through the answers with the whole class.

◎ Practise the intonation of some of these phrases.

◎ For further practice, SS could use some of these phrases to make a short dialogue of their own.

> **1** b   **2** e   **3** c   **4** g   **5** f   **6** a   **7** d

Ⓑ

◎ Ask the whole class to look again at the problem-solving expressions on page 38 of the Course Book and in the previous exercise.

◎ Get SS to work in groups of four or five. Tell them to read the problem and the possible solutions. Deal with any questions.

◎ Circulate while SS discuss the problem and solutions and make a note of the good expressions they use, as well as five or six language points for correction.

◎ Bring the class to order and go through the correction work with the whole class, asking SS to model the correct phrases.

◎ Ask one or two groups for feedback. What other solutions did they come up with. What were the best solutions?

Unit 5 Employment trends

Ⓐ

◎ Get SS, in pairs, to read the sentences and cross out the extra word.

◎ Circulate, monitor and help where necessary, pointing out where SS have or haven't identified the extra word correctly and giving them an opportunity to look again.

◎ Early finishers can check their answers against the Useful language box on page 47 of the Course Book.

◎ Bring the class together and go through the answers with the whole class.

> 1 Let me see if I follow ~~to~~ you, you're saying that the booking is incorrect.
> 2 From ~~in~~ your point of view, the situation has got worse.
> 3 Let me ~~I~~ make sure I understand you correctly.
> 4 I'm sorry, I missed ~~out~~ that. Could you please repeat it?
> 5 I'm not sure I ~~following~~ understand you. Could you say that again?
> 6 Please ~~you~~ go on. I'm interested to hear what you think.
> 7 I appreciate how you feel ~~like~~.
> 8 I can see ~~reason~~ why you feel that way.
> 9 Yes, you have a ~~true~~ point when you say there was a long delay.
> 10 Here's how it looks ~~me~~ from my angle, we both made mistakes.

Ⓑ

◎ Before the class, photocopy and cut up the role cards for A and B. Make as many photocopies as there will be pairs of SS.

◎ Ask the whole class to look again at the expressions in Exercise A or the Useful language box on page 47 of the Course Book. Model and drill the intonation of some of the phrases.

◎ Tell SS they are going to role-play two situations between call-centre agents and clients at Delaney call centre in Dublin. If necessary, look back at pages 48 and 49 of the Course Book to remind SS about the case study.

◎ Allow SS one or two minutes to highlight or make a note of the expressions they might use before doing the role-play.

◎ As this is a telephone role-play, SS should not sit facing each other. Circulate and help where necessary during the role-play, noting down examples of good language used and five or six points for correction, including pronunciation and intonation.

◎ Bring the class to order and go through feedback with the whole class.

◎ SS then swap roles to do the second role-play. Repeat the procedures above.

Unit 6 Business ethics

(A)

◎ Get SS to read the sentences and find the errors. Elicit the first one as an example. Circulate, monitor and help where necessary, pointing out where SS have or haven't identified the incorrect word and giving them an opportunity to look again.

◎ Get SS to compare their answers in pairs.

◎ Early finishers can check their answers against Exercise F on page 51 and the Useful language box on page 54 of the Course Book.

◎ Bring the class together and go through the answers with them. Deal with any difficult vocabulary, e.g. *whistle-blower* (someone who tells people in authority or the public about dishonest or illegal practices at the workplace). This expression also features in Exercise B of the Resource bank.

---

1 If I had to define corporate citizenship, I **would** / **'d** say it's all to do with payback.
2 Let's **face** it, not many companies have the time to write proper CSR reports.
3 Many fashion retailers only pay lip service **to** business ethics.
4 The time has **come** for corporate responsibility to be taken seriously by businesses.
5 I disagree that the **bottom** line about business ethics is making it commercially viable.
6 If it were the **case** that our company was unethical, I'd hand in my resignation.
7 Having **said** that, I'd discuss the situation with my manager first.
8 There are a lot of **issues** at play with bad business practice: firstly, as an individual, are you prepared to be the whistle-blower?

(B)

◎ Refer SS to the words in the box. Deal with any difficult vocabulary (e.g. *whistle-blowers*).

◎ Get SS to read through the guidelines and complete the text.

◎ Circulate and monitor, helping where necessary.

◎ Bring the class together and go through the answers with the whole class.

◎ Drill the pronunciation of some of these words.

---

1 affected; environment   2 harm; mitigate   3 deceptive
4 conflicts; Transparency   5 behave; whistle-blowers; refrain

---

(C)

◎ Ask SS to brainstorm other words in the unit related to business ethics. Write these words on the board.

◎ Ask SS to discuss the guidelines for evaluating ethical behaviour in pairs or small groups. Refer them to the Useful language box on page 54 of the Course Book for problem-solving.

◎ Circulate and help where necessary during the discussion, noting down examples of key language used and five or six points for correction, including pronunciation and intonation.

◎ Bring the class to order and go through feedback with them.

◎ Ask early finishers to add their questions to the board.

◎ To round off the activity, ask SS to vote on removing or adding points to the framework.

Unit 7 Finance and banking

◎ Before the class, photocopy and cut up the role cards for SS A and B. Make as many photocopies as there will be pairs of SS.

◎ Ask the whole class to look again at the language for describing trends on page 126 of the Course Book.

◎ Tell SS they are going to be business newsreaders. Allow them a couple of minutes to highlight or make a note of the pronunciation of their three news items before reading them aloud to their partner.

◎ Circulate and help where necessary during the information gap, noting down examples of good pronunciation and intonation and three or four points for correction.

◎ Bring the class to order and go through feedback with the whole class.

◎ Alternatively, photocopy all four bar charts / graphs for SS, but not the news items. Read the six news items yourself. (Two of the news items are distractors.) Ask SS to match the news extracts to the four bar charts / graphs.

News item 1: There is no graph/bar chart on the Australian banking sector.
News item 2: Allianz, **bar chart A**
News item 3: Mitsubishi Motors, **graph B**
News item 4: Microsoft, **graph D**
News item 5: There is no bar chart on the UK economy.
News item 6: ING Direct, **bar chart C**

Unit 8 Consultants

(A)

◎ Tell SS they are going to do a quiz to find out if they would make good consultants.

◎ SS do the quiz individually.

◎ Circulate and monitor, helping where necessary with vocabulary.

◎ When SS have completed the quiz, they check their scores.

◎ Bring the class together and ask SS, with a quick show of hands, who would make a good consultant.

◎ As a follow-up, ask SS what they thought of the results.

(B)

◎ Before the class, photocopy and cut up the exercise for SS. Make as many photocopies as there will be SS.

◎ Ask the whole class to look again at the expressions and skills in Exercise A on page 74 of the Course Book, if necessary.

◎ Get SS to do the exercise individually and go through the answers with the whole class.

> 1 c   2 d   3 e   4 a   5 b

◎ Ask SS which of these extracts could be a bluff (where the person is only pretending in order to get a better price). (extract b)

◎ Divide the SS in pairs. Tell them they are going to continue one of the negotiating situations. SS A are sales people and SS B, potential buyers. Allow SS a minute or two to choose a situation and highlight or make a note of any of the expressions they might use before doing the role-play. Tell SS they will need to decide what they are buying or selling, but they can be as absurd as possible (e.g. tins of sardines, pet snakes, chocolate hair dryers, designer diamond flip-flops, drills for dentists, etc.). This drama technique often helps SS to learn the key language being used and makes the task more memorable. Tell SS not to worry about the prices being realistic, but they need to be as persuasive as possible. You may decide to act out one of the conversation first with one of the more confident SS in the class.

◎ Circulate and monitor, helping where necessary during the role-play, noting down good examples of negotiating language and five or six points for correction, including pronunciation and intonation.

◎ Bring the class to order and go through feedback with the whole class. Ask SS who managed to sell their product at a good price.

◎ SS may repeat the activity, swapping roles and partners. SS should also choose a different situation and ridiculous product to sell.

Unit 9 Strategy

(A)

◎ Ask the whole class to look again at the expressions in the Useful language box on page 83 of the Course Book and model the intonation of the phrases.

◎ Get SS to read and correct the expressions in Exercise A.

◎ Circulate, monitor and help where necessary. If extra help is needed, put the correct words on the board in random order.

◎ Bring the class together and go through the answers with the whole class.

◎ Practise the intonation of some of the new expressions which might be difficult for SS.

> 1 Would anyone like to get the ball **rolling**?
> 2 What a coincidence. I **was** just going to say that!
> 3 What a fabulous idea! Why didn't I think **of** that?
> 4 Has anyone else got a contribution to **make**?
> 5 Let's see … I'm sorry, my mind's **gone** blank.
> 6 That's not exactly what I meant. I was thinking more **along** the lines of …
> 7 Very interesting, but can I come back to you later **on** that one?
> 8 You've taken the words right out of my **mouth**!

(B)

◎ Before the class, photocopy and cut up the the text on the client and the challenge for SS.

◎ As a lead-in to the activity and for vocabulary revision, ask SS to quickly brainstorm in pairs ten words or expressions related to growth and strategy. Go through the answers with the whole class, writing them up on the board.

◎ Tell SS they are going to brainstorm some growth strategies for a global company interested in expanding its presence in Asian markets.

◎ Allow SS two or three minutes to highlight or make a note of possible strategies and expressions they might use before doing the role-play.

◎ Circulate and help where necessary during the role-play, noting down good examples of language used and five or six points for correction. Highlight to SS who are experiencing difficulty with the task that they need to think both locally and globally and mention some of possible strategies (e.g. recruiting local managers and/or relocating senior managers; product development, etc.).

◎ Bring the class to order and go through feedback with the whole class.

◎ You may like to refer SS to the document entitled 'Thinking locally to grow globally'. Otherwise, summarise the main points for the SS and ask them to compare their ideas with that of the real outcome.

◎ This case study is based on one carried out by the Boston Consulting Group. For further reading, refer SS to consultant websites such as: http://www.bcg.com

◎ With one-to-one students, take on one of the roles, e.g. the CEO of the client company.

Unit 10 Doing business online

(A)

◎ Get SS to look again at the expressions in the Useful language box on page 94 of the Course Book before doing this exercise.

◎ SS match the sentence halves and then the expressions to the correct function.

◎ Circulate, monitor and help where necessary.

◎ Bring the class together and go through the answers with the whole class.

◎ Practise pronunciation and intonation of these expressions.

| 1 i   2 e   3 f   4 j   5 h   6 g   7 d   8 c   9 a   10 b |

Ⓑ

◎ Before the class, photocopy and cut up the quiz cards for SS A and B. Make as many photocopies as there will be pairs of SS.

◎ Ask SS to look again at the expressions for asking and dealing with questions in the Useful language box on page 94 of the Course Book and model the intonation of some of the questions.

◎ Tell SS they are going to do a quiz to find out whether they are technophobes or technophiles. Allow SS a minute or two to look at their questions and make a note of any indirect questions they might use before doing the quiz.

◎ SS do the quiz in pairs and give each other their scores. If they need a more rigid structure, you could make the questions multiple choice (see below).

◎ Circulate and help where necessary as they ask and answer the questions, noting down examples of key language used and five or six points for correction, including intonation.

◎ Bring the class to order and go through feedback with the whole class. Ask SS whether they agree with their scores or not.

◎ With one-to-one students, take on one of the roles.

Suggested multiple-choice options for questions

Student A

1 a) What's the difference? (0 points)
   b) I think Macs are easier to work with. (1 point)
   c) Although Macs are more user-friendly, PCs are more universal and have a greater range of compatible software. (2 points)

2 a) They let a lot of light in. (0 points)
   b) I think it crashes too often. (1 point)
   c) It's pretty user-friendly, as it's based on the desktop system and icons. (2 points)

3 a) Do I what? (0 points)
   b) Yes, I usually use Google. (1 point)
   c) I usually use either Google or Yahoo, but sometimes I use a specialist search engine. (2 points)

4 a) My mobile phone. (0 points)
   b) My iPod. (1 point)
   c) It's difficult to choose. I love my Blackberry, but then my PalmPilot is really useful, too. (2 points)

5 a) Recording my favourite TV programme. (0 points)
   b) Setting up broadband on my computer. (1 point)
   c) Building my computer. (2 points)

Student B

1 a) A laptop? That's a portable computer, isn't it? (0 points)
   b) Yes, but I don't use it very often. (1 point)
   c) Yes, I couldn't live without it! (2 points)

2 a) A plasma-screen TV. (0 points)
   b) A home cinema system with surround sound. (1 point)
   c) An M-987 optimised system. (2 points)

3 a) I can talk to my friends any time. (0 points)
   b) I can talk, text and send photos. (1 point)
   c) I can send e-mails, surf the Net and download the latest music. (2 points)

4 a) They're so complicated! (0 points)
   b) There's so much to choose from! (1 point)
   c) As soon as you buy something, it's out of date again! (2 points)

5 a) Not saving my documents. (0 points)
   b) When my hard disk crashed and I lost all my data. (1 point)
   c) When I tried to rewrite some software, and the whole network went down for days. (2 points)

Unit 11 New business

Ⓐ

◎ Get SS to match the expressions with the responses.

◎ Circulate, monitor and help where necessary.

◎ Bring the class together and go through the answers with the whole class.

◎ Practise the intonation of these phrases.

| 1 f   2 d   3 a   4 e   5 b   6 c |

Ⓑ

◎ Before the class, photocopy and cut up the role cards for SS A and B. Make as many photocopies as there will be pairs of SS.

◎ Ask the whole class to look again at the expressions in the Useful language box on page 102 of the Course Book and model the intonation of some of the phrases that are likely to cause difficulties.

◎ Allow SS a few minutes to make a note of the expressions they might use before doing the role-play.

◎ Circulate and help where necessary during the role-play, noting down examples of key language used and five or six points for correction, including pronunciation and intonation.

◎ Bring the class to order and go through feedback with the whole class.

Unit 12 Project management

Ⓐ

◎ Get SS to read the expressions and add the missing word to each.

◎ Circulate, monitor and help where necessary. If extra help is needed, put the extra words on the board in random order.

◎ Bring the class together and go through the answers with the whole class.

◎ Practise the intonation of some of these phrases, which might be difficult for SS.

1	Good morning, everyone. Who do we have **with** us today?	a
2	OK. It's nine o'clock. Let's start by **taking / doing** a roll call.	a
3	Our programmer, Dave Scott, has also joined **us / me** today.	a
4	Hello. **This** is Émile Piaget from the Paris office.	a
5	I'd like **to** direct a question to Hannah.	b
6	May I add to **what** Enrique has just said?	b
7	Helen Stevens **will** be here shortly.	a
8	Could we **go / talk** over the action points again?	c
9	Is **it** correct to say that Teresa Romero is responsible for that?	c
10	May I make a comment **on** the results of product testing?	b
11	May I ask Nikolay a question **at** this stage?	b
12	Can I just check who's in charge **of** what?	c

Ⓑ

◎ Get SS to read the information. Deal with any questions.

◎ Get SS in small groups of three or four to brainstorm their ideas.

◎ Call the class together and go through their ideas.

Suggested answers
A Singaporean might feel a British person is not being polite by getting down to business before spending sufficient time on small talk in order to establish a relationship. He / she might also feel frustrated if he / she isn't given enough time to respond to questions. He / she might not understand the British use of ironic humour, and this could cause embarrassment and loss of face. A Singaporean might not be aware that the British person has given an instruction if it was made indirectly.

A British business person might feel frustrated that a Singaporean takes a long time to get down to business, seems evasive and takes a long time to respond to questions. He / she might wonder why a Singaporean person doesn't respond to attempts at self-deprecating humour.

Ⓒ

◎ Before the class, photocopy and cut up the role cards for SS A and B. Make as many photocopies as there will be pairs of SS.

◎ Ask the whole class to look again at the expressions in the Useful language box on page 111 of the Course Book and model the intonation of the phrases.

◎ Allow SS a minute or two to highlight or make a note of the expressions they might use before doing the role-play.

◎ Circulate and help where necessary during the role-play, noting down examples of key language used and five or six points for correction, including pronunciation and intonation.

◎ Bring the class to order and go through the corrections and feedback from the role-play with the whole class.

UNIT 1 Being international

Networking

A Choose the most suitable thing to say at a conference reception – a, b or c – in response to items 1–10.

✂

Student A

1 So, what did you think of the plenary talk?
  a) I'm afraid I've run out of business cards.
  b) Well, it's not exactly what I was expecting.
  c) Really? That's a coincidence! So did I.

2 Andreas, can I introduce you to a colleague of mine? This is Djamshid.
  a) Could you spell that, please?
  b) We really must get together again some time.
  c) I'm sorry, I didn't quite catch your name.

3 How long have you been working for this organisation?
  a) I must admit, time flies, doesn't it?
  b) Must be getting on six years now.
  c) How about you?

4 So, Martin has told me some great things about you.
  a) I'm sorry, I don't get on well with him.
  b) Martin Amos, my line manager?
  c) How about giving us a job, then?

5 What do you think of our new offices?
  a) Original design, but I'm not sure about the water feature.
  b) Ssh! Don't talk now, the boss is listening.
  c) Did you build them yourself?

Key 1b 2c 3b 4b 5a

Student B

6 Could you recommend some places to visit while I'm here?
  a) I'm afraid that wouldn't be possible, no.
  b) You're joking, aren't you?
  c) Istanbul's a very big city, let me see …

7 I hear the company's due for some major restructuring.
  a) I'm afraid it isn't what I was expecting.
  b) Really? So, am I.
  c) I think you'll find that's just office gossip.

8 Would you be interested in a game of golf some time?
  a) Great idea, what's your handicap?
  b) Could I introduce you to a colleague of mine?
  c) Friday at 3 p.m. would be lovely, thanks.

9 It's been a real pleasure talking to you.
  a) I'll look forward to hearing from you.
  b) Would you please call me soon?
  c) No, no, I insist on paying. It's my round.

10 I don't suppose you know where the next talk is taking place?
  a) I'm sorry, I'm new around here. Bye.
  b) I'm told the canteen is on the ground floor. Hello, Mike!
  c) No, I don't, but those people look as if they know where they're going.

Key 6c 7c 8a 9a 10c

B Work in pairs. You have five minutes to complete the following tasks.

✂

Student A

• Find out your partner's favourite hobby or sport.

• Ask your partner to recommend somewhere to eat .

• Borrow 10 euros (or the equivalent).

• Swap business cards.

• Arrange a future meeting.

Student B

• Find out your partner's favourite holiday destination.

• Ask your partner to recommend a company to invest in.

• Ask your partner where they bought their shoes, tie or handbag.

• Swap business cards.

• Arrange a future meeting.

UNIT 2 Training

Telephone strategies: clarifying and confirming

 An external trainer phones the Human Resources Department to discuss the details of a course she's about to do there. Match the two parts of the expressions she uses.

1 Would you mind going	a) start at nine o'clock and finish at five?
2 Could I ask you to give	b) was that I'll bring a video camera for the session.
3 Let me just make sure	c) confirm that we'll be in conference room B.
4 So that's now 11 participants with	d) the company chairman, then?
5 Can I just check that we	e) that I can get access to the room half an hour before we start.
6 I'd like to	f) over the audio-visual equipment?
7 Well, actually, what I meant	g) me those details about the break times again?

B **Work in pairs. Student A is an external trainer about to do a one-day course on presentation skills with a group of staff at a finance company. Student B is the manager in Human Resources who has organised the training session. The trainer phones the HR manager to discuss some last-minute details.**

Student A: External trainer

Use some of the expressions above, and others, to clarify and confirm the following.

Number of participants: Ideally there should be ten to 12 participants. In the last e-mail you received (s)he said there were ten people. Can (s)he confirm the ten attendees on your list?

Time: Confirm the session starts at 9 a.m. and finishes at 5 p.m. There is an hour for lunch, from 1 to 2 p.m.

Location: Confirm the training session will be held in conference room B. How do you get there? You'd like to be there 30 minutes before to set up the room.

Equipment: You asked HR to arrange for audio-visual equipment in the room. Is there a TV and DVD player? You have your own digital camera to record the presentations.

Student B: Human Resources Manager

Reply to the trainer's requests and questions using this information.

Number of participants: One participant, Hilary Driver, has had to drop out due to work commitments. However, the company chairman, Stelios Remos, now wants to attend, although it may only be for part of the day.

Time: Start time is now half an hour later – some people have a divisional meeting to attend first. Finish time is unchanged at 5 p.m. Tea and coffee will be served in the conference room at 11 a.m. and 3.30 p.m.

Location: Conference room B is on the second floor. Call from reception and someone will escort you there.

Equipment: You have booked audio-visual equipment, including a TV, a DVD player and a video camera, so that the trainer can record some parts of the session.

Resource bank

Negotiating: Being vague and being precise

A Put the following conversation between a supplier and a client about delivery dates in order.

Amanda:	I can confirm that your order has been received and we're processing it as quickly as we can.
Tobias:	Yes, but I really need to have an exact date of delivery of the shipment. I mean, do you have any idea when it's going to be?
Amanda:	Well, if I'm honest, delivery for December 20th doesn't look very likely, Tobias.
Tobias:	Couldn't you be more specific, Amanda? We really need to have this model in stock again by December 22nd.
Amanda:	Well, before the Christmas rush is looking tricky, then there's the holiday period, which takes us into January.
Tobias:	Are you saying that you won't be able to deliver this order until the New Year?
Amanda:	Realistically speaking, that's the way it's looking.
Tobias:	If that's the case, I'd like to cancel our order, then.
Amanda:	Look, I'm sure we can work something out here. How about a discount for the inconvenience caused?
Tobias:	What did you have in mind, exactly? I really don't think we'd be happy with anything less than 10%.
Amanda:	Fine, we can work with that.
Tobias:	OK, so we're agreed on 10% then. I'll put that in an e-mail to you today.

UNIT 3   Partnerships

Negotiating: Being vague and being precise

B   Correct one word that is incorrect in each of these useful expressions for negotiations.

1   We're seeing at an initial order of two to three thousand.
2   Would you be will to come down a bit on that?
3   Somewhere in the area of 500 euros.
4   I think we could work on that.
5   Supposing we are to make that 12 free samples.
6   Giving that we are likely to be placing large orders, we'd like a 10% discount.
7   Are you said that you can handle an order of that size each month?
8   Where would you say to a display of your products in our toy department?
9   Seen that you'd like some free samples, we'd like our logo to be visible.

C   A sales manager for a toy manufacturer and the buyer for a leading department store are negotiating a contract to supply toys to the store.

Student A

You are the buyer for a department store in the negotiations. Use some of the expressions above to negotiate the following agreement.

Delivery: You want guaranteed delivery within 48 hours of order.

Discount: Ideally, you'd like a discount of 10% on catalogue prices of all orders worth 300 euros or more. But you are willing to be flexible on this point.

Display: You may be able to display the manufacturers' products in a prominent position in the toy department, but not in the shop window, as another toy manufacturer has already paid for that privilege this year. Be vague about this fact, though.

Free samples: You'd like about a dozen free samples of the company's best-selling toys for the children's play area in the store.

Size of orders: You think the initial order for soft toys will be 2,000 or 3,000, but you can't be precise at this stage. Further orders will depend on sales. You'd like to know if the manufacturer can handle monthly orders of this size.

Payment terms: It's your company's policy to make payment 60 days from date of invoice. You may agree to less if the company can make some sort of concession.

Student B

You are the sales manager for the toy manufacturer in the negotiations. Use some of the expressions above to negotiate the following agreement.

Delivery: You can generally deliver within 48 hours, but it depends on the time of year. In the holiday season, it can take up to 72 hours. You want to keep this point a little vague for fear of losing the contract.

Discount: You might agree to a discount of 5%–7% on catalogue prices on all orders worth 500 euros or more.

Display: You'd like a display of your toys to take prominent position in the store windows during periods when toy sales are high.

Free samples: You can offer five or six free samples for the children's play area in the store, provided the company's logo is clearly visible as a sponsor of the play area.

Size of order: You'd like to know how large the orders for soft toys will be. Monthly orders greater than 2,000 may mean you'll need to step up production in that area, but don't mention this fact to the buyer though.

Payment terms: You'd like payment to be made 30 days from date of invoice, although you realise that most companies want 60 days. You can offer a further 2% discount for prompt payment.

Resource bank

UNIT 4   Energy

Problem-solving

A   Match the expressions (1–7) with the functions (a–g).

1   It could be that her baby isn't sleeping very well at night. b
2   It's too soon to jump to any conclusions. e
3   What if we were to introduce flexi-working? c
4   I'll just have a quiet word with her. It's the best thing to do. g
5   Do you think it would be a good idea to send her an e-mail about it? f
6   I notice that Jill was late for work again today. a
7   I'd say we should remind all the staff that punctuality is important. d

a)   introducing a problem
b)   suggesting the cause of a problem
c)   propose a solution
d)   giving an opinion about a problem
e)   avoid making a decision
f)   asking for an opinion about a problem
g)   making a decision

B   **You represent shoe manufacturers in your country and civil servants and politicians from the Department of Industry. Discuss the following crisis in the shoe industry in your country. Look at the possible solutions. Add some of your own ideas as well and decide the best solutions to the problem. Use the expressions on page 38 of the Course Book.**

Problem

The leather-shoe manufacturing industry has a long tradition in your country. However, in recent years, cheap imports from overseas have had a major impact on sales. The industry is now in crisis. Many factories have already closed down, and there is widespread industrial unrest.

Possible solutions

- Devise a national and international advertising campaign and get famous actors and other celebrities to endorse your shoes.
- Provide government subsidies to help the national shoe industry to compete and increase the import tariffs on all imported goods.
- Sponsor sports events to raise the profile of the industry.
- Differentiate your product by concentrating on the luxury end of the market.
- Diversify and move into other leather goods areas that are less affected by foreign imports, e.g. bags and belts.
- Accept that the demise of the industry is inevitable and construct a compensation package for industry owners and retraining programmes for staff.

UNIT 5   Employment trends

Resolving conflict

A Cross out the unnecessary word in each of these expressions.

1   Let me see if I follow to you, you're saying that the booking is incorrect.
2   From in your point of view, the situation has got worse.
3   Let me I make sure I understand you correctly.
4   I'm sorry, I missed out that. Could you please repeat it?
5   I'm not sure I following understand you. Could you say that again?
6   Please you go on. I'm interested to hear what you think.
7   I appreciate how you feel like.
8   I can see reason why you feel that way.
9   Yes, you have a true point when you say there was a long delay.
10   Here's how it looks me from my angle, we both made mistakes.

B Work in pairs. These role-plays are based on the Delaney call centre in the case study. Student A is a Delaney call-centre customer phoning about a car-hire booking. Student B is the agent who takes the call.

Role-play 1

Student A: Customer

You're in a very bad mood. You've had a very stressful day at work, and to top it all, you're had to shorten your trip to Brussels by a day. You'll only need a car for six days from 5 November.

You made your booking yesterday with Tricia. Your booking reference is DR395BV. You want to deal with Tricia again today to make the changes and you insist on dealing only with her.

You also want an upgrade from a class A two-door car to a class B four-door car.

Role-play 1

Student B: Call-centre agent

You haven't been doing this job long and don't have much experience of call-centre work. You've agreed to work extra hours today because your colleague Tricia is off sick. Your typical response to anger is to fall silent, but that only seems to make angry clients worse.

Remember to say the company name and your first name when you answer the caller. The first thing you need is the client's booking reference.

Your computers are very slow at the moment, so you can't complete the client's booking. Apologise, offer to take their phone number and offer to call back at a suitable time.

Role-play 2

Student A: Call-centre agent

You haven't been doing this job long and don't have much experience of call-centre work. You've agreed to work extra hours today because your colleague Tricia is off sick. Your typical response to anger is to fall silent, but that only seems to make angry clients worse.

Remember to say the company name and your first name when you answer the caller. To make a booking, you need to ask for the customer's full name, the type of car the client wants and the dates and times and pick-up and drop-off points.

Your computers are very slow at the moment, so you can't complete the client's booking. Apologise, offer to take their phone number and offer to call back at a suitable time.

Role-play 2

Student B: Customer

You're been trying to get through to hire a car all morning, but the phone is constantly engaged. You feel very frustrated and you want to let off some steam when an agent finally does answer the phone. You want a class B four-door car.

You're travelling to Heathrow Airport and will pick the car up at 11 a.m. on 3 November, dropping it off in the same place at 12 noon on 6 November.

UNIT 6   Business ethics

Ethical problems

A Correct the errors in these sentences related to giving opinions and ethical problem-solving.

1 If I had to define corporate citizenship, I had say it's all to do with payback.

2 Let's argue it, not many companies have the time to write proper CSR reports.

3 Many fashion retailers only pay lip service at business ethics.

4 The time has flown for corporate responsibility to be taken seriously by businesses.

5 I disagree that the top line about business ethics is making it commercially viable.

6 If it were the suitcase that our company was unethical, I'd hand in my resignation.

7 Having told that, I'd discuss the situation with my manager first.

8 There are a lot of subjects at play with bad business practice: firstly, as an individual, are you prepared to be the whistle-blower?

B The following ethical questions provide a framework for dealing with corporate responsibility and individual (un)ethical behaviour. Complete them with words from the box.

affected	behave	conflicts	deceptive	environment	harm
mitigate	refrain	transparency	whistle-blowers		

AN ETHICAL FRAMEWORK

1 Who are all the people _____ by this business decision: from employees, shareholders, and clients to the wider community and _____ ?

2 Does this decision cause _____ to any of those affected and are there reasonable things you can do to _____ this harm?

3 Is your behaviour _____ ? Would you regard it that way if you were in the position of the opposite party?

4 Are there any disguised _____ between yourself, shareholders and those affected by the business decision? _____ can help reinforce ethical behaviour.

5 What would happen if everyone were to _____ in the same way in relation to each player in the transaction? This is like every driver at an intersection deciding to jump the traffic lights. If harm would be caused by everyone treating clients, other parties, _____ and shareholders as you do, you should _____ from doing it.

C Discuss these questions in pairs or small groups.

• Do you think these guidelines are appropriate for using in your company or sector? Why (not)?

• How would you improve these guidelines? Which points would you change?

• What other questions could you add?

UNIT 7   Finance and banking

Business vocabulary

Do this role-play in pairs.

Student A

a) You are a radio newsreader. Look at these business news items, then read them to your partner.

News item 1

Australian banks are lending more cash and growing rich off the proceeds. Annual earnings at the top banks are up 7–15 per cent, with the largest – National Australia Bank – unveiling an 11-per-cent rise in exceptional net profits on Wednesday.

News item 2

This autumn's hurricanes failed to knock the wind out of Allianz. Even after absorbing €750m of catastrophe losses in the third quarter, the German insurer should more or less double net profits to €4bn this year. Allianz is targeting another 10-per-cent profit rise next year.

News item 3

The remnants of DaimlerChrysler's Asian car strategy have finally yielded a profit. A tripling of Mitsubishi Motors' share price this year has changed Daimler's mind about hanging on to its 12.4-per-cent stake.

b) Listen to your partner reading some extracts of business news on the UK economy, Microsoft and ING Direct. Match the two graphs below to the correct news item. (There is one extra news item.)

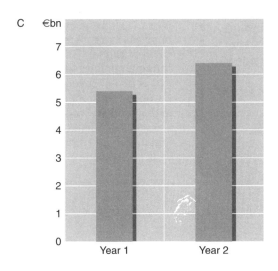

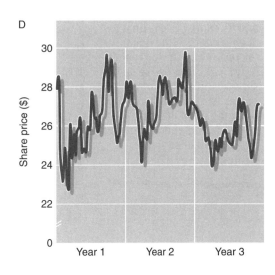

Resource bank

UNIT 7 Finance and banking

Business vocabulary

Do this role-play in pairs.

- ✂

Student B

a) Listen to your partner reading some extracts of business news on the Australian banking sector, Allianz and Mitsubishi Motors. Match the two graphs to the correct news item. (There is one extra news item.)

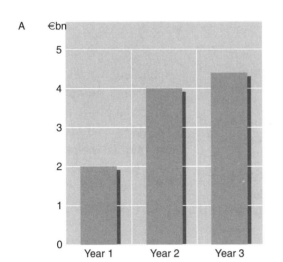

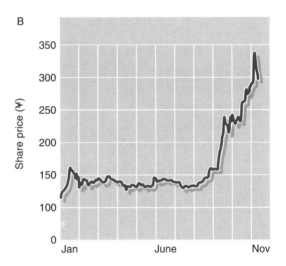

b) You are a radio newsreader. Look at these business news items, then read them to your partner.

News item 4

Microsoft is getting ready for another five-yearly change, and its share price is up again at 27.2 cents to the dollar. Microsoft has started reacting to Google's impressive search service and offer of new online services, with its reorganisation into three divisions and appointment of a new head of services strategy.

News item 5

Growth in the UK economy is worse than expected, and inflation is higher. That being so, the Bank of England decided on Thursday to leave interest rates unchanged at 2.4% for the third consecutive month, surprising no one.

News item 6

New chief executive at ING Direct knocked the company into shape last year, selling 14 businesses and freeing up €3bn of capital. This year, he is demanding growth, and ING is one of several European insurers doing well in this market. Pre-tax profits are up 17 per cent to €6.4bn in the first nine months of the year.

- ✂

UNIT 8   Consultants

Consultant's quiz / sales negotiations

A   **Would you make a good consultant? Answer the following questions, circling true or false, and then check your score. Discuss your results with your partner.**

1	I usually like to work by myself.	T F
2	When I have a tough problem, I usually need to ask someone else for advice.	T F
3	I'm a good listener.	T F
4	I prefer doing number problems rather than word problems.	T F
5	When a friend has a problem, I like to offer ideas about how to solve it.	T F
6	As a student, I found it very stressful when I had homework in several subjects all at once.	T F
7	I'm a creature of habit. I find a way to do something and stick with that method.	T F
8	I am pretty sure of myself, even in unfamiliar situations.	T F
9	I tend to think before I talk.	T F
10	When I hand in a report or other assignment, I know I've done my best.	T F

> Give yourself one point for matching for each of these answers:
>
> 1 T   2 F   3 T   4 F   5 T   6 F   7 F   8 T   9 T   10 T
>
> If you scored 7 or more, you would probably make a good consultant. If you scored 4 or fewer, consulting may not be a good match for you.

B   **Match these negotiating skills (1–5) to the five extracts of different sales negotiations (a–e).**

1   Explaining the value of a concession
2   Testing the situation
3   Checking facts or figures
4   Responding to an unacceptable concession
5   Checking with a higher authority

a)   I'd like to do business with you, but I'm afraid we are simply too far apart. Maybe I could get in touch with you in a few weeks' time to see if things have changed.

b)   Let me understand. I'm offering 74,000, and you are at 80. This means we are only 6,000 apart. You're saying you'll take 77,000, is that correct? It's a real shame that we can't agree over such a small amount. Let me run this by my boss and I'll get back to you tomorrow ... You know, my boss is really tough on these deals. She went through the numbers and said we shouldn't even be at 74,000, but she'll honour it. She won't go for 77, as I thought she would.

c)   If you order 1,000 units at a time, we'll actually pay for the delivery. Now, in real terms, that's a saving for you of about $500 in transport costs.

d)   Buyer: What if I take 4,000 units over the next year? How much would they cost me then?"
     Salesperson: Assuming I can quote you a satisfactory price, are you prepared to sign an agreement to go ahead on that quantity today?"

e)   Buyer: Your asking price of 9,000 is way out of line. I saw at least three of these at prices from 7 to 7,800. You'll have to do better than that.
     Salesperson: What's the name of the places where they were for sale? Were they new or used? What sort of condition were they in? And when was that exactly?

Brainstorming

A **Correct the errors in these sentences related to brainstorming. There is one wrong word in each.**

1 Would anyone like to get the ball kicking?
2 What a coincidence. I were just going to say that!
3 What a fabulous idea! Why didn't I think in that?
4 Has anyone else got a contribution to do?
5 Let's see ... I'm sorry, my mind's been blank.
6 That's not exactly what I meant. I was thinking more of the lines of ...
7 Very interesting, but can I come back to you later from that one?
8 You've taken the words right out of my throat!

B **Work in pairs. Look at the information and brainstorm some possible strategies that the client company could adopt, using some of the expressions in Exercise A.**

Student A: You are a strategic management consultant.
Student B: You are the CEO of a US-based global high-technology manufacturer.

The client
A leading European business-to-business and business-to-consumer high-technology manufacturer with operations in more than 40 countries. The client wishes to grow its already-strong business in Asia by more than 20 per cent a year.

The challenge
The company's business is focused on the United States and Europe, but Asia already accounts for 25 per cent of global sales. The CEO believes that the company needs to significantly expand its market share in Asia (China, India, Korea, Japan amongst others) and wants a strategy for doing so.

The client and consulting team are certain that the key to success in the region is the development of a localised approach to products and management skills. This would entail a significant commitment from the company's senior executives. However, many of them are unfamiliar with Asian markets and tend to shy away from large-scale – and potentially higher-risk – growth initiatives there.

Thinking locally to grow globally

Strategies for growth included the following:

1 Members of the company's board of directors made various trips to Asia during the project to get a better understanding of the opportunities and to demonstrate their support of the strategies.
2 In one country, there was strong demand for specific features of the company's top-selling consumer product lines. The team created a plan for capitalising on this through investment in R&D and new-product development.
3 Another country offered opportunities in the middle and low-end segments of one of the company's business-to-business markets. (The company had focused exclusively on the high end.) The team therefore developed a strategy to close this gap through the acquisition of a local manufacturer and new R&D facilities.
4 Local trade agreements among members of ASEAN (a private business organisation formed by the US and ten Asian countries) meant that locally manufactured goods had an edge over those imported from low-cost neighbouring countries, such as China and India. The team developed a plan for establishing local manufacturing by transferring existing assets to these markets, producing goods at a lower cost and obtaining increased profit margins.

UNIT 10 Doing business online

Presentations

A Match the two parts (1–10, a–j) of these expressions for summarising and dealing with questions at presentations.

1 Let's take another look at some ι

2 As I've said before, usability e

3 You'll find a summary of what f

4 My main point really is, what j

5 I was just wondering what you thought about h

6 Well, that's not exactly my department, but I g

7 I'm not sure I entirely understand. Are you saying d

8 I'd like to know why you didn't mention cyber crime. c

9 Of course, I'd say it's as vital as other security issues, but a

10 I'm often asked that, but I really believe b

a) it wasn't the focus of my talk.

b) we haven't yet realised the full potential of online purchasing.

c) Don't you think it's important?

d) the sales department is usually in conflict with the designers?

e) is about content, design, navigation and effectiveness.

f) makes successful web design in the handbook.

g) think Clive will be happy to discuss that question.

h) copywriting in respect to online sales.

i) of the key factors in successful website design.

j) do you want your online customers to do?

B Technophile or technophobe? Work in pairs.

Questioner must decide if 0,1,2 points

- -

Student A
Ask your partner these questions to find out if he/she is a technophile or a technophobe.

1 Do you prefer PCs or Macs?
2 What do you like most/least about Windows?
3 Do you 'Google', or use other search engines?
4 What's your favourite technological gadget at the moment?
5 What's been your biggest technological success?
6 *Add a question of your own.*

Give your partner 1–2 points for each question, depending on their answers:
0 = technophobe; 1 = average technical competence; 2 = technophile

Tell them their score (out of 12) and why you think they are a technophile or a technophobe.

Student B
Ask your partner these questions to find out if he/she is a technophobe or a technophile.

1 Do you have a laptop? How often do you take it with you?
2 If money were no object, what technological equipment would you buy?
3 What do you like best about cell phones?
4 What annoys you most about new technologies?
5 What's been your biggest technological disaster?
6 *Add a question of your own.*

Give your partner 1–2 points for each question, depending on their answers:
0 = technophobe; 1 = average technical competence; 2 = technophile

Tell them their score (out of 12) and why you think they are a technophile or a technophobe.

Telephone strategies

A Match the expressions (1–6) with possible responses (a–f).

1 Good morning. This is Angela Schulz. I'm calling from PZ Iberia.
2 Could you give me that invoice number again?
3 Can you tell me when delivery will be?
4 I'm sorry, but we'd expect payment sooner.
5 We can dispatch that within 48 hours. Would that be acceptable?
6 Are you saying that the order can't be fulfilled on time?

a) We're looking at the end of the month.
b) Yes, that would be fine.
c) Well, there will be a delay due to the transport strike.
d) Yes, it's PZ915/7S, dated 15 November.
e) I'm sure we can work something out. How about within 15 days?
f) Hello. Barry Jordan speaking. How can I help you?

B Work in pairs. Use expressions from Exercise A and the Useful language box on page 102 of the Course Book. Student A phones Student B about some outstanding payments.

Student A: You are Angela Schulz from the Accounts Department of the packaging company, PZ Iberia.
Student B: You are Barry Jordan from one of PZ Iberia's main clients, Hobart Foods.

Student A
Angela Schulz, PZ Iberia
- Explain that you are calling about two outstanding invoices: PZ915/7S, dated 15 November, and PZ943/6B, dated 2 December. Remind your client that payment is now overdue on both.
- Remind your client politely but firmly of the credit terms they agreed to (within 60 days) and that you would like both invoices settled immediately.
- Sympathise with the client and apologise for the delay due to a transport strike. Explain that as the problem has now been resolved, payment is due.
- Ask for an exact date when the payments will be made. You would like both invoices within seven days; you will be more flexible about the second invoice if necessary, but don't tell the customer this.

Student B
Barry Jordan, Hobart Foods
- Check and confirm the invoice number and dates.
- Acknowledge the payments are overdue and explain that it is standard practice for companies to pay up to 90 days after the invoice date.
- Explain that you have been withholding payment because the deliveries were not made on the agreed date.
- Agree to pay the invoices as soon as possible. You'd like to pay the first invoice within 15 days and the second one within 30 days, but don't tell the supplier this.

Functions and culture

A There is one word missing from each of these expressions for teleconferences. Find the missing word in each. Which expressions are a) making presentations, b) ways of making a contribution or c) checking action points?

1 Good morning, everyone. Who do we have us today?

2 OK. It's nine o'clock. Let's start by a roll call.

3 Our programmer, Dave Scott, has also joined today.

4 Hello. Is Émile Piaget from the Paris office.

5 I'd like direct a question to Hannah.

6 May I add to Enrique has just said?

7 Helen Stevens be here shortly.

8 Could we over the action points again?

9 Is correct to say that Teresa Romero is responsible for that?

10 May I make a comment the results of product testing?

11 May I ask Nikolay a question this stage?

12 Can I just check who's in charge what?

B Read the information about Singaporean and British business cultures. What type of misunderstandings could arise between these nationalities if they were working on a project together?

Singaporean business culture

Singaporeans never disagree with someone who is senior to them in rank, as this causes both parties to lose face and can destroy a business relationship. They have an indirect non-confrontational style of communication. Singaporeans will not overtly say 'no'; likewise their 'yes' does not always signify agreement.

Singaporeans always hesitate before replying to a question. This hesitation can take up to 15 seconds, so it is important not be too quick to speak or you will miss the reply. In business meetings, it is common to engage in small talk to establish a relationship before getting down to business.

British business culture

Punctuality and courtesy are important elements of British business culture. In meetings, an extended period of small talk is not necessary. The meeting can proceed quickly from introductions to the business at hand. First names are used almost immediately with all colleagues. Exceptions are very senior managers. However, you should always wait to be invited to use first names before doing so yourself.

Remember the British have an indirect style of communication, and therefore instructions are often disguised as polite requests. An important element of British culture is the renowned British sense of humour. The importance of humour in all situations, including business contexts, cannot be overestimated. Humour is often in the form of self-depreciation or irony.

UNIT 12 Project management

Functions and culture

 C Work in pairs. An IT manager makes the teleconference call.

Student A: You are the British IT manager.
Student B: You are the Singaporean head of programming.

Student A

IT Project Manager, Manchester, UK

You are Michael Harwood, the IT Project Manager for a large bank. You are based in Manchester, England. In the last ten years, the company has outsourced most of its routine administrative work to call centres in India. More recently, more complex operations, such as IT projects, have also been outsourced to India and Singapore. You are now in charge of various teams of programmers whom you have rarely met face-to-face. One team in Singapore is currently working on the implementation of a new database system.

Read the agenda for the meeting and your notes. Make the telecon call to Garry Yew, the Head of Computer Programming, based in Singapore. Remember to start the call by engaging in some friendly small talk as a mark of respect to your Singaporean colleague.

> **Agenda**
>
> **Objective: Get a status report on the new database**
>
> System testing
> *Have the errors picked up in the tests now been resolved?*
>
> Revised schedule
> *We need the system up and running by 1 March next year.*
>
> Cost overrun
> *I've estimated we're about 5% over budget at this stage.*
>
> Staffing problems
> *Have they recruited enough experienced programmers?*
>
> Face-to-face meeting
> *I'd like to go over to Singapore in the last week of January.*

Student B

Head of Programming, Singapore

You are Garry Yew, the Head of Computer Programming, based in Singapore. You are working for a large UK bank which has outsourced most of its IT projects to India and Singapore, although the IT Project Manager, Michael Harwood, whom you've only met twice, is based at the bank's headquarters in Manchester, England. Your team of 12 staff is currently working on a new database system for the bank.

Read the agenda for the meeting and your notes. Michael Harwood calls you.

> **Agenda**
>
> System testing
> *Most errors picked up in the tests have now been resolved, but not all. We'll be running more tests this month.*
>
> Revised schedule
> *Implementation likely to be delayed until late March.*
>
> Cost overrun
> *About 7–8% over budget at this stage because the bank revised the specifications and introduced new requirements at a late stage.*
>
> Staffing problems
> *We're still two programmers short, but others are working extra hours and hoping to recruit people by end of month.*
>
> Face-to-face
> *Looking forward to IT Project Manager's visit. Business shuts down here for the last week of January because it's the Chinese New Year.*